Reclaiming Nature

Anthem Studies in Development and Globalization

Reclaiming Nature

Environmental Justice
and Ecological Restoration

Edited by

James K. Boyce, Sunita Narain, and Elizabeth A. Stanton

ANTHEM PRESS
LONDON · NEW YORK · DELHI

Anthem Press
An imprint of Wimbledon Publishing Company
www.anthempress.com

This edition first published in the UK and U.S. 2007
by ANTHEM PRESS
75-76 Blackfriars Road, London SE1 8HA, UK
or PO Box 9779, London SW19 7ZG, UK
and
244 Madison Ave. #116, New York, NY 10016, USA

British Library Cataloguing in Publication Data
A catalogue record for this book is available from the British Library.

Library of Congress Cataloguing in Publication Data
A catalog record for this book has been requested.

1 3 5 7 9 10 8 6 4 2

ISBN 1 84331 235 2 (Hbk)
ISBN 13 978 1 84331 235 2 (Hbk)

Printed in India

CONTENTS

LIST OF FIGURES AND TABLES

ACKNOWLEDGEMENTS

Reclaiming Nature is an outcome of the Natural Assets Project, a collaborative research initiative based at the Political Economy Research Institute (PERI) at the University of Massachusetts, Amherst. An earlier book, *Natural Assets: Democratizing Environmental Ownership* (Washington, DC: Island Press, 2003), edited by James K. Boyce and Barry G. Shelley, explored natural asset-building strategies in the United States. This book does the same on an international canvas.

We are grateful to the Ford Foundation for its support to the Natural Assets Project. In particular, we thank Michael Conroy who played a catalytic role in shaping the project while he was serving as a programme officer at the Foundation.

Most of the chapters in this book were first presented at the International Conference on Natural Assets held in Tagaytay City, the Philippines, in 2003. We are grateful to the other conference participants for many helpful comments and suggestions: Mubariq Ahmed, Ruperto Aleroza, Josefina Aranda, Tasso Azevedo, Paul Baer, Charles Bailey, Oscar Castillo, Pisit Charnsnoh, James Fahn, Xu Jianchu, Fatima Jibrell, Budhita Kismadi, Maria Elena Martinez, Dumela Mohlaba, Dani Wayyu Munggoro, Elena Nikitina, Ran Singh Parmar, Tran Phuong Mai, Ferenc Poós, Carlos Porras, Ujjwal Pradhan, Chandrika Sharma, Barry Shelley, Mvusy Songelwa, Susan Stonich, Isabel de la Torre and Zhao Yaqiao.

We owe special debts of gratitude to Simon Doolittle, who served as administrative assistant for the project; Angel Mateo, who helped organize the conference; and Judy Fogg, PERI's administrative manager, who helped to make it all run smoothly.

We are also grateful to Tej Sood, Paolo Cabrelli and their colleagues at Anthem Press for their enthusiasm and support.

Finally, we want to acknowledge the inspiration provided by the countless people around the world who are demonstrating in their work and daily lives that poverty reduction, environmental protection and environmental justice can and must go hand-in-hand.

J.K.B., S.N., E.A.S.
November 2006

The natural world is not a mere backdrop to the human economy:
it is an indispensable form of wealth.

INTRODUCTION

Reclaiming Nature offers a hopeful new vision of the relationship between people and nature. The contributors to this volume have nothing in common with the see-no-evil optimists who dismiss the reality of the world's mounting environmental problems. But neither do they succumb to the bleak pessimism of many 'environmentalists'. Charting a course between denial and despair, they realize that human activities can have positive impacts on nature's wealth as well as negative ones. The crucial question is how we can tip the balance in favour of the positive.

The relationship between humans and nature is shaped by relationships among people. To understand *what* we do to nature, we must ask *who* does what *to whom*. Among the myriad species on Earth, we are distinctive not only in our power to use reason and learn from experience, but also in the fact that we live in differentiated societies where some, in George Orwell's phrase, are 'more equal than others'. Not everyone has the same impact on the environment, nor do all bear the same environmental consequences. The distribution of environmental benefits and costs has profound effects on our overall environmental impact.

This book puts forward three core propositions:

- First, environmental degradation is not the result of an inherent conflict between humans and nature; it is a result of conflicts among people.
- Second, every person has an inalienable right to share in nature's wealth, including the right to a clean and safe environment.
- Third, we do not face a grim choice between protecting the environment and reducing poverty. Instead the two can, and often must, go together.

These propositions form the cornerstones of a new environmentalism that is taking shape across the globe.

Natural Assets

The natural world is not a mere backdrop to the human economy: it is an indispensable form of wealth. Nature is the source of raw materials, the 'sink' for the disposal of wastes and the ultimate foundation of public health. Like all forms of wealth, these natural assets can grow over time, or they can shrink.

As the *source* of raw materials, nature provides food, fiber, water, energy and minerals. The stock of these resources can be depleted by deforestation, over-fishing, soil erosion, the burning of fossil fuels and so on. Yet we can add to this wealth, too, not only by reversing past damages, for example by reforestation and the restocking of fisheries, but also by investing to increase nature's wealth above and beyond what would otherwise exist. Beginning some 10,000 years ago, for example, our ancestors domesticated wild animals and cultivated wild plants to create wheat, rice, maize, potatoes, cattle, and other species of crops and livestock on which we rely for our sustenance. The wealth of agricultural biodiversity bequeathed to us by earlier generations is sustained today in the fields of small farmers around the world.

As the *sink* for wastes generated by production and consumption, nature absorbs and decomposes pollutants and recycles nutrients that are the building blocks of life. The capacity of soils, air and water bodies to perform these vital services is by no means unlimited. By overfilling nature's sinks, we deplete these assets. Yet here, too, there is scope for adding to nature's wealth, both by reducing pollution loads and by enhancing waste absorption capacities. For example, we can manage lands so as to increase 'carbon sequestration', the storage of atmospheric carbon in plant life, as one way to combat global warming.

As the foundation of *public health*, nature's role extends beyond serving as the source of our raw materials and the sink for our wastes. Ecosystems can be more or less healthful for human beings. The prevalence of malaria, for example, depends on whether the environment is hospitable to mosquitoes that transmit the disease. Where human activities create a more mosquito-friendly environment by pooling stagnant water, malaria's incidence may rise. On the other hand, modifications of aquatic habitats to reduce mosquito breeding historically have played a major role in reducing the geographical range of the disease, which as late as a century ago was common in Europe and North America.[1]

When we speak of adding to nature's wealth, or subtracting from it, we must have some criterion by which to define gains and losses. Ours is the ability of the environment to sustain long-term human well-being. In this respect, we are unabashedly 'anthropocentric', or people-centered. We do not regard humans as just another species, whose well-being merits no more concern than that of any other. At the core of our value system is the fate of humankind. Yet once we understand our dependence on nature's wealth, this translates into an abiding concern for the environment.

Reclaiming Nature

This book is about 'reclaiming nature' in a double sense. First, by exploring the possibilities for positive as well as negative interactions between humans and nature, we seek to reclaim nature as our home, the place where we belong. Second, by advancing strategies to secure a more equitable distribution of nature's wealth, we seek to reclaim nature as belonging to us all.

Reclaiming nature as our home means seeing humans as a part of nature, not apart from nature. It means rejecting the notion that human beings are like a cancer on the face of the planet, a malignant growth that threatens to destroy its host, and instead recognizing that we can improve our home or degrade it. It means that the task of environmentalism is not merely to contain human impacts within nature's self-healing capacities, but also to enhance nature's capacity to sustain human welfare.

No species can multiply its numbers forever, and as a part of nature we are not exempt from this law. But this does not mean that at this time human population growth is necessarily harmful for the environment. Humans are not simply 'mouths to feed', nor are we mindless fools whose 'ecological footprint' must relentlessly crush nature's fragile shoots — images that were all too common in the environmentalism of the late 20th century. We have hands. And we have brains. Our net effect on nature's wealth depends on the balance between our positive and negative impacts. This book is about rebalancing.

Reclaiming nature as an asset that belongs to us all in common means restructuring property rights to share nature's wealth more fairly. No immutable law — natural or divine — dictates that access to natural resources or a safe environment is a privilege to be allocated on the basis of wealth and power, rather than a right shared by every woman, man and child. The stark inequities we find in the distribution of nature's wealth are man-made. And both history and common sense tell us that man-made laws can be changed.

Rights come with responsibilities. To say that someone has a right to share in nature's wealth is not to say that he or she has the right to dissipate it. With the right to use nature's wealth comes the responsibility not to abuse it. With the right to inherit nature's wealth comes the responsibility to pass it on to our children and grandchildren, and to those who will come after them.

From 'Natural Capital' to Natural Assets

Nature's wealth is often taken for granted. Mainstream economists, for example, do not count subtractions from it when they calculate a country's gross national product (GNP). If trees are extracted from the forest, or oil is pumped from beneath the ground, the market value of these resources is simply added into GNP, with no corresponding entry for the deductions in nature's wealth. In recent years, some economists have sought to correct this defective vision by introducing the idea of 'natural capital', and incorporating measures of its depreciation in an effort to 'green the national income accounts'.[2] More ambitiously, some have attempted to calculate the total value of ecosystem services such as waste treatment and nutrient cycling, coming up with answers that range from being roughly equal to total world GNP to three times higher.[3] This exercise has the virtue of putting nature's wealth into perspective, even at the risk of being derided for putting a price tag on the priceless.

In this book, we use the term 'natural assets' rather than 'natural capital' to convey broader notions of both wealth and human well-being. Capital often is regarded as a *thing* — an object that people buy, sell and consume. The returns yielded by capital are simply one kind of *income*. 'Asset' denotes something more. It refers to a relationship between people and things, not to the thing itself. And implicitly, it refers to relationships among people, since these define a person's assets.[4] Moreover, the returns yielded by assets go beyond income: they include health, social status, political power and security.

At the outset, we want to emphasize that the term 'natural assets' does not imply that nature can or should be seen as a mere commodity. Indeed, in many instances — as in the cases of clean air and water — commodification would be inimical to the principle that access to nature's wealth is a fundamental human right shared by all, not a privilege apportioned on the basis of purchasing power. This same principle extends to other natural assets, from the rattan harvested by indigenous people in Kunming, China, to the camel milk traditionally shared by pastoralists in Somalia. But to say that something is not a commodity is not to say that it has no economic value.

Values and Value

The essays in this book share an understanding of human well-being that is wider and deeper than that of mainstream economics. The differences are rooted in core values that in turn define what makes assets have 'value'.

Today's economic orthodoxy, neoclassical economics, adopts a breathtakingly narrow view of human welfare. At the level of the individual, well-being is equated with 'utility', an idea that dates from mid-19th century Britain. People who have more utility — roughly the same as happiness — are considered to be better off. As Nobel laureate Amartya Sen has argued eloquently, this is a less-than-complete notion of the good life: it leaves out personal liberty, one's ability to control one's own destiny, and commitments to ethical principles that transcend self-interest.[5]

At the level of the society, neoclassical economics espouses two notions of welfare that co-exist somewhat awkwardly. Both are built on the base of individual utility. The first, adopted in 'theoretical welfare economics', is Pareto optimality, defined as a situation where no one can be made better off without making someone else worse off. This is sometimes called 'efficiency'. Whatever its appeal, this criterion has little cutting power when it comes to choosing among alternative courses of action. Apart from 'free lunches' — about whose existence economists are notoriously sceptical — projects and policies invariably generate some losers who are made worse off, as well as some winners who are made better off. There is no way to avoid the attendant distributional conflicts.

The second notion of social welfare, adopted in the 'applied welfare economics' of cost-benefit analysis, uses a 'compensation test' to get around this difficulty. After translating gains and losses into monetary terms, the cost-benefit analyst asks whether the gains to the winners are large enough to compensate the losers and still leave the winners better off. A project or policy that passes this test is deemed a 'potential Pareto improvement', and judged to be desirable, even though compensation remains a purely hypothetical possibility and is seldom if ever paid. By this sleight of hand, 'efficiency' morphs into the simple rule that the size of the pie should be maximized, no matter how it is sliced.[6]

The view of human well-being adopted in this book goes beyond efficiency to embrace equity, sustainability, resilience and 'non-economic' dimensions of welfare:

- *Equity* refers to how the economic pie is sliced: how wealth and income are distributed among individuals, groups and classes. We regard a more equitable distribution as preferable not only on ethical grounds of fairness, but also on the pragmatic grounds that equity helps to foster efficiency, sustainability, resilience and other dimensions of human well-being.

- *Sustainability* projects equity over time. A sustainable economy is one that does not compromise the ability of future generations to live at least as well as the current generation. This affirmation of inter-generational responsibility stands in marked contrast to the practice of using 'discount rates' in cost-benefit analysis, which whittles down future costs and benefits to get their 'present value' — a value that approaches zero as the time horizon is extended.

- *Resilience* refers to the ability of an economy to withstand 'shocks', be these accidents of nature or consequences of human actions. A resilient agricultural system, for example, sustains diverse crop varieties so that the advent of a virulent new insect, pest or plant disease is less likely to cause a catastrophic harvest failure. Similarly, a resilient energy system has built-in redundancy and dispersed power sources so that if one component fails, the entire grid will not crash.[7] The logic of resilience puts value on diversity and decentralization, in contrast to the relentless 'optimization' of neoclassical economics that prescribes putting all eggs in the single most 'efficient' basket.

- *'Non-economic' dimensions* of human well-being include health, environmental quality, psychological and social satisfaction, and personal freedom. Cost-benefit analysts have devised ingenious methods to impute monetary values to some of these. The cost of noise pollution, for example, can be inferred from gradients in property values as one moves closer to an airport. Whatever the merits of such techniques, we believe that some dimensions of human well-being cannot and ought not to be reduced to monetary measures. Just as all societies outlaw slavery without recourse to cost-benefit analysis, we believe that human rights to a safe environment should lie outside the market calculus.

Equity, sustainability, resilience and the 'non-economic' dimensions of human well-being are missing in the dominant economic ideology's exclusive focus on 'efficiency'. But we believe that most people around the world share these core values.[8]

Environmental Ownership

Natural assets, like forms of wealth, are governed by property rights. Natural assets may be owned by individuals or firms, governments, or communities;

that is, they can be private, public, or common property. Different rights to a given resource — such as the right to enter a forest, to hunt in it, to harvest trees or other forest products, to manage the land and to exclude others — may belong to one single owner, or different 'sticks' in the property-rights bundle may belong to several different parties.[9] Property rights may be codified in formal laws, or informally recognized.[10] The distribution of property can be very egalitarian, very unequal, or anything in between. The structure of these rights can be regarded as legitimate by all concerned, or their legitimacy can be a matter of heated dispute. Wherever property rights are situated on these various continuums, they are never frozen for all time. Rather they are subject to an open-ended process of construction by societies.

Constructing Rights to Nature's Wealth

When there are no property rights to a given resource, there is 'open access'. This can be a recipe for environmental and economic disaster. In an open-access pasture, for example, each cattle herder reaps the individual benefit of letting an additional animal graze, while bearing a negligible fraction of the social cost of reducing the forage available to other animals. Unless the pasture is superabundant, the result is overgrazing. Similarly, each polluter reaps the individual benefit of discharging wastes into an open-access sink, while bearing a negligible fraction of the social cost of fouling the air or water.

Economists typically advocate either state control or privatization as solutions to this 'tragedy of open access'. But a growing number of studies have shown that there is a third option: common property, in which communities regulate access and use, often by means of informal but effective rules. Indeed, in some circumstances common property turns out to be more successful than private or public property in promoting efficiency, equity, sustainability, resilience and other dimensions of well-being.[11]

'Open access' is not necessarily *equal* access. In practice, the door often is open wider to some than others. In an open-access marine fishery, for example, the advantage goes to mechanized trawler fleets that are able to deploy the most 'efficient' technologies for stripping fish from the sea. Small-scale fisherfolk who use less ruthless techniques lose out. Similarly, the poor families who lived nearby nominally had the same 'open access' to the air as the Union Carbide chemical plant in Bhopal, India, but they did not face a level playing field. Hence, open access often leads to not one tragedy but two: not only the abuse of resources, but also the abuse of some people by others.

Property rights do not provide a magic cure for either of these tragedies. The extent to which property successfully protects people and the environment is always a matter of degree. No matter how elaborately property rights are specified, there are bound to be grey areas, especially in periods of technological and institutional change.[12] And no matter how rigorously property rights are enforced, there are bound to be contests over who controls what. The incomplete definition and imperfect security of property rights mean that employment opportunities in the legal professions will never disappear. These attributes also mean that property rights can and do change over time.

Wealth and Power

Wealth is a source of power, and vice versa. From the enclosure of the English commons to the enslavement of Africans and expropriation of Native American lands, history offers plenty of examples in which raw power was the midwife of property. Compared to earlier eras, the scope for coercion and theft may be somewhat diminished today, but it has by no means disappeared, as was illustrated when land grabbers arrived on the scene in coastal Thailand in the wake of the December 2004 tsunami seeking to take advantage of the weakened circumstances of the local populace.[13]

History also offers counter-examples in which the advance of democracy has propelled movement toward more just and equitable distributions of wealth. The abolition of slavery is a case in point. As Friedman (2003, 33) observes, the emancipation of slaves in the United States was 'one of history's largest expropriations of property'. When property is seen as illegitimate, it soon ceases to be property.

Indeed, the loss of legitimacy can transform assets into liabilities. Under the United States 'Superfund' legislation, for example, polluters are liable for the costs of hazardous waste-site remediation regardless of whether their discharges were legal at the time they occurred. In effect, the law reallocated property rights from polluters to the public.[14] In an act of political theater that built on such possibilities, a British group called the 'Yes Men' issued a mock press release in the name of Dow Chemical Company (which had acquired the assets of Union Carbide) on the 20th anniversary of the Bhopal disaster, accepting responsibility and promising more generous compensation to its victims. The BBC took the announcement at face value, and broadcast the ostensible corporate spokesman's statement. Dow quickly disavowed it as the invention of 'irresponsible hucksters with no regard for the truth'.[15] But the prank's success rested on its credibility: enough people believed that such a thing could (or should) happen.[16]

A stripped-down version of the relationship between wealth and power, espoused by ideologues of the 'free market', contends that private property is the best guarantee of democracy. While there is a connection between property rights and democracy — that is, between wealth and power — this formula misrepresents the relationship in four ways.

First, it glosses over the crucial question of how property is distributed. If, by 'democracy', we mean that power ultimately rests with the people — being defined, in other words, not only by institutions such as free elections but also by an egalitarian distribution of power — then an equitable distribution of wealth is more conducive to democracy than a very unequal one. To take a hypothetical case, if all property belonged to a single individual, the political setup would be closer to dictatorship than democracy: we can guess who will be head of state.

Second, the conflation of private property with democracy ignores the role for public property and common property. Some property cannot be private, and some that could be, shouldn't. Examples of the former include national defence and clean air; examples of the latter, we believe, include marine fisheries and the agricultural biodiversity bequeathed to us by earlier generations.

Third, free-market fundamentalism misses the feedback from democracy to property. Secure private property rights do not fall from the sky, nor is their permanence assured: they rest on the distribution of power. Where power is concentrated in the hands of a few, the property rights of others are always under the threat of usurpation.

Finally, any sanctification of property rights erases their history — not only their origins, often in less-than-immaculate circumstances, but also their subsequent unfolding in response to society's changing demands and opportunities. Obscuring history dims our vision of how we can shape the future.

Democratizing Environmental Ownership

This book analyzes strategies for fighting poverty by building natural assets in the hands of low-income individuals and communities. In some cases, as in 'water harvesting' in the semi-arid zones of rural India, this can be accomplished by investing in the creation of new wealth. In some, as in the Brazilian land reform spearheaded by that country's Landless Workers' Movement, it involves the redistribution of existing assets. In some, as in the certification of forest products, it means devising new systems to reward producers for generating environmental benefits. And in some, as in the environmental justice movement, it involves establishing new *de facto* or *de jure* property rights to supplant open access. Each of these strategies helps to bring about a more equitable distribution of nature's wealth.

In many countries across the globe, the principle that all people have equal rights to share in nature's wealth is enshrined in the most fundamental of legal texts, the national constitution. 'Every person shall have the right to an environment which is not detrimental to his or her health or well-being', proclaims South Africa's constitution, adopted after the fall of the apartheid regime. Where the national constitution is silent, as in the United States, state constitutions often contain comparable affirmations (see the following box).

Even where the constitution does not explicitly guarantee the right to a safe environment, the principle has been endorsed in judicial decisions. In India, for example, the Supreme Court declared in 1991, that the 'right to life' guaranteed in the nation's constitution 'includes the right to enjoyment of pollution-free water and air for full enjoyment of life'.[17] Pakistan's Supreme Court likewise has ruled that the dumping of nuclear waste in coastal areas would violate the constitutional right to life.[18]

This ethical and legal principle is radically different from the stance adopted by orthodox economists. The latter was articulated with brutal clarity in a 1992 memorandum penned by World Bank chief economist Lawrence Summers, excerpts of which were published in *The Economist* under the title, 'Let them eat pollution'.

'Just between you and me', Summers asked, 'shouldn't the World Bank be encouraging more migration of the dirty industries to the LDCs [less developed countries]?' He answered his own question in the affirmative, on the grounds that the economic costs of pollution are lower where wages are low and life expectancies short. 'The economic logic of dumping a load of toxic waste in the lowest-wage country is impeccable', he asserted, 'and we should face up to that.'

Whether environmental quality is a basic human right that ought to be allocated equally to all on the basis of law, or a commodity that should be allocated on the basis of purchasing power, is a matter that every society must decide. The choice between rights-based and wealth-based approaches cannot be settled by recourse to science or the dictates of 'efficiency': this is a normative question of values.[19] The rights-based approach, upheld by the contributors to this book, is a powerful lever for natural asset-building strategies.

Democratizing Environmental Ownership: Constitutional Guarantees

'All residents enjoy the right to a healthy, balanced environment.'
    - Constitution of Argentina
'Every person shall have the right to a wholesome environment.'
    - Constitution of Belarus
'Every person has the right to a healthy, satisfying and lasting environment.'
    - Constitution of Benin
'Citizens have the right to a healthy and favourable environment.'
    - Constitution of Bulgaria
'The right to a healthy environment shall be recognized.'
    - Constitution of Burkina Faso
'The Constitution guarantees to all persons: ... The right to live in an environment free from contamination.'
    - Constitution of Chile
'Every individual has the right to enjoy a healthy environment.'
    - Constitution of Colombia
'All persons have the right to a clean and healthy environment.'
    - Constitution of Ethiopia
'All citizens shall have the right to a healthy and pleasant environment.'
    - Constitution of the Republic of Korea
'Citizens of the Kyrghyz Republic shall have the right to a healthy safe environment.'
    - Constitution of Kyrghyz
'Every human being has the right to live in an environment that is ecologically safe for life and health.'
    - Constitution of Moldova
'Everyone shall have the right to a healthy and ecologically balanced human environment and the duty to defend it.'
    - Constitution of Portugal
'Every person shall have the right to an environment which is not detrimental to his or her health or well-being.'
    - Constitution of South Africa
'Everyone has the right to live in a healthy, balanced environment.'
    - Constitution of Turkey
'The people shall have the right to clean air and water.'
    - Constitution of the Commonwealth of Massachusetts (US)
'All persons are born free and have certain inalienable rights. They include the right to a clean and healthful environment.'
    - Constitution of the State of Montana (US)

Sources: Popovic 1996; Boyce and Pastor 2001.

Strategies for Building Natural Assets

In the following chapters, a diverse and distinguished group of authors explore strategies for building natural assets in the hands of low-income individuals and communities. The book is partitioned into four parts, each of which focuses on one broad avenue for building natural assets: *adding value*, or investing to increase the stock of natural assets; *democratizing access*, or distributing existing natural assets more equitably; *capturing benefits*, or rewarding environmental services that support human well-being; and *defending the commons*, or appropriating rights to environmental 'sinks' hitherto abused as open-access resources. In practice, many of the chapters consider a range of approaches that span several of these avenues, all of which can be mutually reinforcing. Such complementarities are just as important in human affairs as they are in natural ecosystems.

Adding Value

Part I focuses on strategies for adding value to nature's wealth, or 'investing in natural capital'. These strategies build on the scope for positive human impacts on the environment, not only by restoring damaged environments but also by enhancing the diversity, productivity and healthfulness of ecosystems.

In 'The Blessing of the Commons', John Kurien uncovers the practices that have sustained small-scale fishing communities in the coastal areas of developing countries for many generations. Kurien juxtaposes the success of their common property institutions to what Hardin (1968) called the 'tragedy of the commons' (more accurately, the tragedy of open access). He also underscores the threat these communities now face from mechanized fleets that ignore traditional rights. Among the strategies adopted by fishing communities in the south Indian state of Kerala is the construction of 'people's artificial reefs', underwater structures that simultaneously improve fish habitat and impede the nets of the trawlers — an example of defending the commons along with adding value.

In 'Natural Resource Management and Poverty Alleviation in Mountain Areas', Narpat Jodha presents a compelling critique of the 'poverty-environmental resource degradation' narrative that ascribes environmental ills to the actions of the poor. Rather than blaming poverty for natural resource depletion, he puts the blame squarely on the social and economic inequalities that allow the relatively well-to-do and powerful to degrade the environments and undermine the livelihoods of the poor. Jodha's geographical focus is the Himalayan mountains, where the incorporation of upland communities into the economic and political structures of the lowlands has precipitated the breakdown of traditional resource management. At the same time, he points to the scope for regenerating landscapes and livelihoods by building new institutions for community-based forestry.

In 'Harvesting the Rain', Sunita Narain and Anil Agarwal explain how the Indian government's mismanagement of forests and grazing lands has alienated rural people and exacerbated resource degradation. Through four case studies, the authors document how these trends can be reversed when local people reassert control over local resources. In semi-arid regions, where water is the most precious natural resource, villagers have devised innovative techniques to capture and store rainfall, bringing impressive gains in environmental quality and economic well-being.

In 'Net Benefits', Mokhlesur Rahman and Stephen Minkin take us to the floodplains of Bangladesh, once described by the Food and Agriculture Organization of the United Nations as 'possibly the richest country in the world as far as inland fishery resources are concerned'. Fish are a key part of the Bangladeshi diet, and open-water capture fisheries are especially important for the nutrition of the rural poor. As ill-conceived flood control embankments have degraded aquatic ecosystems and disrupted fish migrations, government investment and foreign aid have focused on fish farming in ponds. This closed-water aquaculture is a not an adequate substitute for open-water capture fisheries, however, because it erodes biodiversity by replacing many species with a few and because it undermines the access of the poor. The authors describe pioneering efforts to implement an alternative model of fisheries development that is based on reopening waterways and restoring deltaic ecosystems.

Democratizing Access

Part II focuses on strategies for democratizing access to nature's wealth: reconfiguring property rights to achieve a more equitable distribution. Such strategies build on the scope for modifying property rights to advance society's goals — assuming, of course, that these goals include poverty reduction and environmental protection. Strategies for democratizing access are bound to be controversial, since they create losers among the rich as well as winners among the poor. But as these chapters show, this can be a major avenue for building natural assets in the hands of the poor.

In 'Land Reform and Sustainable Development', James Boyce, Peter Rosset and Elizabeth Stanton examine strategies for redistributing farmlands, ranging from the post-World War II reforms that helped set the stage for economic development in East Asia to the 'bottom-up' land reform now happening in Brazil. Land reforms can reduce rural poverty in two ways: by channeling a larger share of agricultural income to the poor, and by improving land productivity to increase the size of the pie. At the same time, the environmental comparative advantages of small farms mean that land reform can foster a transition to sustainable agriculture.

In 'Extractive Reserves', Anthony Hall recounts the efforts of Brazilian rubber tappers to protect the Amazonian forests on which their livelihoods depend. After a protracted struggle, they have persuaded the government to establish reserves where local people have the right to harvest forest products sustainably. The extractive reserve model stands in marked contrast to 'protected areas' that exclude local people and subvert their livelihoods. By forging national and international alliances, the rubber tappers have won victories in the face of powerful opposition from cattle barons bent on clearing ever more land for ranching. To safeguard these gains, the main challenge now is to ensure that the defenders of the forest can earn decent livings.

In 'Mining Rights and Community Rights', Karyn Keenan, José De Echave and Ken Traynor examine the challenges faced by communities impacted by the mining activities that have boomed in the global South in recent years. The central issue is who has what rights — the right to extract minerals (or to leave them in the ground), the right to share in mining income and the right to decide environmental impacts are acceptable. In Canada and Peru, local communities are asserting these rights in efforts to increase their benefits and decrease their costs from mining. In so doing, they are attempting to resolve a paradox: how to turn an inherently unsustainable activity into a springboard for sustainable development.

In 'Natural Assets and Participatory Forest Management in West Africa', Kojo Sebastian Amanor debunks the myth, dating from the colonial era, that the land-use practices of West African farmers have deforested the region. He documents how, on the contrary, traditional practices that combine farming, agroforestry and pastoralism maintain and increase tree cover. These practices have been undermined, however, by powerful commercial interests and by government policies that abrogate community rights. In an unsettling echo of British 'indirect rule', which co-opted local chiefs as instruments of colonial administration, recent 'participatory forest management' schemes often empower local elites at the expense of ordinary farmers. Amanor contends that the restoration of rights to rural producers who create and preserve forest assets is a basic prerequisite for sustainable development and poverty reduction.

Capturing Benefits

Part III focuses on strategies for capturing benefits generated by environmental management. Many low-income households struggle to earn a living, even while their work creates (or could create) valuable 'positive externalities', benefits to others for which they receive no compensation. Examples include watershed management, biodiversity conservation, and the recycling of urban wastes. The ability of households to continue providing these cannot be taken for granted. Nor should society expect to receive them for free. Strategies to reward these producers — to 'internalize' positive externalities — could improve their livelihoods, while strengthening their incentives to protect the environment.

In 'Compensation for Environmental Services and Rural Communities', Herman Rosa, Susan Kandel, Leopoldo Dimas and Deborah Barry review recent initiatives in the Americas — in Costa Rica, Mexico, Brazil, El Salvador and New York — where local governments are compensating landowners who provide environmental services. The authors explore the conditions under which such initiatives help to reduce poverty as well as protect the environment, and conclude that while it is possible to serve both goals, the combination is not automatic. If compensation policies are to become an effective vehicle for helping low-income people, they must be designed with this goal firmly in mind.

In 'Certification Systems as Tools for Natural Asset Building', Michael Conroy arrives at a similar conclusion. He explores another new strategy for capturing benefits: systems to label goods that have been produced following socially and environmentally responsible practices. Two of the most successful examples worldwide are the Forest Stewardship Council and the Fair Trade Network. These enable consumers to harness their values to their purchasing power, and give producers preferential markets and higher prices. Conroy argues that certification systems can bring significant benefits to low-income individuals and communities, especially if this is an explicit objective in their definition of social responsibility.

In 'Wastes as Assets', Eugene Gonzales takes us to the biggest municipal dumpsite in the Philippines, a vast mountain of garbage on the outskirts of metropolitan Manila where thousands of men, women and children live and work as scavengers. By recycling materials, they not only earn their living but also help to ease the country's solid waste disposal crisis. Gonzales calculates that if the scavengers were paid for the service they provide by conserving scarce landfill space, their incomes would go up by roughly 30 per cent. Using this case as an illustration, he explores policies that could make waste recovery and recycling a more effective route to poverty reduction.

In 'Community Rights and Wildlife Stewardship', James Murombedzi explores the tensions between conservation efforts and local communities in Zimbabwe. He focuses on the Communal Areas Management Programme for Indigenous Resources (CAMPFIRE), an experiment that has sought to devolve rights and responsibilities for wildlife management to nearby communities. Murombedzi finds that despite laudable intentions, CAMPFIRE largely failed to appreciate and build upon local institutions and livelihood strategies, and that most of the benefits have been captured by urban-based safari tour operators. As a result, government wildlife protection continues to rely on coercion more than cooperation. He argues that effective community-based wildlife management will require better integration with local land-use practices as well as steps to retain a larger share of wildlife benefits in local communities.

Defending the Commons

Part IV focuses on strategies for defending the commons, appropriating rights to air and water resources that polluters have treated as open-access resources. Strategies that compel polluters to reduce their emissions yield economic benefits in the form of lower medical costs, fewer days lost from work due to illness and higher property values, as well as gains in public health and the quality of life. There is also scope for innovative strategies that charge a price for the use of environmental 'sinks', providing a further incentive to cut emissions and yielding revenues that can be recycled to the rightful owners of these sinks: the public.[20] In this way, the 'polluter pays' philosophy can be married to the principle that nature's wealth belongs to all.

In 'International Environmental Justice', Krista Harper and Ravi Rajan introduce us to social movements across the world that are fighting for more equitable access to natural resources and environmental quality. In Chinese cities, residents are organizing to demand clean air. In South Africa, mine workers and villagers are pressing for the clean-up of hazardous wastes from the asbestos mining industry and compensation for past damages. On Sakhalin Island in Russia's far east, fishing communities are fighting pollution from offshore oil exploration. These and other examples illustrate the new environmental activism gathering momentum around the world — an activism that aims to protect people as well as nature.

In 'Environmental Justice: Reflections from the United States', Manuel Pastor traces the history and achievements of the environmental justice (EJ) movement in the United States. A major focus of the movement has been resistance against the disproportionate siting of hazardous facilities in low-income communities in general, and those with high percentages of African-Americans, Latinos and other minorities in particular. Pastor argues that these EJ struggles not only help overcome environmental deficits, but also lay the basis for wealth-building strategies that can bring lasting economic gains.

In 'Equitable Carbon Revenue Distribution under an International Emissions Trading Regime', Nathan E. Hultman and Daniel M. Kammen turn to a global natural asset: the biosphere's capacity to absorb and recycle the carbon released by the burning fossil fuels. Overfilling of this sink is the main cause of global warming. The Kyoto Protocol, an international treaty that limits carbon emissions from most of the industrial countries (with the notable exception of the United States, which has refused to ratify it), was an initial step in response to this tragedy of open-access. Hultman and Kammen propose a further step: charging a price for carbon emissions and distributing the revenue equitably among and within countries. Building on the principle of common ownership of the Earth's atmosphere, such a system would help to curb emissions while augmenting the wealth of low-income people worldwide.

In 'Greenhouse Justice', Sunita Narain and Matthew Riddle also address the threat of global warming, with a focus on the prospects for a transition to renewable energy technologies. They argue that the developing countries of the global South are in a good position to become leaders in this transition, as they are well-endowed with solar energy potential and not yet locked into extensive carbon-based power grids. The South, therefore, has a chance to bypass the North's fossil fuel-based pattern of industrialization. To make this a reality, however, we will need to construct an equitable international framework for carbon-emission entitlements that provides the South with resources and incentives to 'get it right the first time'.

None of these authors underestimates the twin challenges of fighting poverty and protecting nature's wealth. Readers in search of easy answers to hard questions will not find them here. What readers will find in these pages, however, is hope for a better tomorrow, inspired by examples of people across the world who are building natural assets by adding value, democratizing access, capturing benefits and defending the commons. Reclaiming nature is not easy, but neither is it impossible. We believe that the strategies presented in this book can do much to advance human well-being in the 21st century.

Notes

1. For discussions of the role of environmental modifications in the control of vector-borne diseases, see Kitron and Spielman (1989), Spielman (2003); Willott (2004).
2. For an early initiative, see Repetto *et al.* (1989); for reviews of subsequent efforts, see Bartelmus (1999) and Lange (2003).
3. See Costanza *et al.* (1997). For a critique of these calculations, see Toman (1998).
4. As Bromley (1993, 653) remarks, 'What I own is a function of what other members of the polity say I own.'
5. See Sen (1987, 1999).
6. From an equity standpoint, this marks a retreat from the 'utilitarian social welfare function' embraced by mainstream economists prior to World War II. The latter defined social welfare as the sum of individual utilities, not the sum of monetary values. Allowing for 'diminishing marginal utility of income' — the idea, retained in neoclassical theory, that a given sum of money is worth more when a person is poor than when she is rich — this implies that a more equitable division of a given pie yields greater social welfare.
7. For discussion of the role of crop genetic diversity in agricultural resilience, see Boyce (2006). For discussion of resilience in electric power systems, see Lovins and Lovins (2001).
8. For accounts of the environmental ethics of diverse religious traditions, see the website of the Forum on Religion and Ecology based at Harvard University: http://environment.harvard.edu/religion/main.html.
9. In the forests of the northeastern United States, for example, the public traditionally has enjoyed access for recreational purposes, while private companies hold rights to manage the land, extract trees and sell the land to others (Brighton 2003). Similarly, the British countryside is crisscrossed by footpaths that preserve public access to private lands; for a description, see http://www.ramblers.org.uk/.
10. As an example of informal property rights, Hernando de Soto (2000) remarks that dogs in rural Peru bark when a stranger crosses into their owner's land, even though the boundaries are not demarcated in official documents.
11. For discussion, see the chapters by Agarwal and Narain on water management and Kurien on fisheries in this volume. See also Ostrom (1990); Bowles and Gintis (2002); Baland and Platteau (2003).
12. For discussion, see Bromley (1991); Barzel (1997).
13. For accounts, see Vatikiotis (2005); Montlake (2005).
14. For discussion, see Dixon (2003); US Environmental Protection Agency (2000).
15. For Dow's disavowal, see http://www.dowethics.com/r/about/corp/bbc.htm.
16. The Yes Men's account and video of the BBC broadcast can be found at http://www.theyesmen.org/hijinks/dow.
17. Subash Kumar vs. State of Bihar, 1991 A.I.R. 420, 424 (India Sup. Ct. 1991), cited by Popovic (1996, note 118). For discussion, see also Anderson (1996).
18. See Popovic (1996, notes 116 and 117); Lau (1996).
19. For further discussion, see Boyce (2002, ch. 2).
20. An example is the proposal to create a 'sky trust' for recycling revenues from carbon charges. For discussion, see Barnes (2003); Barnes and Breslow (2003); Brenner *et al.* (2005).

References

Agrawal, Arun and Clark Gibson (1999) 'Enchantment and Disenchantment: The Role of Community in Natural Resource Conservation', *World Development* 27(4): 629–649.

Anderson, M.R. (1996) 'Individual Rights to Environmental Protection in India', in A.E. Boyle and M.R. Anderson, eds., *Human Rights Approaches to Environmental Protection*, Oxford: Clarendon, 199–225.

Baland, Jean-Marie and Jean-Philippe Platteau (2003) 'Economics of Common Property Management Regimes', in Karl-Göran Mäler and Jeffrey Vincent, eds., *Handbook of Environmental Economics*, Volume 1. Amsterdam: Elsevier, 127–190.

Bardhan, Pranab (2002) 'Decentralization of Governance and Development', *Journal of Economic Perspectives* 16(4): 185–205.

Barnes, Peter (2003) *Who Owns the Sky?* Washington, DC: Island Press.

Barnes, Peter and Marc Breslow (2003) 'The Sky Trust: The Battle for Atmospheric Scarcity Rent', in James K. Boyce and Barry G. Shelley, eds., *Natural Assets: Democratizing Environmental Ownership*, Washington, DC: Island Press, 135–149.

Bartelmus, Peter (1999) 'Greening the National Accounts: Approach and Policy Use', New York: United Nations Department of Economic and Social Affairs, Discussion Paper No. 3. Available at http://www.un.org/esa/esa99dp3.pdf.

Barzel, Yoram (1997) *Economic Analysis of Property Rights*, 2nd edn., Cambridge: Cambridge University Press.

Bollier, David (2003) *Silent Theft: The Private Plunder of Our Common Wealth*, New York: Routledge.

Boyce, James K. (2002) *The Political Economy of the Environment*, Cheltenham, England and Northampton, MA: Edward Elgar.

— (2003) 'From Natural Resources to Natural Assets', in James K. Boyce and Barry G. Shelley, eds., *Natural Assets: Democratizing Environmental Ownership*, Washington, DC: Island Press, 7–28.

— (2006) 'A Future for Small Farms? Biodiversity and Sustainable Agriculture', in James K. Boyce, Stephen Cullenberg, Prasanta Patnaik and Robert Pollin, eds., *Human Development in the Age of Globalization*, Northampton, MA: Edward Elgar, 83–104.

Boyce, James K. and Manuel Pastor (2001) *Building Natural Assets: New Strategies for Poverty Reduction and Environmental Protection*, Amherst, MA: Political Economy Research Institute.

Bowles, Samuel and Herb Gintis (2002) 'Social Capital and Community Governance', *Economic Journal* 112: F419–F436.

Brenner, Mark, Matthew Riddle and James K. Boyce (2005) 'A Chinese Sky Trust? Distributional Impacts of Carbon Charges and Revenue Recycling in China', Amherst, MA: Political Economy Research Institute, Working Paper No. 97. Available at http://www.umass.edu/peri/pdfs/WP97.pdf.

Brighton, Deborah (2003) 'Land and Livelihoods in the Northern Forest', in James K. Boyce and Barry G. Shelley, eds., *Natural Assets: Democratizing Environmental Ownership*, Washington, DC: Island Press, 227–242.

Bromley, Daniel (1991) *Environment and Economy: Property Rights and Public Policy*, Cambridge, MA: Blackwell.

— (1993) 'Regulatory Takings: Coherent Concept or Logical Contradiction', *Vermont Law Review* 17(3): 647–682.

Costanza, Robert *et al.* (1997) 'The Value of the World's Ecosystem Services and Natural Capital', *Nature* 387: 253–260.

De Soto, Hernando (2000) *The Mystery of Capital*, New York: Basic Books.

Dixon, K.A. (2003) 'Reclaiming Brownfields: Form Corporate Liability to Community Asset', in James K. Boyce and Barry G. Shelley, eds., *Natural Assets: Democratizing Environmental Ownership*, Washington DC: Island Press, 57–76.

Economist, The (1992), 'Let Them Eat Pollution', 8 February, p. 66.

Friedman, Gerald (2003) 'A Question of Degree: The Sanctity of Property in American Economic History', in James K. Boyce and Barry G. Shelley, eds., *Natural Assets: Democratizing Environmental Ownership*, Washington DC: Island Press, pp. 29–56.

Kitron, Uriel and Andrew Spielman (1989) 'Suppression of Transmission of Malaria Through Source Reduction: Antianopheline Measures Applied in Israel, the United States and Italy', *Reviews of Infectious Diseases* 11(3): 391–406.

Lange, Glenn-Marie (2003) *Policy Applications of Environmental Accounting*, Washington, DC: World Bank Environment Department, Environmental Economics Series, Paper No. 88.

Lau, M. (1996) 'Islam and Judicial Activism: Public Interest Litigation and Environmental Protection in the Islamic Republic of Pakistan', in A.E. Boyle and M.R. Anderson, eds., *Human Rights Approaches to Environmental Protection*, Oxford: Clarendon, 285–302.

Lovins, Amory and L. Hunter Lovins (2001) *Brittle Power: Energy Strategy for National Security*, revised edn., Snowmass, Colorado: Rocky Mountain Institute.

Montlake, Simon (2005) 'In Thailand, a "Land Grab"', *The Christian Science Monitor*, April 8.

Ostrom, Elinor (1990) *Governing the Commons: The Evolution of Institutions for Collective Action*. Cambridge: Cambridge University Press.

Popovic, N.A.F. (1996) 'In Pursuit of Environmental Human Rights', *Columbia Human Rights Law Review*, 27: 487–620.

Repetto, Robert, Magrath, William, Wells, Michael, Beer, Christine, and Rossini, Fabrizio (1989) *Wasting Assets: Natural Resources in the National Income Accounts*, Washington DC: World Resources Institute.

Sen, Amartya K. (1987) *On Ethics and Economics*, Oxford: Oxford University Press.

— (1999) *Development as Freedom*, New York: Knopf.

Spielman, Andrew (2003) 'Recent Approaches in the Development of Interventions against Vector-borne Infection', *Journal of Environmental Biology* 206: 3727–3734.

Toman, Michael (1998) 'Why Not to Calculate the Value of the World's Ecosystem Services and Natural Capital', *Ecological Economics* 25: 57–60.

US Environmental Protection Agency (2000) *Superfund: 20 Years of Protecting Human Health and the Environment*, Washington DC: EPA Office of Solid Waste and Emergency Response. Available at http://www.epa.gov/superfund/action/20years/20yrpt1.pdf.

Vatikiotis, Michael (2005) 'Greasing Palms in Asia', *International Herald Tribune*, January 27, p. 7.

Willott, Elizabeth (2004) 'Restoring Nature, Without Mosquitoes?' *Restoration Ecology* 12(2): 147–153.

PART I:

ADDING VALUE

Fishing on the coast in India.
Photo credit: International Collective in Support of Fishworkers.

CHAPTER 1
THE BLESSING OF THE COMMONS: SMALL-SCALE FISHERIES, COMMUNITY PROPERTY RIGHTS AND COASTAL NATURAL ASSETS

John Kurien

Introduction

Following the influential article by Garrett Hardin titled 'Tragedy of the commons', it is part of both popular and scholarly belief that unless natural resources are strictly in the domain of private or state property, their fate is an inevitable ruin (Hardin 1968). Closer examination of the actions of low-income communities who depend on natural resources for their daily livelihoods has recently brought to the fore a more positive view about human proclivity for caring and nurturing common resources found in nature.

A good example is found in the state of Kerala, in India, where small-scale, community-based fisherfolk initiated collective action to invest in rejuvenating the natural assets of the sea that had been destroyed by the incessant fishing operations of large-scale bottom trawlers in the region. They went about erecting artificial reefs at the sea bottom in coastal waters to create anthropogenic marine environments. Reefs act as fish refugia and become sources of food for them as the structures are soon covered with bottom-dwelling biomass. Artificial reefs placed in strategic positions in the coastal waters can in time increase the overall biomass and the fish stock in the local ecosystem. An unintended side-effect of sufficiently large artificial reefs is that they act as barriers to the operation of bottom trawl nets, effectively performing the role of a sea-bottom fence against incursions of trawlers into coastal waters. Such reefs have not yet healed the wounds inflicted on the coastal ecosystem of the area, nor can the fishing communities depend exclusively on them as a major source of livelihood. But such community investments by small-scale fisherfolk, and their appropriation of coastal sea area to form community property rights, point to the potential for strategies for visualizing natural resources in a new light — as *natural assets* that can contribute significantly to sustainable resource use, community empowerment and well-being. Only with such strategies can we have the blessing of the commons.

Natural Assets of the Oceans and Seas

Life on our planet began in the oceans and seas. It is widely recognized that humanity's present and future will continue to depend very significantly on the way we are able to identify, understand and foster life in this vast watery milieu of our planet (Lovelock 1987). From time immemorial, many millions of persons the world over, living in coastal communities, have obtained food, work and income for a decent livelihood from the vast stocks of living resources of the oceans and seas. Nurturing these resources as natural assets that are the common heritage of humankind can ensure their effective and sustainable use.

The coastal fishing communities in the developing maritime states and numerous native communities in the developed countries, using small-scale fishing equipment, continue to depend on these resources as their primary source of subsistence. These communities are the repositories of traditional knowledge, skills and cooperative fishing techniques that exhibit a highly nuanced ecological sophistication. This is particularly evident in the Asia-Pacific region, where large human populations exert pressure on all manner of natural assets. In this region, the current relatively 'free access' to the seas and oceans often make coastal waters the avenues of last resort for the poor to eke out a living.

It is difficult to establish property rights to the living, predominantly mobile and wandering natural assets of the oceans. Through their long and continuous association with the oceans, however, coastal communities devised a variety of rules and norms — institutional arrangements — with regard to territorial claims and the manner in which living resources were to be harvested. These arrangements were especially important in societies where coastal resources constituted a significant part of daily livelihood. An elaborate array of such arrangements was typically found in island societies and regions where bays and lagoons constitute a significant feature of the coastal morphology. Where these economic and geographic conditions co-exist, some of these arrangements still remain vibrant despite the passage of time.

It is customary to refer to such collective rights over resources as 'common property rights' — meaning the private property of a group of individuals. In this paper, however, I refer to such collective rights as 'community property rights', to stress the role of the group *as a community* and not simply as a number of individuals.

These community property right regimes were largely traditional, unwritten arrangements that were respected and adhered to by the coastal communities. They were not necessarily egalitarian or democratic institutions, but were part of the 'moral economy' of the community (Scott 1978). Consequently, they typically ensured that the benefits from the use of the natural assets of the coastal seas, *as a matter of first importance*, were utilized to ensure food and livelihood for *all* before any surplus was utilized for sale outside the community or for other ceremonial and extravagant uses. The community used a variety of arrangements to modulate the manner in which its members tapped the flow of the resource from its stock. These included the design of equipment for harvest, taboos on its use, controls over times of access and cultural norms of distribution of the harvest. These arrangements often contributed indirectly to the conservation and sustainability of the resource (Akimichi 1984; Amarasinghe *et al.* 1997; Berkes 1999; Doulman 1993; Dyer and McGoodwin 1994; Freeman *et al.* 1991; Hviding and Jul-Larsen 1993; Lim *et al.* 1995; McConney 1997; Normann *et al.* 1998; Johannes 1978, 1982; Pomeroy 1995; Ruddle 1988, 1993; Swezey 1997). Yet the diverse technologies, skills, knowledge and institutional arrangements that evolved over the centuries to harvest these living and mobile natural assets are now not always easy to maintain or restore. They are also no match for recently introduced new technologies, modern scientific knowledge and property right arrangements — particularly when viewed from the perspective of 'extraction efficiency'.

In the latter half of the 20th century, when most developing countries began to get or wrest their political independence, they started on various paths of 'planned modernization and development'. It was optimistically assumed that modern science and technology could serve as a major force in stimulating and sustaining development in the countries of Africa, Asia and Latin America. Development strategies in tropical coastal fisheries followed much the same assumption. There was a considerable amount of blind imitation of the large-scale fishing technology that was fabricated in temperate marine ecosystems and in a social milieu marked by greater urbanization, centralization and capital intensity. Much of this technology transfer was based on the mistaken presumption that the existing rich heritage of small-scale technologies was 'primitive and inefficient'. The rural, spatially dispersed settlement structure in these coastal regions was also viewed as inimical to economies of scale. Conservationist resource-use principles and community property rights over the fishery resources were seen as contrary to the individualistic, entrepreneurial ethic needed to maximize economic growth and raise the throughput from the coastal marine ecosystem. Abandoning what existed due to these perceived weaknesses, and replacing it with large-scale technologies, more centralization of activities and settlement, and an ethic of unfettered access to living resources, spurred and was further spurred by the extension of the fish economy. This took place first through the aegis of development aid and then international trade. But the initial euphoria of increased harvests, enhanced revenues, and higher profits was followed by ecosystem changes and resource depletion. At the same time, this strategy led to economic marginalization of coastal fishing communities and reduced their autonomy for participation in the new structure of the fish economy. It ruined the commons and the commoners (Kurien 1992).

The need of the times is for alternative strategies to revive locale-specific, small-scale technologies, coupled with community-oriented, participatory measures to protect the ecological integrity of the living coastal resources. Such approaches will return the natural assets of the coastal sea to the hands of the poor, empowering them to reduce their poverty. There is an element of 'going back into the future' in this approach. In this context, it is appropriate to examine the relevance, potentials and limitations of four strategies for coastal natural asset building: *investment* to increase the total stock of natural assets; *internalization* to increase the ability of the poor to capture benefits generated by their stewardship of natural assets; *redistribution* to transfer natural assets from others; and *appropriation* to establish community rights for the poor to erstwhile open-access resources (Boyce 2001). These are visualized as routes for rebuilding the living natural assets of the coastal seas and through this ensuring more secure and convivial livelihoods for the labouring poor in coastal communities.

The remainder of this chapter is divided into two main parts. The first part sets the scene by further describing the nature of the oceans and human use of the living natural assets therein. It discusses technology and institutional arrangements through which coastal communities interacted with these living resources, and the political economy of the movement from small-scale to large-scale fishing operations and from community rights to open access. The second part of the chapter examines the potentials of natural asset-building strategies. I draw upon examples from the Asia-Pacific region to highlight how small-scale, community-based fishing is both ecologically and economically suited to make a blessing of the coastal commons that simultaneously will ensure sustainable natural resource use and community well-being.

Part I: From Community Rights to Open Access

For millennia the oceans have been a source of livelihood to millions of humans who settled along their shores, and an important source of food to wider populations in the hinterlands. The interaction between humans and nature resulted in the evolution of patterns of life and livelihood supported by suitable technologies and community-based institutions. The hallmark of these patterns was the widespread prevalence of small-scale fishing communities, whose limited geographic extension was matched by great control over their natural resource base. The establishment of modern nation-states and the formation of the League of Nations and then the United Nations led to greater formalization and statutory laws regarding rights to use the living resources of the oceans. At the same time, international aid and trade led to the import of new ideas and large-scale technologies into the Asia-Pacific region, with the aim of enhancing the flow of living resources out of the oceans and into the marketing channels of the food supply of the developed world. While the stated intentions of these initiatives were to promote overall economic development, the end results were more ambiguous. The most adverse and unintended impacts were on the integrity of the living natural resources of the coastal seas and the well-being of coastal communities.

Living Marine Resources

The living resources of the oceans, if harvested sustainably, hold promise as a major source of quality food for the future. The yearly world ocean production of organic matter is about 130 billion metric tons, most of which is recycled and reused within the food chain composed of plants, prey and predators. Humans harvest only a small fraction of the total production, about 100 million metric tons per year.

The natural capital of the world's marine and terrestrial systems has been estimated to provide services worth US$33 trillion annually (Costanza *et al.* 1998). The marine ecosystems are subdivided into open ocean and coastal areas. The latter include estuaries, seagrass/algae beds, coral reefs and the continental shelf systems. Other than food production, marine ecosystem services include disturbance regulation, such as storm protection and flood control; nutrient cycling; provision of wildlife refugia; raw materials; recreation and cultural services. As much as 36 per cent of the total value of global ecosystem services — an estimated US$12 trillion per year — is contributed by coastal areas.

The mobile nature of the living resources of the ocean distinguishes them from many terrestrial resources. Contrary to popular notions, these resources are not evenly distributed across the 362 million square kilometre area of the ocean. Some regions, particularly those waters close to the coastline into which sunlight penetrates easily, are characterized by higher biological productivity. In fact, roughly 65 per cent of the living resources of the oceans are concentrated in the near-shore zone, which accounts for just six per cent of the total ocean area. Much of the vast ocean area far from land is virtually an aquatic desert.

These characteristics of mobility and uneven spread constitute both a barrier to and an important opportunity for the sustainable utilization of these living resources. The barrier is that while it may be possible to constitute a framework of property rights over marine spaces, it is difficult to institute a framework of rights over the mobile living resources in this milieu. When such frameworks are adopted, they are generally hard to define, often contested and invariably subject to change over time. The resulting 'fuzziness' of rights impedes achieving optimum harvests from the oceans.

The opportunity is that the large share of living resources close to the coastline can be designated as a source of livelihood and food to many millions, particularly in the developing countries of the Asia-Pacific region. Coastal communities, often loosely defined as small-scale fishing communities, have pursued a full-time avocation of fishing from time immemorial. These 'ecosystem people' (Dasmann 1988) or 'marine biomass communities' (Kurien 2002) share a strong 'connectedness' to the resource and have a long-term stake in its secure future as their lives depend on it. Given an appropriate structure of incentives and encouragement, they can become the stewards and protectors of the 'sea ecosystem' (Kurien *ibid*).

Small-scale Fishing Communities

Small-scale fisheries flourish in the marine, riverine or lacustrine ecosystems of many developed and developing countries. They can be found from the inshore sea of Atlantic Canada, the Amazonian floodplain of Brazil, the fjords of northern Norway and the Mediterranean waters of Spain, to the lakes of the eastern Africa, the backwaters of India, the rivers of China, the bays of the Philippines and the lagoons of the Pacific islands. An accurate estimate of the number of persons directly and indirectly dependent on small-scale fisheries is hard to come by. After gleaning data from the Food and Agriculture Organization of the United Nations, Berkes *et al.* (2001) conclude that 'of the more than 51 million fishers in the world, over 99 per cent are small-scale fishers.' They estimate that 250 million people in developing countries are directly dependent upon the fisheries for food, income and livelihood, and that some 150 million people in developing countries depend on associated sectors such as marketing, boat building and gear making.

In most of the developing countries, fishing has been a hereditary occupation in coastal communities. This has resulted in an accumulation of knowledge about the marine environment and its resources through a process best described as 'knowledge-through-labour' (Kurien 1990), and a plethora of technologies for fish harvesting attuned to specific seasons and species. These long-term interactions have also led to the creation of institutional arrangements that modulated collective behaviour vis-à-vis the resources. The resulting technologies and institutions created objective conditions for the sustainable harvesting of the resources.

Their Technologies

Most marine fishing requires the use of a craft on which to go to sea, together with nets, hooks and traps (collectively referred to as gear) to catch the fish. The casual observer normally sees only the craft (and not the gear) on the shore or at sea. Fishing crafts of the small-scale fishing communities of the world are marked by a vast diversity of design. This is sometimes attributed to the 'insular' nature of many coastal communities that have given rise to culturally conditioned variations in the construction of traditional fishing craft (Chaudari 1985). Cultural influences have certainly played an important role in features such as colours, the curves of the prow of the boat and the shape of the sails. But two major constraining factors also influence the technical design of fishing craft. The first is the availability of appropriate woods or other construction materials such as reeds or bamboo. The second is the set of location-specific physical oceanographic factors, including the structure, the texture, and the slope of the sea bottom and the nature of the surf and waves approaching the coast — the latter being a function of the former. It is these factors, rather than cultural insularity, that largely explain the diversity of craft-building traditions.

The diversity of the fishing gear is often 'invisible' to the outside observer, as it is stored away when not in use and immersed in the sea while in operation. Gear forms, materials and designs are the result of centuries of learning and doing. Fishing gear of small-scale fishermen is by and large passive — they wait for the fish to be entrapped in them. They are selective — constructed to catch a specific species and size of fish. They are used seasonally — only at the time when that specific species is available according to the rhythms of nature. In size and extension they are small — making them capable only of catching relatively small amounts of the concerned species, and laying emphasis on the quality of the catch, such as its freshness, rather than on the quantity of throughput. Fishing gear of small-scale fishing communities reflects a sophisticated understanding of complex 'sea ecosystem' considerations related to the behaviour of fish over space and time, and in relation to attributes of the sea such as colour, smell, surface movements and sub-surface currents.

Their Institutions

The interactions of fishing people with the natural assets of the sea have also given rise to rules and norms — that is, institutional arrangements — that circumscribe their actions both on the resources and among themselves. These arrangements have likewise evolved over long periods of time, although some have fallen into disuse and neglect in the context of modern legal developments. They are 'characterized on the one hand by having firm roots in local history, practice and space, and on the other by being unwritten and non-codified, thus permitting continuous interaction, with constant dual reference to continuity and change, to past generations as well as to present challenges...' (Ruddle *et al.* 1992, 259). To illustrate the past rationale of these institutions and their continued relevance, I provide two examples, one from Kerala State in India and the other from the Maluku Islands of Indonesia.

Kadakkodi: The Court of the Sea in Kerala, India

Kadakkodi or the 'sea court' is an age-old community institution among the Hindu fishing communities in the northern part of Kerala State, India, closely associated with temples located on the beach. This coastal region is known for its teeming pelagic fishes — large shoals that inhabit the surface layers of the sea and migrate over long distances. The sea 'court' consists of village 'elders' and a certain number of functionaries who implement its decisions. It meets on the open beach. All the fishermen of the village gather to participate in the discussions on issues relating to access, conservation and conflict resolution. The elders make the decisions and these are considered final. Monitoring their implementation is the responsibility of the whole community. The elders can impose sanctions against offenders, ranging from a mere warning to total social ostracism. Conflict resolution is handled cost effectively and amicably, thanks to open, systematic procedures, quick decisions and effective implementation.

The *kadakkodi* institution has been subjected to considerable pressure from the early 1980s due to several factors. Some enterprising investors from outside the traditional fishing communities introduced new fishing gear for catching pelagic species, patterned on temperate ecosystem gear. These large-scale gears were more effective in encircling shoals of fish, making their operations more profitable in the short run. Initially, the elders of the *kadakkodi* proclaimed a ban on the use of such nets, but with the greater involvement of more educated youth in fishing operations such decisions were questioned as attempts to preserve traditional, old-fashioned technologies. At the same time, new government-promoted organizational forms such as cooperatives, and new political divisions among fishing communities, gave rise to new leadership that further questioned the authority of the elders. Yet the basic scaffolding of the *kadakkodi* is still in place. In many villages it continues to play an important role in solving the socio-economic conflicts that followed new technological and organizational changes. Fishing communities in this region now express interest in reviving the institution, albeit in a new form. The Government of Kerala (1997) is placing a new emphasis on *panchayat* (village) level resource management and governance with full participation of the people. In this context, communities with a history of traditional institutions have an important edge in any new stewardship contract between the state and community.

Sasi: Fishing Rights and Rules in Maluku

Sasi is a traditional community-based coastal resource management system prevalent in the Maluku province of Indonesia. *Sasi* means 'to prohibit', and it is part of the Maluku culture. The *sasi* system prohibits the harvesting of certain biological resources in the estuarine and near-shore coastal areas, in an effort to protect their quality and population. *Sasi* also operates to maintain patterns of social life, through the equal distribution among all local citizens of the benefits from the surrounding natural resources (Kissya 1995). As an institution it has never been static, but has changed with the times. With the coming of state and church organizational structures into the islands, the *sasi* practices have varied from village to village. The governing and enforcing authorities may be traditional, church, local government, or private individuals holding the harvest rights to coastal land and aquatic resources. In certain areas *sasi* has evolved to accommodate significant commercial transactions involving the natural resources and a spectrum of claimants. Consequently the rules that define how the players in *sasi* work together are a mixture of tradition and modern innovations. This has been important to the resilience of the institution.

The modern state apparatus in Indonesia was keen to make marine fisheries an important source of foreign-exchange earnings. Extending state control over the coastal waters of the archipelago was a prerequisite for this. State patronage of modern fishing technologies (such as the bottom trawl), with investors from the Chinese communities taking the lead in the mid-1960s, resulted in the gradual spread of widespread and bitter conflict with coastal fishermen using small-scale, artisanal techniques. Institutions like *sasi* were initially deemed irrelevant to handling these new forms of conflict. State-supported legislation and zoning arrangements were introduced to contain the conflict, but these centrally administered regulatory regimes were costly to implement and largely ineffective in enforcement given the geographic spread of the islands of Indonesia. Moreover, they who had no legitimacy in the coastal communities were marginalized from their traditional fishing grounds. This led to a revival of interest in the coastal villages for more community-oriented arrangements for protection and nurturing of the natural assets of the coastal waters. The *sasi* system attains a new meaning in this context.

Sasi does not cover the entire fishery. It is applied only in small inshore areas and to a few species. However, these areas and species can be considered to be keystones to the health of the ecosystem. This important ecological fact, together with the socio-cultural foundations of *sasi* in Maluku, provides a robust rationale for supporting *sasi* where it continues to be vibrant, and for efforts to revive it where it faces the threat of extinction. Since collaboration, trust and legitimacy are the pillars of the *sasi* system, these are also crucial elements of any new institutional arrangements (Novaczek 2001).

In sum the integral reciprocal relationships between the living resources, technology, institutions and people were not just arrangements that dealt only with rights to the fish. Rather, they were broad enough to embrace rights and duties over the other system features that determined the long-term sustainability of the fishery. To a considerable extent, this may be due to the fact that the relationships were premised on a custodial rather than a possessive attitude towards the living resources. The distribution of benefits tended to cater to the needs of all, before the surplus — where it did exist — was consumed and/or accumulated by a smaller minority. Interdependence rather than competition was the norm. The threat from 'outsiders' was restricted because societies were organized on a basis where each community or occupation group had its respective niche in the economy.

The Political Economy of Living Ocean Resource Depletion[1]

There is a long history to the evolution of rights to living ocean resources. In the Asia-Pacific region, the periods prior to the western colonial expansion were marked by claims to near-shore living resources by their respective coastal communities. These localized customary rights gave communities the freedom to make decisions about harvesting the resources, in particular the nature of technology used, and the responsibility to protect the resource from harm.

Colonial powers were often involved in setting up fishery administrations and in documentation of the fauna of coastal waters. Significant efforts were made to improve the processing of the resources such as fish, seaweeds, shellfish and shark liver oil. In the first half of the 20th century, efforts were also made to organize the export of fish and fishery products to Europe and Japan. This phase also saw greater attention to the non-living resources of the oceans, such as minerals.

At the 1930 League of Nations conference on the codification of international law, nations raised issues regarding jurisdictional frontiers, with an eye on claims to both the living and non-living resources of the oceans. In 1945, President Truman of the United States took unilateral steps to proclaim rights over resources located in the continental shelf — the ocean floor extending out from the land. This action brought a spate of new claims by countries such as Chile, Peru, Ecuador and Argentina, proclaiming exclusive sovereignty over a maritime zone extending 200 miles from their coastlines, including the fish, the subjacent soil and the subsoil.

After World War II, the UN General Assembly, sensing the potential for anarchy in ocean governance, instructed the International Law Commission to prepare draft articles and conventions for a law of the sea. These conventions formed the basis for discussions at the first and second United Nations Conferences on the Law of the Sea (UNCLOS I and II), held in 1958 and 1960, respectively. The debates at UNCLOS I and UNCLOS II gave rise to two important concepts. First was the concept of the 'special interest' of a coastal state with regard to the maintenance of the productivity of the living resources in the coastal waters. The second was the 'preferential right' of coastal states vis-à-vis other states in respect to allocation of fishery resources. Countries such as Vietnam, Philippines and Iceland advanced the argument that in cases where the resources are used primarily by coastal communities who are overwhelmingly dependent upon fisheries for livelihood, there is greater chance of success for resource conservation and management. It was recognized during UNCLOS I that communities whose fishing methods are mainly limited to local fishing from small boats deserve special attention. Had such concerns been articulated into the emerging law of the sea, the chances of greater community control of coastal resources might have become a reality. However, UNCLOS I and II could not produce the necessary consensus among the nations of the world to make this possible.

The stalemate led to further unilateral actions by several developing and developed nations making a variety of claims of rights over coastal waters. This trend towards creation of a mosaic of state property claims, often far beyond their capabilities to care for the resources so claimed, became a cause of concern to statesmen and the world community alike. Ambassador Arvid Pardo of Malta best expressed these concerns in his now famous speech in the UN General Assembly in 1967. He appealed for treating the oceans and the resources therein, beyond the narrow stretch of territorial sea that extends up to 12 nautical miles from the shoreline, as the common heritage of humanity. This, he opined, was the only way to provide a satisfactory framework for an equitable international order, and at the same time to ensure the preservation of the marine environment for the interests of all. Pardo's speech was the motivator for UNCLOS III convened in 1973 and concluded nine years later in 1982.

Under UNCLOS III, coastal states are given sovereignty over a large patch of sea termed the Exclusive Economic Zone (EEZ) — that area of the sea measured out from the coastline up to a distance of 200 nautical miles. These EEZs account for 32 per cent of the total area of the planet's oceans, and contain 85 per cent of the living natural assets of the oceans. The creation of state property rights over the EEZ in effect negated all other *de facto* and *de jure* claims of rights in this zone. Traditional community rights to resources, which were not acknowledged in the first place by most nation states, were not recognized following the promulgation of EEZs, and fell into disuse. Territories and resources that had been considered precious community assets were now up for grabs. Realms where clear notions of property rights had existed now became open-access domains, where only *possession* rights — rights established by capture and harvest — could be exercised. Those with more financial capital and better technology had a clear edge in asserting such rights. This end result was very far from Pardo's original intent. All that remained in the realm of the common heritage of humanity was the deeper parts of the ocean beyond the EEZs. Although this realm accounted for 68 per cent of the ocean's total area, it contained only 15 per cent of the living resources.

The promulgation of EEZs by states, even before the UNCLOS III was ratified, empowered economic interests with access to financial capital and modern technology to usurp the coastal waters and harvest their living resources with the objective of making quick profits. In developing countries, this often was promoted in the name of modern 'fisheries development' schemes. Small-scale fishing equipment in the tropical waters was replaced with large-scale craft and gear from the temperate-water countries. Given virtual open access in the EEZs, there was uncontrolled expansion of the fishing fleet. This often led to overfishing, with deleterious consequences for fishing grounds and fragile tropical coastal ecosystems. Simultaneously, it resulted in the disenfranchisement and impoverishment of numerous ecosystem people, who for centuries had benign interactions with the natural assets of the oceans and considered them part of their own common heritage and community wealth. This was the real tragedy — that of the commoners.

In a global evaluation of fisheries development schemes, Professor Gerhardsen from Norway (1977) summarized the divorce between modern fisheries development and fishworkers' development:

So far in the second half of the twentieth century, general fisheries expansion and development has brought significant benefits to but a small percentage of the world's fishermen. The great majority of fishermen still exploit the fish resources in much the same manner as did their forefathers. They do not have the opportunity to expand their fishery, for they have neither the incentives, nor the proper means of production, nor the structures through which to unite on problems of common interest. For the majority, productivity and incomes remain critically low, and there is an urgent need to improve their working and home conditions.

In the Asia-Pacific region, one of the most compulsive forces in this unpropitious transition was new international consumer demands for the living resources of the oceans. The most illustrative example of this has been the search for new resources of prawns (shrimp), following the shortage in world markets when Chinese exports to the United States, Japan and Southeast Asia were banned after the victory of the Communist Revolution in China in 1949. This led to the 'discovery' of prawns in the coastal waters of many Asian countries. Development aid projects in India, Thailand, Indonesia and other countries introduced bottom trawl nets and mechanized trawlers in these tropical waters. There was a spurt of investment in these new harvesting technologies, and also in new processing techniques like plate freezing. Much of this investment was undertaken by people who were hitherto unrelated to fishing, or in the past had been involved in fish trade alone. The fish economies of many Asian countries (excluding China) took on a distinct 'export-orientation'. Fish exports rose from 57,000 tons valued at US$17 million in 1948 to 540,000 tons valued at US$236 million in 1958, and reached 1,600,000 tons valued at US$2300 million by 1976[2]. After 1958, the bulk of products reached the markets of the United States, Europe and Japan in frozen form. Within the developing countries there was very strong national governmental patronage for these private investors, who were deemed by the state to be economic heroes responsible for earning precious foreign exchange for their nations.

The consequences were threefold. First, it led to the marginalization of communities that had been traditionally involved in fishing and fish processing. Second, the unregulated use of bottom trawl nets slowly began to cause noticeable ecosystem damage in the coastal waters. Third, the traditional institutional arrangements that conditioned both access rights and technology use were relegated in the process of unconditional state support for granting open access to the coastal waters. Market, state and capital combined to deprive community and despoil nature.

Part II: From Open Access to Community Rights

Moving 'back to the future' to recreate a context where the living resources of the oceans are not threatened by human activity is of paramount importance. Viewing these resources as natural assets and placing the locale-specific needs of the ecosystem people at the center of our development perspective is the need of the times. This approach can guarantee both sustainable resource use and the alleviation of poverty in coastal areas. This will require firm initiatives by the coastal communities, committed action on the part of the state including efforts to modulate the raw forces of the market and widespread support from organizations in civil society. Here, I attempt to spell out this alternative approach, giving examples from across the Asia-Pacific region.

Building Natural Assets in the Ocean

We can consider at least four routes to re-conferring rights to coastal communities and (re)building the natural assets of the ocean. First, it may be possible for these communities, with their own initiative or with the support of the state, to make *investments* that will help to manage and rejuvenate the resource. Second, in contexts where these communities contribute to the larger society by their investment in and management of the resource, there may be possibilities for a greater *internalization* of the positive externalities so rendered by them. Third, there may be *redistribution* mechanisms that will ensure greater and fairer access of these communities to the resource. Finally, where ecosystem people have been effectively excluded by 'open' access to the resource, the social and political feasibility of *appropriation* of access merits consideration.

The current trends towards decentralization of governance and the control of resources by village-communities give greater leeway for such alternative strategies to become a reality. Whether this in fact will happen remains to be seen. In principle, however, initiatives for participatory democracy in the control and management of natural resources can foster greater democratization of the state and the market, by instituting a role for the ecosystem people in modulating both.

Investment: Rejuvenating the Resource

Human activity need not lead inevitably to depreciation and ruin of nature's capital. Instead humans can nurture and invest in resources found in nature. A good example of natural asset-building via investment in marine fisheries comes from Kerala, in south India, where coastal ecosystem people confronted with a 'Hardinian tragedy' of a ruined commons initiated collective action to rejuvenate the natural assets of the sea. This yielded both concrete and symbolic rewards that became important ingredients for their larger struggle for resource protection and a better livelihood for all.

The 130-kilometre stretch of Kerala's southern coastline is known for its highly productive waters. It is one of the world's most important sources of marine prawns. The annual sustainable yield from one square kilometer of these coastal waters is estimated at 35 tons compared to the all-India average of 13 tons. This resource plenitude has made this the coastal zone of India with the greatest concentration of fisherfolk. The zone is not only famous for its productivity and dense settlement, but also for the immense diversity of fish in its coastal waters. The assortment of gear used by the fishermen to harvest these resources is remarkable: specialized small-meshed gill-nets, trammel nets, bottom-set nets, boat seines and a variety of hooks and lines. The fishermen are known for their skill and daring. Their intricate knowledge of the sea and the structure of the sea bottom and their navigational acumen have enabled them to fish even at the margins of the continental shelf with relatively simple technology. Some of the most important fishing spots have been large natural reefs that provide habitat for fish aggregation and breeding.

'Modern fisheries development' in the period from 1960 to 1980 resulted in the state-sponsored introduction of 'efficient' nets, such as bottom trawls, which could be used to fish throughout the year. These nets could be operated only from mechanized boats, which the traditional fisherfolk could not afford. The nets and boats were initially introduced as part of a Norwegian aid project (Kurien 1985). A new class of merchant entrepreneurs and investors entered the fishery, breaking into the traditional preserve of the coastal communities who had viewed the sea as their 'community asset'. Access to the sea became open to anyone who could afford to make the necessary investments in craft and gear. This led to unbridled expansion of a fleet of mechanized boats, whose incessant bottom-trawling resulted in great damage to the natural reefs that were once big fishing spots. Fish harvests initially increased as a result of the more efficient nets, but soon dropped as a result of the damage to the ecosystem.

This prompted two kinds of responses from the fishworkers. The first was a socio-ecological movement aimed at re-establishing their historical rights of access to the coastal waters (Kurien 1992). One of the movements' leaders called this 'our struggle to ensure a future — for us and the fish'. Coastal fishing communities united to form a militant trade union of small fisherfolk and demanded that the state regulate the operation of trawlers in space and time. Their main demands were for a trawl-free coastal zone and for a ban on trawling during the three-month monsoon season when fish species breed in the coastal waters. A decade of struggles led to acceptance of the monsoon trawl ban by the state.

The second response was a search for ways to heal the ecosystem and revive fish stocks. One of the collective strategies adopted to achieve this was the construction of people's artificial reefs (PARs) (Kurien 1995). Artificial reefs are structures erected at the sea bottom in coastal waters. They can take a wide variety of forms — a few granite rocks wrapped in coconut fronds; heaps of truck tires; stripped out bus bodies; or even large, shell-like structures with intricate internal designs fabricated with steel-reinforced cement. The PARs initially serve to lure fish to the vicinity, as they provide shade, act as refugia, and soon become a source of food as they are covered rapidly with bottom-dwelling biomass. If placed in strategic positions in the coastal waters, particularly where there has been evidence of natural reefs and other sea-bottom promontories, they can in time contribute to an increase in the overall biomass in the fish stock in the local ecosystem. Good scientific evidence on whether major investments in creating such anthropogenic marine environments will increase fish stocks is, however, still not available. One side-effect of sufficiently large artificial reefs can be that they double as barriers to the operation of bottom trawl nets, thus acting as a sea-bottom fence against the incursion of trawlers.

Encouraged by a voluntary organization, the fishermen from 22 Kerala villages set to work to establish PARs along the coastline, reviving their inter-generational knowledge of reefs and updating it with knowledge from marine scientists. The evolution of 'erection-access' arrangements started with the case of one individual financing the cost of throwing large amounts of granite rocks in one part of the sea. This resulted in small fish aggregations in the vicinity. He then granted the rights of access to this portion of the sea to a small group of persons. This attempt to privatize the sea was soon shunned. The predominant mode became the 'community erection and community access' arrangement organized under the auspices of a 'sahodara samajam' (brotherhood fraternity). One member of each household in the community was a member of the fraternity. Every household made a financial contribution according to its means. The total thus collected was matched with an equal grant from the church. Some special technical assistance was obtained from an NGO. Between 1984 and 1989 as many as 21 PARs were erected at depths 12–15 metres. After a few weeks of 'test fishing', community norms were evolved to restrict the fishing effort by individuals. Only hook fishing was permitted over the PARs, and a limit was placed on the number and size of hooks. The use of lights to fish over the PARs was prohibited. Priority access was given to older fishermen and to young boys learning to fish. Community sanctions were put in place for those who violated the norms.

There is no claim that PARs healed the wounds inflicted on the coastal ecosystem of the area. Nor can it be said that the fishing communities can depend on PARs as a major source of livelihood. But the experiences of the fishermen of Kerala do challenge the influential predictions that only state or market solutions can allocate and protect common resources. They also call into question the assumption that those who are caught in a 'commons dilemma' will rarely invest time and money in the design and supply of knowledge, institutions and technology to conserve resources. Rather it illustrates that, given the appropriate circumstances, people who have an intimate association with natural resources as a source of livelihood can empower themselves to go beyond macro-level political action aimed at conserving resources to micro-level initiatives for investing in them and rejuvenating them.

In the coastal sea, and even more so in the deeper ocean, such investments have their limits as means of restoring damaged ecosystems and providing alternative incomes for the labouring poor in the coastal communities. But initiatives of this type reaffirm that it is those with a livelihood at stake in the living resources of the coastal seas who have the greatest stake in 'investing' to restore them. They do not, however, always have the financial capital, knowledge, or institutional capacity to undertake such ventures. This gap, between committed intentions and the effective ability to put them into practice, needs to be bridged.

Internalization: Rewarding Collective Action

The coastal ecosystem embraces a land and sea interface. It is, so to speak, a tail-end ecosystem, well-exemplified in the coastal proverb that the sea starts in the mountains. Sustainable management of biotic and abiotic natural resources of the coastal ecosystem results in synergies that can cut across many economic sectors of a coastal state. A well-managed coastal area ecosystem can be the basis of a healthy and economically sound fishing community. At the same time, the rejuvenation of coastal vegetation such as mangroves and seagrass can form an important protection against sea erosion and cyclones. The revival of coastal fauna such as corals and fish nurseries, and marine mammals such as dugongs, can also be the foundation of a vibrant eco-tourism industry. Consequently, coastal communities that take the initiative to conserve, revive and invest in the sustainable management of the ecosystem should be recognized and adequately rewarded by state and civil society for the social benefits or 'positive externalities' of their actions. The available evidence of small but significant measures taken by coastal communities in several parts of the world provides hope for such natural asset-building strategies (Ferrer *et al.* 2001). This is illustrated below with one powerful example of an innovative community effort from Thailand (Cunningham 1998). Small-scale coastal communities throughout the world have made significant contributions to the conservation of coastal ecosystems. Western development strategies —

particularly in the Asia-Pacific region — have often dismissed the 'tiny technologies and local knowledge' as inadequate and inefficient for obtaining a greater throughput from the marine ecosystem. The quick diffusion of new technologies and of the related specialized but compartmentalized knowledge (Kurien 1990), generated considerable wealth for those able to make the large financial investments. However, the negative externalities thereby imposed have led to the degradation of the natural assets of the tropical marine ecosystems. We have now come one complete circle on this account, recognizing that what existed in the past was perhaps more ecologically sophisticated, socio-culturally appropriate and economically appropriable by the people of the tropics. To 'go back to the future' on some of these counts, recognition and adequate reward should be given to those whose actions, undertaken in pursuit of earning a sustainable livelihood, bestow unintended externalities on others. Concretely, this implies providing support for low-impact, ecologically sophisticated fishing technologies and for community activities that consciously safeguard the integrity of the coastal ecosystem. Examples include actions like preservation of mangroves, efforts at keeping estuaries pollution-free and the creation of marine reserves where both resource extraction and protection take place simultaneously.

The work of the Yadfon (*raindrop*) Association in southern Thailand is an interesting example of participatory community action. The work started in seven remote coastal villages of Trang province in 1986. The fishing families were the poorest of the coastal population, and they were generally ignored by government and development organizations alike. The fisherfolk were Muslims in a predominantly Buddhist nation. While there was little open animosity between the two religious groups, the fact that they belonged to the minority group and were also poor made them feel like second-class citizens. Yadfon saw their poverty and the degraded environment as symptoms of a deeper problem. Though the people lived together, they had forgotten how to work together.

Through the work of the Yadfon Association, one of the villages decided to try to revive their badly degraded communal-use mangrove forests. This was part of a larger mangrove swamp that was leased out by the government to private concessionaires for extraction of mangrove wood or conversion into shrimp aquaculture ponds. The villagers initially petitioned the government to prohibit the concessionaires from encroaching into their communal-use mangrove forests. This was the beginning of an intense confrontation. Soon one of the village leaders was shot dead, a not-too-unusual consequence in the Asia-Pacific region when little people challenge powerful business and political interests. This violent turn ended the confrontation. The villagers decided that being politically weak, discretion was the better part of valor.

Faced with an impasse, the village group took a different tack. They started replanting the degraded mangrove areas that had been allotted to them to show their genuine concern for the forest. The mangroves are like the roots of the sea, without which the coastal ecosystem would die. They explained the reasons to fellow villagers, and also invited officials to take part. The provincial governor visited and was shocked and surprised to see such an impoverished community, rife with child malnutrition, with such enthusiasm for conserving natural resources. This action helped to win legal demarcation of the communal-use forests. Within three years, an inter-village network sprang up. Following a series of meetings, village exchange visits, and study tours, an area of about 100 hectares of mangrove forest was designated by the Forest Department as a 'community-managed mangrove forest'. This designation has since been extended to six reclaimed forests in the Yadfon area of work. Mangrove planting parties were conducted twice a year in festive style. Provincial and district fishery and forestry officers were invited to attend.

Following the successful mangrove replantation initiatives, the communities set out to protect corals and seagrass beds. The boundaries of the beds were demarcated with coconut tree trunks until the Fisheries Department contributed buoys. With the tacit backing of the provincial officials, the area was designated by the community as a no-go area for boats with destructive pushnets used largely by people from elsewhere. The rewards of such actions were immediate and obvious. Fish, shellfish, squid and turtles returned. Fishermen needed to travel less far out to sea, thus saving fuel. Children and women could catch enough crabs in the seagrass and mangrove swamps to earn the livelihood they earlier got from chopping down the mangrove trees. The most unexpected consequence of their actions, however, was the return of the dugongs. Dugongs — also called sea cows, since they nurse their young from udders between their pectoral flappers — are highly endangered marine mammals. They returned to their traditional home in the revived seagrass. The dugong has become the mascot that symbolizes the greatest returns — ecological and monetary — to the conservation and rejuvenation efforts of the community. Sensing the strong tourism appeal (a boom industry in Thailand), the return of the dugong resulted in unconditional government support to the effort of the community. This helped to secure another long-standing demand of the village people to enhance the trawler-free zone in the coastal waters.

Government officials who once pleaded lack of manpower to enforce the official trawler ban were now compelled to be more active. No one wanted to be accused of threatening the dugong.

The example of the coastal communities of Trang has yielded a commitment from the government to reward the poor for their actions in protecting the crucial natural assets of the sea. Committed state support in the form of infrastructure facilities and financial grants, which allows communities to internalize positive externalities, is economically viable, ecologically crucial and politically wise. On the part of the communities, the composite strategy of 'struggle for rights' and 'labour to build the alternatives' resulted in payoffs far exceeding the conventional 'waiting for the benevolence of the state'. Their actions not only set right their relationships with nature, but also gave them a new standing within the power equation of Thai society. Both are essential dimensions for ensuring sustainable environmental and socio-economic justice.

International recognition should also be accorded to such initiatives. The Yadfon Association recently received the Goldman Environmental Award. More sustained and ongoing measures could include certification efforts to promote fair and remunerative trade of the products harvested by such communities. Certification of marine-based products, particularly those harvested out at sea, can be more costly and complicated. A significant way forward will be for producer groups to reach markets through the aegis of advocacy by alternative fair trade organizations and concerned consumer groups (Kurien 2000). If sustainable production and harvesting are to increase, they must be linked to sustainable consumption through fair-trade practices.

Redistribution: Call for Aquarian Reforms

The post-1980 *de jure* arrangements of UNCLOS III, and the resultant national legislation spelling out access to ocean resources and space, do not recognize any traditional marine tenure systems that have existed in many maritime societies. The formal recognition of the territorial sea and the EEZ has given the nation-state primacy in the management of the natural assets of the oceans.[3] The expectation of the global community was that following the creation of state property regimes in the oceans, problems relating to the management of the natural resources of these coastal waters would be largely solved. However, this was not to be — not even for the developed maritime states. In the developing world the most important reason for 'state-failure' was the inability to prevent this state property from degenerating into an unregulated open-access regime. Possession rights of those with the capital and political power got precedence over the *de facto* property rights of those with historical livelihood claims.

In many developing countries, this gradually evolved into an ecological, economic and social crisis. What most caught global attention was the issue of overfishing and declining resources. In 1984, the UN Food and Agricultural Organization (FAO) decided to organize a World Fisheries Conference in Rome to discuss the state of fishery resources. A group of concerned persons from around the world approached the FAO with the suggestion that this initiative should extend to discussion of the state of fishworkers, too. When this suggestion did not receive an enthusiastic response from the FAO, a decision was taken to hold a parallel conference in Rome. This conference, called the International Conference of Fishworkers and their Supporters (ICFWS), brought to Rome 60 fishworkers and 40 supporters from 34 countries representing all the continents. One significant outcome of this historic meeting was a resolution calling on the international fisheries community to pay greater attention to the strengths of the small-scale fishing operations, in particular their economic, ecological and social viability.

This resolution (ICFWS 1984) observed that: Small-scale fishery is labour and local-skill intensive, and capital and fuel-saving. Its technology and mode of organization give rise to a decentralized settlement pattern, and do not promote large income disparities. Small-scale fishery operations are well adapted to tropical aquatic ecosystems, and communities frequently possess built-in mechanisms and rules for preventing overfishing. Far from being stagnant, small-scale fishery has amply demonstrated in the past that it is innovative, flexible and easily amenable to efficient improvements. The sector is also well-integrated into small-scale marketing channels that are low-cost, highly efficient and cater to local food needs; in many countries, these are managed by women from the community. Thus, small-scale fisheries and fishing communities should be advocated for economic, ecological, technical, organizational and social reasons.

In developing countries across the globe — including the Philippines, Indonesia, India, Senegal, Brazil and Chile to name a few — a new genre of small-scale fishworkers' organizations evolved after the conference to give substance to this call. One common demand made by all of them to their respective governments has been for a redistribution and redefinition of rights to create exclusive marine fishing zones where they could fish totally unhampered by the class of new operators using more powerful fishing crafts and more throughput-efficient fishing nets. Given the difficulty that developing countries' governments face in policing their EEZ's, this move by fishworker organizations to lay exclusive claim to the near-shore coastal seas (extending up to 3 or 5 nautical miles, or in some cases certain depth contours) was tactically astute.

The basic strategy has been to re-institute a community property rights regime within the territorial sea. By definition, this requires co-owners to engage in community consultation and participation to seek common approval of actions that they may mutually agree thereafter to undertake individually. These would include, among other things, decisions on the nature and the quantity of capital to be invested in fishing; and norms regarding the extent of effort to be expended and the manner in which the produce of one's labour will be disposed. This community property rights regime does not usurp the crucial role played by individuals. It only circumscribes it within collective norms. Since the basic motivation is pursuit of a decent livelihood, the participants tend to have a longer time horizon as regards their relationship to the resource, as well as a keener ecosystem perspective (Kurien 1998). This combination of individual enterprise under a rubric of community norms helps to take advantage of the skill variations among fishworkers. It promotes benign competition in coastal fishing, yet it keeps in check the ills of unbridled freedom, which led to excessive capital investments by outsiders. Community property right arrangements put a cap on private accumulation possibilities. But the benefits, in terms of equity of opportunity and freedom to modulate effort in keeping with the diverse fishery resources in the tropical seas, enhance the social accumulation of wealth from the coastal fishery. Taken together, these actions by fishworkers and state authorities are tantamount to a redistribution of resources to the large numbers of persons who depend on them for a livelihood.

Appropriation: Towards Community Property Rights

Effective redistribution, if it is to be sustainable, should be followed by meaningful appropriation of the natural assets by those who have the greatest stake in them. Such measures call for public action from both below and above, from both the community and the state. These are not 'one-time' actions. Rather, they involve long-drawn adversarial and collaborative interactions between the community and the state.

The struggles of the fishworkers in the brackish waters of Laguna de Bay in the Philippines over the last three decades bear witness to the fact that, in the ultimate analysis, only the real transfer of ownership of the natural assets into the hands of those who earn a livelihood from them will ensure resource integrity and an escape from poverty. The bay covers an area of about 90,000 hectares, and for centuries it provided a large population of fisherfolk with a seemingly unlimited source of livelihood. In 1966, the Laguna Lake Development Authority (LLDA) was created to 'promote development within the lake area, conserve natural resources and promote the socio-economic well-being of its residents'. In 1972, during the Marcos Martial Law period, the LLDA promoted an unprecedented privatization of the bay through the rapid establishment of fish pens to grow milkfish. Despite the purported intention of allowing fishermen's cooperatives to have priority in allocation of the pens, town mayors, military officers and government officials took major control over the Laguna. The bay became a maze of fish pens with watchtowers erected and armed guards protecting the pens from 'poaching' by the fishermen. Deprived of their livelihood and denied access to their traditional fishing grounds, the small-scale fishermen decided to fight back. In 1979, they formed the Organization of Small Fishermen in Cavite, Laguna and Rizal — CALARIZ for short. Their initial forms of collective action were restricted to writing letters of protest addressed to the LLDA and the Office of the President of the Philippines. Drawing on two Presidential Letters of Instruction (LOI) issued earlier that ordered the demolitions of illegal fish-pens, the fishermen pressed government agencies to enforce the LOI directives. With the LLDA unwilling to act in their favour, the CALARIZ then decided to take direct action. The confrontation was brutal. Several leading activists of CALARIZ were killed by the armed guards of the fish pens. The human tragedy and its social and political fallout created widespread tension in the Laguna region.

In an attempt to defuse the tension a new LLDA administrator was appointed. He implemented a zoning and management plan aimed at rationalizing and democratizing the Laguna's resources. The success achieved was limited. However, with the greater democratization of the whole country after the downfall of Marcos in 1986, the LLDA was forced to consider more actively ways and means of involving fishermen's organizations in the development and management of fishery resources.

The experience of collective action, the availability of greater democratic space, and the motivation provided by the fishworkers conference in Rome in 1984 spurred the small-scale fishworkers of CALARIZ to help form a new nationwide network of fishworker organizations called BIKIS–LAKAS. In collaboration with others, BIKIS–LAKAS urged President Corazon Aquino to implement genuine fishery reforms and repeal the decrees of the Marcos regime. Most importantly, it urged her to institute mechanisms to give small-scale fishworkers a say in policy-making and effective control over coastal resources by reappropriating them from the commercial interests. More than a decade later, during the term of President Fidel Ramos, after many twists and turns in the legislative process that was stalled and influenced by the commercial fishery interests, the Philippine Fishery Code of 1998 was passed. This Code led to the appropriation of coastal waters (15 km from the coastline), including the waters of Laguna de Bay, exclusively for small-scale fishworkers.

Under this code, Fisheries and Aquatic Resources Management Councils (FARMCs) were formed in 2002. These are the culmination of two decades of struggles, negotiations, confrontations and reconciliatory actions by small-scale fishworker organizations and state agencies. Unlike in the Marcos era, these local organizations are not front organizations for outside interest groups, but genuine participatory networks created by a coalition of workers, committed social activists and NGOs with a good track record of working with coastal communities. Expressing the significance of this process, the Director of the Bureau of Fisheries and Agriculture states: 'It is really with a sense of pride that we say that only in Fisheries have we legalized, institutionalized and put significant meaning to people empowerment' (BFAR, 2000: 5).

The FARMCs were created to institutionalize the major role of the fisherfolk and other resource users in the management, conservation, protection and sustainable development of fisheries and aquatic resources. The FARMCs are formed by fisherfolk organizations and assisted by the Local Government Units in the area. They assist in the preparation of the fisheries development plan for the area, evaluate its implementation, and recommend and enforce fishery ordinances and rules. The aim is that through the FARMCs 'empowered municipal fisherfolk communities shall be able to exercise control over their fishing grounds and make decisions that should eventually alleviate, if not totally free them from, their poverty, while at the same time protecting and further enriching the very resource that gives them life support' (Quicho et al. 2001).

Conclusion

To move from the tragedy of the commons to the blessing of the commons requires a wide spectrum of committed community efforts. Coastal communities and fisherfolk should certainly be active participants in designing their own future, since they generally have a much clearer conception of the important constraints under which they operate as well as a more holistic understanding of the opportunities before them. Where, however, a tradition for collective action is lacking, or the political space for it is limited, mobilization of communities for participatory planning and action may prove to be a long process. Faced with increasing pressures from the ever-growing vested interests that covet the natural assets of the oceans, local coastal communities will need strong support to defend their priority claims and rights to these resources. Empathy from the state and a variety of civil society agencies is a prerequisite for success (Kurien 1987).

In many developing nations, governments are only now moving from the 'development' mode to the 'management' mode with regard to the living resources of the oceans. The former mode most often has been highly centralized and considerably influenced by western, temperate-ecosystem approaches. These have largely proved to be both ecologically and socio-economically inappropriate. The assumption that the decentralized, small-scale, community-based coastal fishing activities were on their way out, and would be replaced by centralized, large-scale firms, has been belied. The fact is that the former remain vibrant and continue to be the backbone of the coastal fishery in many tropical countries.

These realities have resulted in the growing interest by states to 'look back into the future', particularly with regard to local-level institutional arrangements. This ties up well with the recent trend in many developing countries — India, Indonesia and the Philippines, for example — towards more decentralized governance by the devolution of representative democracy towards the village level. Village communities are being given the rights to restore, use and protect natural resources that were earlier converted into *de facto* open-access resources following hasty *de jure* state appropriation. This trend is providing strong incentives for rural households to devise arrangements for collective management of the resources. The state must now stand by — but not whither away. For state support is needed to ensure that benefits from the local commons are not expropriated by the more powerful in the locale and the community.

Restoring community rights to coastal resources does not necessarily lead to proper management for several reasons. These include disagreements among those who hold the rights over how the resources are to be used; corrupt practices in their use; and a lack of understanding of the ways to restore degraded ecosystem functions. In this context, the role of non-governmental organizations as well as the state attains significance. In many developing countries, the shortcomings of the state apparatus and the inadequacies of community institutions create a social space that can be filled by a plethora of voluntary support organizations. These agencies often play a facilitative role in creating and fostering community action. They play an important function in envisioning new sets of basic ideas, thoughts and beliefs. The significance of considering natural resources as assets and the poor as their guardians is a new paradigm that needs to be shared, converted into an ideal and fed into a community movement. Recent initiatives in South-east Asia testify to the significant role being played by such agencies in enabling the ideals of community-based coastal resource management to take root once again in the region (Ferrer *et al.* 2001).

Reviving ecologically sophisticated fishing technologies is a prerequisite for reviving the perspective of living resources of the seas as natural assets. This is possible only when the harvests made using such equipment are backed by effective demand from the consumers. It was international demand for large quantities of shrimp, for example, that led to the widespread introduction of bottom trawlers in Asian tropical waters. It will now require new international demand for shrimp that does not harm the tropical ecosystem to help revive the passive, selective and eco-friendly nets once widely used by small-scale fishing communities. Consumer movements in the United States, Japan and the EU will have to link up with the community-based fishworker organizations to work out mutually beneficial fair trade mechanisms that link sustainable harvesting with sustainable consumption.

A reality of the development world is that ideas translate more quickly into action when they are supported in international circles. For the past decade, organizations like the UNDP, FAO and World Bank have been emphasizing the merits of small-scale fisheries and the need to ensure participation of fishworkers in the implementation of fishery programmes. More recently, there has been increasing concern about sustainable fishing and the need to address the issue of persistent poverty in coastal communities. These interrelated themes can dovetail well to 'pressure' national agencies to support the presently fragmented initiatives to combine the synergy of coastal communities for reclaiming their rights to the living natural assets of the sea. National political commitment is a necessary condition for the ripples of micro-local actions to coalesce into a sea change in ecological and socio-economic circumstances. This will help restore the blessing of the commons: the ecological integrity of the coastal seas, livelihoods based on the sustainable use of living natural resources, and true community well-being.

Notes

1. This section is drawn from Kurien (1998).
2. Data from FAO/UN *Yearbook of Fishery Statistics*.
3. In the territorial sea the nation-state has absolute sovereignty over the sea space, air above and all living and non-living resources. In the EEZ, the sovereignty of the nation-state is for the purposes of exploring, exploiting, conserving and managing the natural resources, whether living or non-living, of the waters superjacent to the seabed and of the seabed and its subsoil. It also extends to other activities such as exploitation of the EEZ for the production of energy from the water currents and winds.

References

Akimichi, T. (1984) 'Territorial Regulation in the Small-scale Fisheries of Itoman, Okinawa', *Senri Ethnological Studies* 17, Osaka, Japan: National Museum of Ethnology.

Amarasinghe, US, *et al.* (1997) 'Traditional Practices for Resource Sharing in an Artisanal Fishery of a Sri Lankan Estuary', *Asian Fisheries Science* 9: 311–323.

Berkes, Fikret (1999) *Sacred Ecology: Traditional Ecological Knowledge and Resource Management*, Philadelphia: Taylor & Francis.

Berkes, Fikret, *et al.* (2001) *Managing Small-scale Fisheries: Alternative Directions and Methods*, Ottawa: IDRC.

Bureau of Fisheries and Aquatic Resources (BFAR) (2000) *Guidelines on the Creation and Implementation of Fisheries and Aquatic Resources Management Councils.* Quezon City, Philippines: BFAR.

Boyce, James (2001) 'From Natural Resources to Natural Assets', *New Solutions* 11(3): 275–296.

Chaudhuri, K.N. (1985) *Trade and Civilization in the Indian Ocean: An Economic History from the Rise of Islam to 1750*, Cambridge: Cambridge University Press.

Costanza, Robert, *et al.* (1998) 'The Value of the World's Ecosystem Services and Natural Capital', *Ecological Economics* 25(1): 3–15.

Cunningham, Susan (1998) 'A Raindrop Cleans the Wetlands', *Changemakers Journal*, October.

Dassmann, Richard (1988) 'Towards a Biosphere Consciousness', in D. Worster, ed., *The Ends of the Earth: Perspectives on Modern Environmental History*, Cambridge: Cambridge University Press.

Doulman, David (1993) 'Community-based Fishery Management: Towards the Restoration of Traditional Practices in the South Pacific', *Marine Policy* 17(2): 108–117.

Dyer, C.L. and J.R. McGoodwin (1994) *Folk Management in the World's Fisheries*, Colorado: University Press of Colorado.

Ferrer, Elmer, *et al.* (2001) *Hope Takes Root: Community-based Coastal Resources Management Stories from South-east Asia*, Halifax, Nova Scotia: CBCM Resource Centre, Coastal Resources Research Network, Dalhousie University.

Freeman, Milton, *et al.* (1991) 'Adaptive Marine Resources Management Systems in the Pacific', Special issue of *Resource Management and Optimization* 8(3/4): 127–245.

Gerhardsen, G.M. (1977) 'Strategies for Development Projects in Small-scale Fisheries', Rome: FAO. Unpublished paper.

Government of Kerala, State Planning Board (1997) *Report of the Task Force on Livelihood Secure Fishing Communities*, Trivandrum: Government Press.

Hardin, G. (1968) 'The Tragedy of the Commons', *Science* 162: 1243–248.

Hviding, E. and E. Jul-Larsen (1993) *Community-based Resource Management in Tropical Fisheries*, Norway: Centre for Development Studies, University of Bergen.

ICFWS (1984) *Report of the International Conference of Fishworkers and Their Supporters*, Hong Kong: DAGA Publication.

Johannes, R.E. (1978) 'Traditional Marine Conservation Methods in Oceania and Their demise', *Annual Reviews of Ecology and Systematics* 9: 349–364.

— (1982) 'Traditional Conservation Methods and Protected Marine Areas in Oceania', *Ambio* 11(5): 258–261.

Kissya, Elissa (1995) *Sasi Aman Haru-ukui: Traditional Management of Sustainable Natural Resources Haruku*, Jakarta: SEJATI Publications.

Kurien, John (1985) 'Technical Assistance Projects and Socio-Economic Change: The Norwegian Intervention into Kerala Fisheries Development Experience', *Economic and Political Weekly* 20: A70–A87.

— (1987) 'Empathy and Struggle: Elements in a Future for Small-scale Fishing Communities', *ICLARM REPORT 1986*, Manila: ICLARM Publications.

— (1990) 'Knowledge Systems and Fishery Resource Decline: A Historical Perspective', in W. Lenz and M. Deacon, eds., *Ocean Sciences: Their History and Relation to Man*, Hamburg: DHZ Publications.

— (1992) 'Ruining the Commons and the Response of the Commoners: Coastal Overfishing and Fishworkers' Action in Kerala State, India', in D. Ghai and J.M. Vivian, eds., *Grassroots Environmental Action: People's Participation in Sustainable Development*, London: Routledge.

— (1995) 'Collective Action for Common Property Resource Rejuvenation: The Case of People's Artificial Reefs in Kerala State, India', *Human Organization* 54(2): 160–168.

— (1998) *Property Rights, Resource Management and Governance: Crafting an Institutional Framework for Global Marine Fisheries*, Trivandrum: CDS/SIFFS Publications.

— (2000) 'Behind the Label: Are Eco-labels the Answer to Sustainable Fishing?' *New Internationalist* 325.

— (2002) *People and the Sea: A 'Tropical-majority' World Perspective*, Amsterdam: MARE Publications.

Lim, C.P., *et al.* (1995) 'Co-management in Marine Fisheries: The Japanese Experience', *Coastal Management* 23: 195–221.

Lovelock, James (1987) *Gaia: A New Look at Life on Earth*, Oxford: Oxford University Press.

McConney, Patrick (1997) 'Social Strategies for Coping with Uncertainty in the Barbados Small-scale Pelagic Fishery', *Proceedings of the Gulf and Caribbean Fisheries Institute* 49: 99–113.

Normann, A.K., *et al.* (1998) *Fisheries Co-management in Africa: Proceedings from a Regional Workshop on Fisheries Co-management Research*, Hirtshals, Denmark: Institute for Fisheries Management, North Sea Centre.

Novaczek, Irene, *et al.* (2001) *An Institutional Analysis of Sasi Laut in Maluku, Indonesia*, Penang: ICLARM Publications.

Pomeroy, Robert (1995) 'Community-based and Co-management Institutions for Sustainable Coastal Fisheries Management in South-east Asia', *Ocean and Coastal Management* 27(3): 143–162.

Quicho, Rodolfo, *et al.* (2001) 'A Paper on Access to Resources in Coastal Waters for Municipal Fisherfolk', Paper presented at *Workshop on Marine and Coastal Resources and Community-based Property Rights*, Batangas, Philippines, 12–15 June 2001.

Ruddle, Kenneth (1988) 'Social Principles Underlying Traditional Inshore Fishery Management Systems in the Pacific Basin', *Marine Resource Economics* 5: 351–363.

— (1993) 'External forces and change in traditional community-based fishery management systems in the Asia-Pacific region.' *MAST* 6: 1-37.

Ruddle, Kenneth, *et al.* (1992) 'Marine resources management in the context of customary tenure.' *Marine Resource Economics* 7: 249-273.

Scott, James (1978) *Moral Economy of the Peasant: Rebellion and Subsistence in South-east Asia*, London: Yale University Press.

Swezey, S.L., *et al.* (1977) 'Ritual Management of Salmonid Fish Resources in California', *Journal of California Anthropology* 4: 6–29.

Nepal's traditional natural resource management systems offer
lessons on how to combine rural livelihoods with environmental protection.

CHAPTER 2
NATURAL RESOURCE MANAGEMENT AND POVERTY ALLEVIATION IN MOUNTAIN AREAS

Narpat S. Jodha

Introduction

This chapter addresses community-level natural resource management and rural poverty, first by re-examining the mainstream view that blames the poor for natural resource degradation. This is followed by a comparison of the traditional and present-day systems of natural resource management in mountain areas. This helps in the identification of factors and processes contributing to resource degradation. Lessons from past systems and successful experiences of new initiatives on community forest management in Nepal and India are synthesized to suggest possible approaches to rebuilding communities' natural assets. The final section of the chapter looks at concerns and uncertainties relating to new forest-centered initiatives, and at possible ways to address these.

The crucial role of natural asset building in reducing poverty — by conserving, regenerating, upgrading and equitably harnessing natural resources, particularly, forests, pastures and crop lands — stems from the contributions of these resources towards enhancing the livelihood options of the poor (Dasgupta 1996). These include direct availability of seasonally and spatially varying supplies of bio-fuel, fodder, fiber, food items, timber and high-value products such as medicinal herbs, honey, mushrooms and vegetable dyes. The indirect services provided by forests and other natural ecosystems include stability of the micro-environment and the flow of moisture and nutrients to sustain productive farming systems.

This facilitative role of forests is all the more important in mountain regions, where due to limited accessibility and relative isolation, people's dependence on local resources is very high. The forest imparts important protection against hazards and risks associated with slope-induced fragility of landscape, occupies a central place in sustaining diversified land-based activities, and, along with pastures, organically links different biomass-based economic and ecological functions. Ideally, functions and contributions are integrated with positive ecosystem/social-system links, wherein community norms and practices are adapted to attributes of natural resources. However, their nature and magnitude tend to change following increased external state and market interventions in mountain areas.

Poverty and Resource Degradation Link

The physical, economic and ecological benefits of natural resources are not confined to the poor, but the poor do tend to depend more on nature-offered options. Unlike better-off groups, they do not have enough human-made endowments to support them (Agarwal and Narain 1990; Jodha 1992). And yet, this not only continues to be disregarded by development strategies, but its logic often is reversed in the scholarly discourse that attributes natural resource degradation in the developing countries primarily to poverty. I call this the poverty-environmental resource degradation (P-ERD) link.

Before discussing the central issue of poverty alleviation through building natural assets, I question the P-ERD link, and advance an alternative explanation for natural resource degradation. The essence of this argument is as follows: evidence on the correlation between P and ERD cannot be generalized because it does not exist everywhere and at all times; there is an alternative causal interpretation for the correlation, where it does exist, in which environmental resource degradation (ERD) causes poverty rather than the reverse; and the real cause of ERD is inequality rather than poverty. In the following discussion I elaborate on these aspects.

The P-ERD link is premised on the widespread co-existence of poverty and environmental resource degradation in developing countries. However, the reasoning is focused on the consequence rather than the process behind this phenomenon. Natural resource degradation, initiated and accelerated through different processes, has led to situations in which the poor emerge as the principal users of degraded natural resources, because of a lack of other options and a very low opportunity cost of labour in comparison to the rich. In the mainstream discourse on the subject, however, the P-ERD link is emphasized so frequently and effectively (for example, Durning 1989; Mink 1993), that is has acquired the status of a stereotype. This not only diverts attention from several basic issues involved in the process of resource degradation (Panayotou 1990; Metz 1991), but also prevents the recognition and analysis of simple field-level observations.

There is widespread evidence, for instance, that in many areas currently facing severe environmental resource degradation, resource users in the past were poorer than they are today, and yet the natural resource degradation was consciously prevented (Bromley and Chapagain 1984; Sanwal 1989; Pant 1935). Furthermore, in many areas the contribution of richer groups towards resource degradation is currently greater than that of the poor (Jodha 1992; Prakash 1997). A mapping of all districts of Nepal, using 39 indicators of development, reveals that the economically poorer districts ranked much higher in terms of the extent and health of environmental resources, including forests, pastures, soil and perennial water springs (ICIMOD 1997). The neighbouring country of Bhutan is poorer, even by South Asian standards, but has the highest extent of undisturbed natural forests and undepleted soil and water resources (National Environment Commission 1998).

The explanation for the co-existence of poverty and a better status of natural resources lies in the processes influencing patterns of resource use. First, the poor have limited needs and limited resource extractive capacities with which to erode the natural resources. More importantly, they are spared from external interventions and forces that often accompany the rising affluence of communities. Consequently, poor communities have an undiminished stake in the health and productivity of their environmental resources, and they have institutional norms and practices at their command to safeguard this stake. Dilution or disintegration of this community stake, and the erosion of grassroots-level mechanisms to protect and enhance it, constitute the fundamental reason behind natural resource degradation, irrespective of the poverty or richness of communities (Bromley and Chapagain 1984). This critical factor is largely ignored by the generalized mainstream view that attributes resource degradation to poverty. Consequently, the focus tends to be on proximate symptoms (e.g., poverty) rather than the key driving forces causing degradation of natural resources (Prakash 1997). More than poverty, it is inequality in resource ownership, access, power and other endowments that promotes environmental degradation (Boyce 1994).

The line of reasoning behind the P-ERD view is that poverty and scarcity cause desperation, which in turn promotes over-extraction of resources leading to resource degradation, causing still greater poverty and scarcity, which again further accentuate this cycle. A major limitation of this formulation is its assumptions about the poor's approach to natural resources and their resource use behaviour. There are four implicit premises underlying the depiction of poverty as the prime mover of environmental degradation. First, the over-extraction of resources is the only and preferred means of sustenance that poor people know. Second, the poor are ignorant of the limitations of their natural resources and of the consequences of their extractive usage practices. Third, the poor have little stake in the health and productivity of their natural resources. Finally, the poor have high rates of time preference, so that even if they are not ignorant of the limitations of resources, and have concern for the health of the resources, they cannot afford to limit extraction (Jodha 2001).

All these premises can be easily inferred from the current pattern of natural resource use in many poor areas. My contention, however, is that these are only manifestations of the erosion of past arrangements at the grassroots level, where the poor's situation and behaviour were previously quite opposite to the ones implied by the above premises. This can be illustrated with the help of examples from the Himalayan mountain regions of Nepal, India, China and Pakistan.

The Mountain Context

Mountain areas are of special significance in the P-ERD link. Most parts of the Hindu Kush–Himalayan region, extending from Afghanistan to Myanmar and covering eight countries, not only belong to the category of poor areas, but also are faced with the rapid degradation of natural resources. Furthermore, the past situation of these mountain areas in terms of ecosystem/social-system links, where resource users' behaviour was conditioned by bio-physical features or supply-side limitations, contrasts sharply with the present situation, where resource use is demand-driven and ignores limitations of the natural resource base (Jodha 1998). Finally, as elaborated below, these areas have a very high potential for persistence of both poverty and rapid degradation of natural resources.

The biophysical features of mountain areas — their high degree of fragility, marginality, limited accessibility and narrow location specificities of activities — tend to favour the persistence of poverty (Jodha 2000a). Because of these features, the conditions historically associated with enhanced economic performance or reduction of poverty in most parts of the world (e.g., resource use intensification, surplus generation, reinvestment and equitable trade) are rarely satisfied in the mountain areas. For instance, resource use intensification and high input absorption for enhanced productivity are constrained by fragility and marginality; gains associated with a larger scale of activities are not possible because of the high degree of resource diversity that favours a narrow location specificity of activities. These factors restrict the scope for surplus generation and reinvestment. The gains from trade and external exchange are also restricted by limited accessibility and isolation, and conditions also restrict the harnessing of opportunities for internal trade linked with small-scale, diversified production systems. Faced with these objective circumstances, the mountain communities, except for those in well-endowed and accessible valleys, live with limited, low productivity options and high environmental risks. Except for extracting niche resources, such as minerals, timber and hydro-power, the mainstream economic and political systems generally found mountainous areas unattractive and ignored them. Thus, nature and the mainstream economy together generated high poverty in these areas.

The poverty of the people and fragility of natural resources in the mountains make them potentially an ideal place for the operation of the P-ERD link. The failure of this potential to materialize in the past, however, encourages one to question the overemphasis of the P-ERD link. An understanding of the reasons behind the non-working of the P-ERD link in the past can provide useful insights to evolve options for breaking the vicious cycle of poverty-resource degradation-poverty implied by the P-ERD theme today. To facilitate this understanding, I next take a quick look at traditional systems of resource use, based on collective stakes and mechanisms to protect and enhance these stakes.

Past and Present Approaches to Natural Resource Management

Here, I describe some features of traditional natural resource management systems in mountain areas that have direct relevance to the poor's resource use behaviour. It should be added that the purpose of highlighting traditional practices in mountain areas is not to idealize them. The objectives are to indicate the grassroots-level institutional arrangements that helped in balancing the protection and extraction of resources to meet sustenance needs, to reflect on the processes and factors leading to the erosion and decline of these arrangements, and to identify possible lessons from the current initiatives directed at re-building natural assets.

Table 2.1: Natural Resource Use in Mountain Areas: Traditional and Present-Day Systems

Traditional Systems	Present-Day Systems
A. *Basic objective circumstances*:	
(i) Poor accessibility, isolation, semi-closeness: low extent and undependable external linkages and support: subsistence-oriented small populations;	(i) Enhanced physical, administrative and market integration of traditionally isolated, mountain areas/communities with the dominant mainstream systems at the latter's terms; increased population;
(ii) Almost total or critical dependence on local, fragile, diverse natural resource base (NRB).	(ii) Reduced critical dependence on local NRB; diversification of sources of sustenance;
	(iii) High external demand, natural resource extraction.
Consequence: High collective concern for health and productivity of NRB as a source of sustenance.	*Consequence:* Reduced collective concern for local NRB; rise of individual extractive strategies.
B. *Key driving forces/factors generated by (A)*:	
(i) Sustenance strategies totally focused on local resources;	(i) External linkage-based diversification of sources of sustenance (welfare, relief, trade, production etc.);
(ii) Sustenance-driven collective stake in protection and regeneration of NRB;	(ii) Disintegration of collective stake in NRB;
(iii) Close proximity and access-based functional knowledge/ understanding of limitations and usability of NRB;	(iii) Marginalization of traditional knowledge, and imposition of generalized solutions from above;
(iv) Local control of local resources/decisions; little gap between decision-makers and resource users.	(iv) The state imposed legal, administrative, fiscal measures displacing local controls/decisions; wider gap between decision-makers and local resource users.
Consequence: Collective stake in NRB supported by local control and functional knowledge of NRB.	*Consequence:* Loss of collective stake and local control over NRB; resource users respond in a 'reactive' mode.

Traditional Systems	Present-Day Systems
C. *Social responses to (B)*:	
(i) Evolution, adoption of resource use systems and folk technologies promoting diversification, resource protection, regeneration, recycling, etc; covering forest, pasture, cropland and their organic links;	(i) Extension of externally evolved, generalized technological/ institutional interventions; disregarding local concerns/experiences and traditional arrangements; promoting sectoral fragmentation;
(ii) Resource use/demand rationing measures;	(ii) Emphasis on supply-side issues ignoring management of demand pressure;
(iii) Formal/informal institutional mechanisms/group action to enforce the above.	(iii) Formal, rarely enforced measures.
Consequence: Effective social adaptation to NRB.	*Consequence*: Natural resources over-extracted as open-access resources.
D. *End results*:	
(i) Nature-friendly management systems;	(i) Over-extractive resource use systems, driven by uncontrolled external market demands and internal population-driven demands;
(ii) Evolved and enforced by local communities;	(ii) Externally conceived, ineffective and un-enforceable interventions for protection of NRB;
(iii) Facilitated by close functional knowledge and community control over local resources and local affairs.	(iii) Little investment and technology input in NRB.
Consequence: 'Resource-protective/ regenerative' social system-ecosystem links.	*Consequence*: Rapid degradation of fragile NRB; nature pleads not guilty; so do the rural poor.

Source: Adapted from Jodha (1995, 1998).

Table 2.1 summarizes the inferences from various studies of natural resource usage in mountainous areas. Faced with low productivity options, high environmental risks and limited and undependable external linkages, most of the communities in these areas had to evolve their sustenance strategies through adaptations to the limitations and potentialities of their local natural resource base (NRB). Adaptations included seasonally and spatially diversified and interlinked land-based activities such as diversified farming systems, farming-forestry links and common property resources. Despite internal inequities and occupation-specific differences in gains from the NRB, everyone's close dependence on local resources created an integrated collective stake in their natural resources, reflected by group action to protect and manage them (Berkes 1989; Jodha 1998; Leach *et al.* 1997).

In the context of the relative isolation and small size of rural communities, physical proximity to environmental resources imparted knowledge and understanding of the limitations and usability of their NRB. This not only helped in developing folk technological practices to protect and regenerate the resources while using them, but also facilitated the creation of a locally enforceable range of regulatory measures to guide use-intensity, such as rotational grazing, periodic fallowing of lands, combining annual and perennial-based activities, and periodic contributions of labour, grain, etc. towards investment for trenching, fencing and other practices for upkeep and development of the resources (Pant 1935; Jodha 1998; Tamang *et al.* 1996; Bjonness 1983).

Most importantly, enforcement of the above measures was facilitated by social actions, community norms, group action and in some cases feudal arrangements for punishing the defaulters. The ultimate source of strength for enforcement of these arrangements was local autonomy over local resources and local affairs, and the resource users' collective experiences and knowledge of their resource base. Despite the presence of some inegalitarian elements, these collective arrangements worked, because the commonness of the source of supplies helped in integrating the individual stakes into a collective stake in the local natural resources (Jodha 1998; Sanwal 1989; Leach *et al.* 1997; Tamang *et al.* 1996).

The regulatory measures and collective efforts also extended to demand-side aspects of resource use, as indicated by collective sharing arrangements for food and fodder during scarcity and crisis periods, management of demand pressure through periodic migration of people and animals, and restrictions on the size and composition of animal holdings (Jodha 1995; Bjonness 1983; Prakash 1997). In some mountain communities, the demand pressure also was controlled through restricting population growth by requiring eldest sons to become Buddhist monks — a practice that still prevails, to an extent, in countries like Bhutan.

To sum up, the foundations of traditional systems of natural resource management in mountain areas included: communities' collective stake in the health and productivity of local natural resources; physical proximity and practical experience-based knowledge, as a basis for evolving technical and institutional measures to prevent over-extractive resource usage; local control over local resources and adherence to social sanctions that empowered the community to enforce measures that helped in balancing supply and demand aspects of resource use.

These arrangements helped significantly in preventing the operation of the P-ERD link in the past. However, as Table 2.1 also shows, these arrangements got eroded following changes that (except for population growth) were initiated from the outside following the closer physical, administrative and economic integration of mountain areas into the mainstream economy and society. The most critical and common element of these changes has been the conception, design and implementation of external interventions by state agencies without sufficient understanding of the ground realities, including local communities' concerns, capabilities and knowledge systems. These externally designed interventions, directed to the development or transformation of mountain areas without a mountain perspective, created circumstances and perverse incentives (such as individual-centered subsidies for resource use intensification and for the acceptance of external advice and technologies) that finally led to disintegration of communities' stake in natural resources, disempowerment of communities in the management of grassroots-level problems, and marginalization of local knowledge systems and institutional arrangements that helped in enforcing NRB protection in the past (Somanathan 1991; Tamang *et al.* 1996; Guha 1983; Butt and Price 2000; Bromley and Chapagain 1984). Table 2.1 indicates some of the provisions that eroded traditional arrangements without providing effective substitutes. Examples include legal and administrative impositions on resource access and usage, extension of resource-intensive technologies unsuited to mountain areas, and focus on supply promotion ignoring demand control.

The enhanced physical, administrative and market integration of traditionally less accessible marginal areas into the mainstream systems reduced the crucial (if not total) dependence of local communities on local NRB. Integration brought several gains to these areas, including external linkage-based increase and diversification of sources of sustenance through welfare and relief schemes, new production possibilities, increased gains through trade and exchange, infrastructural facilities and social-sector services. But it also had some backlash effects in terms of dilution or disintegration of a community's collective stake in the NRB, disregard and erosion of the traditional arrangements that in the past helped to protect and regulate use of the NRB, and an end to the local communities' roles and responsibilities in managing local resources and local affairs. This happened through the introduction of largely outward-looking and politically-oriented formal institutions such as panchayats (village councils), the empowerment of government revenue officials and forest officials as custodians of natural resources, the replacement of locally evolved institutional arrangements and customary provisions by legal and administrative arrangement evolved at a higher level, and the distortion of community incentive systems by patronage, subsidies and relief. The point here is not to question the integration and its benefits, but to question the process that disregarded and marginalized the traditional arrangements for managing and strengthening the communities' natural assets. The rural poor obviously can not be held responsible for this change.

To reiterate, integration has surely helped the mountain communities (though not all communities or individuals equally) in several ways, including reduction in the extent of poverty and vulnerability. But in most cases this change did not facilitate ongoing community collective involvement in natural resource management.

Another negative side-effect of integration is the shift from supply-driven to demand-driven usage of the extraction of resources. The two-way adaptation process — that is, adapting human demands to resource limitations, and adapting or amending resources to rising human needs through terraced water harvesting, annual-perennial combinations and so on — that characterized traditional systems has become a one-way process. The meeting of uncontrolled demands via enhanced technological capacities and support systems to over-extract resources has become the dominant pattern. As mountain people often say, the 'greed' of the rich rather than the 'need' of the poor has become the driving force behind over-extraction. An associated feature has been the development of unequal highland-lowland economic links, leading to unrealistic pricing and limited compensation for mountain resources, products and services, such as timber, hydro-power, non-timber forest products (NTFPs) and tourism services, flowing from mountains to lowland economies (Jodha 2000a). The integration did not facilitate an internalization of gains for mountain areas availed by the lowland systems.

Lessons for Rebuilding Natural Assets

In view of the visible failures and ineffectiveness of most government efforts to protect natural resources and prevent their degradation, one may be tempted to look for some leads from traditional arrangements. Before venturing in this direction, however, it should be clearly stated that pleading for the revival of traditional arrangements for natural resource management could be dismissed as an exercise in futility because most of the objective circumstances associated with them in the past have completely changed. Market penetration and changes in the attitudes of village communities have promoted values and norms that put a very low premium on collective strategies. Population growth, a rise in factionalism and increased economic differentiation have made it difficult to evolve and maintain a collective community stake in natural resources. Depletion of natural resources and the depletion of the culture of group action (or social capital) tend to reinforce each other, accentuating the community's indifference towards rehabilitation of natural resources for collective gains. Also, the legal, administrative and fiscal mechanisms (despite lip-service for the opposite) have strong tendencies towards centralization and the application of uniform, top-down solutions that ignore diversity at the grassroots level.

However, without pleading for a revival of traditional arrangements in the form that they once existed, one can focus on a search for functional substitutes for traditional arrangements that can fit with the present-day circumstances. To do so, one should focus on the three pillars of traditional systems that in the past played crucial roles in preventing human-induced degradation of natural resources in mountain areas. To reiterate, these were: a strong community stake in their local NRB driven by communities' almost total dependence on the same; local control over local resources resulting from isolation and an inaccessibility-induced degree of autonomy; and resource users' and decision-makers' functional knowledge of the limitations and usability of their diverse natural resources, resulting from people's close physical proximity and access to resources.

The incorporation of the three elements — community stake, local control and functional knowledge of natural resources — into the present resource use systems may help in the rehabilitation and conservation of natural resources, and should be promoted. But revival of historically associated objective circumstances — exclusive and almost total dependence on local resources, semi-closed communities, physical proximity for all stakeholders — is neither possible nor, in some contexts, desirable. Hence, the challenge lies in creating a present-day functional substitute that can promote these key elements and induce communities to protect and develop their natural assets while using them.

In Table 2.2, I briefly summarize the relevant issues, and indicate the constraints to such change with respect to each of the three elements. This is followed by possible remedial measures. The suggested possibilities are supported by small and scattered evidence based on successful initiatives in community forestry in recent years. Accordingly, the following discussion of possible approaches to rebuilding natural assets combines the usable elements of traditional systems of natural resource management with the experiences of recent initiatives on community forest management.

Table 2.2: Approaches to Revival of Key Elements of Traditional Resource Use Systems in the Present Context

(A) Community Stake in Local Natural Resources	(B) Local Control Over Local Natural Resources	(C) Recognition and Use of Resource Users' Perspectives and Traditional Knowledge System
Constraints		
(1) Formal legal, administrative and fiscal controls/ restrictions creating a range of perverse incentives; reactive mode of community behaviour as individuals. (2) Highly depleted status of NRB creating no hope and incentive to have a stake in it. (3) More diverse and differentiated communities with different, individual rather than group-based views on community resources.	(1) State's inbuilt resistance to self-disempowerment through passing decision-making power to local communities; focus on 'proxy arrangements', e.g.,, village panchayats. (2) Faction ridden, rural communities driven by diverse signals and concerns. (3) NGOs as key change-facilitating agents, often governed by own perspectives and concerns.	(1) Top-down interventions with a mix of 'arrogance, ignorance and insensitivity' towards local perspectives and traditional knowledge systems. (2) Focus on (old context-specific) forms of traditional practices rather than their rationale for use in the current context. (3) Rapid disappearance and invisibility of indigenous knowledge.
Possible remedial approaches		
(1) Genuine local autonomy for local resource management (see 'B' for constraints to this); legal framework and support system for natural resource user groups.	(1) Genuine decentralization of decision-making powers and resources to communities; raising latter's capacities to respond to the above (with the help of NGOs).	(1) Promotion of bottom-up approaches to resource management strategies, using participatory methods and NGO help.

(A) Community Stake in Local Natural Resources	(B) Local Control Over Local Natural Resources	(C) Recognition and Use of Resource Users' Perspectives and Traditional Knowledge System
(2) Resource protection, investment and use of new technologies for regeneration/high productivity of NRB (using experiences of successful initiatives).	(2) Rebuilding 'social capital', mobilization and participatory methods using NGO input; focus on diversified, high value products from rehabilitated NRB (using successful experiences).	(2) Focused efforts to identify present-day functional substitutes of traditional measures for resource management.
(3) Collective stake through planned 'diversification' and 'shareholding' system in natural resource development and gains (using experiences of successful initiatives).	(3) Required changes in NGO approaches/ perspectives by introspection; involving small local groups, and unlabelled agencies.	(3) R and D to incorporate rationale of traditional knowledge system (using experiences of successful initiatives).

Source: Adapted from Jodha (1998).

Reviving a Community Stake in Natural Resources

A community stake in local natural resources is central to their protection, development and equitable use. In the present-day context, however, there are more circumstances discouraging this than supporting it. In most cases, local communities simply adjust to external controls and perverse incentive systems, such as government laws and regulations, rather than controlling or planning their own approach to resources. The whole incentive structure — permitting privatization of community resources and illegal extraction with little penalty, giving priority to political patronage, and unrealistically low pricing of high-value natural resources products — acts as a disincentive for community involvement in resource protection and regeneration. Reconciling the interests of diverse groups in the villages constitutes yet another challenge for building a community's collective stake in the health and productivity of natural resources. Internal heterogeneity and inequities are not new things to South Asian villages. As noted in Table 2.1, however, the decline of the culture of group action, increased economic differentiation and socio-political factionalism have greatly increased the differences and divisions in rural communities.

Furthermore, traditional circumstances, like dependence on a common resource base, that facilitate informal inter-group bargaining and reconciliation (Leach *et al.* 1997) no longer exist. In place of a local NRB as a common source of sustenance, now there prevail multiple and diverse sources of sustenance, of internal and external origin. The long lead-time available for internal bargaining and adaptations is no longer available. At times the socio-political links for different groups fall outside the boundaries of local communities' influence, and the organic links between different natural resource-based activities — farming-forestry-livestock complementarities — are broken due to outsourcing of their input needs and product disposal destination (Jodha 2002). All these factors obstruct the evolution or revival of a community's collective stake in natural resources. Moreover, in the context of the present bio-physical and economic status of a community's natural resources, local control over local resources may not induce a positive response from the community. The natural resources in many areas are depleted to a level that does not inspire much hope, let alone community groups' interest in their management. The emerging tendency on the part of people (both rich and poor) is somehow to grab the common property resources as private property, rather than to collaborate in collective efforts to rehabilitate the depleted common resources.

Remedial Measures

Most of the aforementioned constraints to reviving a community's stake in local natural resources are of an institutional nature, requiring different approaches and lead-time periods to resolve them. However, in view of the evidence that people care more about more productive units than unproductive units of the same type of community resource, as reported by Jodha (1992), and considering the people's rising priorities to economic gains (Jodha 2002), one can identify the depleted state of community resources as an entry point for reviving a collective stake. Remedial efforts have to focus on converting depleted natural resources into productive natural assets. Regeneration and development of community resources, equitable access to resources and their gains (including for the poor) and reward or compensation for downstream services of natural assets built and maintained by local communities have to be the integral components of these remedial strategies.

The structure of my reasoning is as follows: Eliminate the conditions that induce people's indifference towards community natural resources; raise resource-productivity to achieve this; promote investment and associated activities to enhance resource productivity; to facilitate this, mobilize communities and their effective participation in resource management; to promote participation, ensure both local control over local resources and equitable access for all groups in the community and enhance local capacities not only to achieve local control, but also to bargain for ensuring an internalization of downstream gains from stable and productive natural resources.

The linchpins of the whole process are community mobilization and participation, including incentive structures to facilitate these, and enhancing local capacities for new tasks, including empowerment to seek macro-level attention and support. The two aspects are interlinked in several ways.

In the context of highly differentiated rural communities, the effective group action implied by the above propositions may be dismissed as wishful thinking. However, the on-the-ground experience of some successful initiatives offers a different perspective and inspires greater hope for change. The Agha Khan Rural Support Programme in mountains and other areas of Pakistan has effectively promoted social mobilization for natural resource development and economic well-being of communities. State-supported community efforts in several parts of India, especially in the states of West Bengal, Gujarat, Madhya Pradesh and Andhra Pradesh, have contributed to the rapid regeneration of forest and other natural resources as revealed by both satellite imageries and field observations (Poffenberger et al. 1996; Hazra et al. 1996; Saigal 2001). The often-cited case of the Sukhomajri Project in India, where community involvement in total watershed restoration includes innovative mechanisms for the equitable use of natural assets (such as sharing gains through water rights to non-land owning households), illustrates the scope for mobilizing diverse groups for collective resource management (Sarin 1996; Agarwal and Narain in this volume). Community irrigation systems and user-group forestry programmes in Nepal, involving the mobilization of communities for local resource development and management, furnish further evidence of the effectiveness of group action in building natural assets (Shivakoti et al. 1997; Joshi 1997).

There are many other success stories of social mobilization not only for natural resource management but also for poverty eradication. A Ford Foundation-supported programme on asset building in various countries (Ford Foundation 2002) offers examples. United Nations Development Programme-supported programmes focusing on decentralization and participation-based rural poverty eradication, such as the Participatory District Development Programme and the Local Governance Programme in Nepal, are another example (PDDP 2001, LGP 2001). International Fund for Agricultural Development (IFAD)-supported projects in uplands and elsewhere have also helped building group action for poverty eradication (IFAD 2002). Social mobilization for natural asset building and other development activities, thus, is not only being increasingly emphasized but has demonstrated effectiveness in several areas.

Focus on Economic Gains

A common feature of most of the successful social mobilization efforts is the visible economic gains perceived by the communities. The mechanisms to ensure that such opportunities are perceived, even in the shortrun, differ from intervention to intervention. They include initial component-specific subsidies (payable before or after accomplishment of the tasks); repayable activity-specific loans (often with collective undertaking for repayment); encouragement for local resource mobilization, sometimes through micro-credit schemes; and support for local demand-driven initiatives rather than top-down, supply-driven activities. In the case of natural assets, the globalization process can also offer much-needed economic incentives for development and efficient management by encouraging the trade in high-value NTFPs like herbs and certified organic products. This can promote diversification and value-adding processes to enhance gains from healthy and productive natural assets, as seen in the case of parts of China, India and Nepal (Jodha 2002). If equitably shared, these changes can further encourage community participation.

One of the most effective means to ensure enhanced economic gains from natural assets is internalization of the benefits from efficient management that accrue to the lowland/external economies almost free of cost. For instance, communities in the Indian Himalayas spend effort on resource conservation that helps prevent downstream floods and silting of dams. The farmers in downstream plains, who use the irrigation water and electricity from these dams, pay no water and electricity charges. Furthermore, the royalties received by the hill states for water and power generated through such projects rarely reach the community levels. There is a partial exception to this pattern in Nepal, where the state shares with the local communities the revenue generated by mountain tourism. Rectification of this situation would call for compensation to the mountain communities for their custodianship of well-managed natural resources. In the natural assets project framework this would be an example of internalization. It would work as an important economic incentive to induce community action to build and manage natural assets.

Considerable conceptual work has been done on assessing the economic value of environmental and other natural resource flows, but compensating mechanisms based on such flows from highlands to lowlands are yet to be attempted in South Asia. Outside the region, however, there do exist some cases where communities and agencies have evolved mechanisms to ensure compensation for environmental services by beneficiary communities to those who facilitate these services. These include: irrigators paying upstream land owners for improvements in stream flow in Colombia; irrigators financing upstream reforestation in Australia; a Watershed Conservation Fund in Quito, Ecuador helping upstream farmers; Perrier Payments for Water Quality in France; Makilink Forest Reserve in the Philippines paying farmers for land retirement; hydroelectric companies paying upstream land owners via FONAFICO in Costa Rica, and New York City paying upstream farmers for protecting its drinking water (Koch-Weser 2002 and Rosa *et al.* in this volume). In South Asia, such efforts to facilitate the internalization of the gains of natural asset building and management are constrained by a lack of awareness, a lack of usable operational mechanisms and the persistence of state-to-state (politically influenced) negotiations on royalty payments without involving or rewarding the communities for their resource conservation efforts.

Local Control over Local Natural Resources

An important facilitative factor that could help in rebuilding communities' stake in natural resources and converting them into natural assets is community control over resources. Traditionally, mainstream decision-makers have permitted greater local autonomy to communities in several mountain areas. However, this was more due to default — that is, their inaccessibility-imposed ignorance and indifference towards mountain areas — rather than a conscious decision. With the increased physical and administrative integration of fragile, remote, marginal areas with the mainstream political-economic systems, most of the local natural resources belonging to the communities have been taken over by the state either through formal law or through disregard of customary laws and practices (Hiremath 1997; Poffenberger *et al.* 1996; Guha 1983). In India, it happened through the colonial British government extending its control over forests and establishing forest departments to manage commercial extraction as property of the Crown. After independence national governments inherited the system, with some recent changes (Hobley 1996). In Nepal, a major change happened with the nationalization of forests in 1957, and the debate on further changes is still continuing (Baral 2002). Lynch and Talbott (1995) analyze similar processes in different Asian countries. The consequent lack of local control prevents community protection and regulation in the use of natural resources. Deprived of forest ownership, communities tend to over-extract resources (Bromley and Chapagain 1984). The importance of changing this situation can hardly be overstated.

Constraints

Genuine and effective devolution or restoration of local control over local natural resources faces several constraints emanating from the state's resistance to self-disempowerment. Despite all the talk of decentralization and 'power to the people', when it comes to the control of a property or productive resource, the state operating through its sectoral bureaucracy typically tries to avoid the issue through different devices (Jodha 2000b). For instance, it tries half-hearted compromises, such as under Joint Forest Management (JFM) in India, where communities are involved in protecting resources and there is limited sharing of specific products like timber, and communities are allowed to use intermediate products such as fodder, fuel and minor forest products that the state finds difficult to use.

Use of proxy arrangements is another approach adopted by the state. This is illustrated by the creation of formal institutions such as the village panchayats, with all legal powers and provisions determined by the decision-makers at the top. In most cases, such small-scale political bodies have very little concern and involvement in natural resource management, except when relief and subsidies can be mobilized by showing the extent of community resources in the village (Jodha 1992; Saxena 2000). Despite the recent focus on decentralization, panchayats may not be a substitute for 'user groups' since their goals are too diversified and natural resource protection constitutes a small component therein. The difference between village commons managed by village elders or user-group leaders and those managed by a panchayat makes this clear. The former pay greater attention to the up-keep of natural resources, while the latter tend to treat them as objects for getting government subsidies. Besides, the latter are largely political bodies (Brara 1987; EERN 2000). Conflict between the elected village councilors and the JFM or forest user group leaders tends to erode the gains of the new participatory initiatives in different parts of India (Jodha

2000b). Faction-ridden and differentiated rural communities, as alluded to earlier, and high dependence on government patronage, complement the constraints originating from the state side.

Remedial Measures: Emerging Scenario

Despite strong resistance to devolution on the part of the state, the current scenario offers some options to gradually alter the situation. To begin with, there are greater awareness and efforts at the national and international levels to promote decentralization and community participation to ensure sustainable development. The latest global thrust, promoted by rich donors such as the World Bank and International Monetary Fund through their Poverty Reduction Strategy Programmes, accords high importance to community ownership of development programmes facilitated by decentralization and participation. The field initiatives by the Ford Foundation, United Nations Development Programme and IFAD mentioned earlier also focus on changes in this direction. Induced by these global thrusts and in some cases by donor pressure, national governments are slowly proceeding with various decentralization initiatives (e.g., in Nepal and India).

Apart from these — largely supply-side factors indirectly favouring local control of local resources and local affairs — there are also some demand-side possibilities. Mainly through the efforts of non-governmental organizations (NGOs) and community organizations, the advocacy and demand for greater control of local resources by local communities is increasing at both national and international levels. This demand is supported by convincing evidence that devolution can help better management and sustainability of natural resources. The state in many cases has positively responded to such demands. This is partly a product of capacity building and empowerment of local communities through institutional interventions supported by NGOs, donors and enlightened government agencies. (For discussion see Krishna *et al.* 1997; Zazueta 1995; Gilmour and Fisher 1991; Saxena 2000.)

Local Perspectives and Traditional Knowledge Systems

Even when community involvement in natural resource management is promoted at national or global levels, in practice it must be implemented at local or micro levels. Hence, approaches to natural asset building have to be sensitive to local perceptions. An important dimension relates to traditional knowledge and experiences about the potentialities and limitations of natural resources and possible ways to address them. Examples may include differences according to slopes in mountain areas in soil treatment, crop combinations, crop fallow rotation and so on. These aspects are often bypassed while initiating interventions for local resource development in Nepal and India (Jodha 1992; Tamang *et al.* 1996). Even global initiatives, such as treaties and conventions on biodiversity conservation, generally ignore local concerns and indigenous knowledge. Macro-level perceptions are rarely linked to diverse micro-level realities. In the process, they lose valuable technical (folk-agronomic) knowledge that could help in enhancing the productivity of natural assets.

Constraints

As reported by Jodha and Partap (1992) and Tamang *et al.* (1996), the important factors obstructing the incorporation of indigenous knowledge in the present-day interventions for natural resource development are the arrogance and insensitivity of the planners towards the local communities as a source of information to solve local problems. This is compounded by the general non-availability of indigenous knowledge in a very articulated form on the one hand, and by the technocrat decision-makers' focus on the form rather than the rationale of traditional practices on the other. Since the forms of traditional practices had been context specific (e.g., extensive farming practices worked well under low population pressure, or total dependence on local resources helped in building a community's stake in a semi-isolation context), they became less feasible or ineffective when the situation changed. Instead of evolving alternative forms or practices to suit the changed situation, the decision-makers have discarded both the form and the rationale of traditional practices such as combining annuals with perennials and husbandry of water springs.

Remedial Measures

The following remedial measures should be encouraged: focus on bottom-up approaches to natural resource management; sensitization of decision-makers to local communities' perceptions through advocacy and participatory approaches; and identification and incorporation of the rationale of traditional practices into new technological and institutional measures planned for natural resources. Some of the ongoing initiatives supported by NGOs, such as water harvesting, bamboo plantation, regeneration of pasture and rehabilitation of commons are already using these approaches (Tamang *et al.* 1996; Sanwal 1989; Saxena 1995). Globally rising concerns for indigenous knowledge systems and practices may help in this regard. In the context of economic globalization, the rising demand for natural and organic products may further promote the case for use of indigenous knowledge systems. For example, agencies collecting medicinal herbs from different areas in Hindu Kush–Himalayan region also collect information on their usage and processing methods (Jodha 2002). Similarly, the increasing attention to indigenous resource use systems in the context of sustainable development strategies can help in incorporating local knowledge into interventions for local resource development.

Recent Initiatives in Community Forest Management: A Critique

Because of various factors — such as adverse downstream consequences like floods and silting of dams following natural resource degradation in mountain areas; rising global concern for protecting mountain natural resources as a source of international public goods like environmental services, unique biodiversity and fresh water; and the state's inability to police these resources, despite increased expenditure on it; and the successful experience of a number of small-scale community initiatives to protect and rebuild natural resources — a number of programmes to conserve, regenerate and protect the natural resources, particularly forests, through the involvement of communities have been initiated during the last two decades in different countries, including in the Hindu Kush–Himalayan region. The details have been analyzed in several studies (Shackleton *et al.* 2002; Brown *et al.* 2002; Butt and Price 2000).

In the following discussion, I focus on the two best-known programmes in this area, Joint Forest Management in India and User Group Forestry (UGF) in Nepal. The JFM programme, initiated over a decade ago in India, has spread to almost all states in the country and covers more than 14 million hectares or over 18 per cent of the total forest land in India. By June 2001, 62,890 JFM groups were involved in managing these forests (Saigal 2001). Through UGF in Nepal over the last 20 years, more than 5,000 user groups have taken control of more than 600,000 hectares of forest for protection and regeneration. With assistance from International Center for Integrated Mountain Development (ICIMOD) they have formed the Federation of Community Forest Users in Nepal (FECOFUN) to promote the interests of UGF. The similar efforts supported by ICIMOD have led to the formation of the Himalayan Forum for Community Forestry to promote dialogue among senior officials of the forestry sector in the Hindu Kush–Himalayan region as a whole (Upadhyaya 1999). I have already referred to some of their experiences in the preceding discussion. Here, I briefly comment on their achievements and limitations, including their possible contribution towards helping the poor while rehabilitating and strengthening the forests as natural assets.

Despite differences in history, scale and complexity characterizing the subject in India and Nepal, as well as inter-area variations in the performance of the intervention in the same country, I comment on some common features of these initiatives. Broadly speaking, the new initiatives are considered a success, particularly, when seen in terms of the improved status of forestry as measured by forest cover and biomass production. Both field observations and satellite images indicate this in most areas. The positive achievements of these initiatives are also indicated by other changes, which are briefly described here. They have resulted from community involvement in protecting forests by controlling encroachments, regulating forest use and promoting conservation and development activities. An important positive change observed in several areas has been the increased degree of trust between communities and forest department officials, the lack of which in the past contributed to the degradation of forests. Through regulated collection of intermediate products such as fodder and fuel, and wage employment on forest conservation and development activities, the earnings of community members have also increased in some areas. In addition, through collection and sale of specific forest products, the management committees of forest user groups have succeeded in building investable funds for undertaking development activities for the communities. A major facilitative role in these successes has been played by NGOs, donor agencies and responsive forest department officials (Upadhyaya 1999; Saigal 2001; Shackleton et al. 2002). One distinctive feature of these programmes is that they require people's input or sacrifice — in terms of foregoing the opportunities to collect bio-fuel, fodder and other supplies, or grazing of animals due to complete closure or restricted access to forest areas to promote conservation and regeneration of resources — before the gains of enhanced supplies and income flow to them after resources are regenerated and rehabilitated, unlike most of the rural programmes that start with bribing (i.e., subsidizing) the people to induce their participation in the programme (Jodha 2000b).

Without minimizing these achievements, these new initiatives have shown rather mixed or limited success in terms of several crucial aspects discussed below. The following assessment, however, is explicitly qualified by stating that inter-area, inter-country differences do exist.

Resource-centered rather than People-centered Focus

From the very beginning, the programmes under review were directed to rehabilitate the degraded forests by providing some incentive and authority to the communities to encourage them to participate in the programme. Consequently, addressing communities' concerns and perceptions was never an explicit part of the initial design. Furthermore, the performance of the programmes is also usually judged in terms of changed status and productivity of the forest, and the factors contributing to the same, such as reduced extent of encroachment, or changed images of and attitudes towards forest officials, rather than changes in people's life and economy. Viewed this way the programmes have helped in rehabilitating and building 'natural assets', but whose assets? (Jodha 2000b; Hiremath 1997; Agarwal 2001)

Goal of Poverty Alleviation: Neither Primacy nor Explicit Focus

This issue emerges as a logical consequence of the feature stated in the previous section. Notwithstanding the fact that community forestry has enhanced the biomass productivity of forests, created occasional wage employment for the community and contributed to the accumulation of investable resources with forest user group councils, the programmes in several areas have also adversely affected the poor, women and other disadvantaged groups.

First, unlike the traditional forms of communal resource management, which typically recognized the use rights of all village residents, the new formal arrangements exclude many, especially women and the poor, both as partners in decision-making and as users of resources (Agarwal 2001; EERN 2000).

Second, despite increased biomass productivity, collection of material is restricted to a few occasions in a year. Besides, they often mechanically use equity norms where per household extent of access is the same irrespective of differences in the economic and occupational needs of the rich and the poor. The poor, especially those who collect and carry head-loads of bio-fuel or fodder for their own use or for sale, having few resources of their own, lose the most, and are compelled to encroach on the forest areas of their own or other villages to meet their barest needs. The time required for fuel collection (a key forest product harvested by women) from distant places has increased many-fold in some areas (Agarwal 2001). The nomadic pastoralists in high mountains who use small ruminants as pack animals in their trading occupation have suffered the most, because of reduced access to common property resources following the imposition of restricted access as a part of UGF in Nepal. This has forced many to abandon petty trading or reduce their herd size (Upadhyaya 1999).

Third, the organic links between farming, forestry and livestock activities — a part of the poor's coping strategies against risk and vulnerabilities — have disintegrated following restrictive provisions that do not allow free and unlimited access to forest resources, in the interest of conservation and regeneration.

Finally, the products preferred and used by the poor, such as fodder and fuel, tend to get lower priority in product composition set by the forest user group councils, who favour products such as timber that have long waiting periods. The poor typically have little voice in changing these priorities.

Exceptions

Despite a lack of explicit concern for the poor, in some areas both under JFM and UGF, the poor, when allowed to harvest, have gained from the increased productivity of community forests (Shackleton *et al.* 2002; D'Silva and Nagnath 2002). Nepal's leasehold forestry programme is the best-known initiative that exclusively focuses on households below the poverty line. The programme, run by the government of Nepal, is supported by IFAD, the Food and Agriculture Organization and the government of the Netherlands, and is implemented in ten districts. It focuses on allocating degraded forest lands to poor households on 40-year leases. The programme is judged quite successful in terms of rehabilitating the forest (with ownership of the trees resting with the state) and building agroforestry and fruit tree-based new opportunities. However, there are some uncertainties in terms of the continuation of the programme once donor support ends, and doubts on the transfer of lease rights to children once parents' lease rights expire. There are also a few other obstacles faced by the programme; for example, it is reported that it takes more than two years to get lease certificates for a forest tract (Mahapatra 2002).

Nature of Community Involvement: Illusion of Autonomy and Empowerment

By design and intention, community involvement in forestry programmes was an arrangement to seek people's participation in policing forests, something the state was unable to do despite increased expenditure. Facilities for collecting intermediate products like fodder, litter and some NTFPs, and for sharing the benefits of final products like timber, were included as incentives. Authority to prevent encroachment and regulation of intermediate product collection were also part of the arrangements.

Beyond these arrangements, however, the rest of the authority rested fully with the forest department, including promotion and recognition of forest user groups, disqualification of groups for certain reasons and the right to approve work plans. Thus, communities' involvement in the forestry programmes has been similar to that of a dignified collective-tenant. There has not been enough real autonomy or devolution of real authority for management of community natural resources (Shackleton et al. 2002; Butt and Price 2000). In effect, communities under these forestry programmes are caretakers of the state's natural assets, where any legal or other change affecting the asset is the sole right of the state. This may not be very conducive to building a community's collective stake in local natural resources. This assessment is further strengthened by recent talk of 'collaborative forestry' or 'corporatization of forestry', where forests could be given to private firms as collaborators. This fuels the communities' suspicions about the intentions of the state vis-à-vis the forestry sector (Saxena 1995; Hiremath 1997).

State-approved Group Formation: A Proxy for Social Capital

Under these programmes the forest department not only provides the broad guidelines for forest user group formation and plans, but also gives a stamp of recognition before the user group is entitled to have any authority. Even existing traditional community groups who are efficiently managing their forests in tribal areas need to be registered by forest officials for their formal recognition (Jodha 2000b).

Such state-sponsored and guided user groups follow the standard top-down norms and procedures about inclusion and exclusion of membership, and have little sensitivity to diversity in the local situation. Except for membership in a user group, the people involved may not have any other commonalities necessary for building trust and confidence within the group. Such groups may not represent what is described as 'social capital'. However, effective mediation by NGOs has helped in converting such formal groupings into 'social capital' in some areas. Recognition and acceptance of any product or service as an important shared item by the community has also promoted genuine group action for natural resource upkeep in many cases (EERN 2000; Butt and Nath 2000; Saxena 2000).

Missing Institutional Perspectives and Conflict Situations

Quite related to the feature mentioned earlier is another dimension of community forestry programmes. The JFM and UGF should be seen as institutional arrangements that attempt to help communities to mobilize themselves to protect and conserve their NRB despite unclear terms and conditions offered by the state. Because of the rather mechanical approach of the state, however, forest user groups are established without sufficient understanding of their institutional context in terms of local history, existing group dynamics, socio-economic differences, power relations and possible ways and processes to address these issues (Jodha 2000b; Agarwal 1997; Gilmour and Fisher 1991). Accordingly, in some sense forest departments seem to treat a 'grouping of people' as not different from a 'bunching of logs' in forest areas. Unless there is active NGO mediation to manage these differences, the composed groups are often faced with a variety of actual and potential conflicts between traditional community groups and new state-formulated groups, between the formal political leadership of the elected representatives of village councils and the leaders of forest user groups, and between intra-community sub-groups based on class, caste, gender, losers and gainers (Saigal 2001; Agarwal 2001). Such conflicts often erode the gains of a community's collective effort to manage forest resources. Community forestry programmes, therefore, need some provisions and preparations to address this problem (Saxena 2000).

Persisting Ambiguities and Uncertainties

The community forestry initiatives are faced with a number of ambiguities and uncertainties that can act as risks in the future (Mahapatra 2002; Saigal 2001; Jodha 2000b; Upadhyaya 1999; Saxena 2000). First, in purely legal terms, in most cases (at least in Indian states) these initiatives and their functioning are the product of administrative orders of the government without any legislative foundation. Unlike written laws, these orders can be withdrawn at any time. The pressure by NGOs, media and communities for changing the situation is already growing (EERN 2000). Second, the provisions about registration and the functioning of community forestry programmes provide forest officials with disproportionately great powers that can be used to limit the initiatives of the communities by several methods including disqualifying the user groups and their work plans.

The third source of uncertainties is government's shifting approach to community forestry. They may relate to sharing the benefits, especially from high-value NTFPs, as in India, or permitting corporatization of community forestry as tried by new law in Nepal for the Terai region and debated in India for last several years. Such prospects of change can shake the people's trust in government initiatives promoting community forestry (Saxena 1995; Hiremath 1997; Brown *et al.* 2002; Shackleton *et al.* 2002). A fourth source of uncertainty relates to the possible withdrawal of donor support to community forestry. In view of the significant performance gaps between the projects with and without donor support, the potential consequences of possible withdrawal are seen with concern (Brown *et al.* 2002). Building local support from within the communities is a major issue that should be addressed in this context. Such uncertainties may create opportunities for rich global corporations to co-opt community forestry programmes with a goal of over-extraction of forests. Fifth, the well-functioning community approaches and collective mechanisms addressed to forests protection and conservation may face serious disruptions once the programmes move from the protection to the production stage of resource management. Levels and modes of extraction as well as distributive arrangements may pose different types of problems. Both processing and marketing requirements may need different management skills. The conflict levels may also change. These problems require forward-looking, pro-active strategies to manage community forests in the future (Jodha 2000b; Saxena 2000; Upadhyaya 1999).

Finally, one of the major sources of uncertainties, associated risks and potential opportunities relates to the process of rapid globalization affecting mountain areas and their economies and communities. Because of an unprecedented primacy accorded to markets and the gradual marginalization of the role of state, the process of change may lead to the following effects: corporations acquiring community resources to the exclusion of communities; over-extraction of resources driven by external demands; profitability-driven selectivity focused on premium products like NTFPs and herbs, and discarding diversity as a source of sustainable forestry; major shifts in forest management favouring individualistic approaches in place of collective efforts; and accentuation of unequal highland-lowland economic links (Jodha 2000a).

Globalization may also generate new potential opportunities for helping community forestry by enhanced trading opportunities and new technologies. Identifying them and enhancing capacities to harness them, however, are major challenges. The aforementioned potential changes have already been recorded for different mountain areas in the Himalayan region (Jodha 2002). For instance, an exploratory exercise on globalization and fragile mountains by ICIMOD in the five Hindu Kush–Himalayan countries revealed that several NTFPs such as medicinal herbs, mushrooms, wild flowers and vegetable dyes have become important high-value export products. In some cases a number of these products are being promoted through multi-national firms from western countries, and the gains to local communities in the process are disproportionately low. Finally, the whole subject of the relationship between globalization and community natural assets is new and has never been addressed by the promoters of community forestry. Another never-addressed issue involving community forestry in mountain areas relates to the irony of some provisions of the Kyoto agreement. Reforestation activities are compensated by a global fund, but activities directed towards protection and promotion of existing forests do not qualify for this support. Poor mountain communities and forest custodians, therefore, are not eligible for support unless they deforest the mountains first.

To understand and address these uncertainties, a forward-looking, proactive approach is required. This can be built upon using the experiences of initiatives tried in different areas, particularly comparisons of successful and unsuccessful initiatives. To be fair to the policy makers, it should be noted that in the case of community forestry initiatives they have been more responsive to the emerging issues in this field compared to many other programmes in rural areas (Jodha 2000b). In the Indian case, this is indicated by new guidelines for the JFM programme issued in February 2000 that try to address several constraints and uncertainties discussed earlier (Saxena 2000). In Nepal's case, issues affecting UGF and Lease Hold Forestry Programmes also have been debated by the law-makers and the media in response to issues raised by FECOFUN and others (Mahapatra 2002; Upadhyaya 1999). The growth of civil society, sensitive bureaucracy, community consciousness as well as mobilization and the global environmental discourse all support genuinely decentralized and participatory management of community natural assets.

Conclusion

This discussion focused on factors helping or hindering community-level natural resource management in the Himalayan region. The chapter first questioned the mainstream view that the poor are responsible for resource degradation by looking into traditional arrangements directed to collectively protect and regenerate communities' resources in mountain areas. The decline of traditional institutional arrangements and the breakdown of the community's collective stake in natural resources often has led to degradation of these resources. This happened as a negative side-effect of increased physical, administrative and economic integration of mountain economies into mainstream lowland economies. For this change, the poor plead not guilty.

An examination of the factors and processes leading to the breakdown of a community's collective stake in their natural assets indicates some possibilities for reviving and rehabilitating community assets. In this connection one should focus on three pillars of traditional systems, namely a community's collective stake in natural resources, local control of local resources, and learning from indigenous knowledge systems and practices. This chapter identified present-day constraints to their revival, and possible remedial measures to address their constraints. The emerging evidence highlights the importance of the economic gains as perceived by communities from different collective initiatives aimed at promoting natural asset building. The chapter elaborated on economic gains of natural assets building through internalization of gains flowing downstream and other mechanisms.

The major operational aspect in this context focuses on social mobilization. Evidence from different ongoing programmes supported by NGOs, donors and government agencies inspires hope in participatory approaches to natural asset building. The discussion is supplemented by comments on recent initiatives such as Joint Forest Management in India and User Group Forestry in Nepal. The chapter highlights their performance, prospects and constraints. Based on this, one can draw the following inferences.

Blaming poverty as a prime-mover of community natural resource degradation amounts to discarding the real factors and processes promoting communities' indifference towards their natural resources. Strategies for promoting communities' natural assets should focus on understanding how traditional arrangements got eroded and identifying the elements that could be re-used in today's changed context. A focus on visible economic gains and social mobilization should constitute the key areas for interventions to promote community involvement in natural asset building. To promote these key areas one can benefit from the experiences of ongoing interventions in this field.

The JFM in India and the UGF in Nepal offer useful lessons. To strengthen them one can venture to make the following policy recommendations for state governments: give more autonomy and authority to communities in dealing with protection and usage of forest resources; provide the means and mechanisms for promoting equity within the programme, with a special focus on improving the condition of the poor and women; ensure an effective facilitative role for NGOs and other agencies in mobilizing forest users to form groups where internal differences and conflicts are mutually settled; ensure increased attention to and understanding of the historical, cultural and economic diversities of forestry user groups; have clear-cut policies and programmes to reduce or eliminate the uncertainties emanating from legal gaps, gaps between the authority of the community and the powers of the state, and changing stages of the programme, such as the shift from the protection phase to the usage phase of resource management; and, finally, have forward-looking approaches and strategies to minimize risks and harness new opportunities associated with globalization.

In concrete terms, this last recommendation will require a shift in the orientation of community forestry away from subsistence and towards commercial enterprise, or to an appropriate mixture of the two. Silvicultural research must be guided by this shift. An equitable partnership between corporate agencies and communities focused on fair trade will be essential, as will enhanced community capacities for such a partnership. The replacement of an ad hoc or reactive approach by a forward-looking, proactive approach to building communities' natural assets, and concrete action towards compensating mountain communities for the environmental services provided to downstream economies by their natural resources management, will also be very important aspects of any forward-looking policy.

Consideration and implementation of these suggestions would not only help in reducing poverty, but also redirect attention away from the spurious poverty to environmental-degradation link that currently dominates so much of the mainstream discourse and instead address the driving forces behind natural resource degradation in mountain areas.

References

Agarwal, Bina (2001) 'Participatory Exclusions, Community Forestry and Gender: An Analysis for South Asia and a Conceptual Framework', *World Development* 29(10): 1623–48.

Agarwal, Anil (1997) 'Community in Conservation: Beyond Enchantment and Disenchantment', *CDF Discussion Paper*, Gainesville: Conservation and Development

Forum.

Agarwal, Anil and Sunita Narain (2000) 'Redressing Ecological Poverty through Participatory Democracy: Case Studies from India', *PERI Working Paper Number 36*, Amherst: Political Economy Research Institute.

Baral, J.C. (2002) 'Who Should Control Forests of Nepal: Reminiscence of the Past Endeavour and Some Thoughts for the Future Action', E-mail Contribution Mountain Forum-Asia Discussion in Connection with Bishkek Global Mountain Summit, October 2002. Available at jbaral@wlink.com.np.

Brara, R. (1987) *Shifting Sands: A Study of Rights in Common Pasture,* Jaipur, India: Institute of Development Studies.

Berkes, F. (1989) *Common Property Resources: Ecology and Community-based Sustainable Development,* London: Belhaven Press.

Bjonness, I.M. (1983) 'External Economic Dependency and Changing Human Adjustment to Marginal Environments in High Himalaya, Nepal', *Mountain Research and Development* 3(3): 263–72.

Boyce, J.K. (1994) 'Inequality as a Cause of Environmental Degradation', *Ecological Economics* 11: 169–178.

Bromley, D.W. and Chapagain, D.P. (1984) 'The Village Against the Centre: Resource Depletion in South Asia', *American Journal of Agricultural Economics* 6(5): 869–873.

Brown, D., Y. Malla, K. Schreckenberg and O. Springate-Baginsky (2002) 'From Supervising "Subjects" to Supporting "Citizens": Recent Developments in Community Forestry in Asia and Africa', *ODI Natural Resource Perspectives* 75.

Butt, N. and M.F. Price (2000) *Mountain People, Forests and Trees: Strategies for Balancing Local Management and Outside Interests,* Synthesis of an Electronic Conference of the Mountain Forum, April 12–May 14, 1999, Kathmandu: Mountain Forum, ICIMOD.

Dasgupta, P. (1996) *Environmental and Resource Economics in the World of the Poor,* Washington, DC: Resources for the Future.

D'Silva, E. and B. Nagnath (2002) 'Behroonguda: A Rare Success Story in Joint Forest Management', *Economic and Political Weekly* 37(6): 551–57.

Durning, A. (1989) 'Poverty and Environment: Reversing the Downward Spiral', *World Watch Paper 92.* Washington, DC: World Watch Institute.

EERN (2000) *Joint Forest Management and Community Forestry in India: Summary Findings of EERN,* Bangalore: Ecological and Economics Research Network.

Ford Foundation (2002) *Sustainable Solution: Building Assets for Empowerment and Sustainable Development,* New York: Ford Foundation.

Gilmour, D.A. and R.J. Fisher (1991) *Villagers, Forests and Foresters: The Philosophy, Process and Practice of Community Forestry in Nepal,* Kathmandu: Sahayogi Press.

Guha, R. (1983) 'Forestry in British and Post-British India: A Historical Analysis', *Economic and Political Weekly* 18(44&45).

Hazra, C.R., D.P. Singh and R.N. Kaul (1996) *Greening of Common Lands in Jhansi through Village resource Development: A Case Study,* New Delhi: Society for Wasteland Development.

Hiremath, S.R. (1997) *Forest Lands and Forest Produce: As if People Mattered,* Dharwad, India: National Committee for Protection of Natural Resources (NCPNR).

Hobley, M. (1996) 'The Four Ages of Indian Forestry: Colonialism, Commercialism, Conservation and Collaboration', in M. Hobley, ed., *Participatory Forestry: The Process of Change in India and Nepal,* London: Overseas Development Institute.

ICIMOD (1997) *Districts of Nepal: Indicators of Development,* Kathmandu: ICIMOD and SNV.

IFAD (2002) *Rural Poverty Assessment Report for Asia and Pacific Region,* Rome: IFAD.

Jodha, N.S. (1992) 'Rural Common Property Resources: A Missing Dimension of Development Strategies', *World Bank Discussion Paper No.169*, Washington, DC: The World Bank.

— (1995) 'Enhancing Food Security in a Warmer and Crowded World: Factors and Processes in Fragile Zones', in T.E. Downing, ed., *Climate Change and Food Security*, London: Springer.

— (1998) 'Reviving the Social System-ecosystem Links in the Himalayas', in F. Berkes and C. Folke, eds., *Linking Social and Ecological Systems: Management Practices and Social Mechanisms for Building Resilience*, Cambridge: Cambridge University Press.

— (2000a) 'Poverty Alleviation and Sustainable Development in Mountain Areas: Role of Highland-lowland Links in the Context of Rapid Globalization', in M. Banskota, T.S. Papola and J. Richter, eds., *Growth, Poverty Alleviation and Sustainable Resource Management in Mountain Areas of South Asia*, Kathmandu: ICIMOD and the German Foundation for Development (DSE).

— (2000b) 'Joint Management of Forests: Small Gains', *Economic and Political Weekly* 35(50): 4396–99.

— (2001) 'Poverty and Environmental Resource Degradation: An Alternative Explanation and Possible Solutions', in N.S. Jodha, ed., *Life on the Edge: Sustaining Agriculture and Community Resources in Fragile Environments*, Delhi: Oxford University Press.

— (2002) *Globalization and Fragile Mountains*, An Exploratory Research Report submitted to the MacArthur Foundation, Kathmandu: ICIMOD.

Jodha, N.S. and T. Partap (1992) 'Folk Agronomy in Himalayas: Implications for Research and Extension', in *Rural People's Knowledge, Agricultural Research and Extension Practices*, IIED Research Series 1(3).

Joshi, A.L. (1997) 'Empowering Local Users in Forest Management of Nepal', Paper presented at EDI (World Bank)–SAARC Workshop on Globalization and Environmental Sustainability at Local Level, Goa, India, 2-7 June.

Krishna, A., N. Uphoff and M.J. Esman (1997) *Reasons for Hope: Instructive Experiences in Rural Development*, West Hartford, CT: Kumarian Press.

Koch-Weser, M. (2002) 'Legal, Economic and Compensatory Mechanisms in Support of Sustainable Mountain Development', Paper presented at the Bishkek Global Mountain Summit, October.

Leach, M., R. Mearn and I. Scoones (1997) 'Environmental Entitlements: A Framework for Understanding Institutional Dynamics of Environmental Change', *IDS Discussion Paper 359*, Brighton: Institute of Development Studies.

LGP (2001) *Year 2001: Local Governance Programme (LGP)*, Kathmandu: MLD/NPC/UNDP/NEP/95/021.

Lynch, O.J. and K. Talbott (1995) *Balancing Act: Community-based Forest Management and National Law in Asia and Pacific*, Washington, DC: World Resources Institute.

Mahapatra, R. (2002) 'Nepal's Poor Carry it Off', *Down to Earth* 10(19): 22–24.

Metz, J.J. (1991) 'A Reassessment of Causes and Severity of Nepal's Environmental Crisis', *World Development* 19(7).

Mink, S. (1993) 'Poverty, Population and the Environment', *World Bank Discussion Paper 189*, Washington, DC: The World Bank.

National Environment Commission (1998) *The Middle Path: National Environment Strategy for Bhutan*, Thimphu: National Environment Commission, Royal Government of Bhutan.

Panayotou, T. (1990) 'The Economics of Environmental Degradation: Problems, Causes and Responses', *Development Discussion Paper No.335, HIID*. Cambridge: Harvard University.

Pant, S.D. (1935) *Social Economy of Himalayans*, London: Allen and Unwin.

PDDP (Participatory District Development Programme) (2001) *Putting People First: 2001 the Year in Review*, Kathmandu: HMG, UNDP, NORAD.

Prakash, S. (1997) 'Poverty and Environment Linkages in Mountains and Uplands: Reflections on the Poverty Thesis', *CREED Working Paper Series No.12*, London: International Institute of Environment and Development.

Poffenberger, M., M.B. McGean and A. Khare (1996) 'Communities Sustaining India's Forests in the Twenty-First Century', in M. Poffenberger and B. McGean, eds., *Village Voices. Forest Choices: Joint Forest Management in India*, Delhi: Oxford University Press.

Saigal, S. (2001) 'Joint Forest Management: A Decade and Beyond', Paper presented at a Workshop at Institute of Economic Growth, Delhi, India, September.

Sanwal, M. (1989) 'What We Know about Mountain Development, Common Property, Investment Priorities and Institutional Arrangements', *Mountain Research and Development*, 9(1): 3–14.

Sarin, M. (1996) *Joint Forest Management: The Haryana Experience*, Ahmedabad: Centre for Environment Education.

Saxena, N.C. (1995) '*Forest, People and Profit: New Equations for Sustainability*', Mussoorie, India: Centre for Sustainable Development LBS, National Academy of Administration.

Saxena, N.C. (2000) Research Issues in Forestry in India. *Indian Journal of Agricultural Economics* 55(3): 359–83.

Shackleton, S., B. Campbell, E. Wollenberg and D. Edmunds (2002) 'Devolution and Community Based Natural Resource Management: Creating Space for Local People to Participate and Benefit', *ODI Natural Resource Perspectives* 76.

Shivakoti, G., G. Varughese, L. Ostorom, A. Shukla and G. Thapa (1997) *People and Participation in Sustainable Development: Understanding Dynamics of Natural Resource Systems*, Kathmandu: Tribhuvan University, Institute of Agriculture and Animal Sciences.

Somanathan, E. (1991) 'Deforestation, Property Rights and Incentives in Central Himalaya', *Economic and Political Weekly* 26(1): 37–46.

Tamang, D., G.J. Gill and G.B. Thapa (1996) *Indigenous Management of Natural Resources in Nepal*, Kathmandu: Winrock International Nepal.

Upadhyaya, M. (1999) 'Greening Hills: Seeing the Forest and the Trees', in K. Dixit, B. Subba and A. John, eds., *Tough Terrain: Media Reports on Mountain Issues*, Kathmandu: Asia Pacific Mountain Network and PANOS Institute South Asia.

Zazueta, A. (1995) *Policy Hits the Ground: Participation and Equity in Environmental Policy Making*, Washington, DC: World Resource Institute.

In semi-arid regions of India, poor communities are restoring degraded ecosystems.
Photo credit: Simon Williams.

CHAPTER 3
HARVESTING THE RAIN:
FIGHTING ECOLOGICAL POVERTY
THROUGH PARTICIPATORY
DEMOCRACY

Sunita Narain and Anil Agarwal

Introduction

In many parts of the developing world, poverty is not so much about a lack of money as a lack of natural resources. For rural people who live off the land, prosperity means plenty of water, crops, animals and timber. Improving the 'gross natural product' is far more important than increasing the gross national product (Agarwal 1985). Building and sustaining a base of natural capital is the key to a robust local economy.

This chapter presents case studies of four rural communities in India that have succeeded in mobilizing natural and human capital to generate economic wealth and well-being through improved management of natural resources. All four studies come from hilly and plateau regions of India, with semi-arid to sub-humid climates (500–1,250 millimetres of rainfall per year). In all cases, important natural resources are held as common property. From the colonial era until recently, these resources were managed, or mismanaged, by government agencies. The key to ecological restoration has been the restoration of community control.

In these regions, watershed management requires cooperative solutions above the level of the individual farm. The ancient art of water harvesting needs to be revived and modernized to provide adequate water for irrigation and household needs. Water harvesting means capturing the rain where it falls by collecting runoff from rooftops, constructing check dams and small reservoirs to capture runoff from local catchments, and replanting degraded watersheds, so as to reduce runoff losses. Local-level cooperation is often critical to success.

In each of the case studies, communities have been able to regain significant control over natural resources and to manage them through local, participatory democracy. They have restored environments that were degraded in the past when *de jure* state management often meant *de facto* open access. The growth of natural capital in turn reinforced community spirit, as villagers recognized their stake in managing their assets wisely.

The first case is Sukhomajri, a village in the sub-Himalayan range in north India. The second is Ralegan Siddhi, a village in the state of Maharashtra. The third is from the dry and hilly Alwar region of Rajasthan state. In these three cases, the impetus for reform came from outside the government. The experiments, which began more than 15 years ago, received much attention, but skeptics dismissed them as exceptional successes that could not be replicated widely. In 1996, however, the state of Madhya Pradesh initiated a statewide programme for watershed development, based on the model of Ralegan Siddhi. This is our fourth case, and it shows that with enough political will, community-based ecological restoration can be initiated on a wider scale.

Sukhomajri: Holistic Watershed Management

Sukhomajri was once like any other village in the foothills of the Shivalik Mountains: sparsely vegetated, with poor farmland, and a great deal of soil erosion and water runoff. Crop yields were uncertain, so villagers kept herds of livestock as a safeguard. Open-access grazing of the livestock kept the surrounding hills and watersheds almost bare.

Heavy logging in the Shivaliks during the 19th century led to severe erosion (Franda 1981). The British responded by passing the 1902 Land Preservation Act, which closed some lands to grazing and provided for various soil conservation measures, such as the construction of bunds (berms to check runoff) and tree planting. But the erosion continued apace because people had no alternative but to graze their animals on these lands. The colonial government made no attempt to involve villagers in the management of these lands, and disregarded the traditional land use systems that earlier had been in place. The result was alienation and opposition to the government's conservation measures by the local populace.

Unfortunately, independence brought little change in state policies. The government recommended soil conservation measures, but the people were determined to graze their animals, and again the conservation efforts failed. By the 1970s, the human-made Sukhna Lake, which is surrounded by the Shivalik Mountains, was filling with silt, as sediment poured from the denuded forest lands. The lake was the main water supply for the city of Chandigarh, the joint capital of the states of Haryana and Punjab. City officials became alarmed and considered digging a new lake. Researchers from the government's Central Soil and Water Conservation Research and Training Institute found that the erosion was concentrated in pockets, including the village of Sukhomajri, 15 kilometres upstream from the lake.

Ecological Poverty in Sukhomajri

The research team arrived in Sukhomajri to find a settlement of 59 families, whose livelihoods depended on raising goats and other livestock, and farming small, drought-stricken plots of land. 37 families owned less than one hectare, 20 owned 1–2 hectares, and only two families owned more than two hectares (Mishra *et al.* 1980). All together, individuals owned a little more than half of the land, and the remainder was *panchayat* land, or village commons. Over the years, villagers had encroached on the common land to cultivate it.

The village had no source of irrigation. The annual rainfall, averaging 1,137 millimetres (45 inches) came almost entirely during the four monsoon months. Because their land holdings were small and not very productive, the villagers were forced to extend cultivation to inferior lands, including steep slopes, exposing the land to further erosion. In the late 1960s, several acres of land had collapsed into a ravine at one end of the village, and since then ravine had been edging closer, destroying more fields each year. The villagers faced an acute shortage of fodder for their animals, and in most years had to buy wheat straw from other villages.

A soil and water conservation team from the institute built check dams and planted trees. But the villagers took the logs and twigs used for the check dams home to burn, and continued to take their animals to graze in the watershed where they ate the saplings. One villager explained to P.R. Mishra, the institute director, 'The people of Chandigarh are very rich. We will continue to send mud, and they will continue to remove it. We are poor and have no other way to survive but to graze our animals and get some milk' (Agarwal and Narain 1990).

Water as the Starting Point

The turning point came in 1976. Institute scientists built a small earthen dam to stem erosion by diverting water into a reservoir. The next year, the rains failed and the wheat crop was withering. Villagers asked the scientists if they could use water from the reservoir, and with the stored water they were able to save crops in nearby fields.

Villagers and scientists alike made the connection between preventing erosion and developing small-scale irrigation. Daulat Ram, an enterprising villager, showed the institute staff another good site for a dam that would serve both purposes, and a second dam was built in 1978, with support from the Ford Foundation. An underground pipeline was laid to take water to the fields, and undulating terrain was levelled to maximize the benefits from irrigation, with farmers willingly sharing the cost.

But the water did not get to everyone. Only half the village was prospering. The arable land was divided in two by the village road, and the irrigation system benefited only the land on one side. Some farmers on the favoured side started to plant water-intensive crops like rice and sugarcane, even though the project was supposed to provide only modest, supplemental irrigation. Furthermore, the water was distributed by a government official who started taking bribes.

The village became divided. Resentful villagers without access to the water kept grazing in the watershed, continuing to undermine efforts to stop erosion. When Madhu Sarin, a social worker employed by the Ford Foundation, asked the women about benefits of the dam water, one responded bluntly, 'What water? We do not get any water. It is given to a few and that also in exchange for a bottle of liquor.' Tensions mounted in 1979, when a severe drought killed the unirrigated maize crop, while the irrigated crops survived. At a village meeting, a woman whose family lacked water threatened to sabotage the dam (Mishra and Sarin 1987).

Equity as a Prerequisite

There was only one solution: make sure that everyone got a share of the water. In early 1980, a meeting was called by the village elders to resolve this issue. After some discussion, the villagers decided that all families would get an equal share of water, regardless of where their lands were situated or how much land they owned. They established a water users' association, comprising all the households in the village, to maintain the dams and distribute the water. Pipes were laid to distribute the water throughout the village, and water was sold at a nominal charge to cover maintenance costs.

Households with little or no land could make use of their entitlement by sharecropping or by selling their water to others. These arrangements ensured that each family had a vested interest in protecting the watershed. Under the rules established by the association, a member whose animals were found grazing in the watershed stood to lose his or her right to water.

The water users' association, later named the Hill Resource Management Society, led to an extraordinary turnaround in Sukhomajri. The Society provided a forum for the villagers to discuss problems, manage their local environment and ensure accountability among members. It made sure that no household allowed its animals to graze in the watershed, and in return it ensured a fair distribution of common resources: water, wood and grass. As crop yields improved, villagers started feeding their buffaloes in stalls, and sold their goats, reducing grazing pressures. The goat population decreased from 206 in 1977 to only 32 by 1983 (Mittal et al. 1983). At first, every head of household in the village was a member of the society. To ensure a greater voice for women, the membership expanded a decade later, to include all adult residents, and the bylaws were amended to require at least two women on the managing committee (Sarin 1996). Any member of the managing committee could be recalled by a majority vote. This crucial clause put power in the hands of the majority and fostered participatory democracy.

The Forest

Providing water to the village was the first step in regenerating the local environment. The second was to give villagers more control over forest lands in the area. India's forests, owned by the government, make up 22 per cent of the country's land. They are an important source of fodder and firewood, but villagers have limited rights to access these resources. Illegal grazing and fodder and firewood collection are widespread. At the same time, villagers generally have little stake in the sustainable management of the lands. Ironically, state ownership — recommended by Hardin (1968) as a solution to the 'tragedy of the commons' — fosters the very resource abuse it ostensibly aims to prevent.

In the past, the forest department auctioned the right to cut grass in forests lands near Sukhomajri to a contractor. The contractor would then sell grass to villagers during the November-to-June cutting season. As the condition of the watershed improved, so did the condition of the forest, and residents thought they were entitled to share in the benefits. In 1985, after a protracted struggle, the forest department agreed to give joint grass-cutting rights the village societies of Sukhomajri and the neighbouring village of

Dhamala. The villagers would pay a fixed royalty based on the average received by the forest department in earlier years, and the village societies would in turn charge individuals a seasonal fee to cut grass (Mishra and Sarin 1987). Now the villagers had a stake in improving the forest, because they themselves would reap the benefits.

The village set the grass-cutting fee at 100 rupees (Rs.) (equivalent, at the time, to roughly US$8)[1] for those who migrated outside the village for work, and Rs. 150 (US$12) for those who worked in the village. Widows and families facing special hardships were not charged at all. In the first year, the village society earned a net profit of Rs. 5,000 (US$400), double the royalty it paid to the forest department (Mishra and Sarin 1987). Since the profits went to their own society, instead of to a contractor, the villagers could use the proceeds to generate more resources for the community. They invested in planting more grass in the catchment, providing more fodder and in turn more milk. This 'cyclic development', as P.R. Mishra calls it, continued to build the natural asset base of the village.

One of the most notable gains to the village came with new rights over a fibrous grass known as *bhabbar*, which is widely used for making ropes and paper. As the forest environment improved, the growth of this grass multiplied. In 1986, again after a great deal of pressure on the forest department, the village societies of Sukhomajri and Dhamala won the right to harvest *bhabbar* in return for a royalty. In Sukhomajri, the society hired a subcontractor in the first year; the following year, villagers harvested 150 tons of *bhabbar* themselves and reaped the profits directly.

To date, however, the villagers still lack the right to harvest the forest's most valuable product: trees. Among the most prized species is the *khair* tree. Harvested at sustainable levels, timber could generate about Rs. 30 million (roughly US$700,000) per year (Dhar 1997).

The Village at a Crossroad

The economy of Sukhomajri has made extraordinary gains since ecological restoration began in the 1970s. Crop yields have risen. Grass and tree fodder from the forest have soared, fuelling higher milk production. Annual household income has increased considerably, and the village has turned from an importer to an exporter of food. Brick and cement have replaced thatch and mud for houses, and many homes now boast televisions, radios, electric fans and sewing machines. 'Who could imagine that televisions, tractors and bicycles could be had for mere grass and water?' asks a villager.

A combination of public, private and community investment in Sukhomajri has produced, according to one analysis, an internal rate of return on the order of 19 per cent annually (Chopra *et al.* 1990). One impressive result has been a 90 per cent reduction in the flow of sediment into Sukhna lake — a 'positive externality' for which the villagers have received no direct compensation.

Despite this remarkable transformation, Sukhomajri's future is precarious. As the land generates more wealth, contests for control intensify. The village has regenerated the forest, but the government is holding onto most of the timber proceeds. At the same time, the neighbouring village of Dhamala has sought to expand its rights to forest resources at Sukhomajri's expense.

At the outset, Sukhomajri and Dhamala shared the forest. But their interests clashed over the *bhabbar* grass. As animal herders, the villagers of Sukhomajri relied heavily on the first flush of the grass for fodder. Dhamala, on the other hand, is a village of larger landowners, who are less reliant on livestock and would rather sell all the *bhabbar* to paper mills. In the 1990s, conflict erupted over this issue. Villagers in Dhamala alleged that the *bhabbar* harvest was declining because Sukhomajri was using it for fodder.

As an upper-caste village, Dhamala had greater influence with the forest department, and persuaded it to ban the cutting of grass for fodder. The forest department then divided the land between the two villages. The villagers of Sukhomajri felt cheated, arguing that Dhamala got the portion where most of the grass grows.

On top of these tensions with Dhamala, Sukhomajri is facing other tensions with the forest department. As sales of *bhabbar* grass have soared, the government has moved to take a bigger share of the profit. In the past, when the forest department leased the land to paper mill contractors, the contractors paid minimal fees. When the village society first won the cutting rights in 1985, the charges were similar. Three years later, with the land improved and *bhabbar* production much higher, the department increased its fees by 7.5 per cent. In the late 1990s, however, the government moved to capture a much larger portion of the profits. Under the current scheme, the village society must pay not only lease fees but also income taxes and sales taxes. It then must turn over 25 per cent of after-tax profits, and deposit another 40 per cent into two accounts controlled by the forest department that are nominally earmarked for the development of the village and forest. The result, after all said and done, is that less than one-third of the income is left for distribution to the villagers (Mahapatra 1998). It remains to be seen whether the villagers of Sukhomajri will surmount these repercussions of their own success.

Ralegan Siddhi: Marshalling Government Resources

The village of Ralegan Siddhi, in Maharashtra state, has become a model for rural development nationwide. Ralegan lies in a drought-prone area. Irrigation facilities were minimal, and with poor soils and erratic rainfall, the villagers produced only 30 per cent of the food that they needed to subsist (Mahapatra 1997). Some 15–20 per cent of the population could eat only one meal a day. Most of the village men migrated seasonally to look for work (Hazare 1997).

Change began with one inspired individual, and took off when the village learned how to take advantage of government programmes in a way that other communities rarely do. The story begins in 1975, when Krishna Bhaurao Hazare, a retired jeep driver from the Indian army, returned to his native village. In the 1965 war between India and Pakistan, his transport unit had been attacked and he was the lone survivor. Hazare considered this a virtual rebirth and decided to devote his new life to social work (Lokur 1996). On his return to Ralegan, he began by repairing the dilapidated village temple, which had been damaged by people who stole wood from the building to use as fuel in illegally distilling liquor. Hazare invested his own money in rehabilitating the temple. As his work proceeded, villagers took interest and offered donations, and the temple was restored.

Anna (meaning 'big brother') Hazare, as he was soon called by the villagers, next turned his focus to farming. He made the rounds of government offices, gathering information about the various state-sponsored schemes available for rural development. He decided to start with watershed development.

Ecological Regeneration

The basic principle of watershed development in semi-arid regions is to conserve both soil and water by planting trees and building water conservation structures. The aim is to ensure that every drop of rainwater that falls in the watershed, from ridge to valley, either percolates into the soil or drains into a reservoir.

As Hazare organized the villagers to build check dams, water levels in the wells began to rise. The village solicited and received funds from the district council to rebuild a faulty reservoir that the government had installed a few years earlier. Water levels rose in the seven nearby wells. 'It was the first time that during summer Ralegan saw a well with water', a villager named Nirmala reported (Mahapatra 1997). With the construction of more storage ponds, reservoirs and gully plugs, the groundwater table rose further. As a further step, the village planted more than 300,000 trees, tapping a government forestry programme that offered free saplings and money for labour to plant them (Chopra and Rao 1996). With more water available for irrigation, land that once lay fallow came under cultivation, and yields of millet, sorghum and onions increased substantially.

Hazare encouraged the villagers to view water as a community resource rather than an individual possession, and to manage the supply judiciously. The villagers formed a co-operative to oversee the wells and distribute water equitably. No farmer gets a second round of irrigation until all families have had their first. A village assembly, or *gram sabha*, was established to oversee all community decisions. The assembly persuaded all landholders to refrain from cultivating water-intensive crops, such as sugarcane. With a sustainable supply and fair distribution of water, farmers can now reliably grow two or three crops a year. Some of their produce is exported all the way to Dubai, in the Persian Gulf.

Institutional Dimensions

As in Sukhomajri, ecological regeneration has gone hand-in-hand with participatory democracy. The village assembly approves all initiatives to protect the watershed, and the elected village council, or *gram panchayat*, carries them out. The assembly also oversees a range of registered societies working on specific concerns including education, youth culture and social activities, and the welfare needs of women. A society providing technical assistance to farmers dispenses advice about fertilizers and seeds, organic practices, and getting financial help, and a dairy society provides comparable advice about the dairy business. Before taking on new projects, these societies must bring their proposals and cost estimates before the village assembly, which must approve them unanimously. Thus, the assembly is a pivotal social force.

Ralegan's investment projects have relied on a combination of voluntary labour from residents, funds from government rural development programmes and, more recently, bank loans. By the mid-1990s, the village had invested a total of Rs. 7.5 million (US$380,000) in development, nearly half of which went to paying for the labour of the villagers. As the village has prospered, women have joined together to help one another financially. They have formed seven self-help groups, with 20 members each, who contribute Rs. 25-100 (US$0.60-2.40) monthly toward a revolving credit fund. Women can obtain loans at 2 per cent interest to start businesses or attend to other needs.

Environment and Jobs

Beginning in the mid-1980s, the government of India sought to link its rural employment programmes to ecological regeneration. The idea was to put the rural poor to work on state projects that would help to promote soil and water conservation. Hence, the state began providing jobs not just to build roads and schools, but also to plant trees, construct small reservoirs and undertake other environmental projects. Despite good intentions, this effort to link jobs with environmental protection has largely failed. The main reason is that villagers have not been given enough stake in building and maintaining natural assets for the long haul. The villagers lack strong community institutions with legal rights to manage natural resources. Thus, new reservoirs are created to harvest water, but their catchments continue to be degraded. Earthen dams are built for soil and water conservation, but they are of poor quality and ultimately wash away. In short, the government generates work, but much of this work is ultimately unproductive.

Ralegan Siddhi turned this pattern on its head. Rather than build government assets, the village built community assets. They contributed free labour, with each individual, rich and poor, providing one day of free labour every 15 days. In addition, poor villagers were employed to work more frequently on these community projects using government funds. For each new project, the assembly gauges how much labour will be required, and the contribution of voluntary labour. Having established ownership over these assets, they have reason to maintain them.

Looking at the Ralegan experience, some have suggested that state employment programmes be restructured to give communities greater power to control local resources. But elsewhere, government bureaucracies have maintained their hold and widespread community control remains a dream. Ralegan was unusual in that it took full advantage of numerous government programmes that were available. The settlement received funds from watershed development from the soil conservation department. The District Rural Development Agency gave funds to build houses for the homeless. Solar panels for heating water and solar cookers were provided by the Urja Gram Udyog Medha (Rural Energy Development Centre), and the Council for Advancement of People's Action and Rural Technology provided funds for a windmill to pump water.

By Indian standards, Ralegan Siddhi today is a rich village. Incomes have risen to the point that more than a quarter of the residents now earn more than Rs. 500,000 (US$11,000) per year. The village is so prosperous that a major bank has opened a branch there. For a village that was once badly degraded, both economically and environmentally, this is truly remarkable.

Alwar: Bringing Rivers Back to Life

Gopalpura is a village at the base of the Aravali Hills in the Alwar region of Rajasthan state. This area, too, is semi-arid, and over the years deforestation has left it practically devoid of vegetation. Most of its rainfall comes in four or five spurts lasting a few days each. All told, the region gets roughly 600 millimetres (24 inches) of rainfall a year, and surface water evaporates quickly in the heat. People in the region struggle to survive. There is hardly any industry, and many villagers migrate to cities in search of work.

In 1986, with help from a local voluntary agency called Tarun Bharat Sangh (TBS) the people of Gopalpura built three earthen structures to collect monsoon rains, irrigate their fields and increase percolation to recharge wells. These water-harvesting structures, called *johads*, are built across a slope, sometimes in a series, and are based on traditional techniques for capturing rainfall.

Gopalpura's *johads* attracted a good deal of attention, and over the next decade, TBS helped to build almost 2,500 water conservation structures in some 500 villages in the region (UN 1998). TBS supplied some materials and equipment, such as cement and diesel fuel, while villagers contributed labour and other materials. The total investment came to Rs. 150 million (US$3.5 million). Despite their poverty, villagers contributed an astounding 74 per cent of the total in cash or in kind.

In each settlement, a village assembly planned the *johad*. The villagers determined which site would receive the most runoff, what size the structure should be, and set guidelines for distribution of water, management of the watershed and maintenance of the structure. To protect their watersheds, some villages instituted penalties for cutting trees.

Hydrological Achievements

Studies of some of the villages by engineers, social scientists and journalists report that these projects have succeeded overall. There has been no comprehensive study of the region, however, so there is not much information about variables that made some experiments work better than others. One study of 36 villages, by G.D. Agarwal (nd), former head of the civil engineering department at the Indian Institute of Technology, Kanpur, found that groundwater tables rose from 10 to 24 feet. He found the structures to be quite cost-effective, with an average cost of one rupee (2.2 cents) per cubic meter of storage capacity. No state engineering organization would be able to build water harvesting structures at this price. They were durable, too: in 1995 and 1996, when unusually heavy rains washed away numerous structures that had been designed by government engineers, the *johads* built by the villagers stood the test.

Water conservation has brought new life to the region's rivers. The Arvari and Ruparel rivers, which flow from the Aravali Hills through hundreds of villages, used to go dry each year after the monsoons ended. Thanks to more than 250 structures the villagers built along these rivers, year by year, the flow lasted a little longer, and today, both rivers are perennial. Villagers talk about the Arvari's revival as they would about the birth of a child. Hydrogeologists consider it to be a marvel.

The increase in water supplies has brought major improvements in agriculture. The Agarwal study found that wheat production had doubled. The villagers still practice subsistence agriculture, but now they have enough to eat. Perhaps most tellingly, 'reverse migration' has begun: some villagers who went to the cities for work now are returning to till lands that lay fallow for decades.

Struggles with Government Agencies

As elsewhere in India, the villagers in the Aravali Hills have had to struggle with the government for control over natural resources. After considerable conflict, they have arrived at an unwritten understanding in which state agencies let them manage their environment.

When TBS built its first *johads* in Gopalpura, the state irrigation department declared them illegal and demanded that they be dismantled. Under the Rajasthan Drainage Act of 1956, all water resources, whether on private or government land, belong to the state. The irrigation agency initially argued that the *johads* would reduce water flows downstream. Later the agency claimed that these structures could be washed away and flood villages. Ironically, the next rains washed away several official structures, while the *johads* built by the villagers endured. After a protracted resistance from the villagers, the administration finally backed down from its effort to remove the *johads* (Agarwal and Narain 1989).

Similarly, when the villagers of Gopalpura planted trees in the catchment of their watershed, they received a notice that they would be fined, on the grounds that legally the land belonged to the state revenue department. The agency eventually dropped the fine, but not before taking control of the land and redistributing it to outsiders, effectively destroying local control over the watershed.

The state likewise intervened to control fishing rights in the Arvari River after its revival. In 1996, villagers in the riverside settlement of Hamirpura received notice that the state had awarded to a contractor a license to fish in the river. The villagers insisted that the river was theirs, and that they were entitled to a voice in its management. In December 1998, TBS organized a forum on the issue, at which eminent jurists and former bureaucrats preached patience and encouraged the villagers to work with the government. But one of the authors of this chapter, Anil Agarwal, urged the people to fight back, and suggested that villagers living along the river form their own parliament.

The villagers took Agarwal's words to heart. In 1999, working with TBS, they formed the Arvari Sansad, or Arvari Parliament, an association of all the villages along the river. The parliament adopted a constitution and formed two houses, one with a representative from each village, the second with a representative from each cluster of villages. It subsequently set rules and regulations for river management, including restrictions on the type of crops that could be grown in the river basin and limits on the installation of tubewells for groundwater extraction. These rules were critical to ensure equitable distribution of the water and to prevent individuals from appropriating excessive amounts to cultivate water-intensive crops such as sugarcane. On balance, the villagers of the Alwar region have scored some remarkable victories in controlling their natural assets. But they have done so in the face of a legal framework that remains exclusionary. Nationwide, policy changes are needed to support rather than obstruct similar initiatives.

Jhabua: When Government Learns

The transformation of Sukhomajri, Ralegan Siddhi and Alwar villages are scattered instances of the regeneration of rural ecosystems led by remarkable leaders and non-governmental organizations. As a rule, government afforestation and watershed management programmes have not been able to replicate such successes. One impediment is that they have been unwilling to hand over power to local communities.

One outstanding exception, however, is in Madhya Pradesh, where the state government has promoted watershed management with extensive public participation. Trees are growing in Jhabua, a district that looked like a moonscape 15 years ago, and wells are filled with water in an area that once was chronically prone to drought.

The change can be credited in large part to the then Chief Minister of Madhya Pradesh, Digvijay Singh. Inspired by the work of Krishna Bhaurao Hazare in Ralegan Siddhi, Singh launched a similar programme across the state after he became Chief Minister in 1993. Drawing on funds from national programmes for rural employment, he established the Rajiv Gandhi Watershed Development Mission (RGWDM) (Agarwal and Mahapatra 1999). Guidelines from the central government encourage state governments explicitly to use this money for watershed development, but few states actually do so.

About 22 per cent of Jhabua District, covering 374 villages, has been brought under this watershed programme. Across the state, the programme has been extended to nearly 8,000 villages spread over 3.4 million hectares, slightly more than one per cent of India's total land area. The agency by 2000 had invested some Rs. 3 billion (US$70 million) since the programme began in 1995–96 (Mahapatra 1999). The cost per hectare has been about one-fifth the cost in prior government afforestation initiatives.

Water conservation measures have brought a wide range of economic and ecological benefits. A study of 18 micro-watersheds (about 500–1,000 hectares) in Jabhua District found that the amount of land under irrigation doubled in four years (Agarwal and Mahapatra 1999). Both stream flows and agricultural productivity increased. The biggest initial benefit to the local people has come from the rapid regeneration of grass for animal fodder. Some estimates suggest there is five to six times as much grass as before the conservation programme began. This increased productivity gives families an incentive to protect the watershed.

Institutional Dimensions

The experience in Jhabua shows what can happen when a government starts working seriously with the people. The state government has created a new institutional framework to ensure that policy is coordinated at the state level, implementation is coordinated at the district level and democratic decisions are made at the village level.

Each 'milli-watershed' (covering about 5,000–10,000 hectares, or 10 times the area of a micro-watershed) has a project officer who is supported by a group of technicians and social workers. This group works with villages in designing and implementing water conservation measures. Villagers engage in a planning process that takes into account the welfare of the village as a whole as well as the preferences of various interest groups. This process includes an initial appraisal in which villagers identify problems and solutions, and consider what conservation structures should be built. Once the plan is approved by a district advisory committee, funds for executing it are transferred to the local watershed committee. Most of the money goes for labour.

Each conservation structure is overseen by a user group, comprising landowners who benefit from the structures. In addition, the landless participate in self-help groups to promote employment, and there are women's groups. The village watershed committee consists of the chairpersons of the user groups, self-help groups and women's groups. The state requires that at least a third of the committee members be women, and if there is a shortfall the village assembly must nominate enough women to fulfil this requirement.

Difficulties Ahead

While the watershed development programme of Madhya Pradesh has scored remarkable gains, big challenges lie ahead. Now that the groundwater is being recharged, there is a danger that the richer and more powerful villagers will begin to exploit this resource through private tubewells. Bureaucratic regulation of groundwater extraction has not worked effectively in India, and water tables are falling rapidly in many parts of the country. In an unprecedented move toward community regulation of water management, state officials in Madhya Pradesh considered proposing that local watershed committees should be given powers to regulate withdrawal of water. The government has not been able to match the successes of Jhabua in other districts, for a variety of reasons. In some cases, the district leadership failed to show enough interest and commitment. In addition, villages in other districts often are more intensely stratified by class and caste, whereas Jhabua is primarily tribal and relatively homogeneous. These problems sometimes have been compounded by weak local participation. If the *gram sabha* holds only a quick meeting to establish a watershed committee, and nominates its members, few people in the village are informed and involved, and the project suffers. Nonetheless, the successes in Jhabua offer great hope, showing that poverty does not make environmental degradation inevitable, and that a combination of a limited, strategic role for state government and local-level democracy can make sound environmental management possible.

Principles for Rebuilding Natural Assets

These case studies of watershed development in semi-arid regions of India suggest four principles of wider relevance for efforts to rebuild natural assets. First, a holistic approach is required. Second, property rights are implicated. Third, democratic institutions are crucial. And finally, external funding can prime the pump for locally-financed investment.

A Holistic Approach

Natural asset building strategies must take into account all the resources of a village, including grazing lands, tree and forest lands, croplands, water systems and domestic animals. Often rural development efforts falter because they are fragmented. A government agency that builds ponds and tanks, for instance, may fail to consider how land-use practices affect their catchments. Likewise, an agency that looks after animal husbandry or promotes dairy operations may pay little attention to how fodder supplies can be increased.

Local plans must address not only the interplay of natural resources, but also the interests of different socio-economic groups, and the interplay of private and common property. The productivity of private lands often depends on the productivity of commonly held resources. While upland watersheds may be held in common, for example, the water harvested from them will affect the yield of private crop lands below. In a similar fashion, the grass from common pastures helps to sustain private animals.

Property Rights

Ecological restoration requires a legal framework that gives communities the right to improve their common natural resources and to benefit from these improvements. Many political reformers in India have focused on the redistribution of private lands from rich to poor. Such land reform is especially important in places where most land is privately held and many rural people are landless, as in the floodplains of the Ganges Valley. In other parts of the country, however, a large share of the land is held in common, usually under *de jure* state ownership. Such is the case in the hilly, mountain, arid and semi-arid regions. Here the main task is to reform the control and management of common lands. This may require legislation that devolves control from government agencies to local bodies.

In rural India, inequality tends to increase as one moves from the hills to the plains, from non-irrigated areas to irrigated ones and from arid regions to humid ones. In those places where water is relatively abundant, most agricultural land is privatized and the ownership is often highly concentrated. In general, the societies that depend more on common lands than on private property tend to be more equal. The cases in this chapter all come from such regions of the country. Here the main inequality — and the main arena for reform in property rights — lies in the relationship between the community and the state, rather than in the intra-village distribution of private holdings.

Institutions for Democracy

Ecological regeneration requires cooperation and accountability. Villagers must refrain from overgrazing their animals in the protected commons. They must conserve the catchments of local water bodies. They must distribute produce from common lands equitably to ensure that all share an interest in their proper management. Villagers can achieve all this only if they have local institutions for democratic participation.

In India, the Gandhian concept of a *gram sabha* is an assembly of all adults in the village. Unlike elected village councils, *gram sabha* assemblies take place in open view, fostering accountability and confidence in decisions. Yet India lacks a legal framework to give *gram sabhas* the power that they need. Instead the law provides for elected councils, or *gram panchayats*, to represent clusters of villages. These *panchayats* have authority to implement schemes for rural development. The law requires regular elections, reserves seats for certain groups and mandates a finance commission to oversee the council's spending.

The flaws in the legislation are many. The state legislatures retain power over the *panchayats* and have the authority to dissolve them, an arrangement that sets the stage for political patronage and rewards sycophants rather than fostering public accountability. The *panchayats* themselves are often products of village factionalism, and generally are dominated by the more powerful in the village. The *panchayat* meets as a closed forum, setting the stage for corruption by village leaders, petty bureaucrats and politicians who can easily siphon off most of the benefits of government programmes. In many cases, villagers are not even aware of the projects that the government has approved. Moreover, since the *panchayat* usually covers several villages, it is often too far removed from the grassroots to be an effective agent for natural resource management.

Because the *panchayats* fail to represent the interests of the community at large, their role in natural resource management is often destructive. For this reason, non-governmental organizations generally bypass the *panchayats* altogether and instead create new village forums for open deliberations. Even the state government of Madhya Pradesh decided in its watershed development programme simply to exclude the *panchayats* and instead give power and funding to informal village assemblies.

In response to public pressure, the Panchayati Raj Act of 1992 established the *gram sabha* as a legal entity. But the law left it to state legislatures to define the *gram sabha*'s powers and state legislatures have been reluctant to devolve control. In some areas, *gram sabhas* have been able to thrive even in the absence of legally defined powers. However, national legislation to strengthen the village assembly as an institution of local governance is critical to promoting better natural resource management countrywide.

Funding

Poor communities often need financial assistance to get started in rebuilding natural capital. Funds from the state or other sources can be critical in mobilizing villagers to invest time and energy in developing a plan for resource management. Even a small pool of funds can often be quite effective, inducing villagers to contribute their own labour and resources to the community and launching an upward spiral. As the village starts to build its common natural assets, the commons supports economic growth by supplying food, fuel, fodder and other raw materials. Once this process is set in motion, the village itself often can raise substantial sums to invest in its land and water resources.

Conclusions

Ecological restoration is not primarily about planting trees or rehabilitating landscapes. It is about deepening democracy. In Sukhomajri, Ralegan Siddhi, Alwar and Jhabua, natural assets began to accumulate only after communities were mobilized and won greater power to manage their environment. In each case, a non-governmental organization or the state played a catalytic role by providing the community funds to invest and helping to find ways around restrictive laws.

Such cases remain few and scattered in India, in large part, because the country's legal framework denies villagers property rights over common lands. In three of the cases described, the villages strictly speaking are managing the common property illegally: they have appropriated control, and after considerable tension and conflict they have reached an unwritten understanding with the government authorities. Even in Madhya Pradesh, where the state government itself initiated change, the laws on the books remain unchanged. Ecological restoration on a large-scale will require changes in national policy. The fight for such changes will require extraordinary perseverance.

As these initiatives have progressed, new demands for institutional innovation have arisen. In Alwar and Madhya Pradesh, for example, watershed protection has made more groundwater available, but this has spurred the sinking of tubewells that threaten to deplete the aquifer and raise the danger of inequities in distribution between those who have pumps and those who do not. In Alwar the villagers have set up a river parliament to contend with these issues, and in Madhya Pradesh the government is considering giving village watershed committees the power to set rules over groundwater usage.

In all these cases, progress has been possible because the communities created local assemblies that deliberate in the open and invite widespread participation. Environmental regeneration demands heavy investments of labour, whether for reforestation, construction of water harvesting structures, or soil conservation. Ordinarily, impoverished people are not motivated to do this kind of work because the economic returns are not immediately apparent. The government's rural employment programme has enormous potential to address this problem. In the late 1980s, the government decided to provide rural employment funds directly to villages rather than routing the money solely through government functionaries. But the crucial error was that the village *panchayat*, not the *gram sabha*, was chosen to receive the money. The *panchayats* failed to ensure that the villagers were informed about the money, let alone consult with them about how it was to be used (Agarwal and Narain 1991). With a more inclusive framework for village participation, the rural employment programme could become a major tool for ecological restoration.

As the natural resource base grows, so do the interests of the rich and the powerful in augmenting their share. Strengthening property rights and village institutions to withstand this threat becomes all the more critical. It has long been held that village institutions fail to protect the poor against powerful vested interests, and that the best solution is to strengthen outside agencies. Over more than five decades of India's independence, however, bureaucracies too have become handmaidens of the rich and powerful. Their closed nature and lack of accountability engender corruption, leading to more inequality, not less.

The answer again lies in fostering democracy. The case studies presented in this chapter show that open and participatory village institutions, with clearly defined property rights, are in the best position to balance competing interests in the community. This does not mean that conflict will disappear, or that all decisions will serve the interests of the poor. But participatory democracy does provide an institutional and legal framework that allows the poor to fight for their rights and defend the natural resources on which their livelihoods depend.

Note

1. US dollar equivalents are based on the exchange rate in the year for which the corresponding Rupee amount is specified. The value of the Rupee has fallen against the dollar over the past 30 years. In the late 1970s, 10 Rupees equalled one dollar. Today, the exchange rate is closer to 45 Rupees to the dollar. For periods covering several years, the average exchange rate for that period is used.

References

Agarwal, Anil (1985) 'Politics of the Environment', In *State of India's Environment 1984–85: Second Citizens' Report*, New Delhi: Centre for Science and Environment.

Agarwal, Anil and Sunita Narain (1989) *Towards Green Villages: A Strategy for Environmentally Sound and Participatory Rural Development*, New Delhi: Centre for Science and Environment.

— (1990) *Strategies for the Involvement of the Landless and Women in Afforestation: Five Case Studies from India*, Geneva: World Employment Programme, International Labour Office.

— (1991) 'Panchayat Bill is Prescription for More of Neta Raj', *Economic Times*, 6 October, New Delhi.

Agarwal, Anil and Richard Mahapatra (1999) 'Madhya Pradesh: Regaining Paradise', in Anil Agarwal, Sunita Narain and Srabani Sen, eds., State of India's *Environment–1999: Citizens' Fifth Report*, New Delhi: Centre for Science and Environment.

Agarwal, G. D (nd) 'An Engineer's Evaluation of Water Conservation Efforts of Tarun Bharat Sangh in 36 Villages of Alwar District', Alwar: Tarun Bharat Sangh. Unpublished paper.

Chopra, Kanchan, Gopal Kadekodi and M. N. Murthy (1990) *Participatory Development: People and Common Property Resources*, New Delhi: Sage Publications.

Chopra, Kanchan and D. V. Subba Rao (1996) 'Economic Evaluation of Soil and Water Conservation Programmes in Watersheds', Delhi: Institute of Economic Growth. Unpublished paper.

Dhar, S. K. (1997) Personal communication from Chief Conservator of Forests, Government of Haryana.

Franda, Marcus (1981) 'Conservation, Water and Human Development at Sukhomajri', Unpublished paper.

Hardin, Garrett (1968) 'The Tragedy of the Commons', *Science* 162: 1243–1248.

Hazare, Anna (1997) *Ralegan Siddhi: A Veritable Transformation*, Ralegan Siddhi: Ralegan Siddhi Pariwar.

Lokur, Vasudha (1996) *Ralegan Siddhi: Rural Transformation through People's Participation*, Ralegan Siddhi: Sant Yadav Baba Shiksham Prasarak Mandal.

Mahapatra, Richard (1997) 'Field Report on Adarsh Gaon Yojana', New Delhi: Centre for Science and Environment. Unpublished paper.

— (1998) 'Sukhomajri at the Crossroads', *Down to Earth*, 15 December 1998, New Delhi.

— (1999) 'Success Spreads', in Anil Agarwal, Sunita Narain and Srabani Sen, eds., *State of India's Environment 1999: Citizens' Fifth Report*, New Delhi: Centre for Science and Environment.

Mishra, P.R., Grewal, S.S., Mittal, S.P. and Agnihotri, Y. (1980) *Operational Research Project on Watershed Development for Sediment Drought and Flood Control—Sukhomajri*, Chandigarh: Chandigarh Central Soil and Water Conservation Research and Training Institute.

Mishra, P.R. and Madhu Sarin (1987) 'Social Security through Social Fencing:

Sukhomajri and Nada's Road to Self-sustaining Development', Paper presented at the *Conference on Sustainable Development, International Institute for Environment and Development, London.*

Mittal, S.P., Y. Agnihotri and R.M. Madhukar (1983) 'Watershed Management and Controlled Grazing Promotes Dairy Development in Hill Areas', Unpublished paper.

Sarin, Madhu (1996) *Joint Forest Management: The Haryana Experience,* Ahmedabad: Centre for Environment Education.

United Nations (1988) *Putting Tradition Back into Practice: Johad Watershed in Alwar District, Rajasthan,* New Delhi: United Nations Inter-agency Working Group on Water and Environmental Sanitation.

Bangladesh has the world's richest inland fishery resources.
Photo credit: Centre for Natural Resource Studies.

CHAPTER 4
NET BENEFITS:
THE ECOLOGICAL RESTORATION OF
INLAND FISHERIES IN BANGLADESH

M. Mokhlesur Rahman and
Stephen F. Minkin

The Centre for Natural Resources Studies (CNRS), since 1992, has implemented community-based environmental restoration projects in Bangladesh that seek to protect and renew floodplain ecosystems. These efforts grew out of a situation where the country's aquatic resources were under assault by massive flood control projects. The CNRS strategy was inspired by research showing that the rural poor in Bangladesh rely on a rich diversity of fish species for their diets and livelihoods. Most of these fish species depend on the annual inundation of flood waters for their reproduction and growth. Yet these crucial social and biological realities were either unseen or ignored by the leading development agencies concerned with water management, flood control and fisheries in Bangladesh. The CNRS projects have shown that an alternative strategy, based on investment in ecological restoration, can benefit both the fish and people.

Inland Fisheries in Bangladesh

In his classic book, *Fish, Water and People: Reflections on Inland Openwater Fisheries Resources of Bangladesh*, the late Dr. M. Youssouf Ali described the link between fisheries and rural livelihoods in the Bengal delta:

Bangladesh has the reputation of being very rich in inland openwater capture fisheries production. A large number of fish and prawns could be captured by men, women, and children at their doorsteps during the monsoon season, when all the low-lying areas of the country remained under floodwater. As a result of the plentiful availability of inland-water fish production, fish constituted the second most important component of the Bengali's diet next to rice. Bengali people have been known to be made up of 'rice and fish' (Ali 1997).

For centuries, the people living in the region that is now Bangladesh have depended on wild aquatic resources for their diets and economic security. Lying in the floodplain delta of the Ganges, Brahmaputra and Meghna rivers (see Figure 4.1), the country has rich and diverse inland aquatic environments that support more than 300 inland species of fish and prawns (Rahman 1989; Rainboth 1990). Seasonally inundated floodlands and *beels* (perennial water bodies) account for roughly three-quarters of the inland open-water fish catch, with rivers accounting for the remainder. In the 1980s, it was estimated that 75 per cent of rural families practiced seasonal consumption fishing, and that about two million Bangladeshis were engaged in commercial fishing and associated activities. Fish accounted for roughly three per cent of the gross domestic product, and more than 11 per cent of the country's export earnings (World Bank 1991, 1–3). Rural families consume fish an average of 3.5 days per week (Minkin *et al.* 1997), and more than 70 per cent of animal protein in the diet comes from fish (Institute of Nutrition and Food Science 1983).

The words 'nutrition' and 'biodiversity' are seldom linked, yet fish species diversity is a critical component of the nutritional profile of the Bangladeshi people. Poor people, in particular, traditionally have relied on a wide variety of species to meet their nutritional needs. A year-long study conducted in 1992 found that poor families consumed between 50 and 75 species of fish annually. Most of these species migrate between rivers, where they find shelter during the dry winter seasons, and floodplains, where they spawn and feed during the summer monsoon. Fish are the principal source not only of animal protein but also of fatty acids in the diet, and they contribute important vitamins and minerals to the diets of children, pregnant women and nursing mothers (Minkin *et al.* 1997). These 'vulnerable groups' suffer the most from nutritional losses caused by impeded fish migration.

Prior to the 1992 study, the dietary contribution of the diverse fish species eaten in Bangladesh was largely ignored. Official documents lumped hundreds of edible species together under the headings 'miscellaneous' or 'other' fish (Department of Fisheries, 1988; World Bank 1991, 144). Fisheries 'experts' dismissed the small fish that play such an important role in the diet of the poor as 'junk fish'. Policy guidelines produced by the government's Flood Plan Coordination Organization referred only to a handful of 'economic species' — larger fish sold in urban markets — implicitly assigning no value to most of the fish produced and consumed in Bangladesh (FPCO 1992).

Figure 4.1: Map of Bangladesh

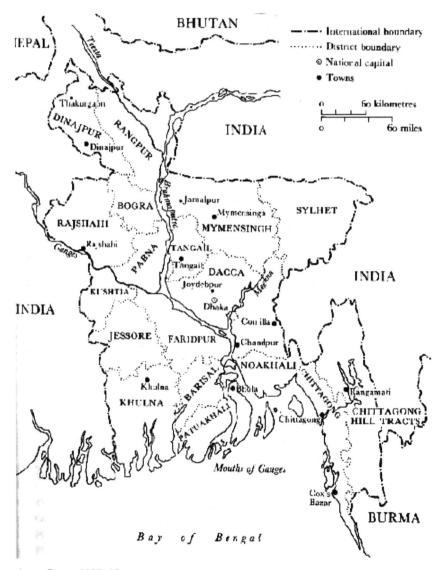

Source: Boyce 1987, 15.

In the 1970s, Bangladesh was described by the Food and Agriculture Organization of the United Nations as 'possibly the richest country in the world as far as inland fishery resources are concerned' (FAO 1973, 31). By the 1980s, however, the central component of those resources—open-water capture fisheries—increasingly was under attack from large-scale flood control projects whose embankments blocked natural routes for fish migration. The 1990s saw a dramatic shift in fisheries production in Bangladesh, with a marked decline in open-water capture fisheries and a vast increase in closed-water pond aquaculture.

Although opportunities are shrinking, substantial numbers of people in Bangladesh still engage in subsistence fishing. In effect, this is a hidden economy. Families interviewed in the study of fish biodiversity and nutrition often initially described members who were engaged in subsistence fishing as 'unemployed'. Each year, large numbers of so-called unemployed individuals, numbering in the millions, enter a wageless labour system and obtain food for their families by catching fish. Inexpensive or free fish effectively subsidize grain production in Bangladesh by allowing labouring families to consume essential nutrients despite low wages and intermittent employment. The loss of subsistence fisheries today is an important but largely unrecognized factor compelling landless labourers and small farmers to leave rural areas in search of work to the cities.

Bangladesh's freshwater fish populations are heavily dependent on seasonal variations in rivers and floodplain ecosystems. During the summer monsoon season, the inundation of the countryside allows fish to migrate from the river to critical floodplain habitats. In the last two decades, however, millions of hectares of open-water resources in Bangladesh have been impacted by flood control projects and road embankments. These structures have blocked fish migration routes and destroyed the natural spawning and feeding grounds of many fish species. As a consequence, some fish species are no longer seen in the floodplains, and many others are at risk.

The importance of species diversity for both floodplain fisheries production and social equity has been largely overlooked in official fisheries development plans. Instead, fisheries management policies have focused on increasing the production of a limited number of commercially valuable species (Minkin and Boyce 1994). In particular, development strategies have promoted large-scale stocking of carp fingerlings, including 'exotic' species introduced from other countries. These costly programmes have altered the country's aquatic ecosystem, favouring a narrow band of species at the expense of biodiversity. The stocked carps, particularly the exotics, compete with local species for food and space, reducing diversity in open waters. The major benefits of the stocking programme go to leaseholders and large farmers, who seek to enclose the aquatic commons and profit from the sale of carp to urban markets (Toufique 1997). This misguided strategy runs directly contrary to the interests of the poor people, for whom easy access to a variety of fish species is of utmost importance.

Community-based Ecological Restoration

The Centre for Natural Resources Studies (CNRS), based in Bangladesh's capital, Dhaka, seeks to address issues of poverty, malnutrition and underemployment by improving the environmental management of aquatic resources. Initially, CNRS aimed to demonstrate the feasibility of community-based ecological restoration as a means of benefiting poor people. A pilot project in Tangail district revitalized a degraded wetland ecosystem by reconnecting the floodplain to local rivers via canals. This project tested both a biological paradigm concerning the response of fish species to potential migration channels and a social paradigm resting on community support and involvement.

The project was built on the observations that fishing in Bangladesh is highly dependent on species diversity; that inland fisheries require movement of water between rivers and floodplains to remain robust and abundant; and that reductions in species diversity and fish movements hurt poor families disproportionately. Based on this diagnosis, the CNRS advanced the following propositions:

- The solution to fisheries problems in Bangladesh depends on management of the movement of water between rivers and floodplains.
- The rehabilitation of blocked and silted canals linking rivers and floodplains can substantially increase both fish production and species diversity.
- Water management programmes to enhance fisheries can also provide agricultural benefits, by allowing effective drainage and increasing the availability of water for irrigation.
- Fish sanctuaries — refuges where fish are protected during the dry season — can enhance the benefits of water management.
- Community-designed interventions and management can ensure sustainable production and use of natural resources in the floodplains.

In sum, the conservation and enhancement of inland fisheries requires wise stewardship, so as to maintain the integrity of aquatic ecosystems of which humans are an integral part.

Site Selection

Intervention began with the selection of low-lying areas with permanent water bodies, known as *beels*, which had the following characteristics:

- The bed of the major link canal had been raised because of siltation, delaying the entry of water and reducing fish migration.
- There were perennial and seasonal wetlands in the area, and fishing was a major economic activity much of the year.
- Poor people enjoyed access rights for fishing in the wetlands as a common property resource.
- Local people believed that the opening of the canal would be beneficial for fish and crops, and the local government (union council) favoured de-siltation.
- Poor people who fished in the *beel* and floodplain were organized.

Several initial project sites were selected. Here we present data from the first site, Sigharagi *beel*, a crescent-shaped wetland covering about seven hectares in the dry season. We then briefly report on experiences at a second site, Bejurnala *beel*.

Participatory Management

A project implementation committee (PIC) was formed for each site. It consisted of around 30 members — 10–15 per cent of whom were women — representing villages located around the *beel*, and included various social strata and CNRS field staff. A respected local person was selected as PIC chairman, and the local union council chairman acted the PIC's adviser. The services of PIC members were voluntary.

Restoration Activities

The reopened canal not only facilitated fish migration, but also allowed more river water into the floodplain. Thus, fish habitats in the Sigharagi wetland were expanded both spatially and temporally. In addition to re-opening canals, CNRS undertakes measures to enhance wetlands to make them more favourable for fisheries and other forms of aquatic life. These include the reintroduction of locally threatened species, the restoration of swamp forest and reed lands, and the placing of brush pilings into the water to provide shelter and safe habitats for fish.

The restoration of 'fish sanctuaries' — the deeper parts of the floodplains and river channels where fish survive during the dry season, and where they grow and attain maturity for spawning in the next monsoon season — is particularly important. Where perennial wetlands have been transformed to seasonal wetlands because of poor land use management and excavation, de-siltation and reforestation can help to restore sanctuaries. The complete draining of seasonal water bodies to catch fish is a common practice, but this is detrimental to fish populations, as it leaves no parent stock in the floodplain for the next year's reproduction. CNRS staff discussed the necessity of fish sanctuaries in seasonal wetlands with fishermen and owners of *pagars* (small ponds and ditches in which fish are trapped at the end of the monsoon season). In March 1995, a *pagar* located in the middle of the Sigharagi floodplain was leased as a demonstration plot, with the aim of raising public awareness about the need to conserve parent brood fish, and kept as mini-sanctuary for *beel* resident species. The villagers volunteered to protect the *pagar* sanctuary. At the onset of early monsoon rains, these fish dispersed on the floodplain and released millions of eggs even before the entry of river water through canals. During the catch survey in the following year, the fishers reported an abundance of species that they attributed to conservation in the *pagar* sanctuary. Based on this experience, the PIC decided to continue the practice of keeping a *pagar* as sanctuary to conserve the parent stock of fish.

Impact Monitoring

Careful data collection and research are standard features of CNRS projects. Data are collected on social parameters including consumption of fish species by different economic groups and involvement in fishing activities, and on biological parameters such as the fish harvest, fishing methods and intensity, and fish migration. In the Sigharagi *beel* project, 56 households were randomly selected for monitoring. Five village women with basic literacy and numeracy skills were trained in the use of structured monitoring formats and simple weighing instruments. The resident monitors visit the sample households for five consecutive days each month and collect data through interviews, direct observation and measurement.

Project Benefits

Beels, chawks and *pagars* are three distinct types of fishing grounds in the Sigharagi floodplains. *Beels* are perennially inundated areas; *chawks* are seasonally inundated lands that are usually cultivated in the dry season; and *pagars* are temporary ponds and ditches dug within the chawks to trap fish. Both *beels* and *chawks* are generally open-access fishing areas for residents of the surrounding villages for at least part of the year. In the pagars fishing is restricted to the landowners or leaseholders, and their designated users. Poor households customarily have been allowed to catch residual fish, however, after the *pagars* have been fished by their owners and leaseholders, a practice akin to gleaning. They are also allowed to fish in low productivity *pagars* where the owners do not even bother to fish. Poor and landless households, therefore, have had some access even to privately held fishing grounds.

Yield and Diversity of Beel and Chawk Catch

Comparison of pre- and post-intervention data from the Sigharagi project site shows roughly a five-fold increase in the catch from the *beel* and the *chawk* in the first year (see Table 4.1). This dramatic rise indicates an underlying increase in wetland productivity. In the project's second year, production fell by about 30 per cent, but it remained more than three times higher than the baseline figure. The decrease in the second year was because of relatively low river-flooding, leading to lower ingress of water and a shorter inundation period. Moreover, spawn fishing in the project-rehabilitated canal had a negative impact on the overall productivity of the *beel* and floodplain. In light of this experience, the PIC launched an awareness campaign to discourage future spawn fishing in canals during the ingress of river water.

The data also show an enhancement of fish species diversity, with the number of species caught increasing from 46 before the project to 59 in year one, and 63 in year two. This reflects the positive impacts of habitat improvement and other conservation measures like the establishment of sanctuaries and restrictions on the use of harmful fishing equipment in the floodplain. Small fish, small prawns, snakeheads and eels continued to make up the bulk of the catch. The share of carps and catfish rose following the canal rehabilitation, however, indicating successful recruitment of these riverine species into the floodplain.

Yield and Diversity of Pagar Catch

Total yield from 19 *pagars* in the Sigharagi *chawk* area, which were monitored before and after intervention, more than tripled in the first year of the project. The production of fish from these *pagars* fell in the following year because of low flooding, but remained 70 per cent higher than the baseline production. Major changes also were observed in the species composition of the *pagar* catch. Prior to intervention, commercially valuable major carp species represented less than two per cent of catch and ranked only seventh in terms of contribution to yield. After intervention, in year one, major carps made up almost 24 per cent of catch and ranked first, while in the second year major carps constituted 15 per cent of the catch and ranked fourth. Similarly, large catfish that were absent from the *pagars* in the baseline year, made up about eight per cent and six per cent of the catch in the next two years, respectively. Exotic species, which include other carps and tilapia, also increased in absolute and relative terms. At the same time, the small fish group also showed impressive yield gains, ranking first and contributing over 24 per cent of the catch in the second year.

Table 4.1: Yield and Species Composition of Beel and Floodplain Catch

Species Group	Baseline (Dec 1994–June 1995)			Year One (Dec 1995–June 1996)			Year Two (Dec 1996–June 1997)		
	Weight (kg)	Per cent of Total Weight	Number of Species	Weight (kg)	Per cent of Total Weight	Number of Species	Weight (kg)	Per cent of Total Weight	Number of Species
Small fish	830	33.5	25	4548	37.2	33	2160	24.8	29
Prawns	709	28.5	1	4052	33.1	2	1495	17.2	3
Snake heads	305	12.3	3	1626	13.3	2	2588	29.8	3
Eels	417	16.8	4	657	5.4	4	181	2	3
Small catfish	143	5.8	7	434	3.6	7	198	2.3	10
Major carps	4	0.2	1	375	3.1	3	1239	14.3	4
Large catfish	1	0	2	345	2.8	3	191	2.2	4
Exotic species	42	1.7	2	135	1.1	2	422	4.9	3
Knife fish	29	1.2	1	34	0.3	1	59	0.7	2
Minor carps	-	-	-	16	0.1	2	160	1.8	2
Total	2,480	100	46	12,222	100	59	8,693	100	63

Human Benefits

Fishing Participation

Men, women and children fish in the Sigharagi wetland, although participation and end-use of the catch vary by age group and gender. Roughly 40 per cent are subsistence fishers, about 35 per cent are part-time professional fishers and 25 per cent are full-time professionals. Survey data show that females make up 7.4 per cent of the fishers, most of whom are children below 15 years of age, fishing for home consumption. Overall, children comprise 28 per cent of all fishers, most of whom fish mainly for subsistence. In contrast, two-thirds of adult fishers sell at least some of their catch.

Table 4.2: Yield and Species Composition of *Pagar* Catch

Species Group	Baseline (1995)			Year One (1996)			Year Two (1997)		
	Rank	Weight (kg)	Per cent of Total Weight	Rank	Weight (kg)	Per cent of Total Weight	Rank	Weight (kg)	Per cent of Total Weight
Snake heads	1	597	41	4	569	11	2	497	20
Small catfish	2	393	27	5	509	10	3	463	19
Small fish	3	177	12	2	1120	22	1	593	24
Knife fish	4	113	8	9	77	1	9	16	1
Eels	5	86	6	7	256	5	7	76	3
Exotic species	6	31	2	3	744	14	5	231	9
Major carps	7	29	2	1	1222	24	4	363	15
Prawns	8	25	2	8	254	5	8	33	1
Large catfish	9	-	-	6	431	8	6	167	7
Minor carps	10	-	-	10	<1	0	10	<1	0
Total		1451	100		5182	100		2439	100

Participation in fishing varies from season to season, being highest during monsoon and post-monsoon months (July–December). In 1995, before the project intervention, fishers altogether spent 690 person-days fishing, with landless households accounting for the greatest fishing effort (see Table 4.3). Fishing effort increased substantially following intervention in response to greater fish availability and the extended spatial and temporal extent of wetland area. Total fishing effort almost doubled to 1,302 fishing days in 1996, with the greatest increase occurring among small farmer households, who spent four times as many days fishing after intervention. In 1997, the second year of the project, the total fishing days fell to 858, less than in the project's first year but still higher than the baseline situation despite the drought.

Table 4.3: Fishing Days by Household Type

Household Type	Fishing Person Days					
	Baseline (Feb–June 1995)		Year One (Feb–June 1996)		Year Two (Feb–June 1997)	
	Days	%	Days	%	Days	%
Landless	434	63	624	48	402	47
Small Farmer	118	17	450	35	300	35
Medium and Large Farmer	138	20	228	18	156	18
Total	690	100	1302	100	858	100

Fishing by landless households fell below the pre-project level in year two. This was not only due to the low flooding, but also to a conflict that arose over access to the *beel*. Previously, the *beel* had been leased to a third party residing outside the project area, who controlled commercial fishing there through a local agent. Subsistence fishers had free access often after the major fish harvest. With project support, the PIC got the lease, but the local agent illegally sought to retain control over access to the *beel*, impeding fishing by villagers, particularly, by the landless subsistence fishers. After he relinquished control, however, the villagers regained open access to the *beel*.

In addition, survey data showed that following the intervention landless households had reduced access to 'gleaning' in the private *pagar* fisheries, as these became even more productive. However, a share of the income from *pagars'* enhanced production does go to poor local fishermen who buy the fish from the *pagar* owners in advance at a relatively low price and, after protecting the *pagars* for 2–3 months, harvest the fish for a profit.

Fish Consumption

Per capita fish consumption for all types of households increased markedly in the year following project intervention. Average daily consumption rose from 24 grams before the project to 30 grams in the first year (see Table 4.4). In year two, per capita fish consumption slipped back to 25 grams, because of lower fish production resulting from low river-flooding exacerbated by the dispute over leasing arrangements in the *beel*.

The sample households consumed more than 60 different species of fish. Small fish species were eaten more than any other group. Before the project, purchased fish accounted for 73 per cent of household consumption; their own catch represented only 27 per cent (see Table 4.5). The project led to a marked increase in the proportion of self-caught fish, to roughly half of the total consumption, with landless and small farm households showing the largest gains.

Table 4.4: Fish Consumption by Household Type

Household Type	Per Capita Fish Consumption (gm/head/day)		
	Baseline (Feb–June 1995)	Year One (Feb–June 1996)	Year Two (Feb–June 1997)
Landless	18	22	19
Small farmers	26	42	26
Medium and Large farmers	40	43	36
All Types	24	30	25

Table 4.5: Sources of Fish Consumed by Household Type

Household Type	Baseline (1995)		Year One (1996)		Year Two (1997)	
	Caught (%)	Bought (%)	Caught (%)	Bought (%)	Caught (%)	Bought (%)
Landless	25.2	74.8	51.6	48.4	43.5	56.5
Small Farmers	22.3	77.7	46	54	55.7	44.3
Medium and Large Farmers	34.2	65.8	37.5	62.5	51.2	48.8
All Types	27	73	46.1	53.9	49.3	50.7

Bejurnala Beel

A CNRS project in Bejurnala *beel,* a 33-acre wetland that borders five villages in north-central Bangladesh, also illustrates the potential for community-based ecological restoration of inland fisheries. The *beel* is owned by the government, but 21 acres have been distributed among the local people on a long-term lease.

In the dry season, the water area of the *beel* remains at least 20 acres, and it is open for both subsistence and professional fishing. In the past, there were several connecting canals between the *beel* and the nearby Singha River, which facilitated fish migration and supported rich fisheries production and species diversity. The *beel* also provided water for irrigation to the adjoining lands in the dry season.

By the mid-1990s, however, the *beel* had become almost seasonal. Both the *beel* and the canal beds had been raised because of siltation over a long period. This not only resulted in a shortage of dry season surface water, but also led to crop losses in the rainy season because of rainwater congestion, and to declining fish production and species diversity. In low-flooding years, the *beel* disappeared in the dry season, leaving water only in privately owned *pagars*. To make matters worse, a local influential person excavated a big pond in the *beel* for fish culture, in effect enclosing part of the aquatic commons. The poor fishers were unhappy about this illegal occupation, but they could not stand against the rich man.

After discussions with CNRS, the local people expressed their desire to re-excavate the main canal between the *beel* and the Singha River. A PIC was formed in 1996, composed of project staff, a schoolmaster, fishers and farmers from the five villages around the *beel*. Under the supervision of the PIC, the link canal was rehabilitated during the dry season in the following year, generating 600 person-days' work in local employment.

After excavation, water and fish entered the canal from the Singha River in April 1997, much earlier than in previous years. By mid-June, the canal was filled with water. Some villagers started rearing ducks in the canal, and farmers began planting a local jute variety in nearby lands with the hope that the canal would reduce drainage congestion. The local people returned to fishing in the canal with fixed nets and enclosures during the monsoon. The project staff convinced them to remove fixed nets during the peak migration period, however, so that fish from the river could move onto the floodplain and into the *beel*.

The total fish catch and species diversity in Bejurnala *beel* increased greatly following the canal re-excavation. Fish production increased from a baseline of 970 kilograms (kg) to 5,700 kg. Particularly dramatic increases in major carp and catfish production were observed, indicating that the project facilitated fish migration from the river. After rehabilitation, the canal retained water for 11 months, compared to seven months before the project. Fish catch in the canal increased substantially, too, from 300 kg to 3700 kg. A particularly remarkable outcome was that more than 1,000 kg of major carps were harvested in the canal, whereas in the preceding year only one fish had been caught. As large, high-priced fish, major carps are rarely consumed by poor people, but the increased catch of these species contributed to higher fishing incomes for poor families. Various species of knife fish, minor carps and large catfish were also found that were not observed in the canal before rehabilitation. The total number of fish species increased from 37 to 51, again indicating that the quality of the habitat had improved.

Conclusion

In recent decades, Bangladesh's physical landscape has been transformed in ways that have dramatically reduced the productivity of open-water floodplain fisheries. The CNRS approach to ecological restoration seeks to reverse this trend by mobilizing local communities to invest in natural assets. The success of this approach has inspired others to follow suit, and ecological restoration has now been taken up as part of the national fisheries policy agenda. Projects funded by the US Agency for International Development and the World Bank have attempted to promote community-based ecological restoration. The success of these endeavours has yet to be independently evaluated. CNRS's own work continues to evolve, incorporating new ideas and lessons learned through participatory research and action. The restoration of submerged forests and aquatic vegetation has become a recent focus in its activities. This work is demonstrating that humans and fish can not only co-exist in Bangladesh's rich delta ecosystem, but also that their relationship can be a mutually supportive one, in which each helps to sustain the other.

References

Ali, M. Youssouf (1997) *Fish, Water and People: Reflections on Inland Openwater Fisheries Resources of Bangladesh,* Dhaka: University Press Ltd.

Boyce, James K. (1987) *Agrarian Impasse in Bengal: Agricultural Growth in Bangladesh and West Bengal 1949–1980,* Oxford: Oxford University Press.

Department of Fisheries (1988) *Catch Statistics for Bangladesh, 1987–88,* Dhaka: Government of Bangladesh.

Food and Agriculture Organization (1973) *Bangladesh: Country Development Brief,* Rome: FAO.

Flood Plan Coordination Organization (FPCO) (1992) *Guidelines for Project Assessments,* Ministry of Irrigation, Water Development and Flood Control, Dhaka: Government of Bangladesh.

Minkin, S.F., M.M. Rahman and S. Halder (1997) 'Fish Biodiversity and Environmental Restoration in Bangladesh', in Tsai C and Al My, eds., *Openwater Fisheries in Bangladesh,* Dhaka: University Press Ltd.

Minkin, Stephen F. and James K. Boyce (1994) 'Net Losses: "Development" Drains the Fisheries of Bangladesh', *Amicus Journal* (New York: Natural Resources Defense Council) 16(3): 36–40.

Institute of Nutrition and Food Science (1983) *Nutritional Survey of Rural Bangladesh, 1981–82,* Dhaka: University of Dhaka.

Rahman, A. (1989) *Freshwater Fisheries of Bangladesh,* Bangladesh: Zoological Society of Bangladesh.

Rainboth, W. (1990) 'The Fish Communities and Fisheries of the Sunderbans', *Agricultural and Human Values* 7(2): 61–67.

Toufique, Kazi Ali (1997) 'Some Observations on Power and Property Rights in the Inland Fisheries of Bangladesh', *World Development* 25(3): 457–467.

World Bank (1991) *Bangladesh: Fisheries Sector Review,* Report No. 8830-BD. Washington, DC: World Bank.

PART II:

DEMOCRATIZING ACCESS

Small farmers in the Andean region sustain potato biodiversity.
Photo credit: CooperAcción.

CHAPTER 5
LAND REFORM AND SUSTAINABLE DEVELOPMENT

James K. Boyce, Peter Rosset and Elizabeth A. Stanton

Introduction

In agricultural economies, land is the single most important asset. With access to arable land, rural people at a minimum can feed themselves and their families. Yet ironically, world hunger is concentrated in the countryside. The United Nations Food and Agriculture Organization (FAO 2004, 25) reports that land-poor and landless households in rural areas account for 80 per cent of the people who are chronically hungry in the world today.

Land reform — here defined as the reallocation of rights to establish a more equitable distribution of farmland — can be a powerful strategy for promoting both economic development and environmental quality. Across the globe, small-scale farmers consistently tend to grow more output per acre than large farms. At the same time, when small family farmers hold secure land rights, they tend to be better environmental stewards, protecting and enhancing soil fertility, water quality and biodiversity. For both reasons, democratizing access to land can be the cornerstone for sustainable rural development.

This chapter provides an overview of land reform as a natural asset-building strategy. First, we sketch the wide variety of changes in agrarian structure that fall under the rubric of 'land reform'. To illustrate, we review the experiences of China, Japan, Korea and Taiwan after World War II, where land reforms helped to set the stage for rapid economic growth. We then describe of one of the most vibrant land reform movements of the present day: the Landless Workers' Movement of Brazil. Drawing on these and other examples, we then discuss the effects of land reform on both poverty reduction and environmental quality.

Varieties of Land Reform

Land reform comes in many shapes and sizes. In this chapter, we are concerned with the redistribution of rights from relatively wealthy landowners, who cultivate primarily by means of hired labourers or tenant farmers, to relatively poor people who cultivate primarily with their own family labour. Even then, land reforms can and do vary in a number of dimensions:

- *Rights:* Property rights are a 'bundle of sticks', not all of which necessarily belong to the same party.[1] For example, a tenant farmer may hold an 'occupancy right' to cultivate the land in return for payment of rent, while the landlord has the right to sell the land. Land reforms may redistribute certain sticks in the bundle but not others. Reforms that strengthen the rights of tenants, for example, by prohibiting arbitrary evictions or putting a ceiling on rents, are less far-reaching than 'land-to-the-tiller' reforms that expropriate landlords and transfer land titles to the tenants.
- *Security:* Property rights are never perfectly secure. In many times and places, small farmers have been dispossessed by legal chicanery or outright force; in the words of American folksinger Woody Guthrie, 'Some rob you with a six-gun, some with a fountain pen.' Land reforms can be reversed over time by these or more 'normal' processes of land concentration, particularly, if large landowners enjoy preferential access to inputs, subsidies and other advantages.[2] Some land reforms have kept such processes in check by distributing non-saleable *use rights* to farmers, while the community or the state retains title to the land. After the 1910 revolution in Mexico, for example, ownership of roughly half the country's farmland was vested in communities called *ejidos*, in which families hold use rights to individual plots as long as they continue to till them.[3]
- *Structure:* The new agrarian structure established by a land reform can be based on family farms, small-scale cooperatives, large-scale collectives, or state farms. Strategies shift over time. For example, the Chinese revolution initially redistributed land to individual families and then

organized them into cooperatives and later into large communes; but a generation later, use rights were reallocated to households. Similarly, in Nicaragua the Sandinista government initially created state farms on large holdings expropriated from the former dictator and other estate owners; in an effort to consolidate their political base, they later experimented with cooperatives and issued individual titles to peasants.[4]

- *Egalitarianism:* The degree to which land reform programmes yield a more egalitarian agrarian structure is, well, a matter of degree. During British rule in India, for example, a series of tenancy reforms in Bengal redistributed rights from large landlords to the upper stratum of the peasantry, while doing little to expand the land rights of the poor.[5] The post-war land reforms in East Asia, described in the next section, had much stronger egalitarian impacts.

- *Gender:* Land reform can also affect disparities between men and women. In El Salvador, for example, a US-backed reform in the 1980s that transferred titles from landlord to tenants actually had the effect of worsening women's (already inferior) position: women comprised only 10 per cent of the beneficiaries, but they accounted for 36 per cent of those whose lands were expropriated, the latter being mostly 'elderly widows and single women who did not work the land directly themselves, but rather share-cropped it or rented it out' (Deere and León 2001, 98). In contrast, Colombia's land redistribution programme in the late 1990s improved women's land rights by mandating joint titles for couples instead of exclusive titles for male household 'heads'. Moreover, women in Colombia received nearly one-third of the land titles that were distributed to individuals rather than couples (Deere and León 2001, 195–197).

- *Compensation:* Land reforms also vary in their treatment of those whose land rights are redistributed to others. In some cases, as in the Chinese revolution, land simply is confiscated without compensation. In others, as in Guatemala's 1954 land reform that was aborted quickly by a CIA-backed coup, large landowners are compensated at a fraction of the market value of the land (in this case, compensation was to be based on the value that the landowner had declared for tax purposes, which usually was well below the land's market price).[6] In still other cases, as in Guatemala after the 1996 Peace Accord, former landowners receive full (or even inflated) compensation from the government, and beneficiaries are supposed to repay part or all of the cost in future years. As a general rule, successful redistributive land reforms have featured what Griffin *et al.* (2002, 279) term a 'high degree of land confiscation'.

- *Macro-economic environment:* While land reform can make a tremendous difference in the lives of the rural poor, it is not a panacea for rural poverty. In the absence of broader macro-economic policies that support agriculture in general and small-scale producers in particular, land reform alone will not bring substantial income gains to the poor. Indeed, if the macro-economic context is quite adverse to agriculture — for example, if exchange rate overvaluation and trade policies make agricultural imports so cheap that local growers cannot compete — then to encourage the poor to seek to earn a living in farming is to lure them into debt and penury. For this reason, Acevedo (1996, 209) observed that in El Salvador in the 1990s, 'a small farm (particularly one encumbered by debt for its acquisition) and access to agricultural credit is an economic curse to be wished only on one's worst enemy'.[7]

- *Process:* A genuine land reform requires a profound social transformation. The processes by which land reform has come about have included 'top-down' initiatives like that of General Douglas MacArthur's administration in post-war Japan, 'bottom-up' popular movements like today's Landless Workers' Movement in Brazil and combinations of the two like the Chinese revolution. But a feature that all successful land reforms share in common is 'a transformation in the balance of power within the rural community and in society at large' (Sobhan 1993, 7). Attempts to implement land reforms without changing the balance of power — what Sobhan calls 'inegalitarian reforms without social transition' — at best yield only modest results.

Land Reform and the East Asian 'Miracle'

Despite wide differences in their political regimes and economic policies, the East Asian countries that emerged in the second half of the 20th century as the world's fastest-growing economies — China, Japan, South Korea and Taiwan — had one thing in common: all implemented highly egalitarian land reforms after World War II. Land reform not only helped to reduce rural poverty and unleash agricultural growth, but also helped to lay the social foundation for rapid industrialization.

In *China*, the Agrarian Reform Law of 1950 institutionalized the land-to-the-tiller redistributive reforms that were begun in communist-controlled territories during the revolution. Landlords — whom the Chinese defined as the rural 'gentry' who did not work in the fields — were expropriated, and sometimes killed, and their properties were transferred to landless and poor peasants. Individual peasant proprietors, including these land reform beneficiaries, were free to buy, sell and rent land. According to Meisner (1986, 140), in the early years of the revolution 'the traditional Chinese ideal of a system of more or less equal family-owned and -operated farms... was probably more fully realized than it ever had been in China's long history'. The Chinese Communist Party initially advocated a gradual, voluntary transition from individual farming to collective farming. Starting in 1955, however, the party embraced a more aggressive collectivization strategy with the aims of increasing agricultural output, extracting bigger surpluses for industrial investment and heading off the reemergence of inequalities in the countryside. This culminated in the establishment of 'people's communes', each of which comprised roughly 5,000 households. The collectivization strategy proved disastrous: it contributed to what has been termed 'the largest famine in human history' in 1959–1961, in which millions perished (Smil 1999, 1620). Ultimately the communes were dissolved, in the new wave of agrarian reforms begun in the late 1970s. Under the 'household responsibility system', individual families in China now have the right to till the land, but not to buy or sell it.[8]

In *Japan*, a far-reaching land reform was initiated after World War II by US occupation authorities under General Douglas MacArthur. American backing for land reform reflected two motives: to dismantle the traditional rural power base of Japanese militarism, and to ward off the appeal of communism by reducing agrarian discontent (Putzel 1992, 69–78). The chief architect of the land reform described it as 'a drastic redistribution of property, income, political power and social status at the expense of the landlords' (Ladejinsky 1977, 356). The reform put a 1-hectare ceiling on ownership of tenanted lands, and a 3-hectare ceiling on self-cultivated lands. Holdings above these limits were expropriated and redistributed to the tillers of the soil. Former landlords received partial compensation in government bonds. Tenants participated in the local land commissions that implemented the reforms, but most tenants and landlords alike saw it as a top-down transformation imposed 'from the heavens above' (Dore, 1959, 172).

In *Taiwan*, Chiang Kai-Shek's post-war government similarly sought to win the support of the peasantry and weaken the island's traditional landowning elite, first by imposing a rent ceiling and then by introducing a land-to-the-tiller reform. The latter required landlords to relinquish excess land (defined, in the case of medium-quality land, as anything above three *chia*, roughly nine acres). The state then sold this land to the tenants. Landowners were compensated with government bonds and shares in public enterprises that had been expropriated from the Japanese. Thanks to the reform, the share of agricultural income accruing to farmers increased from

67 per cent to 82 per cent, the share received by the government rose from 8 per cent to 12 per cent and the share going to landlords and moneylenders fell from 25 per cent to 6 per cent.[9]

In *South Korea*, the US military authorities and the new post-war government also instituted a land-to-the-tiller reform. Prior to this, most farmland was cultivated by tenant farmers, who paid half or more of their crop to Japanese and Korean landlords. The reform transferred ownership rights to former tenants. The ceiling on land ownership was set at three hectares (about 7.5 acres). Korean landlords (but not their Japanese counterparts) received compensation, nominally equal to the 'market price' of the land. In practice, the market price already was deflated by landowner fears of expropriation, and the value of the compensation was further curtailed by stretching payments over time, with no interest or inflation adjustments. The former tenants made in-kind payments (in rice) to the government in return for the land. The government used the income from sale of the rice not only to compensate landlords, but also to invest in rural water supply systems (Jang 2004).

By redistributing rights to the most important rural asset, East Asia's post-war land reforms did much to reduce poverty in the countryside. At the same time, the land reforms helped to set the stage for the rapid industrialization that one day would be hailed as 'the East Asian miracle' (World Bank 1993). Two links between land reform and industrial growth were particularly important. First, farmers' improved economic security meant that they could afford to send their children to school, providing a skilled workforce for industry (Shin, 1998). Second, compared to the landed oligarchies that dominated political life in the pre-reform era, the reforms brought about a more egalitarian order. This helps to explain why government efforts to promote industrialization did not degenerate into a mere pretext for looting state resources and capturing policy-generated 'rents', as so often happened in countries where traditional landed elites retained their grip on power.[10] Analyzing how and why the state succeeded in promoting industrial growth in South Korea and Taiwan, economist Dani Rodrik (1995, 92–93) concludes that the 'initial advantage' conferred by an egalitarian distribution of wealth and income was 'probably the single most important reason why extensive government intervention could be carried out effectively, without giving rise to rampant rent seeking'. In other words, land reform was one of the keys — arguably *the* key — to East Asia's economic 'miracle'.

Land Reform from 'Below': Brazil's MST

Brazil has long had one of the most unequal patterns of land distribution in the world. Since the mid-1980s, however, the country has also given birth to a vibrant land reform movement. As in East Asia, the Brazilian land reform movement strives to redistribute land from the rich to the poor so as to lay the basis for more inclusive economic growth. Unlike the East Asian cases, however, in Brazil the driving impetus for land reform comes not from the state but instead from a popular organization, the Landless Workers' Movement (*Movimento dos Trabalhadores Rurais Sem Terra*, or MST for short).[11]

The origins of the MST can be traced to Catholic liberation theology, which spread in the Brazilian countryside and urban shantytowns in the 1960s. In the 1970s, the Pastoral Land Commission, organized by the National Council of Catholic Bishops, supported a number of land occupations by landless workers. In the mid-1980s, leaders of these occupations from around the country came together to found the MST.

In Brazilian property law, land ownership is governed by the 'principle of effective use'. This principle, based on moral foundations that go back to Saint Thomas Aquinas and John Locke, provides a legal opening for land occupations. Under the law, landowners who do not use their land productively — thereby, failing to fulfill the 'social function' of property — are subject to expropriation (Wright and Wolford 2003, 23–24). This principle was affirmed in the Land Statute passed by Brazil's new military rulers in 1964, and again in the National Agrarian Reform Plan that was passed upon the return to civilian rule in 1985. The latter defines a 'productive farm' as one in which at least 80 per cent of the acreage is effectively used, environmental and labour standards are respected and the use of the land is 'of common benefit to landowners and workers' (Deere 2003, 262).

Although farms that do not meet these criteria can be expropriated, in practice Brazilian government authorities 'generally do not act unless direct action forces their hand' (Hammond 1999, 473). This is where the MST plays a crucial role. After identifying an unproductive estate that it considers eligible for expropriation, the MST recruits 200–2500 landless families, sometimes from rural areas and sometimes from towns and cities, to carry out an occupation. Over a period of several months, the families are trained and prepared in meetings of 'origin groups' in their places of residence. The occupation is then conducted at a single stroke, mobilizing 'thousands of people overnight, some of them from substantial distances' (Hammond 1999, 474). The landowners typically respond with lawsuits, and sometimes with violence. If they are evicted, the occupiers often erect temporary shelters on nearby state-owned land while the litigation proceeds, receiving material support from the MST while they attempt to win legal title to the land.

The MST's strategy is founded on the reality that property rights are never perfectly defined, nor perfectly secure. Instead they are created, and recreated, in an ongoing process of social construction:

> Though an occupation is a militant act requiring ideological commitment and a willingness to undertake significant risks, the MST nevertheless assumes and benefits from a public posture embracing moderation and legality. Occupiers demonstrate their willingness to work. They actively mobilize both solidarity (through urban movements including trade unions) and public opinion, claiming that giving the land to those willing to work it could solve the problems of unemployment and food shortage.... The occupation *per se* is illegal, but they can accurately claim that their aim is to secure enforcement of the law which provides for expropriation of the property, and they are often legally vindicated. (Hammond 1999, 475)

To date, MST-led occupations have enabled some 300,000 Brazilian families (more than a million people) to win legal recognition for more than eight million acres of land reform settlements.[12] While this represents only a fraction of the land held in large estates in Brazil, it is an impressive beginning that could mark a historic break from Brazil's highly unequal agrarian structure.

At first, the MST encouraged settlers to undertake collective production on the occupied lands. These efforts often failed. In subsequent years the MST has evolved a flexible system that promotes 'cooperation' in multiple forms, from true collective farming to various kinds of marketing cooperatives that serve individual family farms. A typical settlement of several hundred families may include some groups who farm collectively, as well as several different cooperatives. All families participate together in the political governance of the settlement.[13]

The MST has only recently begun to stress the importance of securing land rights for women. Earlier the organization considered gender issues to be potentially divisive and a diversion from the central issue of class. Under Brazilian law, joint titling to couples is not mandatory, and title to the land often is held by the male 'household head'. At a national seminar in Curitiba in 1997, almost 100 landless women from across the country debated the role of gender issues in the MST. A gender collective within the MST and a national rural women's organization were subsequently organized. Today the MST has begun to pay more attention to the gender dimension of land reform, prompted by growing awareness that 'the failure to recognize women's land rights is prejudicial to the development and consolidation of the *assentamentos* (settlements) and thus the movement' (Deere 2003, 284; Martins 2004).

How has 'bottom-up' land reform in Brazil affected the country's environment? In many cases, the large landowners have managed to hang onto their most fertile lands, surrendering those tracts that have been most degraded by past practices. Hence, many settlers have realized, as Branford and Rocha (2002, 212) report, 'that unless they can return the land to a state of ecological health, the long-term economic viability of their settlements is threatened'. Once they win secure land rights, the settlers have a powerful incentive to invest in ecological restoration. Nevertheless, in many cases they instead have imitated the chemical-intensive farming techniques of larger farms. The shift to environmental-friendly farming practices has been slow, but with experience and education, new 'agro-ecological' practices are gaining ground in the MST settlements. These include tree replanting, the use of crop rotations and manures to build soil fertility, and organic farming with some of the produce fetching a price premium in urban markets.[14] To assist in this transition, the MST has set up an organic seed company, called Bionatur, which sells to settlements around the country.

Land Reform and Poverty Reduction

By expanding the land rights of the poor, land reform adds to their wealth and thereby reduces asset poverty. This, in turn, helps to reduce income poverty in two ways: first, by increasing the poor's share in the agricultural income pie and second, by increasing the total size of the pie.

The first effect is straightforward. Assets are stocks of wealth, and these generate flows of income. By redirecting an important flow — the returns to land — into the hands of the poor, progressive land redistribution augments their incomes. At the same time, assets enhance a person's social status and political power. Land reform reduces these 'non-economic' dimensions of poverty, too.

The second effect is more complicated, and less certain. In the short run, land reforms can have 'transaction costs' that reduce agricultural output, particularly if accompanied by political instability that disrupts input supplies or access to markets. Moreover, it may take some time for the beneficiaries to learn how best to manage their new assets. But in the long run, land reforms can increase the size of the agricultural income pie by promoting more labour-intensive farming. In other words, land reform can be a 'win-win' strategy that improves both equity and efficiency.

Farm Size and Land Productivity

Evidence from around the world demonstrates that small, owner-operated farms typically produce more output per acre than large farms cultivated by means of wage labour or tenants. A recent report on the relationship between farm size and total output in 15 countries in the global South found that in all cases relatively smaller farms were more productive per unit area, by a factor of 2–10 times (Rosset 1999).

This higher output per acre takes four forms:

- *Higher cultivation intensity:* In any given year, small farms tend to cultivate a bigger percentage of their land than do large farms. In Latin America, in particular, large farms often leave a substantial proportion of their lands uncultivated — a fact that helps to open the legal space for the MST's land occupations in Brazil.
- *Higher cropping intensity:* Likewise, small farms tend to have a higher cropping intensity; that is, they grow more crops per year on a given piece of land. In Bangladesh, for example, 79 per cent farms of half an acre or less grow two or three crops per year, while only 41 per cent of farms larger than 25 acres do so.[15]
- *Higher-value crop mix:* Small farms also tend to grow crops that are higher-value and more labour-intensive than those grown on large farms. The cultivation of vegetables, for example, usually requires much more labour per acre than the cultivation of grains; at the same time, vegetable cultivation yields much greater value per acre.
- *Higher yields per acre:* Finally, small farms often get higher yields per acre for any given crop, simply by virtue of putting more time and care into their farming. While it is not negligible, this differential generally is less important to overall land productivity differences than the other three.[16]

These four effects combine to create a significant advantage, even when the political environment favours larger farmers in multiple ways. In Brazil, for example, family farms account for 40 per cent of the total national value of production, while occupying just 30 per cent of agricultural land area. They generate 77 per cent of Brazil's agricultural employment, while receiving only 25 per cent of farm credit (Pengue, 2005).

These land productivity differences can be traced above all to differences in the use of labour. As a rule, small farmers get more output by applying more labour per acre. Labour productivity — output per unit labour — is often lower on small farms. But in settings where land is scarce and labour relatively abundant, land productivity is the more relevant indicator of overall efficiency.

Why do small farms use more labour per acre? Three main reasons can be advanced. The first is what economist Amartya Sen (1975a) calls the 'labour cost' explanation: working on one's own land is not the same as working for someone else. Small farmers may be willing to work on their own land even when the return (the extra product from a day's work) is less than the daily wage. For example, performing a task like irrigating the crop may only take an hour or two, but if this precludes getting work that day as a wage labourer, the small farmer may put more time into other farm tasks rather than taking the rest of the day off. Or farmers simply may prefer to be their own boss, and be willing to accept a lower 'wage' in return for the satisfaction and status this confers. In this respect, as Sen (1975b, 199) has observed, labour differs fundamentally from other inputs: workers 'are endowed with minds and with ideas and preferences', and these can include a preference to work on their own land.

A second explanation is based on the need for supervision of hired labourers. In the absence of concern for the well-being of their employers, wage labourers have an incentive to work hard only in so far as their jobs depend on it. In agriculture, it is often difficult to tell how much effort a labourer has expended simply by looking at the field. For this reason, employers spend time and money to supervise their farm workers. If there were no incentive problem or if supervision were costless, hired labour would be just as efficient as family labour. But if neither of these conditions holds, large landowners who rely on hired labour will use less labour per acre than owner-operated farms.[17]

A third explanation is based on the observation that local labour markets are often partitioned by natural and social boundaries into 'an archipelago of small, fragmented labour markets' (Griffin *et al.* 2002, 287). In such settings, individual employers wield monopsony power — if they demand more labour, wages go up, and if they demand less, wages go down. This means they have an incentive to employ less labour than would be the case either in competitive labour markets or on owner-operated farms.

These three explanations are not mutually exclusive. In any given place, the lower cost of family labour, the supervision problem with hired labour, and local monopsony power of large landowners may all be at work, contributing in varying degrees to the phenomenon of more labour-intensive practices and higher output per acre on small farms.

The Limitations of Markets

This raises a further question: if small farmers are able to use land more productively than large landowners, why don't markets reallocate land to them? Assuming that farmland is worth most to those who can use it best, over time we could expect market forces to channel it to the highest bidder. Yet, in reality, land sales by large landowners to small farmers are the exception, not the rule. There are two main reasons. The first is the familiar chicken-and-egg problem: the poor need credit to buy land, but without land they lack the collateral to secure loans. The second is that in practice the distribution of land often is determined by political power rather than purchasing power. Historically, inequitable land ownership patterns rarely originated in the free play of market forces; rather they emerged through processes involving conquest, fraud and outright force. Today political power and land rights remain fused in rural societies, each reinforcing the other. For landed elites, the value of land lies therefore not only in its agricultural productivity, but also in the power, status and economic advantages that land ownership confers.[18] Efforts to promote 'market-assisted land reform' by earmarking credit for land purchases for small farmers often founder on this stumbling block.

Nor do land rental markets provide an adequate solution. Tenancy arrangements do allow the surplus land of the rich to be combined with the surplus labour of the poor, bypassing the drawbacks of hired labour discussed earlier. But at the same time, tenancy creates a new set of incentive problems that again depress labour use and land productivity. The most widespread form of tenancy in many parts of the world is share-cropping, in which the landlord takes a share of the harvest (often half) as rent and the share-cropper gets the rest. As far back as the time of Adam Smith, economists have pointed out that this reduces the tenant's incentive to put labour into the land, since the tenant bears the full cost of each unit of labour but receives only a fraction of the resulting output.[19] Fixed rents avoid this problem, but leave the tenant to bear all the risks of output and price fluctuations. Moreover, tenants have no incentive to make investments that enhance the long-term productivity of the land, unless they have 'occupancy rights' that protect them from eviction. Granting such rights to tenants is itself a land reform, since it redistributes one important stick in the property-rights bundle. The landowners' fear of losing property rights is one reason that long-term land rentals are uncommon.[20]

Neither hired labour nor tenancy arrangements successfully resolve the inefficiencies that result from a dichotomy between the ownership of land and labour on it. By ending this dichotomy, land reforms can bring forth higher agricultural output as well as a more egalitarian distribution of that output. 'In most cases', the International Fund for Agricultural Development (2001, 71) concludes, 'if the poor get a bigger share of asset control or benefits, efficiency and economic growth also improve'. By creating a bigger pie as well as a wider slice for the poor, land reform offers a potent strategy for reducing rural poverty. If land reform has positive spillover effects on the urban economy, too, as the East Asian experience suggests, then its contribution to poverty reduction can be even greater.

Land Reform and the Environment

What about the environmental impact of land reform? If land reform does promote labour-intensive farming and higher land productivity, will this accelerate land degradation?

Land Use and Land Abuse

The answer to this question hinges on the difference between *land use* and *land abuse*. Not all agriculture is tantamount to environmental degradation; on the contrary, sustainable farming practices can increase nature's wealth. For example, while myopic farming practices often deplete soil nutrients and cause soil erosion, sustainable farming can increase both the depth of soils and their fertility. Let us illustrate by means of two examples.

The first is from the southwestern United States. Starting in the 16th century, Spanish farmers began to settle in the upper Rio Grande valley, the territory that now spans northern New Mexico and southern Colorado. To irrigate the semi-arid lands, the settlers built channels called *acequias* that carry water from upstream to valley slopes below. This gravity-fed irrigation system transformed local landscapes into a mosaic of wetlands, cultivated fields, orchards and riparian corridors for wildlife movement. Over the generations, the land stewardship of these Hispano farmers and their descendants has created deep and fertile soils. Anthropologist Devon Peña (2003, 169) describes humans as the 'keystone species' of this *acequia* ecosystem: without the people, many other species in the ecosystem would not survive.

The second example comes from South America's Amazon basin. Notwithstanding Amazonia's lush rainforests, most of the region's soils are nutrient-poor and subject to rapid erosion if the forest cover is removed. However, roughly 10 per cent of Amazonia — an area roughly the size of France — has fertile soil known as *terra preta do indio*, the 'dark earth of the Indians'. Researchers believe that *terra preta* is not a random anomaly, but rather a deliberate creation of indigenous farmers who long ago practiced 'slash-and-char' agroforestry in the region.[21] A noteworthy feature of *terra preta* is its remarkable capacity for self-regeneration, which scientists attribute to soil microorganisms. 'In a process reminiscent of dropping microorganism-rich starter into plain dough to create sourdough bread', (Mann, 2000b, 52) explains, 'Amazonian peoples inoculated bad soil with a transforming bacterial charge.' Today researchers are investigating whether *terra preta* can be used to improve soil fertility elsewhere, including in sub-Saharan Africa.[22]

These examples illustrate the fact that agriculture can add to — as well as subtract from — nature's wealth. The question, then, is what determines the balance between positive and negative effects? Why do farmers enrich the environment in some times and places, and degrade it in others? In particular, how might land reform affect this balance?

Environmental Advantages of Small Farmers

No iron rule ensures that small farmers will invest more in natural capital, or manage their lands more sustainably, than large farmers. Outcomes in the field depend on the opportunities and incentives farmers face, and the cultural and institutional environment in which they operate. But there are four good reasons to believe that land reform not only is compatible with sustainable agriculture, but also can help to promote it:

- First, environmentally beneficial land-use practices are often more labour-intensive than environmentally costly land abuse. For example, manual weed control takes more labour than using herbicides. Integrated pest management often is more labour-intensive than simply blasting the fields with insecticides. Similarly, applying bulky organic manures takes more work than applying concentrated chemical fertilizers. Small farms have a comparative advantage in these and other labour-intensive practices for the reasons discussed above, and this translates into a comparative advantage in environment-friendly farming.
- Second, intimate knowledge of the local environment — including soils, weather, crop varieties, insects and plant diseases — is a key input in

sustainable agriculture. A dichotomy between the ownership of land and labour on it often leads to a dichotomy between decision-making and local knowledge. Absentee landowners, in particular, generally lack the accumulated knowledge of small-scale family farmers.

- Third, small farmers not only have greater *ability* to care for the land; they also have greater *willingness* to do so. As owners of the land, they clearly have a stronger incentive to maintain its long-term productivity than do tenant farmers or hired labourers. Apart from self-interest, the ownership of the land often instills a moral sense of duty to safeguard it. For family farmers, land is not just another input: it is an asset to be passed to future generations.[23]

- Finally, farmers who cultivate the land by means of their own family's labour have a much stronger incentive to worry about occupational health and safety, including exposure to toxic pesticides. The people who bear the highest costs from environmentally destructive farming practices often are those who toil in the fields. In farming as other occupations, protecting workers' health goes hand-in-hand with protecting the environment.

Small Farms and Agricultural Biodiversity

The environmental advantages of small farmers are illustrated by their vital role in the evolution and conservation of agricultural biodiversity. The food crops on which we depend for survival are not simple gifts of nature: they are the fruits of interactions between humans and plants that began 10 millennia ago when the inhabitants of Asia Minor began cultivating wheat and barley. Their counterparts in South and East Asia gave us rice, an extraordinarily versatile plant that can survive in continuously flooded fields. In the Andean mountains early Americans evolved the potato, the world's most important root crop, and in Mesoamerica the forebears of today's *campesino* farmers evolved maize from its wild relative, teosinte. With few exceptions, the centres of origin of humankind's food crops are in the global South.[24]

Over the millennia, the process that Charles Darwin termed 'artificial selection' has continued in the farmers' fields. At harvest time, they saved seed from those individual plants that fared best on their lands, for replanting in the next season. In this way, new varieties co-evolved to grow in diverse habitats and adapt to changing environments. This monumental process of investment in natural assets gave us the thousands of crop varieties that exist today. In terms of human well-being, the crop genetic diversity given to us by generations of small farmers unquestionably ranks among the most important sources of biodiversity on the planet, the storehouse from which plant breeders draw to adapt all crops to changing insect pests, plant diseases and climatic conditions.

As a rule, it is small farmers who practice high-diversity agriculture today. In so doing, they generate a 'positive externality' by conserving crop genetic diversity *in situ* (in the field). Not only do different small farmers in a given locality often cultivate different varieties of the same crop, but also individual small farmers often cultivate several different varieties. Large farms, on the other hand, often sow a single variety over a large acreage. The result is an inverse relationship between farm size and varietal diversity.

One reason for this is the comparative advantage of small farms in labour-intensive farming practices. It takes more time and effort to grow multiple varieties with different sowing dates, cultivation requirements and harvest times than to grow a single, uniform variety. Considerable labour is also needed to maintain the physical infrastructures — such as watercourses and terraces — that often accompany high-diversity agriculture.

A second reason is again the importance of local knowledge. Small farmers are repositories of wisdom about the characteristics of different crop varieties. They know which varieties grow best in what locations, which are most resistant to what pests and diseases, which are best suited to what culinary purpose. Without the farmers, it not only would be harder to sustain agricultural biodiversity, it also would be harder to know what is being sustained. In many parts of the world, women play a particularly important role in managing agricultural biodiversity and maintaining this knowledge. In the indigenous communities of the Guatemalan highlands, for example, it is often women who select the seed for the next production cycle, doing so on the basis of culinary requirements and Mayan cosmology as well as agronomic characteristics.[25]

There is also a historical reason why small farmers today are the main cultivators of biodiversity: they tend to predominate in 'marginal' agricultural environments where the spread of 'modern' crop varieties has been held in check by less favourable growing conditions. Hilly terrain, like the highlands of southern Mexico and Guatemala, is less suited to varietal monoculture and agricultural mechanization; similarly, the deeply flooded parts of the Bengal delta are unsuitable for the new short-statured, high-yielding rice varieties. Such lands have been relatively unattractive as targets for appropriation by landed elites, while at the same time having environmental conditions that favour varietal diversification.

This is not to suggest that small farms are or should be living museums.

On the contrary, a hallmark of traditional agriculture is its dynamism. Varietal selection proceeds unabated in farmers' fields, which continue to serve as 'evolutionary gardens' (Wilkes 1992, 24–26). In this evolutionary process, the dividing line between 'traditional' and 'modern' agriculture often becomes blurred. Traditional varieties co-exist with new varieties, and cross-pollination and mutation give rise to successive generations adapted to local conditions and tastes.[26] Indeed, given the dynamic character of small-scale agriculture, the 'traditional-modern' distinction is better described as a contrast between high-diversity and low-diversity agricultural ecosystems.

Nor do we mean to suggest that small farms are immune to the appeal, or threat, of varietal monoculture. Where 'high yielding varieties' (more accurately, highly fertilizer-responsive varieties) of rice and wheat are suited to the lands of small farmers, as in much of Asia, they have displaced large numbers of traditional varieties. Moreover, imported grain from industrialized countries — artificially cheapened by the ecological subsidy from high-diversity agriculture as well as monetary subsidies from Northern governments — is now displacing local production in many developing countries. Both phenomena are contributing to the erosion of crop genetic diversity.

If the environmental advantages of small farms are to translate into competitive advantages in the marketplace, a supportive policy environment is necessary. This includes policies to reward farmers for generating 'positive externalities' like the conservation of agricultural biodiversity, and policies to incorporate 'negative externalities' like pollution and soil erosion into the costs of production and the resulting output prices.[27] Land reform alone does not guarantee a move toward sustainable agriculture, but it can and should be a part of the policy mix.

Conclusions

There is no single road to successful land reform. It takes different forms in different physical and human environments. Nevertheless we can identify several common ingredients in successful experiences:

- Secure rights are critical. Without them, families and communities will remain unwilling and unable to invest in land improvements, and the gains of land reform will remain vulnerable to reversal.
- Women's rights to land must be part of the mix. When land titles are vested exclusively in male 'heads-of-household', divorce and widowhood can lead to the destitution of women and children. Moreover, women's

labour and knowledge often are crucial in small-scale farming.

- The rights of indigenous communities to land, forests, water and other common property resources must be guaranteed and protected, as must their right to manage them using customary law and tradition. While property rights are crucial, no single form of property is universally the best.
- The land distributed must be suitable for farming and free of disputed claims by other poor people.
- When families receive land, they must not be saddled with heavy debt burdens to pay for it. This can be accomplished by limiting the amount of compensation paid to former owners.
- Small farmers need more than land if they are to make a living. They also need a supportive policy environment, including access to credit on reasonable terms, fair prices for their products and access to infrastructure and social services.
- Policies to reward farming practices that generate environmental benefits, like the conservation of agricultural biodiversity and the protection of watersheds, can strengthen rural livelihoods and the competitive advantages of small farms.
- At the same time, policies to discourage farming practices that generate environmental costs, like the profligate use of pesticides, can further enhance the competitive advantages of small farms.
- In today's neo-liberal political environment, strong grassroots movements like the MST are critical to the land reform process. Land occupations that capitalize on the legal and political space to contest property rights can be a particularly effective method of pressing governments to act.

Experience shows that pro-poor land reform is possible. For example, it was done successfully in the mid-20th century in East Asia. And it is being done successfully today in Brazil. When done well — with genuine grassroots engagement, the redistribution of power as well as land, and a supportive social and policy environment — land reform is a powerful strategy to reduce poverty, while improving environmental quality.

Notes

1. Adams *et al.* (1999, 9) observe: 'Land rights may include one or more of the following: rights to occupy a homestead, to use land for crops, to make permanent improvements, to bury the dead, and to graze animals, have access for gathering fuel, fruits, grass, minerals etc.; rights to transact, give, mortgage, lease, rent and

bequeath areas of exclusive use; rights to exclude others from the above; rights to enforcement of legal and administrative provisions in order to protect the rights holder.' For discussion, see also Ross (1989), Schlager and Ostrom (1992); Sterner (2003, ch. 5).

2. De Janvry, Sadoulet and Wolford (2001, 294) cite the case of Chile as an 'archetypal occurrence' of land reconcentration. Among other factors, they point to the land reform beneficiaries' inadequate access to credit and inputs; their high debts incurred for land acquisition; an unfavourable macro-economic environment for traditional crops because of trade liberalization and exchange-rate appreciation; and the greater capacity of larger farmers to participate in the fruit and vegetable export boom by making heavy capital investments with long maturation periods.

3. In 1992, however, Article 27 of the Mexican constitution was amended to allow *ejidos* to vote to grant individual titles to plots that can then be sold, rented, or mortgaged, a change that critics fear has opened the door to greater land concentration.

4. See Deere, Marchetti, and Reinhardt (1985); Enríquez (1991, 1997) for discussion of the Nicaraguan land reform experience. A similar policy shift took place in Cuba in the 1990s, motivated by the country's economic crisis and the need for greater food self-sufficiency coupled with less reliance on petroleum-intensive technologies; see Funes *et al.* (2002).

5. For an account, see Abdullah (1976).

6. See Schlesinger and Kinzer (1982, 54); Sobhan (1993, 53-4).

7. In a similar vein, De Janvry *et al.* (2001, 5) remark: 'Access to land is … not sufficient to secure higher incomes. This is the case when the policy context is adverse to farm profits, competitiveness is undermined by a lack of supportive institutions, assets transferred are not valorized by complementary public goods (e.g., access roads) and investment is deterred by insecurity regarding conditions for access.'

8. In principle, as noted above, such a system of use (or 'usufruct') rights can prevent land concentration and the reemergence of landlordism. In practice, however, it can leave farmers vulnerable to landgrabbing by politically powerful interests — a problem that has become evident in China in the last decade, as real estate development on the periphery of urban areas has pushed millions of farmers off the land (Yardley 2004).

9. Fei, Ranis and Kuo (1979, 44). For discussion, see also Campos and Root (1996, 51–53).

10. An example is the Philippines, where the failure to carry out a serious post-war land reform had far-reaching consequences for the distribution of political power and the fate of economic development strategies; for discussion, see Putzel (1992); Boyce (1993); Hutchcroft (2005).

11. For more on the MST and 'and reform from below', see Rosset (2001a, 2001b).

12. Personal communication with João Pedro Stédile, MST, Brazil, 2004.

13. Interviews conducted on MST settlements by Rosset in 2001–2005. See also Branford and Rocha (2002, 216).

14. For examples and discussion, see Branford and Rocha (2002, 211–239).

15. According to the 1996 agricultural census of Bangladesh, among farms of ½ acre or less, 21 per cent of the land is single-cropped, 67 per cent is double-cropped and 12 per cent is triple-cropped. The corresponding figures for farms of 25 acres or more are 59 per cent, 37 per cent and 4 per cent (Government of Bangladesh, 1999, 25).

16. For extensive reviews of evidence on the size-productivity relationship, see Berry

and Cline (1979); Netting (1993); Tomich *et al.* (1995); Binswanger *et al.* (1995); Rosset (1999).

17. For further discussion of labour supervision as an explanation for the inverse relation between farm size and labour use, see Sen (1981); Boyce (1987, 39–40).

18. These economic advantages include access to subsidized credit, favourable tax treatment of agricultural incomes, and landholding as a hedge against inflation. For discussion, see Binswanger *et al.* (1995, 2710–11).

19. See Smith (1904 [1776], 366–7). For discussion of the efficiency impacts of sharecropping, see also Boyce (1987, 41–44, 213–220).

20. 'The history of land reform', Binswanger *et al.* (1995, 2694) remark, 'shows that long-term rental of entire farms often implies a high risk of loss of land to tenants.'

21. See Mann (2002a). Brookfield (2001, 96–97) discusses this and other examples of 'manufactured soils'. See also Amanor (in this volume).

22. For discussion, see Mann (2007).

23. For further discussion, see Rosset (1999, 2001a, 2006).

24. For discussions of the origins of these and other crop plants, see MacNeish (1992); Harlan (1995); Smartt and Simmonds (1995); Smith (1995).

25. FAO/IPGRI (2002, 22, 39–40). See also Howard (2003).

26. For examples, see Biggs (1980); Brush (1995, 2003); Bellon *et al.* (1997).

27. For further discussion, see Mann (2004), Boyce (2006), and Rosa *et al.* (in this volume).

References

Abdullah, Abu (1976) 'Land Reform and Agrarian Change in Bangladesh', *Bangladesh Development Studies* 4(1): 67–114.

Acevedo, Carlos (1996) 'Structural Adjustment, the Agricultural Sector and the Peace Process', in James K. Boyce, ed., *Economic Policy for Building Peace: The Lessons of El Salvador,* Boulder: Lynne Rienner, 209–231.

Adams, Martin, Ben Cousins and Siyabulela Manona (1999) 'Land Tenure and Economic Development in Rural South Africa: Constraints and Opportunities', *Working Paper No.125,* London: Overseas Development Institute. Available at: http://www.odi.org.uk/publications/working_papers/wp125.pdf.

Bellon, M.R., J.-L. Pham and M.T. Jackson (1997) 'Genetic Conservation: A Role for Rice Farmers', in N. Maxted, B. Ford-Lloyd and J.G. Hawkes, eds., *Plant Genetic Conservation: The In Situ Approach,* London: Chapman & Hall, 263–289.

Berry, R. Albert and William R. Cline (1979) *Agrarian Structure and Productivity in Developing Countries,* Baltimore : Johns Hopkins University Press.

Biggs, Stephen D. (1980) 'Informal R&D', *Ceres* (Rome: Food and Agriculture Organization) 13(4): 23–26.

Binswanger, Hans P., Klaus Deininger and Gershon Feder (1995) 'Power, Distortions, Revolt and Reform in Agricultural Land Relations', in J. Behrman and T.N. Srinivasan, eds., *Handbook of Development Economics, Volume III,* Amsterdam: Elsevier Science, 2559–2771.

Boyce, James K. (1987) *Agrarian Impasse in Bengal: Institutional Constraints to Technological Change,* Oxford: Oxford University Press.

— (1993) *The Philippines: The Political Economy of Growth and Impoverishment in the Marcos Era,* London: Macmillan and Honolulu: University of Hawaii Press.

— (2006) 'A Future for Small Farms? Biodiversity and Sustainable Agriculture', in James K. Boyce, Stephen Cullenberg, Prasanta Pattanaik and Robert Pollin, eds., *Human*

Development in the Age of Globalization, Cheltenham: Edward Elgar, 83–104.

Branford, Sue and Jan Rocha (2002) *Cutting the Wire: The Story of the Landless Movement in Brazil*, London: Latin American Bureau.

Brookfield, Harold (2001) *Exploring Agrodiversity*, New York: Columbia University Press.

Brush, Stephen B. (1995) 'In Situ Conservation of Landraces in Centres of Crop Diversity', *Crop Science* 35: 346–354.

— (2003) 'The Lighthouse and the Potato: Internalizing the Value of Crop Genetic Diversity', in James K. Boyce and Barry G. Shelley, eds., *Natural Assets: Democratizing Environmental Ownership*, Washington, DC: Island Press, 187–205.

Campos, Jose Edgardo and Hilton L. Root (1996) *The Key to the Asian Miracle: Making Shared Growth Credible*, Washington, DC: Brookings Institution.

Deere, Carmen Diana (2003) 'Women's Land Rights and Rural Social Movements in the Brazilian Agrarian Reform', *Journal of Agrarian Change* 3(1/2): 257–288.

Deere, Carmen Diana and Magdalena León (2001) *Empowering Women: Land and Property Rights in Latin America*, Pittsburgh, PA: University of Pittsburgh Press.

Deere, Carmen Diana, Peter Marchetti and Nola Reinhardt (1985) 'The Peasantry and the Development of Sandinista Agrarian Policy, 1979–1984', *Latin American Research Review* 20(3): 75–109.

De Janvry, Alain, Gustavo Cordillo, Jean-Philippe Platteau and Elisabeth Sadoulet (2001) 'The Changing Role of the State in Latin American Land Reforms', in Alain De Janvry et al., eds., *Access to Land, Rural Poverty and Public Action*, Oxford: Oxford University Press, 279–303.

De Janvry, Alain, Elisabeth Sadoulet and Wendy Wolford (2001) 'Access to Land and Land Policy Reforms', in Alain De Janvry et al., eds., *Access to Land, Rural Poverty and Public Action*, Oxford: Oxford University Press, 1–26.

Dore, Ronald P. (1959) *Land Reform in Japan*, London: Oxford University Press.

Enríquez, Laura J. (1991) *Harvesting Change: Labour and Agrarian Reform in Nicaragua, 1979–1990*, Chapel Hill: University of North Carolina Press.

— (1997) *Agrarian Reform and Class Consciousness in Nicaragua*, Gainesville: University Press of Florida.

Fei, J.C.H., G. Ranis and S. Kuo (1979) *Growth with Equity: The Taiwan Case*, New York: Oxford University Press.

Food and Agriculture Organization of the United Nations (FAO) (2004) *The State of Food Insecurity in the World 2004*, Rome: FAO. Available at: ftp://ftp.fao.org/docrep/fao/007/y5650e/y5650e00.pdf.

Food and Agriculture Organization of the United Nations (FAO) and International Plant Genetic Resources Institute (IPGRI) (2002) *The Role of Women in the Conservation of the Genetic Resources of Maize*, Rome: FAO/IPGRI.

Funes, Fernando, Luis García, Martin Bourque, Nilda Pérez and Peter Rosset (2002) *Sustainable Agriculture and Resistance: Transforming Food Production in Cuba*, Oakland, CA: Food First.

Government of Bangladesh (1999) *Census of Agriculture, 1996: Agricultural Sample Survey 1997, Volume 2*, Dhaka: Bangladesh Bureau of Statistics.

Griffin, Keith, Azizur Rahman Khan and Amy Ickowitz (2002) 'Poverty and the Distribution of Land', *Journal of Agrarian Change* 2(3): 279–330.

Hammond, John L. (1999) 'Law and Disorder: The Brazilian Landless Farmworkers' Movement', *Bulletin of Latin American Research* 18(4): 469–489.

Harlan, Jack R. (1995) *The Living Fields: Our Agricultural Heritage*, Cambridge: Cambridge University Press.

Howard, Patricia L. (2003) *Women and Plants: Gender Relations in Biodiversity Management and*

Conservation, London: Zed Books.

Hutchcroft, Paul (2005) *The Power of Patronage: Capital and Countryside in the Twentieth-Century Philippines*, Cambridge: Cambridge University Press.

International Fund for Agricultural Development (IFAD) (2001) *Rural Poverty Report 2001— The Challenge of Ending Rural Poverty*, Rome: IFAD. Available at: http://www.ifad.org/poverty.

Jang, Sang-Hwan (2004) 'Land Reform and Capitalist Development in Korea', paper presented at the Economic History and Development Workshop, University of Massachusetts, Amherst, May.

Ladejinsky, Wolf (1977) 'Land Reform', in Louis J. Walinsky, ed., *Land Reform as Unfinished Business: The Selected Papers of Wolf Ladejinsky*, New York: Oxford University Press, 354–366.

MacNeish, Richard S. (1992) *The Origins of Agriculture and Settled Life*, Norman: University of Oklahoma Press.

Mann, Charles (2002a) 'The Real Dirt on Rainforest Fertility', *Science* 297: 920–923.

— (2002b) '1491', *Atlantic Monthly*, March, 41–53.

— (2004) *Diversity on the Farm*, New York: Ford Foundation and Amherst, MA: Political Economy Research Institute. Available at http://www.peri.umass.edu/fileadmin/pdf/Mann.pdf.

— (2007) 'New Hope for Shattered Earth', *National Geographic*, forthcoming.

Martins, Monica (2004) 'Aprendendo a Participar', in Monica Dias Martins, ed., *O Banco Mundial ea Terra: Ofensiva e Resistência na América Latina, África e Ásia*, Sao Paulo: Viramundo, 61–74.

Meisner, Maurice (1986) *Mao's China and After: A History of the People's Republic*, New York: Free Press.

Netting, Robert M. (1993) *Smallholders, Householders: Farm Families and the Ecology of Intensive, Sustainable Agriculture*, Stanford: Stanford University Press.

Peña, Devon G. (2003) 'The Watershed Commonwealth of the Upper Rio Grande,' in James K. Boyce and Barry G. Shelley, eds., *Natural Assets: Democratizing Environmental Ownership*, Washington, DC: Island Press, 169-185.

Pengue, Walter (2005) 'Agricultura industrial y agricultura familiar en el Mercosur: El pez grande se come al chico… siempre?' *Le Monde Diplomatique, Edición Cono Sur* 71: 7–9.

Putzel, James (1992) *A Captive Land: The Politics of Agrarian Reform in the Philippines*, London: Catholic Institute for International Relations and New York: Monthly Review Press.

Rodrik, Dani (1995) 'Getting Interventions Right: How South Korea and Taiwan Grew Rich', *Economic Policy* 20: 55–107.

Ross, Thomas (1989) 'Metaphor and Paradox', *Georgia Law Review* 23: 1053–1084.

Rosset, Peter (1999) 'The Multiple Functions and Benefits of Small Farm Agriculture in the Context of Global Trade Negotiations', Oakland, CA: Institute for Food and Development Policy, *Food First Policy Brief* No. 4. Available at http://www.foodfirst.org/media/press/1999/smfarmsp.html.

— (2001a) 'Access to Land: Land Reform and Security of Tenure', Paper prepared for the FAO World Food Summit Five Years Later. Available at http://www.landaction.org/display.php?article=179.

— (2001b) 'Tides Shift on Agarian Reform: New Movements Show the Way', Oakland, CA: Institute for Food and Development Policy, *Food First Backgrounder* 7(1).

— (2006) 'Moving Forward: Agrarian Reform as a Part of Food Sovereignty', in Peter Rosset, Rajeev Patel, and Michael Courville, eds., *Promised Land: Competing Visions of Agrarian Reform*, Oakland: Food First Books.

Schlager, Edella and Elinor Ostrom (1992) 'Property-rights Regimes and Natural Resources: A Conceptual Analysis', *Land Economics*. 68(3): 249–262.

Schlesinger, Stephen and Stephen Kinzer (1982) *Bitter Fruit: The Untold Story of the American Coup in Guatemala*, Garden City, NY: Doubleday.

Sen, Abhijit (1981) 'Market Failure and Control of Labour Power: Towards an Explanation of Structure and Change in Indian Agriculture', *Cambridge Journal of Economics* 5(3): 201–228.

Sen, Amartya (1975a) *Employment, Technology and Development*, Oxford: Oxford University Press.

— (1975b) 'The Concept of Efficiency', in M. Parkin and A. Nobay, eds., *Contemporary Issues in Economics*, Manchester: Manchester University Press, 196–210.

Shin, Gi-Wook (1998) 'Agrarian Conflict and the Origins of Korean Capitalism', *American Journal of Sociology* 103(5): 1309–1351.

Smartt, J. and Simmonds, N.W. (1995) *Evolution of Crop Plants*, 2nd edn., Harlow: Longman Scientific & Technical.

Smil, Vaclav (1999) 'China's Great Famine: 40 Years Later', *British Medical Journal* 319(18–25 December): 1619–1621.

Smith, Adam (1904 [1776]) *An Inquiry into the Nature and Causes of the Wealth of Nations* (Cannan edn.), London: Methuen.

Smith, Bruce D. (1995) *The Emergence of Agriculture*, New York: Scientific American Library.

Sobhan, Rehman (1993) *Agrarian Reform and Social Transformation: Preconditions for Development*, London: Zed Books.

Sterner, Thomas (2003) *Policy Instruments for Environmental and Natural Resource Management*, Washington DC: Resources for the Future.

Tomich, Thomas, Peter Kilby and Bruce F. Johnston (1995) *Transforming Agrarian Economies: Opportunities Seized, Opportunities Missed*, Ithaca: Cornell University Press.

Wilkes, Garrison (1992) *Strategies for Sustaining Crop Germplasm Preservation, Enhancement and Use*, Washington, DC: Consultative Group on International Agricultural Research.

Wright, Angus and Wendy Wolford (2003) *To Inherit the Earth: The Landless Movement and the Struggle for a New Brazil*, Oakland: Food First Books.

Yardley, Jim (2004) 'In Rural China, Unrest Over Land Seizures', *International Herald Tribune*, 9 December, p. 2.

This portrait of the late Chico Mendes hangs in the Chico Mendes Environmental Park in Xapurí, Brazil.
Photo credit: Anthony Hall.

CHAPTER 6
EXTRACTIVE RESERVES: BUILDING NATURAL ASSETS IN THE BRAZILIAN AMAZON

Anthony Hall

Introduction

Brazil occupies four-fifths of the Amazon Basin and is home to the world's largest remaining area of tropical rainforest, 3.5 million square kilometres (km^2). Despite three decades of settlement and intensive development, the forest is still relatively intact compared with similar areas elsewhere. The region is an increasingly important source of natural assets for both regional and national economic growth, and provides livelihood support to a population of several million. In addition, the Amazon supplies key environmental services in terms of the conservation of biological diversity, climate regulation and watershed management, as well as sequestering an estimated 10 per cent of global carbon emissions.

Traditional forest-dwelling populations such as rubber tappers and indigenous groups have been stewards of the natural resource base in Amazonia through their use of non-destructive technologies at low demographic densities. As the frontier has advanced, however, they have come under growing peril from rent-seeking interests that threaten to destroy the forest and people's livelihoods with it. Official policies have tended to reward such predatory forms of occupation through generous subsidies, while ignoring the ecological services provided by local populations. Brazil's rubber tappers were the first social group to pose a major challenge to this 'development' model. Making a pre-emptive strike against cattle ranchers and land speculators, they have appropriated for themselves large areas of forest at risk of becoming 'open access' to all comers seeking profits. They defended their lands, and proposed a strategy to consolidate their hold by setting up 'extractive reserves'; that is, protected areas (known in Brazilian legislation as 'conservation units') where local communities can harvest non-timber forest products, such as latex and nuts.

The 'extractive reserve' model attempts to reconcile objectives previously considered incompatible under mainstream environmental policy in Brazil; namely, the protection and conservation of forests alongside their sustainable economic use for the benefit of local populations. It aims to achieve this through a strategy of joint management involving local communities, representative bodies, government institutions, non-governmental organizations (NGOs) at domestic and international levels, aid donors and the private sector. It is hoped that over time these extractive reserves will build economic strength, managerial competence and social unity. In the long run, however, the viability of the reserves may require that locally generated income from the sale of forest products be supplemented by the establishment of fiscal and other revenue transfer mechanisms to reward these guardians of the forest for the environmental and social benefits they produce.

People and Nature in Amazonia

Ever since the first colonial explorers set foot in Brazilian Amazonia during the 16th century, the region has been perceived as an infinite resource pool that could be tapped at will regardless of the consequences. Perhaps because of its sheer size (5 million km² — see Figure 6.1) and its vast natural wealth, Brazil's Amazon region effectively has been treated as an open-access resource that can be exploited unashamedly to serve a range of economic, social and geopolitical interests, both public and private.

As Slater (2002) notes, images of the Amazon have been created and manipulated by outsiders bent on appropriating its natural assets for their own benefit. The Conquistadors portrayed it as a hostile wilderness inhabited by warrior-like women, promptly named 'Amazons' after the Greek legend. Following the military coup of 1964, Brazil's generals projected images of the region as an uninhabited frontier, 'empty spaces' urgently in need of occupation in the name of national integration and development. Conservationists similarly have tended to ignore the long-standing presence of indigenous populations and their role in managing what is in many respects an 'anthropogenic forest' rather than the 'virgin' rainforest of popular myth. To some extent, the assumption of a demographic vacuum was based on sheer ignorance, but it was also convenient in that it allowed outsiders to ignore the interests and rights of pre-existing occupants in their search for land, forest and mineral assets to exploit.

Figure 6.1: Map of Brazil-Amazonia

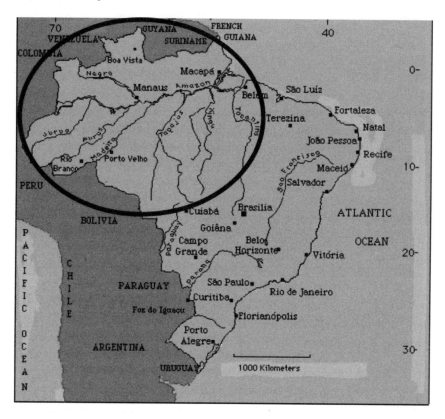

Until the 1960s, Brazil's Amazonia remained relatively isolated, being considered a distant and primitive backwater of little relevance to the nation's quest for economic progress and industrial power. Its rural population comprised some 100,000 Amerindians (the descendants of an original indigenous population estimated at several million at the time of the Conquest) as well as other 'traditional' mixed-race populations, known locally as *caboclos*, formed over the centuries through the mixing of Indians with a small but steady stream of white and Afro-Brazilian immigrants to Amazonia. Their livelihoods were (and, to a large degree, still are) based on a combination of 'extractivism' (the harvest of non-timber forest products), fishing and subsistence farming. From the late 1960s, these groups were complemented by waves of small-farmer settlers from north-eastern and southern Brazil, attracted to Amazonia by government promises of land. According to the 2000 census, Brazilian Amazonia's rural population of almost four million (of 13 million in the region as a whole) includes about 200,000 indigenous people, thanks to an annual growth rate in recent decades of 3.5 per cent, three times the national average (ISA 2000). *Caboclos* probably account for a further million-plus (or some 25 per cent), and newer settlers now account for the remaining majority in the countryside.

'Developing' the Amazon

During the Brazilian 'economic miracle' years of the 1970s, when Amazonia was subjected to intensive settlement, traditional groups were viewed by government authorities and most urbanites with indifference or outright hostility. At best they were perceived as vestiges of a bygone age to be tolerated for their exotic value, and at worst as obstacles to modernization who had to be dragged into the 20th century or, if necessary, eliminated. Generations of social, cultural and racial prejudice had portrayed Amazonia's traditional populations as 'poor', 'inferior', 'backward' and a burden on society. These notions were reinforced when Brazil's military regime, which came to power in the coup of 1964, began the process of 'integrating' Amazonia into the mainstream of economic and political life. Official development policies at that time, heavily influenced by thinking emanating from Brazil's military college, adopted a nationalistic and expansionist strategy with regard to Amazonia to advance a number of economic, social and geopolitical goals (see Hall 1989; Gross 1990; Becker and Egler 1992; Schminck and Wood 1992).

First, investments in large-scale commercial livestock, agriculture, logging, mining and infrastructure enterprises were expected to bring rapid economic progress to the region and generate valuable export revenues. Underpinned by then-dominant modernization and 'growth pole' theories, with their 'trickle-down' assumptions, it was thought that such a strategy would benefit all sectors of the population. So-called 'primitive' technologies such as extractivism were considered an anachronism by policy-makers, and received no official support. Instead resources were directed at the 'modern' sector. Generous government inducements were given to entrepreneurs and especially political allies from southern Brazil, as well as to foreign corporations such as Volkswagen. From 1971 to 1987, a staggering US$5 billion in tax credits were granted for Amazonian cattle ranching alone (Schneider 1992; Mahar 1989). In addition, vast subsidies were used to encourage large-scale mining of iron ore, bauxite and other minerals in schemes such as the Greater Carajás programme (Hall 1989).[1]

A second driving force behind the settlement of Amazonia was social rather than economic. The government used the region as a 'safety-valve' in an attempt to create employment and ease social tensions elsewhere. The polarization of land ownership and growth of land conflicts between peasant farmers and estate owners had created increasingly volatile situations in various parts of the country. In North-east Brazil, the spread of subsidized cattle ranching within an already volatile property structure led to violent confrontations over access to land. Furthermore, periodic droughts drove landless and land-poor farmers to seek livelihoods elsewhere (Hall 1978). In southern Brazil, the rapid extension of large-scale mechanized wheat and soybean production for export made family farming increasingly difficult. Many small farmers were unable to compete with the larger subsidized producers and were driven out of business. Some left farming altogether, but, encouraged by government promises of support, many others were attracted to Amazonia in the early 1970s. The government undertook aggressive publicity campaigns to promote official colonization schemes along the newly opened Trans-Amazon Highway and in the *Polonoroeste* programme in the north-western state of Rondônia, even providing free bus and air transportation. Economic and social infrastructural support in these schemes fell far short of the original promises, however, leading to high rates of farmer turnover, internal migration and deforestation (Hall 1989; Mahar 1989). Following in the wake of officially sponsored settlers, many more poor farmers spontaneously settled in Amazonia.

A third major factor that underpinned official strategies to penetrate and settle Amazonia was geopolitical. The strongly technocratic federal state, under the direction of the generals, was anxious to contain the power of regional oligarchs who, it was thought, could resist change and undermine central government attempts to modernize Amazonia. Furthermore, military occupation of the region was seen as important to help contain the dangers of guerrilla insurgency, as occurred in the Araguaia region of eastern Amazonia in the early 1970s. Hard-line nationalists within the armed forces and Ministry of Foreign Affairs also considered it essential to boost Brazil's border defences to consolidate the country's strategic domination of the Amazon Basin and defend against possible foreign incursions (Becker 1982; Dreifuss 2000).

Deforestation and Conflict

Official Amazon development policy has had major implications for the use and abuse of the region's natural assets. The level of deforestation, arguably the most important indicator of ecological degradation, has increased steadily. According to government statistics, in 1970 total forest loss stood at just 2.4 per cent in Brazilian Amazonia, rising to more than 10 per cent by 1993 and 17 per cent in 2005. Recorded annual deforestation rates have fluctuated from an average of 21,000 km² during the 1980s to a peak of 29,000 km² in 1994–5, and an average of 18,000 km² a year since then (INPE, 2000). Research suggests that forest fires and illegal logging damage a further 15,000 km² of forest every year, bringing the annual total to over 30,000 km² (Nepstad et al. 1999). Furthermore, increased fragmentation, in which the forest is reduced to isolated patches rather than a contiguous expanse, substantially worsens biodiversity loss because of the inability of small areas to support the populations of flora and fauna (Lovejoy 2000). Although the various causal factors overlap, it is generally accepted that cattle ranching has been directly responsible for the majority of overall forest loss (some 60 per cent), small-scale farming for about 30 per cent, and commercial logging and mining for the remaining ten per cent (Mahar 1989; Fearnside 1993; Margulis 2003). Destruction has been concentrated along the so-called 'deforestation arc' on the southern and eastern borders of Amazonia, but its impacts have been felt throughout the region.

From the inception of Brazil's official 'assault on the Amazon' (Bourne 1978), political and military leaders assumed that 'modernizing' initiatives would generate economic progress with a minimum of ecological and social disruption. Little regard was given to the compatibility of land-use models imported from north-east and southern Brazil with the circumstances of Amazonia. Slash-and-burn farming, for example, although viable at low population densities, became unsustainable and a threat to the rainforest ecosystem in significant sections of the Brazilian Amazon following large-scale settlement by farmers from north-eastern and southern Brazil (Fearnside 1990). Similarly, cattle ranching on Amazonia's generally poor soils led to rapid land degradation and soil erosion, reducing the life expectancy of pastures to a few years (Hecht 1985).

Livestock development, fueled by huge government subsidies that encouraged property speculation, exacerbated land conflicts between cattle barons on the one hand and small farmer colonists and resident traditional populations on the other. The result was a dramatic increase in land struggles and displacements of small producers, and a sharp rise in the death toll from such conflicts, with over 1000 fatalities from 1980–6 alone (Branford and

Glock 1985; Hall 1989). Since the mid-1990s, Brazil's 'Movement of the Landless' (*Movimento dos Trabalhadores Rurais Sem Terra* — MST) has become increasingly active in Amazonia as small farmers have struggled to secure permanent access to land (Branford and Rocha 2002). Land occupations have on the whole been relatively peaceful, but violence is never far below the surface. For example, in 1995 military police killed 14 people during an occupation at Corumbiara in the western state of Rondônia. In April 1996, at Eldorado do Carajás in the eastern Amazon state of Pará, military police massacred 19 members of the MST during a demonstration. During 2005, of 37 deaths from rural conflict officially recorded in Brazil, 22 occurred in Amazonia. 16 of these were in the state of Pará alone, including that of Sister Dorothy Stang (CPT, 2005).

The outside observer could be forgiven for thinking that such conflicts reflect a land shortage in the Amazon. With some five million km² (including 3.5 million km² of rainforest) and covering 60 per cent of national territory, land itself is plentiful. What is in shorter supply is land close to roads and highways. The more accessible the land, the higher its price and the greater the competition over tenure. Just 17 per cent of land in the Amazon is officially classified as 'occupied' under private property, and many of these titles are fraudulent (INCRA 1997). Around 10 per cent (54 million hectares) of Brazil's Amazon region lies in 120 federally and state administered protected areas of various kinds. A further 6.5 million hectares were set aside in February 2006 in the heavily deforested state of Pará. In addition, 20 per cent of Brazilian Amazonia is covered by about 370 officially identified indigenous reserves with over 100 million hectares. Regularization of half of the area in question was financed through the indigenous lands component of the Group of Seven Pilot Programme to Conserve the Brazilian Rain Forest (PPG7) (ISA 2000; FUNAI 2006; Lisansky 2005).

Thus, about one-third of Brazil's Amazon region is under some form of officially decreed protection, a far higher proportion than in any other large tropical or temperate landscape (Cleary 2005), while also benefiting from significant financial aid through programmes such as the PPG7, discussed next, and ARPA.[2] Discounting protected areas and private property, the remainder of Amazonia (over half of the total) is categorized as state land under the jurisdiction of the federal government. The one million-plus Amazonians who engage in extractive activities such as rubber tapping, nut gathering and fishing do so largely within protected areas and on state-owned land. There is also a small but growing number of private landowners adopting extractivist and related agroforestry technologies, as discussed next.

The most intensive processes of land conflict and deforestation occur in easily accessible areas close to highways, as in southern Pará and Rondônia. Over 60 per cent of forest loss occurs within a 100-km corridor along major roads in the region. From 1992–8, 105 million hectares (an area four times the size of the United Kingdom) was incorporated within the agricultural frontier, much of it in large properties, producing soybean for export and livestock. Private distribution in Amazonia is heavily skewed, reflecting the polarized land ownership structure in Brazil generally. Just 53 properties of over 100,000 hectares account for 30 per cent of land ownership in the region. Properties in the Amazon of over 1,000 hectares account for five per cent of farms but 76 per cent of the land, while properties of less than 100 hectares make up 62 per cent of farms and six per cent of the land (INCRA 1997).

Small and poorer producers struggling for survival at the margins have in many respects paved the way for larger settlers as they have opened up the frontier. For example, small farmers have commonly entered into agreements in which they are allowed by larger landowners to deforest and cultivate land for a limited period before moving on to allow the owner to sow pasture and raise cattle. Similarly, small settlers often cede logging rights on their land to commercial companies in exchange for the bulldozing of access roads.

Deforestation adversely impacts upon the provision of key environmental services, including the maintenance of biodiversity, climate control, soil conservation and watershed management. In addition, and most critically for the present analysis, deforestation undermines the position of traditional populations such as extractivists and indigenous groups whose livelihoods depend to varying degrees on intact forests. Indigenous and traditional groups have suffered at the hands of both large and small settlers, as newcomers have occupied land, often with little or no concern for customary or legal property rights. Environmental policy in Brazil during the 1970s and 1980s was limited to the protection of designated conservation areas in which human habitation was either prohibited, as in national parks and ecological stations, or carefully controlled, as in national forests (Hall 2000). There was no concern for incorporating local livelihoods into environmental policy instruments.

As the livestock frontier advanced westwards into the Amazon, the rubber tappers of southern Acre state (situated close to the Bolivian border) found themselves increasingly under threat, their interests completely ignored by the State. Their struggle for survival, described in the next section, led to the establishment of extractive reserves as an innovative, sustainable land-use model and a potential precursor to a range of environmental policy instruments that would attempt to involve directly local populations in the process of resource governance.

The History and Struggle of Brazil's Rubber Tappers

During the late 19th century, extraction of latex from Brazil's native rubber tree expanded in response to growing world demand for rubber, especially from the new automobile industry following discovery of the vulcanization process (Hall 1996, 1997a). Businessmen set up rubber estates throughout Amazonia, especially in the states of Amazonas, Rondônia and Acre, which was annexed from Bolivia in 1903. Poor peasant farmers fleeing the periodic droughts of north-east Brazil were brought in to make up the labour force. After the collapse of the rubber boom in 1912 as the result of competition from Malay plantation rubber (a venture initiated by the British with seedlings taken from Brazil), the rubber economy fell into decline. Estates were abandoned by their owners leaving their former labourers to eke out a living as best as they could. By the 1960s, many of the latter had become small producers, operating autonomously on their respective areas of forest throughout which rubber trees were scattered. These rubber tappers held no property titles, but they exercised effective usufruct rights. They were linked through a system of debt-bondage to a new class of intermediaries, itinerant traders who plied their way along the rivers and purchased cured latex and supplied household goods. Isolated and with little access to public services, tappers survived through a combination of latex production and subsistence farming. Poverty has been the norm, with high levels of malnutrition, illiteracy and diseases such as malaria and lieshmaniasis.

During the 1970s, the already precarious lives of rubber tappers came under further pressure from the advancing cattle front, part of the government's drive to 'integrate' the region into the mainstream economy. Business interests from São Paulo used hired gunmen and violent tactics to grab land from local populations. In southern Acre, a rural trade union movement was started in the 1970s by activists such as Wilson Pinheiro and Francisco 'Chico' Mendes to oppose this invasion. They developed a strategy of peaceful resistance, called an *empate* or stand-off, in which men, women and children confronted labourers hired by ranchers and logging companies to clear the forest and attempted to persuade them to leave. It was a highly effective tactic: between 1976 and 1988, 45 *empates* reputedly saved more than one million hectares of forest from destruction (Mendes 1989).

At the same time, Amazonia was coming under international spotlight. From 1983, a network of environmental activists based in the United States started to monitor the impacts of development schemes funded by multilateral banks in the region. This culminated in a campaign against the World Bank's sponsorship of the *Polonoroeste* programme, and led to the temporary suspension of loans in 1985, pending reformulation of the project to include provision for local conservation and development initiatives.

As democratization gathered pace in Brazil, the Rubber Tappers' Council (CNS) was set up in 1985, the year that marked the formal end of military rule. By this time it had become evident that the rubber tappers' survival ultimately would depend on developing a long-term strategy to manage their natural assets in a fashion that would both preserve the forests and strengthen people's livelihoods. With official development policies for Amazonia coming in for intense criticism, the time was ripe to develop an alternative model. The CNS and environmental activists thus began to formulate a proposal for extractive reserves, loosely modeled on the concept of indigenous reserves (Indian reservations in the United States) or protected areas for the exclusive use of indigenous groups.

Chico Mendes had become world renowned, receiving two international environmental awards for his work, including the UN Global 500 prize, and in 1987, he addressed the annual meeting of the Inter-American Development Bank (IDB) in Washington, DC. Soon after this visit to the United States, the World Bank and the IDB both formally endorsed the extractive reserve proposal. That same year, Brazil's agrarian reform ministry created a legal instrument by adapting existing land-reform legislation to set up 'extractive settlement projects' (PAEs) under the jurisdiction of the National Institute for Colonization and Agrarian Reform (INCRA). Ten private rubber estates were expropriated under Brazil's National Land Reform Programme, to form PAEs covering a total of 900,000 hectares with some 3000 families. The authorities dragged their heels on the issue of setting up extractive reserves.

In December 1988, Chico Mendes was murdered at his home in southern Acre by local cattle ranchers. The resulting international outcry drew together diverse groups fighting for conservation and social justice, now increasingly perceived as two sides of the same coin (Keck 1995). The outgoing administration of President Sarney rushed through legislation to allow the creation of extractive reserves. The 'extractive reserve' was legally instituted early in 1990 under the auspices of a new department within the national environmental control agency (IBAMA), known as the National Centre for the Sustainable Development of Traditional Peoples (CNPT).

Four federal extractive reserves were set up, home to 14,000 people, covering over two million hectares. Since then, another eight federal extractive reserves have been decreed in Amazonia, covering a further million hectares, and several states have taken steps to create locally administered units (Brazil 2002). Other notable cases include the *babaçu* nut gatherers of eastern Amazonia, the movement to set up community-based floodplain fisheries management schemes in 'lake reserves' along the Amazon River and several marine extractive reserves (McGrath 2000; Hall 1997a).

The extractive reserve was a major policy innovation, since it officially incorporated local populations for the first time into the process of natural resource management. Until then, extractivists had remained politically 'invisible'. Their recognition represented a major conceptual break from the crude protectionist principles of the past that assumed all human presence in conservation areas to be inherently harmful to the environment. Rubber tappers set up local associations to help design and implement an environmental management plan for each reserve, to serve as the basis for a 60-year lease contract between IBAMA, and the reserve population. The local associations then sub-lease rubber stands to individual households. Land transfers to outsiders are prohibited, as are destructive forms of asset-use such as clear-felling of trees. Areas that had previously comprised common property resources, governed very loosely and informally by local populations, and thus vulnerable to appropriation by outsiders, would now be transformed into clearly defined legal units to be administered by extractive populations jointly with government agencies under a new form of cooperative, private usufruct.

The four federal extractive reserves initially set up in the early 1990s — Chico Mendes and Alto Juruá in Acre, Rio Ouro Preto in Rondônia and Rio Cajarí in Amapá — were earmarked for financial and technical support under the PPG7, which was officially launched at the Houston Summit of 1990. Some US$9 million was granted for 1995–9 to implement the four reserves (which until then existed only on paper), and a second five-year grant of the same size was approved from 2000. With foreign funding, and support from the Ministry of the Environment and other authorities, a number of major steps have been taken to transform these units from 'paper reserves' into viable concerns (CNPT 2000).

Measures so far have included demarcation and legalization of reserve boundaries, as well as baseline socio-economic and biodiversity surveys. In addition, there have been improvements in production, transport, health and education infrastructure. In view of the huge areas covered by the reserves (almost one million hectares in the case of the reserve named after Chico Mendes) and their dispersed population, some 80 community centres have been built to act as meeting points. On these four reserves, seven local associations and five cooperatives have been set up and training given to local leaders in basic production and management skills. Apart from the four supported through the PPG7, other federal and state extractive reserves have received little, if any, financial support either from Brazilian authorities or outside donors.

Current Challenges Facing Extractive Reserves

The extractive reserve is, in theory, an ingenious solution for the problem of protecting inhabited forests. To make it viable in practice, however, a number of hurdles must be overcome. At the time of writing, there has been no detailed, systematic, independent evaluation of the performance of extractive reserves. Yet research suggests that extractive reserves face several major challenges in their quest for sustainability: (1) defending protected areas from illegal invasions as well as internal abuse; (2) generating higher household incomes through diversification of productive activities; (3) harnessing and strengthening social capital on the reserves; (4) creating a more favourable macro-policy environment; and (5) rewarding forest stewardship through non-market as well as market incentives. This section discusses each of these in turn.

Defence and Vigilance

The legal establishment of a protected area such as an extractive reserve is itself a strong disincentive to potential deforesters, often forming an effective buffer between encroaching settlers and loggers and the intact forest. Especially where the protected area in question is populated by traditional resource users anxious to defend their livelihoods, a human presence usually acts as a significant brake on deforestation. This is so even when compared with total conservation units that, although covered by stricter protection regimes, may in practice be quite vulnerable. The immediate challenge faced by the rubber tappers and other extractivists has been to protect their new reserves from abuse, whether by outsiders or insiders. In the past, violent threats from cattle ranchers and loggers undermined security of tenure and induced tappers to engage in short-term, destructive activities such as slash-and-burn farming or to abandon their plots altogether. These were rational responses in view of the fact that it was impossible to guarantee a long-term, secure income flow under such conditions. After their successful resistance to land-grabbing through the *empates* led by Chico Mendes and others, it was expected that the legal recognition of collective land rights together with a system of vigilance would discourage such short-term practices. The reserves would thus avoid a 'tragedy of the commons' scenario in which the land is treated as open-access. Community-based monitoring systems have been set up on the four reserves and around 400 reserve inhabitants have been trained and are paid as environmental wardens to police their areas. The passage of the federal 'Environmental Crimes Law' in 1998 has also made IBAMA sanctions more effective.

The main danger comes from outsiders undertaking illegal timber extraction, but the wardens check for abuse by reserve dwellers as well. In terms of territorial defence and protection, the existence of extractive reserves as an official conservation unit, together with a grassroots monitoring system, seems to have been effective. Satellite images between 1990 and 1998 show that forest loss on the four reserves remains very low, ranging from 0.23 per cent (Alto Juruá) to 3.7 per cent (Rio Ouro Preto). The losses are accounted for largely by subsistence farming and some cattle raising. These figures compare very favourably with deforestation levels for the states in which these reserves are located: nine per cent for Acre and over 20 per cent for Rondônia. Furthermore, rates of deforestation on the extractive reserves have been falling since they were established (CNPT 2000).

Boosting Household Incomes

A second requirement for reserves to be sustainable in the long term is enhanced income-generating capacity. This would provide economic incentives for rubber tappers to participate actively in collective resource governance, and help persuade them to stay on the reserves. Research data show that extraction of latex and Brazil nuts remains the mainstay of people's livelihoods on the four reserves. They constitute complementary parts of an 'agro-extractive' production cycle. Rubber tapping takes place during the dry season (April–December) while subsistence agriculture and nut gathering are undertaken during the wet months (December–March).

There are two opposing schools of thought regarding the long-term feasibility of extractivism. The first sees it as an archaic remnant of traditional society that is essentially exploitative and traps people in poverty. Extractivists are seen as unable to compete with 'modern' plantation and synthetic products, especially in the case of rubber, forcing them into agriculture or off the land altogether (Homma 1994). The second stance questions this assumption of linear, evolutionary decline, arguing instead that potential economic returns from extractivism are considerable, comparing favourably with those from subsistence farming and cattle raising. Market-based strategies, in this view, can reconcile forest conservation and development (Gradwohl and Greenberg 1988; Anderson 1990; FOE 1992). More efficient exploitation of native rubber and Brazil nuts would underpin the new strategy (Allegretti 1994a, 1994b; Anderson 1994). In addition, this school of thought highlights the social roles performed by extractivists as they supply vital ecological services to the wider community (Emperaire 1996).

Since the heady days of the early- and mid-1990s, it has become apparent that rubber and Brazil nuts on their own are most unlikely to generate adequate levels of income to support households or contribute significantly towards project overheads. Competition on world markets from Bolivia has seriously undermined production of Brazil nuts on extractive reserves, still a mainstay, which complements income from rubber. Brazil's neighbour is able to produce nuts more cheaply because of a system of vertical integration of production, economies of scale and labour exploitation — including use of migrant Brazilian workers (Assies 1997). At the same time, Amazon rubber production has declined in the face of competition from Malaysian rubber and synthetic substitutes, while government subsidies have been gradually withdrawn. The price of latex fell from US$1.80 per kg (kilograms) in 1980 to US$0.40 per kg in 1992, and Amazonian rubber as a proportion of national production declined from 85 per cent to 28 per cent over the same period. These trends suggest that the first, pessimistic scenario might be an accurate prediction.

In 1998, however, under pressure from civil society, the federal government re-introduced subsidies for Amazon latex through the 'Chico Mendes Law'. Funds are channeled through rubber processing factories, which pay suppliers of the raw material over 50 per cent more than the market price. The state of Amazonas also has established its own scheme for 1500 families in 86 communities, which pays rubber tappers directly through their associations, although these are not organized into extractive reserves. Such measures have been instrumental in boosting rubber production and value-added tax receipts as well as in persuading rubber tappers to return to the reserves from nearby towns where they had sought informal sector employment (*Gazeta Mercantil* 2001).

Improvements in latex production techniques also have been introduced, targeting niche markets such as surgical goods, aircraft tires and computer mouse pads. New products such as 'organic leather' (sheets of cotton coated in latex) have been created and used to make clothes, accessories and car seat covers. Small factories have been set up on various reserves to process rubber, Brazil nuts and heart-of-palm. There were early but generally ill-fated efforts to improve the efficiency of Brazil nut production on the Chico Mendes reserve, funded by a range of external agencies (including the Ford Foundation, Cultural Survival, WWF and NOVIB) and efforts to market high-profile specialty products such as Ben and Jerry's 'Rainforest Crunch' ice cream. Brazil's federal government has also provided further financial support to agro-extractivist activities through special credit lines. Yet despite this support to traditional extractive production, it is now widely agreed that additional, diversified forms of production are urgently needed.

There are plenty of examples of relatively successful attempts at developing alternative, sustainable activities in Amazonia in the field of agroforestry, albeit on a small scale (Hall 1997a; Smith *et al.* 1998). On the four reserves, over 170 tree nurseries have been set up, along with seed distribution systems and individual and community gardens. Studies are under way to explore the potential for expanding production of agroforestry and other non-timber forest products, including fruit pulp, medicinal and cosmetic plants, handicrafts, aromatic oils, Brazil nut biscuits and heart-of-palm. Commercial contracts have been signed with a range of private and non-governmental organizations (NGOs) to assist in the marketing of these goods, and extractive reserves have been represented at many national and international trade fairs (CNPT 2000).

In a related development in March 2002, the 24,000 hectare Chico Mendes agro-extractivist settlement project, adjacent to the extractive reserve in southern Acre, was given a seal of approval by the Forest Stewardship Council (FSC) for its community forest management scheme. FSC certification, started in 1995, now covers five per cent of the world's working forests (Conroy 2001). In Brazil, a rapidly growing network has emerged to satisfy the thriving niche market for certified timber (FOE 2001). Agroforestry and selective timber extraction are beginning to offer alternative economic options and to discourage internally induced deforestation by the reserve population (Vianna 2002). It is predicted that this could boost the annual incomes of rubber tappers by some US$1500 a year per household (FOE 2002).

There is growing official commitment to integrating extractive production into regional economic development strategies, particularly in states such as Amapá and Acre that have environmentally sensitive political administrations. In April 2002, for example, the government of Acre launched a business agency to stimulate the production and marketing of 'green' products such as heart-of-palm, guaraná (a tree fruit used widely in the Brazilian Amazon to make a stimulating, high-caffeine drink) and Brazil nuts. The agency hopes to attract some US$12 million in funding over four years from central government and multilateral sources.

It is evident, however, that the reserves face many formidable obstacles, including the high transaction costs associated with setting up production in the Amazon, collectively nicknamed 'the Amazon factor' in popular parlance. Problems include distance from urban markets, inadequate quality control, perishability of tree products, market saturation at given points for popular fruits such as *cupuaçú*, power cuts affecting refrigerated warehouses, and the lack of ongoing technical and financial support (Smith *et al.* 1998; Richards 1997; Plotkin and Famolare 1992). Furthermore, poor management capacity has on occasion undermined economic potential. For example, the nut-processing cooperative in Xapuri, Acre, serving the Chico Mendes reserve and funded by large foreign donations, in the past suffered from severe mismanagement (Hecht 1994; Hall 1996, 1997a). Given these problems critics have accused the extractivist movement of creating 'unrealistic expectations' based on 'environmental interventionism', and of shamefacedly using extractive reserves 'as a way of attracting foreign investment' (Homma 1994, 51–3).

Strengthening Social Capital

A third vital issue relating to the sustainability of extractive reserves is how far it is possible to strengthen 'social capital' so as to enable the local population to perform the functions for which it is responsible under this new model. Social capital refers to the networks of relationships and values that bind people together in forms of collective action, both within groups (bonding capital) and with other groups (bridging capital). Strengthening the weak organizational skills of reserve populations is a vital prerequisite for carrying out key reserve management activities, like vigilance and monitoring against external and internal abuses, and for forming alliances and negotiating with other government agencies, non-governmental organizations, the private sector, and international donors. As noted above, local vigilance has been effective in limiting deforestation on the reserves.

Outside observers sometimes assume that extractivists are akin to the 'noble savage' — homogenous, egalitarian and imbued with a spirit of collective action for the common good. During the early struggles against land grabbers, there was indeed a strong collaborative spirit of working together against the common external enemy. Yet in the longer term, many factors conspire against the permanent attainment of such ideals. Populations are widely scattered over huge areas, with the nearest neighbours often being several days away on foot or by river. Families settle in individual households, each with its rubber stands, frequently having to relocate because of seasonal flooding. There are few nuclear communities, and it is not uncommon for individuals to go for years without seeing close friends or relations, such are the obstacles of distance and poor communications. The installation of short-wave radios in some reserve community centres has helped to overcome these barriers.

The social structure of the rubber economy traditionally has been based on vertical ties of patron-clientage and debt-bondage between tappers and estate owners or intermediary merchants, rather than on horizontal bonds of solidarity. Landowners did their utmost to maintain their workers in conditions of poverty, dependence and ignorance, backed by violence in the event of any protest from below (Mendes 1989). Until the *empates* of the 1970s and 1980s — which took place only in southern Acre, around Xapurí — there had been no history of organized struggle by tappers against the brutal conditions under which they lived. This was what inspired Chico Mendes and his colleagues to start a rural union movement in 1975.

Democratization and unionization have opened up new rifts along party political lines, however, creating additional conflicts of interest among local rubber-tapper groups (Cardoso 2002). Traditional patronage may also be replaced by new forms of favouritism. There is evidence to suggest that some rubber-tapper communities, which are better organized politically and loyal to the CNS leadership and Workers' Party, may benefit disproportionately from new economic projects over which the CNS has decision-making control, placing other reserve members at a disadvantage (Hecht 1994; Hall 1997a, 1997b). This could exacerbate the already unequal distribution of household wealth within the reserves, leading to further resentment and disunity. Such developments could undermine the formation of social capital and collective resource governance on extractive reserves, unless new forms of organization can be instituted to overcome this obstacle.

The Macro-policy Environment

Historically, the macro-policy environment of official Amazon settlement and occupation has been dismissive of traditional production technologies such as extractivism. It is now widely recognized in Brazil that Amazon development policies have encouraged widespread destruction of the region's natural asset base, as a result of the deforestation induced by cattle ranching, commercial logging, mining, and unplanned or badly planned farmer settlement. This process is quiet likely to continue, however, as successive governments have outlined ambitious infrastructure development plans for Amazonia; *Avança Brasil* ('Forward Brazil') under Fernando Henrique Cardoso, now re-labelled *Brasil, Um País de Todos* ('Brazil, One Country for All') under the administration of Luiz Inácio Lula da Silva. Designed to stimulate economic development in the industrial, agricultural, mining and timber sectors, and to integrate the Brazilian Amazon into continental markets through *Mercosul*, this is very likely to accelerate substantially current rates of forest loss (IPAM 2000; Laurance *et al.* 2001; Hall 2005).

In this context, the positive externalities generated by conservation units such as extractive reserves are becoming increasingly apparent and are being officially acknowledged for the first time. In its Amazon development policy statement (Brazil 1995), the Brazilian government recognizes the interdependence of economic, social and ecological dimensions of the environment and the need to incorporate local populations into resource management. The importance of protected areas for conserving genetic diversity and other ecological functions is highlighted in official proposals for a national biodiversity policy (Brazil 2000). A new National System of Conservation Units, which entered the statute books in 2001, incorporates the 'extractive reserve' as a form of sustainable development unit.

Thus, there is evidence of a gradual change in official perceptions, both within and outside Brazil, regarding the potential contribution of Amazonia's traditional and extractivist populations to the process of sustainable economic development. Yet specific instruments for rewarding the providers of ecological services remain ad hoc. As discussed below, systematic mechanisms are required to internalize the environmental benefits generated by extractive reserves, so as to reward them for preventing deforestation and for their long-term stewardship of ecosystem services.

Rewarding Forest Stewardship

Internalization mechanisms can be broadly divided into market-based mechanisms of environmental services and the use of public resources to reward non-market provision of environmental services. Market-based mechanisms have already been discussed at length earlier. The Brazilian government and NGOs have been actively involved in assisting reserve associations and cooperatives to explore marketing possibilities for non-timber forest products and for sustainably harvested (FSC-certified) timber. Consumer demand for these products reflects a desire to support ecologically sound production processes, and the resulting 'green' price premia in national and international markets can represent a modest but significant way for producers to internalize some fraction of the 'positive externalities' they generate through forest stewardship. At the same time, an important side-benefit of such initiatives is that they can raise public awareness of the importance of environmental services, such as biodiversity conservation and carbon sequestration, thereby, helping to set the stage for more supportive public policies.

Since many of these commercial activities are embryonic, it is difficult to judge their long-term viability in the Amazon context. Yet it seems unlikely that locally generated, market-based extractive revenues will ever fully compensate rubber tappers for the ecological services performed by the reserves. It seems inevitable, therefore, that the onus will fall on public institutions to provide complementary financial support to reward forest stewardship. This is very likely to require funding from both central government and international sources.

In terms of Brazilian public policy, various existing mechanisms could be more effectively harnessed. For example, fiscal instruments could be sharpened to favour conservation (Haddad and Rezende 2002). The *Fundo Constitucional de Financiamento do Norte* (FNO) a subsidized credit scheme introduced under the 1988 Constitution to finance small-scale agriculture in Amazonia, benefited some 120,000 borrowers from 1989–2000. In 1999, about 24,000 farmers received FNO loans worth over US$200 million (Andrae and Pingel 2002). However, the distribution pattern of FNO funds has been questioned (see below), and there is evidence to suggest that the scheme could be better designed and implemented to reach extractivist and agroforestry groups.

The government is obliged by law to redistribute a proportion of federal income — tax revenues through state and municipal 'participation funds'. These were designed to compensate for biases as the result of poor local levels of economic activity and small tax bases in conventional central government mechanisms for allocating revenues. By including environmental quality indicators among the criteria, states and municipalities that support conservation activities such as extractive reserves could receive a greater share of these revenues. A first step in this direction was taken when the Brazilian Senate approved a proposal to earmark two per cent of the state participation fund to states according to their area in protected and indigenous reserves.

Brazil's rural land tax was originally designed to discourage speculative and non-productive use of land by penalizing owners who kept their land idle. 'Productive use' is defined as conversion to farming or pasture, while standing forest is considered 'unproductive' and taxed accordingly at higher rates. Extractive reserves currently fall into the latter category and hence are penalized for their lack of 'productivity' (Haddad and Rezende 2002). This provision has encouraged proprietors to convert large forested areas to pasture to reduce their tax liability. In the Amazon context, there is an urgent need for the land tax law to be modified to acknowledge the potential economic value of standing forests in terms of both market-based agroforestry as well as non-market environmental benefits. Indeed, the law could be reoriented to reward forest stewards through tax breaks and concessions.

Another available tool is the 'ecological value-added tax' (ICMS-E), which has been applied successfully in the states of Minas Gerais and Paraná in central and southern Brazil (May et al. 2002). The ICMS-E allocates 2.5 per cent of value-added tax revenues to compensate municipalities that have standing forests in protected areas, and it has been shown to be effective in encouraging the expansion of conservation units. Its impact could be enhanced further by increasing the ecological share of tax allocations. This could be a useful tool to strengthen extractive reserves, although states with a weak commercial tax base would still need other options, such as the municipal participation fund discussed earlier. In some municipalities, however, large landowners have been the prime beneficiaries of the tax, whereas in others poor rural households that manage their forests collectively have been prioritized. If extractive reserves are to benefit from this mechanism, there would have to be a clear political commitment from local government to this end, and greater transparency in the allocation of such tax revenues.

A major initiative to provide rural producers with financial incentives to reduce deforestation has been the government's recent Sustainable Development Programme for Rural Family Production in Amazonia (*Proambiente*). Small producers engaged in conservation activities, including reforestation and cultivation of perennial tree crops, receive subsidized loans and compensation payments through an 'environmental service fund'. An explicit aim of the programme is to increase the rate of carbon sequestration in Amazonia, where deforestation currently releases an estimated 200 million tons of carbon every year, three times the amount generated by the burning of fossil fuels in the country. Although this programme is targeted not at extractive populations but at individual smallholders in Amazonia, it sets a precedent that could be applied more widely — especially if Brazil manages to agree on a position with regard to the inclusion of standing forest within the Clean Development Mechanism (CDM) of the Kyoto Protocol.

As these examples reveal, there is increasing interest within Brazil in exploring ways of using fiscal mechanisms to internalize the environmental benefits of conservation and development efforts, such as extractive reserves. To date, however, most financial support for natural asset building and environmental protection in Amazonia has come from foreign sources. Until 1995, when the PPG7 got off the ground, the four federal extractive reserves existed only on paper. A PPG7 grant of US$9 million (renewed in 2002) has underpinned their operationalization, with government counterpart funding of around 10 per cent. Without such external support, it is most unlikely that the reserves would have reached their present stage of development.

It can reasonably be argued that the PPG7 and similar forest conservation projects supported by the World Bank, the Inter-American Development Bank, bilateral agencies and NGOs are vehicles for internalizing environmental benefits. In terms of promoting species preservation, climate control and carbon sequestration, it could be said, pure market mechanisms are not sufficient and it is the duty of the international public sector to seize the initiative and directly reward forest dwellers. Yet the amounts involved are minor (if not insignificant) when compared to the volumes of public and private investment for economic development activities that accentuate deforestation. In the case of the PPG7 at any rate, the hope is that pilot initiatives will stimulate the dissemination of valuable lessons for promoting resource conservation and development, while helping to leverage government policies in a more environmentally-friendly direction.

A further possibility for external support is the international funding under the CDM of the Kyoto Protocol on climate change. Forests act as biological 'sinks' for carbon dioxide emissions, mitigating the process of global warming and thus performing a valuable environmental service for humanity. The 1997 Kyoto Protocol requires industrialized countries who sign it to accept binding targets to reduce greenhouse gas emissions. Countries need not achieve these reductions solely by taking direct measures to reduce domestic emissions. Instead, they may achieve these targets indirectly by paying other countries to undertake net emission-reducing activities, such as the planting of new trees. The CDM would allow for sales of carbon credits generated by human-induced changes in land use and management (Brown *et al.* 2001). In Brazil's case, it has been argued that reduced-impact logging and avoidance of deforestation (more than reforestation) have tremendous potential for yielding carbon benefits (Fearnside 2001a).

It appears very likely that the role of Brazil's extractive reserves (and other conservation units such as National Forests) — in avoiding deforestation, controlling anthropogenic disturbances such as forest fires, and managing forest-use — could qualify as legitimate carbon-reducing activities under the CDM. However, during climate change negotiations the Brazilian Ministry of Foreign Affairs has rejected the suggestion that standing forests (as well as plantations) should be included in the CDM. Avoided deforestation was excluded from the CDM in the first commitment period of the Kyoto Protocol (2008–2012), but the issue could be revived later. Reasons offered for the Brazilian government's stance vary from concerns about the undermining of national sovereignty and fears about the 'internationalization' of the Amazon to holding out for higher carbon-trading prices. Paradoxically, major international environmental NGOs have also opposed the inclusion of Brazilian avoided deforestation in the CDM on the grounds that it would alleviate pressure on the USA to reduce its own carbon emissions (Fearnside 2001b).

Although public resources offer some scope for internalizing the ecological benefits of extractive reserve management, there are implementation and distribution issues that have to be faced. The funds made available to support extractive reserves have generally been considered 'participatory', with close involvement of grassroots organizations in their design and execution. Projects funded under the auspices of the PPG7, including extractive reserves and agroforestry schemes, are portrayed as having been 'demand-driven', considered a positive feature and an indicator of democratic processes (World Bank 2001). 'Demand' may reflect the evolution of strong social capital capable of articulating felt needs. That is, projects benefit those who have sufficient political connections and influence to impact decision-making. It is an open question, however, whether such 'demand' reflects the needs or interests of local resource users themselves, as opposed to outsiders such as NGOs and politicians with their own agendas. As noted above, the allocation of resources for some extractive projects has apparently been subject to political bias (Hecht 1994; Hall 1996). Similarly, local managers have been known to manipulate project funds to further their own electoral ambitions (Hall 1997a). The rich have no monopoly over corruption.

Micro-finance schemes also have been widely used as a form of social welfare in Brazil to subsidize political allies. Although such schemes have disbursed quite large amounts, their impact on poverty alleviation has been questioned. High rates of loan default have been recorded (50–70 per cent) while wealthier borrowers have captured the lion's share of subsidies. Borrowers tend to be regarded as 'beneficiaries', as political patronage often dictates loan policy and there is scant regard to financial or technical soundness (Hall 1997a; Andrae and Pingel 2001; World Bank 2001). Clearly, if public policy instruments are to be more equitable and effective as vehicles for internalizing environmental benefits, their design and execution will have to be streamlined.

There are further potential problems in using official bilateral and multilateral assistance as compensatory mechanisms. Donors still operate largely within the confines of the standard project cycle. Their programmes tend to be limited in duration, with fixed, predetermined objectives and quantitative indicators of progress. This format is not ideal for supporting long-term processes in which variables and objectives may change during implementation. Donor funds are also typically characterized by high overhead costs and slow execution. In the case of the PPG7, for example, overall administrative costs account for 40 per cent of actual spending, and after seven years the Pilot Programme had spent just 29 per cent of committed funds (Indufor Oy and STCP 2000). Generating additional funds is therefore only part of the answer. Spending funds promptly and efficiently is an even greater challenge.

Conclusion: The Future of Extractive Reserves

The extractive reserves in Brazilian Amazonia were born of the rubber tappers' opposition to a rapidly advancing army of predatory loggers, land speculators and cattle ranchers in search of quick profits. This army, like most armies in a state of open conflict, had no concern whatsoever for the environment, let alone for respecting and preserving the natural asset base upon which local populations depended to sustain their livelihoods. The people themselves had to seize the initiative. Had they remained passive in the face of this onslaught, it would have been only a matter of time before the rubber stands were gradually clear-felled and the forest dwellers forced off the land into urban penury. The fact that the local people managed to put a halt to deforestation in certain areas of Amazonia is testimony to their resolve and determination, as well as to the logistical and political support they received from key Brazilian NGOs and unions and from international campaigning in the wake of the 1980s 'decade of destruction' and the murder of Chico Mendes.[3]

Winning this battle was difficult in one sense, yet easy in another. Having a common enemy united extractive populations against the destroyers of the Amazon, their short-term survival providing a common purpose, a clear goal. But the challenge of turning extractive reserves from 'paper protected areas' into units of 'productive conservation' is undoubtedly the biggest battle of all; namely that of consolidating existing protected areas (Hall 1997a; Cleary 2005). Since the mid-1990s, significant achievements have been made on various fronts. In the reserves, deforestation at the hands of outsiders has been reduced to a minimum through effective local policing. Decentralized management gradually is being implemented, with the setting up of local community associations and capacity-building through special training programmes. Economic strengthening and diversification is taking place through improvements in traditional production as well as new ventures in agroforestry and community forests.

However, there are still serious potential problems to be faced. These include limited markets for forest products, their vulnerability to price fluctuations and the generally high transaction costs of establishing such ventures in Amazonia. Moreover, the difficulties of inducing self-governance in hitherto poorly educated, geographically isolated and socially fragmented traditional populations should never be underestimated (Rosendo 2005). Even if environmental and social stability are attained in the medium- to long-term, economic self-reliance is in most cases probably unrealistic, unless it includes transfer payments to forest stewards in return for the environmental benefits generated through their activities.

Some analysts have warned of the dangers of creating a negative dependency of extractive reserves on outside funding, arguing that this removes their incentive to become self-reliant. This danger undoubtedly exists, but there is a strong counter-argument in favour of financially compensating conservationists for the environmental services that they provide. The expansion of 'productive conservation' initiatives in Brazil is bringing about a gradual change in official perceptions in this respect. It is becoming recognized that traditional populations have borne most of the costs of conserving natural assets and providing environmental services, but have reaped relatively few of the benefits. Federal and state governments have moved to establish fiscal and other instruments to help internalize these benefits. These include targeted credit lines, price support for strategic products such as native rubber, technical assistance and provision of social welfare services. New tools such as 'green' taxes and special environmental funds also could be harnessed to support extractive reserves.

The international aid community has provided major assistance through such programmes as the PPG7, and additional support has been forthcoming through the non-governmental sector. Preliminary lessons are emerging from these programmes, although it would be premature to draw definitive conclusions at this stage. One clear lesson has been that it is dangerous to make unfounded assumptions about the availability of stable markets for forest products. Another is the need for greater investment at the early stages of project design and implementation in capacity building in financial and administrative matters, both for NGO staff and community managers, to avoid mismanagement and wasted resources.

The extractivist movement is now well-established in Brazil's national policy framework as underpinning the model of 'sustainable development' conservation units. Following in the wake of the rubber tappers, other extractivist groups have kept up the pressure for federal intervention to protect threatened ecosystems and develop jointly managed reserves. The governance of key natural assets in a growing number of areas in Brazilian Amazonia depends on co-management operations being successfully implemented and sustained. National and international institutions, working with local stakeholders, have a responsibility to assist in this process. Federal extractive reserves have benefited from international aid, but there are a growing number of small reserves at state level that are in desperate need of support. These remain largely 'paper reserves' that urgently require basic physical and social infrastructure, as well as investment in production, marketing and administration. In addition, overseas organizations could argue the case for international transfer payments more strongly through such mechanisms as the CDM of the Kyoto Protocol. International NGOs should target their resources and expertise in these key areas to help make extractive reserves a viable policy instrument for sustainable development. These lessons of the Brazilian experience are relevant elsewhere in the world, wherever natural assets are to be governed by local resource users.

Notes

1. Many of these enterprises, especially in the livestock sector, were subsequently discovered to have been fronts for land speculation and corruption. For example, a mere 16 per cent of funded cattle ranches were found to be commercially viable, leading to the conclusion that most such enterprises had been fronts for obtaining cheap credit that was then diverted into other areas of economic activity, such as urban real estate speculation and personal consumption (Gasques and Yokomizo 1985).

2. The US$400 million Amazon Protected Areas Programme (ARPA), supported by the Global Environmental Facility, World Wildlife Fund for Nature (WWF), the

World Bank and German bilateral aid among others, will provide major support for conservation over a period of at least 10 years to 2013.
3. 'The Decade of Destruction' is the title of the documentary film series on Amazonia by British director Adrian Cowell. See also his book of the same title (Cowell 1990).

References

Allegretti, Mary (1994a) 'Reservas Extrativistas: Parâmetros para uma Política de Desenvolvimento Sustentável na Amazônia', In Ricardo Arnt, ed., *O Destino da Floresta: Reservas extrativistas e o desenvolvimento sustentável na Amazônia*, Rio de Janeiro: Relume Dumará.

— (1994b) 'Policies for the Use of Renewable Resources: The Amazon Region and Extractive Activities', In Miguel Clusener-Godt and Ignacy Sachs,.eds., *Extractivism in the Brazilian Amazon: Perspectives on Regional Development*, Paris: UNESCO.

Anderson, Anthony (1990) *Alternatives to Deforestation: Steps Towards Sustainable Use of the Amazon Rain Forest*, New York and Oxford: Columbia University Press.

— (1994) 'Extrativismo Vegetal e Reservas Extrativistas', In Ricardo Arnt, ed., *O Destino da Floresta: Reservas extrativistas e o desenvolvimento sustentável na Amazônia*, Rio de Janeiro: Relume Dumará.

Andrae, Silvio and Kathrin Pingel (2002) 'Rain Forest Financial System: The Directed Credit Paradigm in the Brazilian Amazon and its Alternative', Free University of Berlin, Institute of Latin American Studies.

Assies, Willem (1997) 'The Extraction of Non-timber Forest Products as a Conservation Strategy in Amazonia', *European Review of Latin American and Caribbean Studies* 62: 33–53.

Becker, Bertha (1982) *Geopolítica da Amazonia*, Rio de Janeiro: Zahar.

Becker, Bertha and Paulo Egler (1992) *Brazil: A New Regional Power in the World Economy*, Cambridge: Cambridge University Press.

Bourne, Richard (1978) *Assault on the Amazon*, London: Gollancz.

Branford, Sue and Oriel Glock (1985) *The Last Frontier: Fighting Over Land in the Amazon*, London: Zed Press.

Branford, Sue and Jan Rocha (2002) *Cutting the Wire: The Story of the Landless Movement in Brazil*, London: Latin America Bureau.

Brazil (1995) *Integrated National Policy for the Legal Amazon-Brazil*. Brasília: Ministry of the Environment.

— (2000) *Política Nacional de Biodiversidade: Roteiro de Consulta Para Elaboração de uma Proposta*, Brasília: Ministry of the Environment.

— (2002) *Reservas Extrativistas na Amazonia*, Brasília: IBAMA. Available at http://www2.ibama.gov.br/resex/amazonia.htm.

Brown, Katrina and Sérgio Rosendo (2000) 'Environmentalists, Rubber Tappers and Empowerment: The Politics and Economics of Extractive Reserves', *Development and Change* 31: 201–227.

Brown, Sandra, Ghillean Prance, Norman Myers, Ian Swingland and Robin Hanbury-Tenison (2001) 'Carbon Sinks for Abating Climate Change: Can They Work?' Unpublished paper.

Cardoso, Catarina (2002) *Extractive Reserves in the Brazilian Amazon*, London: Ashgate.

Cleary, David (2005) 'Extractivists, Indigenes and Protected Areas: Science and Conservation Policy in the Amazon', in Anthony Hall, ed., *Global Impact, Local Action. New Environmental Policy in Latin America*, London: Institute for the Study of the Americas, University of London.

Cowell, Adrian (1990) *The Decade of Destruction: The Crusade to Save the Amazon Rain Forest*,

NewYork: H. Holt.

Conroy, Michael (2001) 'Can Advocacy-led Certification Systems Transform Global Corporate Practices? Evidence and Some Theory', *PERI Working Paper Series 21*, Amherst, Massachusetts: University of Massachusetts, Political Economy Research Institute.

CNPT (National Centre for the Sustainable Development of Traditional Peoples) (1998) *Extractive Reserves: Business Opportunities without Environmental Destruction*, Brasília: CNPT/IBAMA.

— (2000) *Projeto Reservas Extrativistas: Relatório Final da 1ª Fase, 1995–1999*. Brasília: CNPT/IBAMA.

CPT (2005) 'Assassinatos no campo Brasil jan-nov 2005', Comissão Pastoral da Terra. www.cptnac.com.br

Dreifuss, René Armand (2000) 'Strategic Perceptions and Frontier Policies in Brazil', in Anthony Hall, ed., *Amazonia at the Crossroads: the Challenge of Sustainable Development*, London: Institute of Latin American Studies, University of London.

Emperaire, Laure (1996) *La forêt en jeu: L'extractivisme en Amazonie central*, Paris: ORSTOM/UNESCO.

Fearnside, Philip M. (1993) 'Deforestation in Brazilian Amazonia: The Effects of Population and Land Tenure', *Ambio* 22(8): 537–545.

— (2001a) 'The Potential of Brazil's Forest Sector for Mitigating Global Warming Under the Kyoto Protocol', *Mitigation and Adaptation Strategies for Global Change* 00: 1–19.

— (2001b) 'Environmentalists Split over Kyoto and Amazonian Deforestation', *Environmental Conservation* 28(4): 295–99.

FOE (Friends of the Earth) (1992) *The Rainforest Harvest*, London: Friends of the Earth.

— (2001) *Certificação Florestal no Brasil: Alguna Dúvida?* São Paulo: Friends of the Earth.

— (2002) 'Chico Mendes viveu no futuro', São Paulo: Friends of the Earth. Available at http://www.amazonia.org.br/noticias/print.cfm?id=8768.

FUNAI (2006) Data on Indigenous Lands. Available at www.funai.gov.br.

Gasques, José Garcia and Clando Yokomizo, 'Avaliação dos Incentivos Fiscais na Amazônia', Brasília: IPEA. Unpublished paper.

Gazeta Mercantil (2001) 'Subsídio à borracha tem resultados positivos no Acre', 7 November.

Gradwohl, Judith and Russell Greenberg (1988) *Saving the Tropical Forests*, London: Earthscan.

Gross, Anthony (1990) 'Amazonia in the Nineties: Sustainable Development or another Decade of Destruction?' *Third World Quarterly* 12(3-4): 1–24.

Haddad, Paulo and Fernando Rezende (2002) *Instrumentos Econômicos para o Desenvolvimento Sustentável da Amazônia*, Brasília: Ministry of the Environment.

Hall, Anthony (1978) *Drought and Irrigation in North-east Brazil*, Cambridge: Cambridge University Press.

— (1989) *Developing Amazonia: Deforestation and Social Conflict in Brazil's Carajás Programme*, Manchester: Manchester University Press.

— (1996) 'Did Chico Mendes Die in Vain? Brazilian Rubber Tappers in the 1990s', in Helen Collinson, ed., *Green Guerrillas: Environmental Conflicts and Initiatives in Latin America and the Caribbean*, London: Latin America Bureau.

— (1997a) *Sustaining Amazonia: Grassroots Action for Productive Conservation*, Manchester: Manchester University Press.

— (1997b) 'Peopling the Environment: A New Agenda for Research, Policy and Action in Brazilian Amazonia', *European Review of Latin American and Caribbean Studies*. 62: 9–32.

— (2000) 'Environment and Development in Brazilian Amazonia: From Protectionism to Productive Conservation', in Anthony Hall, ed., *Amazonia at the Crossroads: The Challenge of Sustainable Development*, London: Institute of Latin American Studies, University of London.

— (2005) 'Introduction', in Anthony Hall, ed., *Global Impact, Local Action. New Environmental Policy in Latin America*, London: Institute for the Study of the Americas, University of London.

Hecht, Susanna (1985) 'Environment, Development and Politics: Capital Accumulation in the Livestock Sector in Eastern Amazonia', *World Development* 13(6): 663–684.

— (1994) 'Decentralization, Women's Labour and Development in Extractive Reserves', Unpublished paper.

Homma, Alfredo (1994) 'Plant Extractivism in the Amazon: Limitations and Possibilities', in Miguel Clusener-Godt and Ignacy Sachs, eds., *Extractivism in the Brazilian Amazon: Perspectives on Regional Development*, Paris: UNESCO.

INCRA (Instituto Nacional de Colonização e Reforma Agrária) (1997) *Atlas Fundiário do Brasil*, Brasília: Instituto Nacional de Colonização e Reforma Agrária.

Indufor Oy and STCP (2000) *Mid-term Review of the Pilot Programme to Conserve the Brazilian Rainforest*, Brasilia: Indufor Oy and STCP.

INPE (Instituto Nacional de Pesquisas Espaciais) (2000) *Deforestation data 1998–99*, Brasilia: INPE. Available on the worldwide web at http://www.inpe.br.

IPAM (Instituto de Pesquisa Ambientas da Amazônia) (2000) *Avança Brasil: Os Custos Ambientais para Amazonia*, Belém and São Paulo: Instituto de Pesquisa Ambientas da Amazônia (IPAM) and Instituto Socio-Ambiental (ISA).

ISA (Instituto Socioambiental) (2000) *Povos Indígenas no Brasil 1996/2000*, São Paulo: Instituto Socioambiental.

Keck, Margaret E. (1995) 'Social Equity and Environmental Politics in Brazil: Lessons from the Rubber Tappers of Acre', *Comparative Politics* 27(4): 409–424.

Laurance, William, Mark Cochrane, Scott Bergen, Philip M. Fearnside, Patricia Delamônia, Christopher Barber, Sammya D'Angelo and Tito Fernandes (2001) 'The Future of the Brazilian Amazon', *Science* 291: 438–439.

Lisansky, Judith (2005) 'Fostering Change for Brazil's Indigenous People: The Role of the Pilot Programme', in Anthony Hall, ed., *Global Impact, Local Action. New Environmental Policy in Latin America*, London: Institute for the Study of the Americas, University of London.

Lovejoy, Thomas E. (2000) 'Amazonian Forest Degradation and Fragmentation: Implications for Biodiversity Conservation', in Anthony Hall, ed., *Amazonia at the Crossroads: The Challenge of Sustainable Development*, London: Institute of Latin American Studies, University of London.

Mahar, Dennis J. (1989) *Government Policies and Deforestation in Brazil's Amazon Region*, Washington DC: World Bank.

Margulis, Sergio (2003) *Causes of Deforestation of the Brazilian Amazon*, Washington DC: World Bank.

May, Peter, Fernando Veiga Neto, Valdir Denardin and Wilson Loureiro (2002) 'The 'Ecological' Value-added Tax: Municipal Responses in Paraná and Minas Gerais, Brazil', in Stefano Pagiola, Joshua Bishop and Natasha Landell-Mills, eds., *Selling Forest Environmental Services: Market-Based Mechanisms for Conservation*, London: Earthscan.

McGrath, David (2000) 'Avoiding a Tragedy of the Commons: Recent Developments in the Management of Amazonian Fisheries', in Anthony Hall, ed., *Amazonia at the Crossroads: The Challenge of Sustainable Development*, London: Institute of Latin American Studies, University of London.

Mendes, Chico and Anthony Gross (1989) *Fight for the Forest: Chico Mendes in His Own*

Words, London: Latin America Bureau.

Nepstad, Daniel, Adriana Moreira and Ane Alencar (1999) *Flames in the Rain Forest: Origins, Impacts and Alternatives to Amazonian Fire,* Brasilia: Pilot Programme to Conserve the Brazilian Rain Forest.

Plotkin, Mark and Lisa Famolare (1992) *Sustainable Harvest and Marketing of Rain Forest Products,* Washington: Island Press.

Richards, Michael (1997) *Missing a Moving Target? Colonist Technology Development on the Amazon Frontier,* London: Overseas Development Institute.

Rosendo, Sergio (2005) 'Extractive Reserves in Rondônia: The Challenge of Collaborative Management', in Anthony Hall, ed., *Global Impact, Local Action. New Environmental Policy in Latin America,* London: Institute for the Study of the Americas, University of London.

Schmink, Marianne and Charles Wood (1992) *Contested Frontiers in Amazonia,* New York: Columbia University Press.

Schneider, Robert (1992) *Brazil: An Analysis of Environmental Problems in the Amazon,* Washington DC: World Bank.

Slater, Candace (2002) *Entangled Edens: Visions of the Amazon,* Berkeley and London: University of California Press.

Smith, Nigel, Jean Dubois, Dean Current, Ernst Lutz and Charles Clement (1998) *Agroforestry Experiences in the Brazilian Amazon: Constraints and Opportunities,* Brasília: The Pilot Programme to Conserve the Brazilian Rain Forest/World Bank.

Vianna, Virgílio (2002) 'Seringueiros, Certificação e Desmatamento', *Folha de São Paulo,* 15 April, 2002.

World Bank (2001) *Estudo Sobre os Fundos Sociais Ambientais Apoiados Pelo Banco Mundial no Brasil,* Brasília: World Bank.

The Tintaya copper mine in Espinar, Peru.
Photo credit: CooperAcción.

CHAPTER 7
MINING RIGHTS AND COMMUNITY RIGHTS: POVERTY AMIDST WEALTH

Karyn Keenan, José De Echave and Ken Traynor

Introduction

In the 1990s, the global mining industry experienced unprecedented expansion, establishing a presence in countries with no prior history of commercial mining, particularly, in the global South.[1] Latin America became the world's most important destination for mining-related investment capital.[2] The regions of West Africa and South-east Asia also experienced rapid growth in mining activity (Chalmen 1999, 2000). Expansion was driven by rising mineral prices in response to growing demand, and was also promoted by the policies of the international financial institutions, which favoured privatization and permitted foreign investors to enter economic sectors and exploit natural resources that had previously been inaccessible.

The boom has imposed high environmental and social costs on communities in the global south. In some cases, mining threatens the very survival of local subsistence economies. Consequently, conflict between mining companies and communities has grown in parallel with the industry. This poses enormous challenges for communities, who often lack the skills and tools that are needed to address conflict adequately and constructively.

Communities have begun to develop a number of strategies to secure greater control over mining activity. In some cases, communities seek to impede the development of mining projects in their territories, judging them to be incompatible with local development. In other cases, communities have accepted the presence of mining activity and have attempted to establish a new, more equitable relationship with industry that integrates mining with local strategies for sustainable development.[3]

Non-governmental organizations (NGOs) are increasingly involved in these struggles. This chapter draws on the experiences of CooperAcción, a Peruvian NGO that works directly with communities that are affected by commercial mining activities, and the Canadian Environmental Law Association (CELA), a legal aid clinic in the province of Ontario. For several years, these organizations have collaborated to promote the sustainable development of mining-affected communities. We discuss the costs and benefits of mining activity for affected communities, and describe the recent experiences of communities and NGOs that seek to transform mining from an activity that is often at odds with sustainable development to one that contributes to local, regional and national sustainable development strategies.

Mineral Assets and the Poor

The World Bank and other international financial institutions promote commercial mining activities in less-developed countries as a mechanism for economic development and poverty alleviation. Through the International Finance Corporation (IFC), the World Bank has helped to finance, and in some cases has become part-owner of, important mining projects.[4] Yet there is growing evidence that mining projects do little to reduce poverty.

A recent study prepared by Michael Ross (2001) for Oxfam America shows that many mineral-rich developing countries are among the poorest nations in the world. Ross discusses the strong links between mineral dependence and both lower standards of living and increased poverty rates. Twelve of the world's 25 most mineral-dependent states are classified by the World Bank as 'highly-indebted poor countries'. The study also reveals that there is a strong correlation between mineral dependence and income inequality. The author suggests that mineral exports not only fail to alleviate poverty, but appear to *exacerbate* it.

The Peruvian experience conforms to Ross's analysis. The Peruvian government regularly produces a 'poverty map' that displays the relative poverty classifications for the country's different geographical regions (Compensation Fund for Social Development 2000).[5] Mining activity is carried out in 45 of Peru's 194 provinces. When the poverty classifications for these provinces are examined, we find that 12 per cent rank as extremely poor, 40 per cent are very poor and 36 per cent are poor. Only 1 per cent of the Peruvian provinces that support mining activity have an 'acceptable' level of poverty. It is clear that in many areas with long histories of mining activity, this has not resulted in an improvement in the principal indicators of development or in the quality of life.

The failure of mineral development to lessen poverty is due to a number of factors. Mining is capital-intensive, as opposed to labour-intensive. Few local people are hired at mines. Employees are generally skilled labourers who are often expatriates. Mining generates significant social and environmental impacts that are disproportionately borne by the poor and that hinder their development. Mining is highly localized, restricting the flow of wealth. Because of high international tariffs on value-added mineral products, less-developed countries generally export unprocessed concentrates, restricting opportunities for spin-off industries. Finally, mineral-dependent countries are vulnerable to the vagaries of global mineral prices, which are known for their volatility, often leading to boom-and-bust cycles (Ross 2001).

Although mineral activities, as currently undertaken, largely fail to benefit local communities, this result is not inevitable. Mining generates significant wealth. In some countries, such as Canada and Australia, mining companies have begun to negotiate agreements with impacted aboriginal communities so that the latter receive a share of the benefits that are created from mining activity. These benefits can take the form of employment opportunities, a share in mine profits, and investment in local development and infrastructure projects such as roads, schools and clinics. To increase employment opportunities, mining companies can provide training and apprenticeship programmes, scholarships, career support including counseling, flexible work schedules that accommodate traditional activities, facilities that permit the preparation of traditional local food, the use of local languages and subsidized transportation between communities and the work site. Monetary benefits to communities can include royalties, profit shares or fixed cash amounts.[6] They may also include equity interests in the mining project, with possible representation of local parties on the company's board of directors.

The Impacts of Mining

Mining operations routinely cause serious social, health and environmental impacts. In virtually all cases, these are disproportionately borne by local communities who depend on the natural resource base for their livelihoods. Frequently, indigenous people are among those most seriously affected by mining operations. For example, it is estimated that by the year 2020, 60–70 per cent of world copper production will take place in the territories of indigenous people (Moody 2001).

Environmental Impacts

The environmental effects of mining operations can be dramatic and wide-ranging. Toxic contamination is a frequent problem, generated by a variety of means. Mining activity often involves the use of chemicals to extract minerals. These chemicals are not always transported or handled properly. For example, mercury is an extremely toxic substance that is a by-product of the gold extraction process at the Yanacocha mine in Peru.[7] A truck carrying mercury from the mine spilled its load in 2000. At least a thousand *campesino* people in the small village of Choropampa were poisoned by the spill. Unaware of the danger, many residents collected the mercury, believing it to be valuable.[8]

Contamination is also frequently caused by inadequate tailings containment. Tailings are the rock wastes left behind following ore extraction. They often contain heavy metals, acid-forming minerals and residue from toxic chemicals used in the extraction process, including cyanide and sulphuric acid. Tailings disposal has been a historical problem for the mining industry. The Omai gold mine in Guyana is a telling example.[9] When the dam wall on its tailings holding pond failed in 1995, over three billion liters of cyanide and heavy metal-laced effluent was released into the Essequibo River, the country's main waterway and the source of livelihood for most of the country's Amerindian population.[10] In other cases, to avoid the expense of containment, tailings are simply dumped into rivers or the ocean, with disastrous consequences for aquatic life and the human populations that depend on these resources. This is the case at BHP Billiton's OK Tedi mine in Papua New Guinea. Since operations began in 1984, millions of tons of waste rock and tailings have been dumped into the Fly River system, devastating that ecosystem and neighbouring indigenous communities.[11]

The environmental impacts of mining operations may damage local natural assets to such an extent that communities are no longer able to sustain themselves, threatening their survival. For example, on the Philippine island of Marinduque, 12,000 families supported themselves from the biological wealth of Calancan Bay. For more than 25 years, the Marcopper mining company used the bay as a tailings dumping ground, devastating fishing grounds and jeopardizing food security for local communities.[12]

Social Impacts

The arrival of a mining company can have dire social consequences for local communities, including outright displacement. In some cases, communities are forcibly relocated to make way for mine development. In other cases, communities are displaced as they seek refuge from the adverse effects of a mine. For example, the Wassa traditional area of western Ghana experienced a gold boom in the 1990s. During that time, the residents of the communities of Atuabo, Mandekrom and Sofo Mensakrom were forcibly evicted by armed soldiers and police to clear the way for a gold mine owned by the South African company Goldfields Ghana (Appiah 1999).[13]

Mine construction and operation usually involve the arrival of outsiders. Mining activity may introduce or greatly enhance the cash economy, and local communities may be unprepared to navigate this system. These and other conditions routinely generate tension within communities and threaten traditional practices. It is not uncommon for prostitution, alcoholism, domestic violence, family breakdown and health problems to increase in communities that coexist with mining. These impacts are often most acute when the affected communities are indigenous (Innu Task Force on Mining Activities 1996; MiningWatch Canada *et al.* 2000).

In some cases, the impacts of mining activities on local communities generate social unrest that is met with military repression or the use of private security forces. An infamous example is the Grasberg gold and copper mine in Irian Jaya, Indonesia, owned by the American company Freeport. As local opposition to the mine grew, the mining concession became increasingly militarized and reports emerged of appalling human rights abuses against the local indigenous population (Project Underground 1998).

Enhancing the Natural Assets of Mining Communities

At CooperAcción and CELA, we seek to transform mineral development from an activity that largely benefits industry, lending institutions and first-world shareholders, to one that constitutes an integral component of sustainable development at the local, regional and national levels. This requires discarding the current *modus operandi*, that at best compensates locally affected communities for mining-related damages, and replacing it with a scenario where local communities are active participants in the process of deciding whether and how mines are developed, and are beneficiaries of mineral development. Such a scenario requires respect for the rights of communities to natural assets, including the right to land and resources, to be adequately informed and to participate in decision-making processes.

The primary aim of CooperAcción's work is to strengthen local actors so that they can work to ensure that their rights are respected. This involves providing opportunities for knowledge and skill development, improved organization and the development of stronger linkages between and within communities. It also involves the articulation by communities of their development objectives and strategies. To achieve these goals, CooperAcción facilitates a variety of participatory processes. These include workshops, community assessments, strategic planning exercises, environmental monitoring, community surveys and experience in the protection and recuperation of natural resources (De Echave 2001). CELA provides information and analysis on strategies to secure local participation in decision-making and local benefits from mining, particularly those that are used in Canada.

These efforts focus on the protection and enhancement of natural assets. The transition to a scenario where communities are involved in decision-making and benefit from mineral development requires that they appropriate mineral and land rights. When communities refuse mineral development that they judge to be too harmful, they effectively invest in non-mineral natural assets, including clean water and air, pastoral land and wildlife habitat. Such investment can also occur when communities permit mining activity, and have a role in how that activity unfolds. In such cases, mining activities tend to be more environmentally benign and non-mineral assets better preserved. Community participation in decision-making can also result in the internalization of otherwise uncompensated environmental services that community members provide, such as the recuperation of damaged and contaminated pasture lands.

The case studies that follow provide more details regarding the experiences of communities impacted by mining, and their strategies to protect and enhance their natural assets.

La Oroya: Investing in Environmental Recovery

The province of Yauli La Oroya was established as an important mining area when a poly-metallic smelter was built in the city of La Oroya in 1919. Under the indifferent eyes of successive Peruvian governments, this area has experienced profound environmental deterioration ever since. La Oroya is now considered one of the most environmentally threatened areas of Peru: both rural and urban settlements are adversely affected by mining activities, rivers are visibly polluted, farmlands have been rendered unusable and air quality is dramatically impaired by the operation of the smelter.

In response, local residents demanded that the area be cleaned up. The Union for Sustainable Development Consortium (UNES) is a coalition of NGOs that work with affected communities to develop local capacity in environmental monitoring and management. Actions also include investment in local natural assets through environmental rehabilitation. UNES's work has been carried out in phases. In Phase 1, the community conducted an assessment to identify the environmental concerns of the residents, develop an environmental recovery plan and select 'environmental delegates' in each community who serve as local environmental watchdogs. The delegates receive instruction in a number of areas, including environmental law, simple monitoring techniques, basic technical information and the environmental impacts of mining. They monitor environmental quality, organize capacity-building exercises in their communities and mount campaigns. Their environmental assessments unequivocally demonstrate that local air, soil and water resources are seriously polluted. For some contaminants, measured levels exceed the Maximum Permissible Levels established under Peruvian law (UNES 1999).

In Phase 2, implementation of the environmental recovery plan began. In addition, UNES undertook a study that measured blood lead levels in the residents of La Oroya, focusing on children and expectant mothers, two groups who are particularly vulnerable to the adverse impacts of this contaminant. As with the environmental monitoring work, the study aimed to generate scientifically credible data that could be used by the community in its efforts to initiate change. The study found dangerously high blood lead levels, in excess of limits suggested by the US Center for Disease Control and the World Health Organization (UNES 2000).

Phase 3 is ongoing and involves work on the rehabilitation of natural resources, including water sources and grazing lands. These activities have brought together *campesino* communities, government agencies, universities and NGOs. A consensus-building roundtable (*mesa de concertación*) was established with the participation of all interested parties, including the main mining companies. Environmental recovery is an important priority for this body. In the past four years, the communities of Yauli La Oroya have developed a range of strategies aimed at environmental rehabilitation and the sustainable use of natural resources. In some cases, improved environmental management and environmental recovery activities have resulted not only in investment in natural capital, but also resulted in discernable improvements in local living conditions.

Tulsequah Chief Mine: Assessing Sustainability

In 1998, the Canadian province of British Columbia approved the Tulsequah Chief project, which involved the re-opening of an old metals mine situated on the Tulsequah River, near the border between British Columbia and Alaska. This pristine area, which supports exceptional wildlife habitat, is virtually undeveloped. It is also part of the traditional territory of the Taku River Tlingit First Nation.[14]

There are numerous concerns about the mine's potential impacts. The project requires the construction of a 160 kilometres access road through the heart of the Tlingit First Nation's traditional lands. The mine also has high potential for generating acid mine drainage. Both road construction and contamination would significantly impact on the Tlingit's legally-protected right to hunt, fish and gather food, with associated effects on the Tlingit economy and culture.

The Tlingit First Nation was a member of the Project Committee that carried out the environmental review of the project. During the review, Tlingit representatives raised concerns about the mine's impacts on fish and wildlife populations, and on Tlingit rights and interests. Following project approval, the Tlingit initiated a judicial review of the government's decision, arguing that the environmental assessment for the project failed to consider whether the project contributed to sustainability, as required under British Columbia's Environmental Assessment Act.[15] The Supreme Court of British Columbia agreed, revoking the approval and ordering a revised project review that was required to address 'whether the project was a sustainable development in the sense that it would protect Tlingit environmental interests and foster a sound economy and social well-being for the Tlingit.'[16]

A number of NGOs in British Columbia and Alaska collaborated with the Tlingit in their struggle to protect their land and resources. One of these groups is the Environmental Mining Council of British Columbia (EMCBC).[17] In the absence of any legislative or policy guidance regarding how to determine whether a mine contributes to sustainability, EMCBC commissioned a report by economist Tom Green (2001) to examine this issue.

Green began by developing a series of nine criteria that can be used to gauge the contribution that a proposed mine will make to achieving sustainability:

1. the mine contributes to meeting the needs of the present generation;
2. the mine does not impair the ability of future generations to satisfy their needs;
3. the mine has an acceptable environmental legacy, with a low risk of imposing decontamination costs on future generations;
4. the producer covers the full costs of the mine;
5. the mine contributes to economic development;
6. mine benefits are shared equitably;
7. there is local consent for the mine;
8. the mine respects ecological limits; and
9. the producer undertakes restoration work at an abandoned mine so as to offset environmental disturbance.

On the basis of these criteria, proposed mines can be ranked on a continuum that ranges from 'high contribution to sustainability' to 'highly unsustainable'. Applying the criteria to the Tulsequah Chief Mine, Green found that it performs very poorly, in large part because the access road would cross undeveloped wilderness areas that are highly significant to the Tlingit.

Green's framework is noteworthy for several reasons. In British Columbia, the law required sustainability to be considered when approval decisions are made for proposed mine projects. However, if sustainability is poorly defined and there is uncertainty about how it should be assessed, this criterion is rendered meaningless. Such lack of clarity works to the advantage of project proponents, who can then jettison considerations of sustainability and instead focus merely on demonstrating that a given project will not cause unacceptable environmental impacts. The development of clear guidelines for evaluating sustainability minimizes the possibility that this criterion will be overlooked. In other settings, where there is no legal requirement that a mine contributes to sustainability in order to proceed, Green's framework can assist communities and NGOs to advocate the inclusion of this criterion in mine approval decision-making.

Espinar: Building Alliances to Protect and Enhance Community Rights

In 1980, the government of Peru established a public mining company to develop a large copper deposit in the region of Tintaya in the department of

Cusco. The mine was auctioned off in 1994 and eventually became the property of BHP Billiton of Australia. Since its establishment, neighbouring *campesino* communities have lost a great deal of land to the mine through direct expropriation by the government and the sale of land by owners, many of whom were pressured by the company. In 1996, serious conflict broke out between BHP Billiton and surrounding communities. Local residents complained about a number of issues, including the invalidity of the land sales and the environmental impact caused by mine operations. The situation attracted the attention of organizations such as the Peruvian National Coordinator of Communities Affected by Mining (CONACAMI).

CONACAMI is the world's only national organization of communities affected by mining.[18] It emerged from a series of workshops and congresses that CooperAcción and other Peruvian NGOs organized with community representatives from around the country. Regional coordinators have now been established in 13 departments, an area that includes over a thousand communities that are impacted by mining operations.

The goal of CONACAMI is to protect and enhance community rights. It does this through educational and capacity-building exercises with affected populations on the subjects of law, conflict management and advocacy. CONACAMI disseminates information regarding the experiences of Peruvian communities impacted by mining activity and any resulting conflicts. It advocates for policy and law reform. This includes, for example, a campaign for legally-mandated social and economic impact studies for proposed mineral developments. It also intervenes on behalf of affected communities, communicating and negotiating with mining companies. Nationally, CONACAMI seeks the establishment of a tripartite commission with government, the mining industry and affected communities, as a venue for dialogue and conflict resolution.

With the assistance of CooperAcción, CONACAMI and local groups in Espinar undertook a number of activities. First, a participatory community needs assessment was carried out. This was followed by a detailed evaluation of the land sale process and an independent environmental assessment. A survey was undertaken to gauge community perceptions about the mining company's presence in Espinar, and to derive social and quality of life indicators.

The land sale evaluation focused on the sale of communal land in the communities of Tintaya-Marquiri and Alto Huancané. The evaluators concluded that in both communities the process suffered from a number of serious debilities: the company negotiated with individuals who were not authorized to represent community interests; there were significant legal irregularities in the sales; and community members were intimidated by the company during negotiations (CooperAcción 2001). Workshops were convened to disseminate these findings and to improve community understanding of the legislation and regulatory procedures that govern the transfer of communally-held land.

The purpose of the environmental study was to assess whether BHP Billiton's mining and metallurgical activities were having negative impacts on local air, soil and water resources. Water samples failed to meet either Peruvian or World Health Organization standards for human consumption. The water was also found to be of limited use for agricultural and animal husbandry purposes. The study attributed the contamination to mine operations, and concluded that there was a high risk to the local populations (EQUAS S.A. 2000).

Based on these findings, and with the support of groups such as the Canadian Environmental Law Association and Oxfam America, a report was prepared on the practices of BHP Billiton in Espinar. This report was forwarded to the Oxfam Community Aid Abroad (OCAA) Mining Ombudsman in June 2001. OCAA is an Australian non-profit organization that works globally for social justice and poverty eradication. In recent years, OCAA has received an increasing number of requests for assistance from communities in less-developed countries that are affected by the operations of Australian mining companies. In response, OCAA established a Mining Ombudsman in 2000. The Ombudsman helps communities to understand their internationally-recognized human rights and to ensure that the Australian mining industry operates in a manner that respects those rights. OCAA raises particular cases directly with the companies in Australia. The objective is to reach equitable resolutions to mining-related conflicts.

Upon receipt of the report on Espinar, the OCAA Mining Ombudsman visited the *campesino* communities around Tintaya and facilitated a meeting with a number of groups, including BHP Billiton, CONACAMI, Oxfam, CooperAcción and the municipality of Espinar. The Ombudsman also met with BHP Billiton at its headquarters in Australia, and obtained a commitment from the company to enter a process of dialogue aimed at resolving identified conflicts.

The resulting 'Dialogue Group' established four working groups on the issues of land, environment, human rights and sustainable development. The lands committee is working to resolve the ongoing land conflict by identifying properties that can be given to the affected communities, in exchange for areas lost during the expansion of the mine. The environmental committee has agreed to develop a baseline study as the first step in an environmental monitoring and management strategy for the areas that are affected by the mine. The willingness of BHP Billiton to participate in the Dialogue Group indicates that the company recognizes the need to address existing conflicts. Communities have great expectations that the Group will lead to the resolution of outstanding conflicts with the company, and to the recovery of their economic, social and cultural rights. They also view it as an opportunity to initiate a process of environmental recuperation in their regions.

Ekati: Gaining a Voice and Sharing in Benefits

In 1998, BHP (now BHP Billiton) opened Canada's first diamond mine, in the far reaches of the North-west Territories.[19] BHP's proposal to develop the Ekati mine was met with great concern on the part of local First Nations, who had several outstanding and overlapping land claims in the area. Not surprisingly, First Nations were concerned about how their interests would be addressed during project approval and operation. They also had significant environmental concerns. Ekati is in an area that supports important wildlife habitat and has experienced little industrial development. It is a traditional hunting, trapping and fishing area for First Nations. Moreover, the public, including First Nations, considered the government's record on environmental regulation to be poor. There was concern that existing regulatory systems were inadequate to manage a large mining project with the potential to generate significant environmental impacts.

The approval process for the mine was unique, and included a number of innovative instruments aimed at addressing these concerns. Exercising ministerial discretion, the federal Minister of Indian Affairs and Northern Development made project approval contingent on the negotiation of several legally-binding agreements. This intervention demonstrated a recognition on the part of the federal government that aboriginal people and northerners should benefit from mineral development, and that the environmental impacts of such development should be managed responsibly (CIRL 1997).

Parties to the 1997 Ekati Environmental Agreement included the federal government, the territorial government and BHP. Although not signatories, affected aboriginal groups participated extensively in the negotiations. The Environmental Agreement imposes obligations on the company that surpass existing legal provisions. It requires that BHP develop environmental management plans and monitoring programs, and includes compliance reporting requirements.

The Agreement also mandates the establishment of the Independent Environmental Monitoring Agency, a non-profit organization that acts as a public watchdog over the implementation of the Environmental Agreement. The Agency, which is funded entirely by BHP, has seven directors who are appointed by the government, BHP and First Nations, but act independently. Directors are generally chosen for their environmental expertise. The Agency reviews and advises on the company's environmental management and monitoring activities, as well as government regulatory activity. The Agency also facilitates aboriginal and public involvement in the regulatory process.

The Environmental Agreement is a marked improvement over the existing environmental regulatory system. Many credit the Agreement's strength to aboriginal participation in the negotiations, backed by good legal and technical advice (Macleod Institute 2000; O'Reilly 1998). Similarly, there is broad consensus that the Independent Agency has improved environmental monitoring and management (Macleod Institute 2000). However, the decision of the federal government to require the negotiation of an Environmental Agreement and the creation of an Independent Environmental Monitoring Agency was wholly discretionary. There is no legal requirement in Canada that mandates the adoption of such instruments, and hence no guarantee that this precedent will be followed in the future.[20] There is also concern regarding the ongoing development of project-specific environmental agreements and accompanying agencies. Limitations include the lack of oversight regarding the cumulative impacts of these mines. Finally, some believe that agreements between select parties, negotiated behind closed doors, are not an appropriate instrument for achieving public policy goals (Kennett 2001).

BHP was also required to negotiate impact benefit agreements with four aboriginal groups affected by the Ekati mine. Impact benefit agreements (IBAs) are negotiated directly between First Nations and mining proponents and are generally treated as binding contracts between the signatories.[21] Their primary purposes are to minimize the adverse impacts of commercial mining activities on local communities and their environments, and to ensure that First Nations benefit from mineral development. These agreements are gaining prevalence in Canada, where First Nations have historically been marginalized from natural resource management and have received few or none of the associated benefits.

IBAs can deal with a diverse range of issues. Provisions regarding the employment of aboriginal people in a mining project are usually a central focus. Such provisions may include a preferential First Nations hiring policy, training and apprenticeship programmes, and requirements that aboriginal languages be used in the workplace. An IBA may also include provisions that promote the development of aboriginal businesses that supply the mining company with necessary goods and services. In addition, mining companies may provide First Nations with economic benefits such as royalties, profit shares, or fixed cash amounts. Compensation can also be provided to individuals, such as hunters, who suffer losses as a result of mine operations. IBAs may also include environmental provisions that supplement other applicable laws and regulations. In addition, provisions may be included to minimize the negative social and cultural impacts of mining projects.

There are several limitations with IBAs, however. For a variety of reasons, they do not always succeed at providing First Nations with anticipated benefits. For example, IBA economic development goals are often unmet, in part because there is often a poor match between the mine's needs and the skills and interests of First Nations people (Kennett 1999b; Cleghorn 1999). Because the negotiation of IBAs is unregulated in Canada, there is great uncertainty regarding when an IBA will be negotiated and what it will contain.[22] Outcomes depend on a variety of factors, including the political power of a particular First Nation, its land and resource rights, the regulatory framework in place in the particular province or territory, and the relationship between affected communities and the mining company.[23] Any concessions that are obtained by a First Nation are dependent on the relative bargaining power of the parties to the negotiation. This situation leads to inconsistency and unfairness, and calls into question the value of the IBA as a tool for achieving public policy goals such as environmental protection and wealth distribution. Despite these and other criticisms, IBAs remain one of few tools available to affected aboriginal communities to secure a role in mine management and to gain a portion of the benefits accrued through mining.[24]

The experience at Ekati demonstrates that aboriginal communities can secure an important role in the environmental management of a mine and can receive significant benefits from mineral development, through direct negotiation with mining companies. Although not without its shortcomings, this approach may have potential for application in other mining countries. Like the Ekati mine, the Tintaya mine in Espinar, Peru, discussed earlier, is owned and operated by BHP Billiton. CooperAcción, the Canadian Environmental Law Association, and the Environmental Mining Council of British Columbia have undertaken a number of collaborative activities aimed at building links between the communities impacted by these mines, and have disseminated information in Peru about the instruments that are being used in Canada. A representative of Espinar visited the North-west Territories, and a workshop was held in Espinar to provide residents with information about the experiences of indigenous communities at Ekati, including an explanation of the Independent Environmental Monitoring Agency and the use of impact benefit agreements.

Tambogrande: The Right to Say 'No'

The conflict in Tambogrande, in the San Lorenzo valley in Peru, is one of the most important mining-related struggles in the country. This case is unique for a number of reasons. The valley was transformed 40 years ago from a desert landscape to a major agricultural area through the construction of an irrigation dam. Prior to the irrigation project, Tambogrande was sparsely settled. After the dam was built, an area of approximately 50,000 hectares was settled by farmers who began to grow fruit (mainly mangoes and lemons) and smaller quantities of other crops. According to farmers' associations, the valley now sustains approximately 2.6 million fruit trees. The valley's land and water resources support approximately 7000 families. Moreover, the surrounding dry forest, a fragile ecosystem that is easily damaged by farming, has been conserved and is sustainably exploited. This area has no history of metals mining, and the local population is firmly opposed to mineral development.

In May 1999, the government of Peru passed a Supreme Decree awarding the Canadian company Manhattan Minerals an option to acquire a 75 per cent interest in the Tambogrande mineral project, which includes high grade gold as well as copper, zinc and silver. Through this decree, Manhattan obtained all of the permits that it needed to begin exploration of the concession, which includes an area of 10,000 hectares in the District of Tambogrande alone. The people of Tambogrande have remained steadfast in their opposition to the mine's development. They have been supported by numerous organizations, among them the Catholic Church, professionals from the largest university in the region, and local and international NGOs. The issues that most concern residents include the fact that the creation of an open pit in the first phase of the mine will require the forced relocation of more than a third of all urban residents (nearly 8,000 people), and the demolition of part of the town. Also of concern are the company's plans to alter the course of the area's principal river, and the environmental effects that mining would have on the valley and its agricultural operations. Despite pressure from the mining company and its efforts to gain the support of area residents, the people continue to reject the project, reaffirming a vision of development for Tambogrande based on agriculture and preservation of the existing ecosystem.

An NGO technical roundtable (*mesa técnica*) was formed to support the community of Tambogrande and has undertaken work to assess the dangers that a project of this type could pose in a region like the San Lorenzo valley. An analysis by US hydrologist Robert Moran (2001) of the company's Environmental Baseline Study revealed that it does not satisfy the reporting standards required in places such as British Columbia (site of Manhattan's offices) or the United States, and that it significantly underestimates the potential environmental impacts of the mine. For example, Manhattan's study does not seriously address *El Niño*, a climatic phenomenon that occurs every three to five years in the area. *El Niño* causes the water levels in the Piura River, which the company plans to divert, to rise dramatically. Concomitant sedimentation causes the riverbed to rise. These conditions create a high risk that mining activity in the Piura River basin would contaminate surface and ground water, and disperse toxic substances on land surfaces.

The people of Tambogrande, and their most representative organization, the Defence Front, along with a range of supporting organizations, have conducted a major resistance campaign in the last three years. In June 2002, a municipal referendum was held in which 97 per cent of the eligible voting population voted against mineral development. The following day, the value of Manhattan's shares on the Toronto Stock Exchange fell by 28 per cent.

The struggle in Tambogrande, and the community's achievements, has promoted a national discussion about the rights of local people to be consulted about proposed projects on their lands. In addition, there is discussion about the need to create environmental management mechanisms that guarantee the responsible use of natural resources and that include the participation of people who live in potentially-affected areas. This represents a significant step in Peru, where the mining sector is extremely important to the national economy.

The conflict in Tambogrande has also generated discussion about whether it is appropriate to mine in all regions and ecosystems in Peru. For example, is it in the public interest to mine in protected areas, or in the few agricultural valleys that are as productive as Tambogrande? The struggles in Tambogrande and other communities affected by mining have brought important issues to the fore, including informed and timely participation, land-use zoning for the exploitation of non-renewable natural resources and the reform of public environmental management mechanisms. These discussions and debates are an essential step in the transition to a scenario where communities have greater control over the natural assets upon which they depend.

Conclusions

Worldwide a growing number of communities, many indigenous, are impacted by the global mining industry. Mining activity rarely alleviates poverty or benefits local communities in a meaningful way. Instead, the social and environmental costs of mining can devastate local communities. Communities and NGOs in diverse locations are making efforts to change these conditions. Communities are attempting to protect their natural asset base through a variety of means. This involves the generation of independent, accurate information about the effects of mineral activities; collaborative efforts with advocacy groups in other countries and the development of new organizational forms, like the Peruvian National Coordinator of Communities Affected by Mining. Communities also enhance their capacities through training and education in areas such as environmental monitoring techniques, the law, communications and conflict resolution. In some cases, such as the Ekati mine, communities enter into agreements with mining companies.

The results of these processes are encouraging. In La Oroya and Espinar in Peru, community members are now engaged in multi-stakeholder processes that include the participation of mining companies. In Tambogrande, residents may succeed in blocking undesired mining development. In the Canadian Northwest Territories, government, First Nations and mining companies are now working collaboratively to improve environmental performance at mine sites.

Despite these gains, many hurdles remain. In most cases, communities remain marginalized from important decisions about mine development, including whether mining projects will be permitted. Community consent for mineral projects is seldom sought. Nor are communities routinely involved in mine management and oversight. While it is important that communities share in the benefits that are derived from local mine operations, this is not sufficient. Communities must also be recognized as legitimate participants in the decision-making about when mining is desirable and under what conditions. Only then can mineral development contribute to sustainable development.

Notes

1. Between 1990 and 1993, mining operations were carried out in 105 countries. By 1994, the figure had increased to 151 nations.
2. In the early 90s, that region accounted for just 12 per cent of global investment. By the end of the decade, however, its share reached approximately 30 per cent.
3. The term 'sustainable development' was coined by the World Commission on Environment and Development in 1987 and is defined as 'development that meets the needs of the present without compromising the ability of future generations to meet their own needs'. The authors would augment this definition with a requirement of self-determinism, meaning that communities should exercise control over their sustainable development.
4. Faced with widespread criticism of its involvement in mineral, gas and oil extraction, the World Bank initiated a review to assess whether it should continue to support these industries. For a list of the mining projects that the World Bank supports, see http://www.ifc.org/ogc/eirprojects/.
5. The map uses a relative poverty index with five different poverty classifications: (1) Extremely Poor; (2) Very Poor; (3) Poor; (4) Regular; and (5) Acceptable.
6. For example, under the 1995 Raglan Agreement, which concerns a nickel mine in northern Quebec, Canada, aboriginal signatories receive a profit share that during the first 15 years of mine operation could amount to between CDN$50 and US$60 million dollars.
7. Yanacocha is a joint venture that includes US mining giant Newmont, the World Bank's International Finance Corporation and the Peruvian company Buenaventura.
8. Guarango Film and Video — a non-profit Peruvian organization — produced an award-winning documentary about the mercury spill entitled *Choropampa: The Price of Gold*. For information, see the Guarango web site at www.guarango.org. See also the Oxfam-America web site at http://www.oxfamamerica.org/art2215.html.
9. The Omai mine is a joint venture involving the Canadian company Cambior and the US company Golden Star Resources.
10. See back editions of the Mineral Policy Institute's publication *Mining Monitor* at http://www.mpi.org.au/mm/mm.html, or Project Underground's publication *Drillbits and Tailings* at http://www.moles.org/ProjectUnderground/drillbits/index.html.
11. The OK Tedi mine was opened by Broken Hill Proprietary Ltd. (BHP). Since its merger with Billiton, the company is called BHP Billiton. For more information on OK Tedi and the issue of submarine tailings disposal, see the Mineral Policy Institute web site at http://www.mpi.org.au.
12. See Probe International's web site at http://www.probeinternational.org/probeint/Mining/placerdome/pdhome.htm and the Global Mining Campaign web site at http://www.globalminingcampaign.org/theminingnews/case_marinduque.html.
13. See also the Third World Network web site at www.twnafrica.org.
14. In Canada, aboriginal or indigenous people are commonly referred to as First Nations.
15. *Environmental Assessment Act*, R.S.B.C. 1996, c. 119.
16. *Taku River Tlingit First Nation* v. *Tulsequah Chief Mine Project*, (2000), 77 B.C.L.R. (3d)

310, 2000 BCSC 1001 at 58. This decision was upheld by the B.C. Court of Appeal in *Taku River Tlingit First Nation.* v. *Tulsequah Chief Mine Project,* (2002), 98 B.C.L.R. (3d) 16, 2000 BCCA 59.

17. See the EMCBC web site at http://www.emcbc.miningwatch.org/emcbc.

18. See the CONACAMI web site at http://www.conacamiperu.org/index.htm.

19. This section draws on a number of sources including Keeping (1998 and 1999); Independent Environmental Monitoring Agency (2001); Kennett (1999a, 1999b, and 2001); Kerr (2000), O'Reilly *et al.* (1999); Pearse (2001).

20. An environmental agreement was negotiated for Diavik, Canada's second diamond mine, also in the North-west Territories. The agreement establishes an Environmental Monitoring Advisory Board that works differently than the Ekati Independent Environmental Monitoring Agency. One important difference is that the Board includes First Nation representatives and not independent appointees with scientific expertise (Kennett 2001).

21. These are also variously referred to as Human Resources Development Agreements, Socioeconomic Agreements, Participation Agreements and Cooperation Agreements.

22. Under the *Nunavut Land Claims Agreement,* some general guidelines are provided regarding the content and procedure for the negotiation of IBAs. In the view of the Kitikmeot Inuit Association, however, there is still too much latitude under the Land Claims Agreement in the negotiation of IBAs and too much uncertainty about the roles and responsibilities of the parties (Kennett 1999b).

23. For details see Sosa *et al.* (2001).

24. The Good Neighbour Agreement of 2000 is a rare example of an agreement between non-aboriginals and a mining company. This contract, between the Stillwater Mining Company and three non-profit citizen groups, aims to reduce the adverse environmental and socio-economic impacts of mines in Montana and to facilitate local oversight. The Agreement provides citizens with access to information, inspection rights and the right to participate in regulatory processes. The company must pay for the technical, scientific and administrative costs associated with meaningful citizen participation in these areas. There are conservation measures and pollution mitigation plans and programmes. The company is required to fund independent environmental performance audits and to implement audit recommendations. The Agreement does not, however, grant monetary benefits to affected communities. Key factors in bringing about the Agreement include the fact that the deposit was very valuable and that the NGO signatories initiated a lawsuit in relation to the mines. The suit was dropped when the Agreement was signed. For more information see Whitney (2000) and the Northern Plains Resource Council web site at http://www.nprcmt.org.

References

Appiah, William (1999) *A Brief Case Study of Wassa Traditional Areas,* For Third World Network — Africa. Available at the Project Underground web site at www.moles.org.

Canadian Institute of Resources Law (CIRL) (1997) *Independent Review of the BHP Diamond Mine Process.* Submitted to the Mineral Resources Directorate, Department of Indian Affairs and Northern Development. Available at the CIRL web site at http://www.ucalgary.ca/~cirl/html/about.html.

Chalmen, Philippe (1999) 'El Informe Cyclope: Les Marchés Mondiaux', *Editorial Económica.*

— (2000) 'El Informe Cyclope: Les Marchés Mondiaux', *Editorial Económica.*

Cleghorn, Christine (1999) *Aboriginal Peoples and Mining in Canada: Six Case Studies,* Prepared for MiningWatch Canada. Available at the MiningWatch web site at http://www.miningwatch.ca.

Compensation Fund for Social Development (2000) *Poverty Map.*

Consorcio Unión para el Desarrollo Sustentable (UNES) (1999) *Evaluación de la Calidad de Aire, Ríos y Suelos en la Provincia Yauli-La Oroya,* Available at the CooperAcción web site at www.cooperaccion.org.pe.

— (2000) *Evaluación de Niveles de Plomo y Factores de Exposición en Gestantes y Niños Menores de 3 Años de la Ciudad de La Oroya.* Available at CooperAcción web site at www.cooperaccion.org.pe.

CooperAcción (2001) *Los Conflictos de Tierra en La Provincia de Espinar: El Caso de BHP y las Comunidades de Tintaya Marquiri y Alto Huancané.* Available at the CooperAcción web site at www.cooperaccion.org.pe.

De Echave C., José (2001) *Construyendo un Proceso de Toma de Decisiones Comunitarias Frente a Operaciones Mineras,* Lima: CooperAcción. Available at the CooperAcción web site at www.cooperaccion.org.pe.

Ekati Environmental Agreement (1997) *Between Her Majesty the Queen in Right of Canada, the Government of the Northwest Territories and BHP Diamonds Inc.* Available at the Independent Environmental Monitoring Agency web site at http://www.monitoringagency. net/website/key%20documents/Environmental%20Agreement/New_Environmental %20Agreement_menu.htm.

EQUAS S.A. (2000) *Evaluación Ambiental Aire, Agua y Suelos: Area de Influencia de las Operaciónes Mineras de BHP Tintaya S.A.* Available at the CooperAcción web site at www.cooperaccion.org.pe.

Green, Tom L. (2001) *Evaluating Mining and its Effects on Sustainability: the case of the Tulsequah Chief Mine,* Final Report, Prepared for the Environmental Mining Council of British Columbia. Available at the Environmental Mining Council's web site at http://www.emcbc.miningwatch.org/emcbc/index.htm.

Innu Nation Task Force on Mining Activities (1996) *Ntesinan Nteshiniminan Nteniunan: Between a Rock and A Hard Place,* Final Report.

Keeping, Janet (1998) 'Thinking about Benefit Agreements: An Analytical Framework', *Northern Minerals Programme, Working Paper No. 4,* Yellowknife: Canadian Arctic Resource Committee.

— (1999) *Local Benefits from Mineral Development: The Law Applicable in the North-west Territories,* Calgary: Canadian Institute of Resources Law.

Kennett, Steven (1999a) *A Guide to Impact and Benefits Agreements.* Calgary: Canadian Institute of Resources Law.

— (1999b) *Issues and Options for a Policy on Impact and Benefits Agreements for the Northern Territories,* Prepared for the Mineral Directorate, Department of Indian Affairs and Northern Development, Calgary: Canadian Institute for Resources Law.

— (2001) *Project-specific Environmental Agreements in the NWT: Review of Issues and Options,* Prepared for Environment and Conservation, Department of Indian Affairs and Northern Development.

Kerr, A. (2000) *Impact and Benefits Agreements as Instruments for Aboriginal Participation in Non-renewable Resource Development. A Report on Selected Case Studies,* National Roundtable on the Environment and the Economy.

Macleod Institute (2000) *Independent Environmental Monitoring Agency Evaluation Report,* Prepared for the Ekati Independent Environmental Monitoring Agency.

MiningWatch Canada and Canadian Consortium for International Social Development

(2000) *On the Ground Research: A Workshop to Identify the Research Needs of Communities Affected by Large-scale Mining.* Workshop Report. Ottawa, Canada, April 14–16, 2000. Available at the MiningWatch web site at http://www.miningwatch.ca/documents/On_the_Ground.pdf.

Moody, Roger (2001) Presentation to the Communities Confronting Mining Corporations Seminar, London, England, May 2001.

Moran, Robert E. (2001) *An Alternative Look at a Proposed Mine in Tambogrande, Peru.* Prepared for Oxfam America, Mineral Policy Center and the Environmental Mining Council of British Columbia. Available at the Oxfam America web site at http://www.oxfamamerica.org/art615.html.

O'Reilly, Kevin (1998) *The BHP Independent Environmental Monitoring Agency as a Management Tool,* Prepared for the Labrador Inuit Association.

O'Reilly, Kevin and Erin Eacott (1999) 'Aboriginal Peoples and Impact and Benefit Agreements: Report of a National Workshop', *Northern Minerals Programme, Working Paper No. 7,* Yellowknife: Canadian Arctic Resource Committee.

Pearse, Tony (2001) Presentation Notes. *CooperAcción Workshop, Lima, Peru, November 20–21, 2001.* Available at the Canadian Environmental Law Association web site at http://www.cela.ca/international/IMGeng.pdf.

Peruvian National Coordinator of Communities Affected by Mining web site at http://www.conacamiperu.org.

Project Underground (1998) *Risky Business: The Grasberg Gold Mine. An Independent Annual Report on P.T. Freeport Indonesia, 1998.* Available at Project Underground web site at http://www.moles.org/ProjectUnderground/motherlode/freeport/tenrisks.html.

The Raglan Agreement (1995) Between Makivik Corporation, Qarqalik Landholding Corporation of Salluit, North Village Corporation of Salluit, Nunaturlik Landholding Corporation of Kangiqsujuaq, North Village Corporation of Kangiqsujuaq and the Société Minière Raglan du Québec Ltée.

Ross, Michael (2001) *Extractive Sectors and the Poor.* An Oxfam America Report. Available at the Oxfam America web site at http://www.oxfamamerica.org/art545.html.

Sosa, Irene and Karyn Keenan (2001) *Impact and Benefit Agreements Between Aboriginal Communities and Mining Companies: Their Use in Canada.* Available at the Canadian Environmental Law Association web site at http://www.cela.ca/international/ibaeng.pdf.

Whitney, Eric (2000) 'Mining Out the Middleman', *High County News,* 32: 14. July 31. Available at the High Country News web site at http://www.hcn.org.

World Commission on Environment and Sustainable Development (1987) *Our Common Future,* Oxford: Oxford University Press.

In northern Ghana, farmers intercrop peanuts and *shea* trees.
Photo credit: Kojo Sebastian Amanor.

CHAPTER 8
NATURAL ASSETS AND PARTICIPATORY FOREST MANAGEMENT IN WEST AFRICA

Kojo Sebastian Amanor

Introduction

Participatory forest management in West Africa became institutionalized during the 1980s as part of the movement towards decentralization under structural adjustment programmes. Most nation states in the region have implemented forest-sector administrative reforms that give greater roles to communities in forest management, and that recognize the importance of building partnerships between communities and forest departments (Brown 1999).

The idea that community participation is central to effective natural resource management has been endorsed in a number of international environmental conventions. It was given a prominent place in both the 1992 Rio Earth Summit and the 1994 UN Convention to Combat Desertification. It was embraced again in 1997, in the United Nations Intergovernmental Panel on Forests' *Proposals for Action*, which called for the establishment of participatory mechanisms to involve all interested parties, including local communities and indigenous people, in policy development as well as implementation.

Although most West African forestry services now have moved beyond previous exclusionary approaches, participatory forest management still generally is situated within a technocentric, top-down framework. The goal is to get rural communities to participate in the programmes designed by global and national agencies, rather than to enable rural people to make their own inputs into natural resource policy. The main concerns, rooted in neo-liberal economic philosophy, are the need to make forestry management more efficient and to lower transaction costs by involving communities. Equity concerns have focused largely on promoting a trickle of minor benefits to communities. These strategies do not get to grips with redressing the past state appropriation of forest resources that benefited industry at the expense of rural dwellers. They certainly do not restore rights in forest resources to rural producers.

Community forestry is typically conceptualized as a response to ecological 'crisis'. The crisis is blamed on inappropriate local resource management strategies, overpopulation, poverty and unsuitable technologies used by peasant farmers. The objective is to introduce efficient regulation by imposing community natural resource management structures in areas where previously there was open access. While such regulation seeks to control the use of natural resources *by the local population*, it does not examine the distortion of forestry policies by industrial interests, nor does it address the sources of alienation of rural people from these policies.

Crisis narratives have long been used as rhetorical devices to justify external interventions (Leach and Mearns 1996). Paradoxically, just as colonialism sought to justify state appropriation by referring to the peasantry's supposed incapacity to manage forestry resources, community forestry proponents now justify the need for participation and community regulation by resorting to the same crisis narratives. In both cases, there is little attempt to understand the full range of human imprints on nature, including positive interactions between rural people and forests, or to base new initiatives upon this history.

This chapter explores West African contemporary forest policy's implications of for relationships among people, their production and the environment. It describes how many West African communities historically have interacted with the environment in ways that have enhanced the natural resource base, and argues that a forestry strategy rooted in a conception of building natural assets — rather than in protecting an ostensibly pristine and threatened nature from human intervention — can best meet the objectives of reducing poverty and protecting the environment. By addressing the alienation of the rural poor from mainstream environmental policies, this alternative approach would be a step in the direction of harmonizing popular aspirations with sustainable forestry management.

Forests and People in West Africa

The West African region comprises several distinct ecological zones that become drier towards the north. The southern coastal zone, with annual rainfall over 1,250 millimetres, is made up of tropical high forest. This zone is particularly rich in timber species, and it is integrated into international high-value timber markets. Beyond this zone, in areas with rainfall under 1,250 millimetres, high forest gives way to a savanna environment with both woodland and grassland. There can be high tree densities in the savanna, but these trees tend to be small and hardy. Timber species are relatively unimportant in this zone, and the trees are used mainly for fuelwood, poles, fruits and other local purposes. Although the savanna zone lies mostly north of the tropical high forest, it reaches to the coast in the Dahomey Gap, between Benin, Togo and eastern Ghana, dividing the eastern and western high forests. The Dahomey Gap was thought by early European botanists and foresters to be a result of forest degradation caused by human activity, but in fact, it was formed more than 2,500 years ago (Maley, 2001). North of the savanna zone is the arid zone with rainfall less than 1,000 millimetres. Cropping is less important in this zone, and pastoralism more dominant.

Figure 8.1: Ecological Zones in West Africa

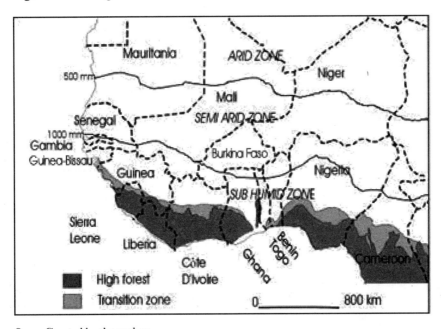

Source: Created by the author.

Charcoal and fuelwood from the savanna woodlands are the major fuel sources in urban areas. Savanna tree species are partially fire-resistant, resulting in slow burning properties that are ideal for fuelwood. Many savanna trees also coppice well — that is, they produce plentiful shoots when cut back — enabling forests to sustain high off-takes of fuelwood (Ribot 2001a). In some areas, as in the vicinity of Kano, Nigeria, fuelwood production mainly occurs on farms, and merchants purchase the wood from farmers. In other areas, as in Ghana and Senegal, fuelwood is harvested mainly on fallow lands by migrant woodcutters and urban merchants (Ribot 2000, 1998). In Ghana, there has been a transformation in charcoal production in recent years. In the past, it was produced by migrant charcoal burners on fallow lands over which they gained extractive rights from chiefs. At present, however, charcoal is mainly produced from the tree resources of farms, and charcoal burners transact with farmers for suitable trees at the beginning of the farm clearing season (Amanor *et al.* 2002).

Sources of non-traditional forest products (NTFPs) are planted, conserved and harvested in West Africa for a wide variety of purposes, including use as foods, medicines, construction materials and habitat for game animals.[1] Forests also provide important ecological services, for example, trees are preserved on river banks and in headwaters to sequester rainfall. In the high-forest zone, the dominant forms of agriculture involve tree crops, such as cocoa and coffee, and food crops grown in rotational bush fallow or variants of slash-and-burn agriculture. In the savanna, the dominant forms involve bush plots that are fallowed as well as permanent cultivation of farm plots with the use of manure to maintain soil fertility. Pastoralism is common in the savanna, and many cattle herders have worked out transhumant strategies in which they move seasonally between dry-season pastures in the south and wet-season pastures in the arid north. In the arid zone, pastoralism dominates since the short growing season makes agriculture a marginal activity. In the semi-arid zone, mixed farming is common, and pastoral populations coexist with sedentary farmers, providing them with livestock, meat, milk, manure and bullock ploughing services in return for staple crops and land for grazing and minor farming. In the sub-humid zone, cattle herding is a relatively recent activity, dating from the 19th century, dependent on the prior clearing of vegetation by farming populations to remove trypanosomiasis (sleeping sickness) vectors, and on the selection and breeding of trypanosomiasis-resistant cattle.

The web of activities of farmers and pastoralists can promote regeneration of environments and biodiversity. Since the early colonial period, however, the activities of both groups have been maligned by government authorities who have portrayed them as destroyers of the environment. From the late 19th century, European accounts began to warn of an impending environmental calamity as a result of the inappropriate cultivation techniques of the African farmers. This crisis narrative helped to justify colonial occupation, the appropriation of uncultivated land as State or Crown land, and efforts to regulate and control activities of African producers. In the first work on West African forestry in the English language, for example, Maloney (1887, 236) painted a picture of mindless destruction of forest resources by shifting cultivators, and called for the protection of nature from 'the wanton mischief of those who take more delight in a good blaze — which they usually originate at night — and in their own ignorance, than in interest in the country.' (Maloney 1885, 233) As evidence, Maloney attributed the savanna salients of the Accra plains and the Togo-Dahomey gap to the activities of shifting cultivators. Yet, historians now believe that the formation of the Togo-Dahomey gap took place some 3,000–4,000 years ago, and that it was related to climatic phenomena rather than human interventions (Maley 1993, 1996).

In the crisis narrative, pastoralists are portrayed as destroying the environment in three ways. First, their cattle are said to strain the carrying capacity of the land. Second, their practice of burning grasses early in the dry season to create a flush of new grass is thought to destroy woodland and thickets. Third, since the cattle herders are mobile, they are believed to have no long-term interest in preserving the environment; instead they exploit the grazing lands as an open-access resource, leading to the 'tragedy of the commons'. National and international environmental policies often are hostile to cattle herders, and attempts to promote individual or community ownership and demarcation of land frequently undermine pastoral livelihood strategies. Moreover, since current 'participatory' frameworks tend to delegate land management to village authorities, they provide little scope for management over wider areas, which is critical for pastoralism (Lane 1998).

Recent studies of rangeland ecology have questioned the assumption that pastoralists degrade the environment. They question the equilibrium approach that pre-supposes the existence of a stage of climax vegetation, instead stressing that arid and semi-arid regions of Africa are characterized by large fluctuations in species composition, biomass and cover, largely due to erratic rainfall. The vegetation has adapted to short-term disturbances, and in the long-term these rangelands are highly resilient. In these environments, 'degradation' can be said to occur only when the vegetation loss crosses a critical threshold that prevents its return to a productive state.

Pastoralists adapt to these conditions by adjusting their livestock numbers to the availability of forage. In wet periods, herds increase; in dry periods, as biomass declines, there is an off-take of large numbers of animals (through sale or slaughter) or movement to other less affected pastures. This practice is often more efficient than conservative stocking strategies based on static concepts of carrying capacity (Behnke and Scoones 1993). In this view, policies should not be judged by their success in preventing periodic crashes in livestock numbers — an inevitable product of an erratic environment — but by the appropriateness of responses to these crashes. This requires a flexible approach to environmental management — one that facilitates mobility of cattle herders, rather than rigidly demarcating pastoral lands and village lands.

The dominant crisis narrative deduces rates of forest loss during the 20th century from presumed homogeneous climax forest belts, seeing forest patches as evidence of deforestation in the surrounding area and assuming that unforested areas were once forest. Yet Fairhead and Leach (1998) have shown that many areas that were presumed to have been pristine forests were in fact settled farmlands in the 19th century and earlier. Forest areas supported settlements and centralized states, and consisted of a mosaic of patches of forest and fallow in different states of regeneration. Indeed, several recent studies have found that forest areas in the transition zones of West Africa have *expanded* rather than declined. These studies indicate that interactions between the techniques of shifting cultivators and the movement of cattle can create favourable conditions for forest regeneration: cattle grazing helps to eliminate grasses that promote the spread of fires into the forest; cattle manure enriches the soil, favouring regeneration of forest species and the early dry-season burning strategies of cattle herders prevent more intense wildfires later in the dry season. To the chagrin of the herders, these strategies often lead to the expansion of woodland and shrubs. Thus Fulani herders in the Adamawa plateau of Cameroon complain that 'the bush has become dense and enclosed' (Basset and Boutrais 2000, 248–249).[2]

In a study in the transition zone of Guinea, Fairhead and Leach (1996) document how people in the Kissidougou area have created 'forest islands' around their villages, as refuse dumps around the perimeters of settlements to provide favourable conditions for the generation of forests.[3] Based on an analysis of aerial photographs and remote sensing data in Côte d'Ivoire's Korhogo transition zone, Bassett and Zueli (2000) estimate that woodlands expanded from four per cent of the land cover in 1956 to 31 per cent in 1989 — a change that farmers attribute to an influx of Fulani herders that brought manure and new fire management techniques. In many regions, forest transgressions into the savanna were common in the 20th century, reflecting long-term recovery from earlier climatic disturbances and favourable human interactions with the environment along the forest-savanna boundary zone (Maley 2001).

The present mosaic characteristic of many West African forests, where evergreen and deciduous formations are juxtaposed with grasslands, is the product of long-term disturbance by fire and human activities (Hawthorne 1996; Van Rompaey 2001). These heterogeneous forests are the richest in biodiversity, and have the highest concentration of timber species. In Ghana, for example, many of the most economically important species, including iroko and several species of mahogany are deliberately preserved by farmers. It is very likely that these trees became common as the result of anthropogenic influences in forest formation. Iroko, one of the major timber species in West Africa, in the past was frequently protected and sometimes regarded as sacred. In a survey in the Onitsha and Owerri provinces of Nigeria, Cousins (1946) found that the preponderance of iroko was directly related to human activity in farmland, fallow lands and remnant village forests, where people eliminated unwanted species and preserved those they liked.[4]

Although farming is still portrayed as a threat to forests in mainstream environmental discourses, this is not reflected in statistics on sources of timber. In the Ghanaian high-forest, 20 per cent of the land has been appropriated by the state for forest reserves. Yet during the 1990s more than 80 per cent of timber originated from off-reserve areas, largely farmland. In other words, in addition to agricultural crops, farming areas continued to produce at least as much timber as the forest reserves. Although farming areas do not contain closed canopy forest, farmers have managed to preserve forest resources of considerable value. Farm production of timber in Ghana is increasingly threatened, however, by the extension of concession systems, in which trees are appropriated by a small number of timber concessionaires, without recognizing the role of farmers in creating these resources. The law does not recognize the rights of farmers to timber trees on their farms. Instead these rights are vested in local chiefs, on behalf of whom the state manages and transacts with concessionaires. Recent legislation criminalizes the exploitation of timber by farmers or by small-scale chainsaw operators who, unlike the logging companies, pay farmers for the timber they exploit on their land. Increasingly alienated from a timber industry that expropriates resources without proper compensation, many farmers now are choosing to destroy timber saplings that regenerate on their farms (Amanor 1996).

In savanna areas, too, farmers have expended considerable energy in refashioning nature and creating valuable forest resources. Again, this investment is not recognized in mainstream forestry policy, which portrays the savanna areas as threatened by desertification. In northern Nigeria, in the densely settled farming area around Kano, Cline-Cole (2000) documents that forest products, especially fuelwood, account for more than one-quarter of the non-agrarian supplementary livelihoods of households. Fuelwood is produced largely for the urban Kano market, on farms rather than forest reserves. Farmers not only preserve trees but also plant them by hand. Yet official forestry policy did not recognize, let alone reward, the skills of farmers in incorporating trees into their farms and meeting demands for forest products. Instead the government introduced regulations to prevent farmers felling trees on their land, in an attempt to halt deforestation, and other policies were instituted to create forest reserves and promote tree plantations (Cline-Cole 1996).

In contemporary northern Ghana, farmers similarly are preserving large numbers of trees on their land, particularly shea because of growing export demand for shea butter, a high-value seed-oil with culinary, cosmetic and medicinal uses. In several areas, the high densities of shea trees resemble plantations, a major achievement since shea is a slow-growing tree that takes up to 15 years before it bears fruit. In the park-like environments they have created, Ghanaian farmers also preserve large numbers of locust bean (a condiment with high protein content), *Acacia albida*, baobab, silk cotton and various species of *Diospyros* trees.

Paradoxically, in colonial times tree cover on farms was interpreted as evidence of environmental degradation. Instead of recognizing that the rich vegetation was the product of farmers' strategies to incorporate particular trees into their farming systems and protect them from fire, colonial foresters assumed that these were areas recently opened for cultivation, with trees that farmers had not yet destroyed. Similarly, uninhabited areas were thought to have been denuded of their cover by slash-and-burn agriculture and then abandoned by farmers as their soils became exhausted, whereas in reality these areas were vulnerable to wildfires precisely because they were not being managed by people, and so their vegetation was constantly checked by fire. The paucity of forest cover was not the product of destructive farming practices, but rather a result of the absence of constructive farming practices. Colonial foresters simply could not conceive that farmers engaged in activities that promoted the regeneration of trees. So rather than build on the most promising aspects of West African agroforestry, the colonial forest departments appropriated land for forest reserves and fuelwood plantations, increasing land pressures (Amanor 2001b).

Today's situation is not much different. Crisis narratives of desertification abound. Ministries of Agriculture, forestry services and non-governmental organizations (NGOs) promote fast-growing exotic agroforestry species, such as *Cassia siamea* and *Leucaena leucocephala* that regenerate so profusely that they often become large nuisance weeds, and do not offer products as useful as those of the species traditionally preserved by farmers. In many areas, these projects seek to involve women, but finding land on which to plant these trees has become a major headache for women's groups since land around settlements is scarce and there are already optimal trees integrated into the farm environment (Amanor 2001b, 2001c). Indeed, environmental projects are in danger of creating an overload of trees in the farm environment. Yet NGOs can readily get funding for promotion of these exotic species, whereas the slower growth of many indigenous species does not fit as well into donor preconceptions of project duration and evaluation. Thus, the indigenous species preserved by farmers tend to be undervalued, and underappreciated, while fast-growing exotics are promoted as a panacea to perceived ostensible environmental problems.

Forest Management in the Colonial Era

Formal systems for natural resource management in West Africa antedate colonial rule. For instance, in the early 19th century the Islamic Fulbe state of the Dina of Macina codified rules for resource use in the Inner Delta of the Niger River in Mali. These rules recognized the rights of Fulbe cattle herders to exploit the floodplains of the delta during the dry season, and the rights of fisherfolk and farmers during the wet season when the floodplains were covered with water, thus establishing a regional land-use system attuned to the needs of multiple production systems (Ba and Daget 1984; Moorehead 1998).

Present-day forestry management, however, has been influenced heavily by colonial policies that were concerned primarily with securing control over resources for the new authorities. The French claimed forests as state property. In 1900, Francophone Africa's first forest code declared state control over all unutilized land ('les terres vacantes et sans maître'), including forests. Rural communities could claim usufructuary rights — rights to use land — but formal ownership was under the trusteeship of the colonial authority. The code of 1935, gave jurisdiction of forests to the forestry service. Rural communities were granted only rights to gather noncommercial forest products for domestic use; commercial rights were allocated through licenses and quotas to urban *citoyen français* (Africans assimilated as French citizens) and French expatriates (Ribot 2001a).

In the British colonies, two different arrangements prevailed. In some territories, including southern Nigeria, the Northern Territories of the Gold Coast (Ghana), Sierra Leone and British Cameroon, forests were vested in the British Crown. In other areas, such as the Gold Coast colony and northern Nigeria, forests were vested in local chiefs. The latter arrangement arose as a result of resistance to colonial rule, and the resulting British alliances with chiefs against more radical resistance forces, the phenomenon known as 'indirect rule'. In the Gold Coast, for instance, attempts to place land under direct control of the colonial authority were met with resistance from local merchants, lawyers and the intelligentsia, who organized the Aborigines' Rights Protection Society (Amanor 1999). The colonial government responded by placing land under the authority of chiefs who were responsible for rural administration. The creation of forest reserves became their responsibility, but legal provisions existed for the Forestry Department to demarcate forest reserves if the chiefs failed to act. By-laws introduced by chiefs had to be ratified by the colonial authority, and the state could intervene if chiefs deviated from official policy.

Under both British and French colonial rule, rural administration in Native Authority districts or *cercles* was based on the authority of the chief. Where chiefs did not exist, they were invented. Where they were not sympathetic to colonial policy, they were changed. The chiefs became responsible for implementing colonial policy. In response to the difficulty that colonial authorities experienced in gaining access to wage labour, the power of chiefs was bolstered to enable them to recruit forced labour for public works and colonial enclaves, and to collect taxes that forced their subjects to seek paid employment or produce export crops. In colonial enclaves, chiefs were responsible for reallocating land to expatriate projects, regulating land use for export crop production, and in some areas coercing peasants to produce export crops. By the 1940s, labour markets, often based on long-distance migrations, had become well-established and forced labour was abolished in the British and French colonies.

The post-war period saw the emergence of an urban African bureaucracy that began to assume administrative functions, but customary rule and chiefly authority continued to define rural administration. Mamdani (1996) argues that colonialism produced a bifurcated state, one that differentiated between a civic sphere, reserved for Europeans and elite citizens, and a customary sphere of Native Authority or the *indigenat*, reserved for Africans and subdivided into distinct 'ethnicities'. While the civic sphere was the domain for the introduction of democratic political processes, the customary sphere was one of despotic rule by chiefs appointed or approved by colonial authorities.

With the transition to independence, the civic sphere became decolonized and Africanized, but in the countryside the 'customary' autocratic institutions remained intact. This colonial framework, taken into the post-colonial political setting, has tempered any moves toward more democratic rural administration based on elected councils. Instead the emphasis has been on participation without representation (Ribot 2001a, 2001b). Communities are expected to participate in the *implementation* of development projects without any voice in their *design*. The state predetermines what constitutes the community and who represents it. Rather than being discarded at the onset of independence as an outmoded institution, chieftaincy not only has continued but has been strengthened in recent years in the name of participatory community development, particularly, in environmental and natural resource management. Although participatory forest management often is portrayed as overturning state-led approaches to forestry, its foundations in West Africa are in fact rooted in colonial policy.

Participatory Forest Management

The origins of participatory forest management in West Africa in the late 1970s and early 1980s can be traced to three concerns:

- *The Sahelian droughts* of the 1970s, led to the resuscitation of colonial desertification narratives and the associated solutions of large-scale tree planting projects in the savanna areas of West Africa.
- *The energy crisis* of the 1970s, sparked fears of a fuelwood crisis, and the promotion of plantations and energy-saving stoves as technical solutions.
- *The failings of forestry policies* throughout the world, and the alienation of rural people as a consequence of exclusionary policies, led to the development of 'social forestry' as a means of winning local support (Westoby 1987; Peloso 1992).

In early social forestry projects, state agencies, in collaboration with NGOs supported tree planting, provided seedlings to farmers and undertook extension activities to encourage more appropriate agriculture in forest fringe communities. An example is the *bosquets villageois* (village woodlands) in

Mali, a response to the drought of the 1970s, in which management plans for reforestation were created by the Water and Forestry Service, and the villages were responsible for planting species chosen by technical services. Since the rural people could not make creative inputs into these projects, and gained few if any benefits from them, they had no incentives to manage these community woodlands, and the projects ultimately failed (Kone 2001).

The next stage of participatory forestry management began in the region with the adoption of structural adjustment programmes (SAPs) by African states in return for external loans and grants. The conditionalities attached to aid included the divestiture of state assets and the decentralization of administration. The World Bank and other international agencies pressed state forest departments to devolve forest management resources to local administrative bodies, communities and private-sector enterprises. During the 1990s, many West African states moved to introduce new forest codes, enact new forest policies and develop national principles of joint forest management with communities. The rationale for participatory forest management is that it can improve administrative efficiency, reduce costs, address equity issues and improve environmental monitoring (Zhang 2001; Kellert et al. 2000; Brown 1999). Behind these interests, however, were other less explicit objectives associated with structural adjustment: rolling back the state, reducing the government budget deficit, shifting the burdens of natural resource management to local authorities and communities, retrenching workers from the forestry service and increasing corporate control over natural resources.

Reform efforts have attributed the alienation of rural people from forestry policy to the top-down approach of state forestry administrations, rather than to the appropriation of forest resources by the state for private industry. Yet in both the Sahelian fuelwood economies and the high-forest export timber economies, state policies have expropriated forest resources through the allocation of permits, licenses, concessions for commercial exploitation and road checks on the movement of forest commodities. The system extends even to the forest products of farmland. While forest resources in West Africa are the product of the actions of rural people on the environment, the fruits of this relationship are appropriated by states and chiefs who act in concert with logging companies, jeopardizing the survival of both rural people and the natural assets they preserve.

Participatory reforms open a role for communities in the management of forest resources, and give them access to the benefit flows that arise from the provision of management services contracted out to them. But such participation does not address the fundamental issues of the control of forest resources and their role in building rural economies. Democracy, downward accountability and recognition of popular struggles and aspirations tend to be absent from the forestry projects backed by international agencies. At the same time, the lack of independent associations representing their interests in forest resources makes it difficult for rural people to organize to voice their own concerns.

Decentralized Fuelwood Management in the Sahel

A major focus of reform in the Sahelian countries has been decentralizing fuelwood resource management. Case studies from Mali, Burkina Faso and Senegal reveal several common features. In Mali, a 1994 Forest Law delegated responsibility for forest management to *Collectives Territoriales Décentralisées* (Decentralized Territorial Collectives), the basic unit of local government. Local government in turn delegates management of specific forest areas to the *Structure Rurale de Gestions de Bois* (SRGB — Rural Woods Management Structure), which are local associations and cooperatives. In collaboration with the forestry service, the SRGBs develop management plans for local government approval. The plan includes annual fuelwood exploitation quotas and sustainable production targets negotiated by an ad hoc commission comprised of four representatives: two from the SRGB, one from local government and one from the forestry service. Once the plan has been approved, the SRGB receives a permit upon payment of a forest exploitation tax (Ribot 2001b; Intercooperation 2001; Kone 2001).

In Burkina Faso, the 1997 Forestry Code distinguishes between public forest lands of national interest and those of local interest, and provides for delegation of management of the latter to *Collectives Territoriales Décentralisées* and local communities or private concerns. Lands of national interest remain under the forestry service, and any exploitation of these areas is based on permits that it issues. The Code aims to balance resource conservation with use to meet the needs of local populations. Community forest groups, implement a management plan devised in collaboration with the forestry service. The groups do not control the cutting of fuelwood, however, for which the forestry service continues to issue permits to merchants. A price fixed by the state is paid by the merchants to the forestry service, which distributes part of the revenue to the community groups (Ribot 2001b, 2000; Dorlochter-Sulser *et al.* 2000).

In Senegal, where the fuelwood industry supplies much larger urban markets than in Mali and Burkina Faso, it is dominated by a few rich merchants (Ribot 1998). In 1994, the government introduced a new forest law that reaffirms state control over forests, and enables the state to retain choice areas as national forests, but makes provisions for the delegation of rights to private concessionaires and local governments (Barro 1998). To participate in forest management, the elected Rural Council (local government) must request that the forestry service draw up a management plan that specified the quantity of wood that can be cut from different locations, the harvest methods to be used and the reforestation measures that should be in place to promote sustainable fuelwood production. The Rural Council in turn can delegate the right to exploit designated areas to individuals, cooperatives and corporations, under terms set by the forestry service. The Rural Council cannot develop its own management plan, nor decide to conserve the forest, nor exploit it for commodities other than fuelwood. If the Rural Council does not accept the management plan, or does not apply for one, the forestry service can allocate rights of exploitation to outside commercial interests. Candidates for election to Senegal's Rural Councils are not chosen at the local level: they are selected by nationally registered political parties and by deputies in the national assembly, resulting in weak downward accountability. Moreover, the distribution of licenses for the transport and sale of fuelwood has not been decentralized to local government, yet it is in this sector that most of the profits in fuelwood are made, as local producers are obliged to sell at low prices to a small number of licensed merchants (Ribot 2001b, 1995).

In all three Sahelian countries, 'participation' thus largely means creating local responsibilities in the management of marginal forests. While communities gain some rights, these are often limited to production for domestic use and local markets. The forestry services retain options of designating the richest areas as national forests and excluding them from community management. Licensing schemes ensure that the preferential access to commercial resources is maintained for non-local elites, and that forest products cannot be transported beyond custom posts without the necessary permits. This allows state agencies to allocate exploitation rights to select clients and allies. In short, 'participation' transfers some of the responsibilities and costs of forest management to local communities, without providing corresponding benefits.

Decentralized Timber Management in the High-forest Zone

In contrast to the Sahelian zone, forest management in the high-forest zone involves highly valuable timber resources traded on international markets. Here attempts at reform are opposed by vested interests, notably the timber concessionaires who control vast forest areas and gain super-profits from their exploitation. In the early stages of structural adjustment, aid donors backed the timber industry as a way of promoting export-oriented economies. This threatened long-term sustainability, and resulted in glaring contrasts between the huge profits made in timber exploitation and the poverty of many forest dwellers. The growing international critique of the negative impact of structural adjustment programmes on the environment and on poverty encouraged forestry sector reforms. International donor policies have sought to build the capacity of forestry services to manage these resources more efficiently, and to build avenues for civil society participation to counter the alliance of industry with powerful politicians (Brown *et al.* 2002). The reform process is complex, with different actors — including multilateral donors, bilateral donors, state agencies and politicians — attempting to impose agendas, protect interests, introduce counter-agendas and deflect policies that are being implemented. The role of participatory strategies in West African timber production has been rather limited, as case studies from Ghana and Cameroon illustrate.

Forestry Reform in Ghana

Ghana's timber industry virtually collapsed during the 1970s and early 1980s under the burden of economic recession. Prior to this, timber had been the country's third largest export, behind cocoa and gold. In 1983, Ghana signed a structural adjustment loan with the International Monetary Fund. The timber sector was identified for special attention in the World Bank's Export Rehabilitation Project, and major donor programmes provided for re-equipping the industry and for transport. The World Bank and the UK government provided loans to private-sector companies, with the selection process coordinated by the Ministry of Land and Natural Resources. Although these resulted in increased export earnings, they also increased the country's external debt and disproportionately benefited a small class of timber concessionaires. 'A seven-fold rise in export earnings to US$80 million a year may seem impressive', an article in the *Financial Times* commented, 'but not when you have US$30 million annual debt repayments on transport alone' (Keeling 1989).

By 1987, it became evident that malpractices were rampant in the revitalized private forestry sector. A government investigation led to the prosecution of many firms for violating concession regulations, felling undersized trees, under-invoicing timber exports, smuggling, bribing officials and illegally moving profits outside of Ghana. Some of these timber operations were local fronts for foreign companies, and others were fly-by-night companies taking advantage of the favourable loans and the large profits to be made in timber trade.

Deeply embarrassed by an exposé published by Friends of the Earth (1992), the aid donors began to re-evaluate their strategies. They recognized that sustainable development could not be promoted by disbursing loans for commercial logging without allocating funds for forest conservation and management. During the early 1990s, they turned their attention to building the capacity of the forestry service. The major foci were establishing inventory systems for monitoring forest resources, reforming systems for allocating timber concessions to promote transparency and better revenue collection, and encouraging community participation in forest management.

As sustainable management plans limited harvesting in forest reserves, timber concessions on farmland expanded. Distressed by the increasing amounts of timber being harvested from their farms by industry and small-scale chainsaw operators without licenses or permits, and by concessionaires who were under no obligation to compensate them, farmers in many areas deliberately destroyed trees and saplings that regenerated on their land to express their anger and prevent loggers from damaging their farms. In response to these concerns, a Collaborative Forest Management Unit was established within the forestry service in 1994.

In Ghanaian law, timber is legally regarded as the property of the local chief. Farmers have no right to sell trees on their land, and they receive no rent or royalty from the exploitation of timber. Instead royalties are divided between paramount chiefs, local chiefs and district councils. These are comparatively recent arrangements. Before the development of the concession system, farmers had rights to the trees on their land (Amanor 1999, 1997, 1996). For example, farmers sold trees to pitsaw operators in return for one-third of the sawn beams or their equivalent value (Foggie and Piasecki 1962). With the expansion of timber exploitation, concessionaires sought to secure the timber on farmland by promoting an invented 'tradition' that timber resources belong to the chiefs rather than the farmers. This was formalized in the Concessions Act of 1962. Nevertheless, small-scale extraction of timber on farmland by pitsawyers, and by the chainsaw operators who came to replace them, continued in many areas until the 1990s. It is only in recent years, as the main source of timber moved from forest reserves to farmlands, that laws preventing farmers from felling trees on their farms have been vigorously enforced.

Participatory forest management has been adopted in Ghana largely in response to the problem of regulating farmland timber. Former Conservator of Forests Johnnie Francois summed up forestry service concerns:

> It was quite clear to me that we were having a difficult time coping on
> the ground, that we needed more support on the 'ground floor'. We did
> not have enough staff to have eyes all over the place. We needed the
> support of local people and yet these are the very people who are
> disillusioned with us... Only when the forests have a real value to the
> local people will we be able to gain their cooperation and energy for
> forest protection and management. Without that cooperation the
> future of the forests cannot be guaranteed, except at the cost of a vast
> army of forest guards. (cited in Boateng 1995)

The 1994 Forestry and Wildlife Policy and the 1995 Interim Measures to
Control Illegal Felling recognized that the future of the forestry industry
depended upon farmers planting and preserving trees. However, the reform
process soon ran into resistance from vested interests. As a compromise,
rather vague Social Responsibility Agreements were introduced, in which
concessionaires agreed to provide payments — set at only 5 per cent of the
stumpage value — for community infrastructure projects, in return for the
right to exploit the timber resources in their community's vicinity. This was
an unsatisfactory solution, not only because benefits of individual farmers'
efforts were redistributed to the community, but also because the chiefs
frequently dominated the process and defined the appropriate forms that the
agreement should take.

Moreover, while the new forestry policy aimed to establish a framework
for participatory management, paradoxically it created the conditions for
the further erosion of farmers' rights by centralizing off-reserve forest
management into the hands of the forestry service. Prior to this reform,
decentralized District Assemblies had issued permits and licenses for
exploitation of forest resources on farmland. Now, with the concession
system extended to farmlands, it is difficult for local timber craft producers
to get access to trees for production of mortars, canoes and wood carvings.
The informal timber sector has been criminalized: legislation bans the use of
chainsaws to process lumber into boards, and the military has launched
punitive campaigns against rural people who continue to produce chainsaw
timber. Nevertheless, timber supplies in the urban market still are mainly
sourced from chainsaw operators, since concessionaires prefer to export
their timber. With prices rising in the urban market, chainsaw timber has
become the preserve of well-organized illegal operations that have the
influence to arrange all the necessary rents to be able to pass through or

evade checkpoints.

In the forest reserves, reform took the shape of a Collaborative Forest Management programme that seeks to involve local communities in planning, implementation and monitoring. In communities around the edge of the reserves, Community Forest Committees enter into contractual relations with the forestry service to perform functions including boundary maintenance, firebreak establishment, tree planting, facilitating and monitoring Social Responsibility Agreements with timber concessionaires, and policing the reserves against illegal encroachers. As the forestry service retrenches its own workforce, forest-edge communities increasingly are drawn upon to provide such services. The emphasis is on the provision of labour services rather than participation in management planning. While communities get some employment benefits, these pale in comparison to the profits being realized by the timber industry.

Forestry Reform in Cameroon

Cameroon was one of the fastest growing economies in Africa during the 1960s and 1970s, with annual growth rates of more than five per cent. Growth was based largely on exports of cocoa, coffee, cotton, aluminium and petroleum. In the 1980s, however, poor management and unfavourable international terms of trade led to a budgetary crisis, forcing Cameroon to accept a structural adjustment programme in 1988. Growing demand in Asia encouraged expansion of the timber industry, and by the 1990s timber accounted for more than a quarter of the country's exports. The government used logging concessions as a way of bolstering its political support, and members of the regime were closely allied with contractors. There were no requirements to manage timber concessions on a sustainable basis (Brunner and Ekoko 2000; Djeumo 2001).

The World Bank targeted forestry sector reform as a criterion for 'good governance' in Cameroon and a condition for disbursement of structural adjustment loans. A draft Forest Law largely drawn up by the World Bank was introduced in 1994 (Brunner and Ekoko 2000). The major focus was the allocation of concessions by an auction process, with 'realistic' fees to enable the government to capture more of the rents from timber exploitation. In addition, the new law required sustainable forest management plans as a condition for exploiting a concession. It also included provisions for local communities to acquire exclusive rights to manage forest areas up to 5,000 hectares, and to gain revenues from logging these community forests or contracting out to logging companies. This was perceived by donors as encouraging local communities to participate in monitoring forest resources, thus, promoting efficiency and transparency. Because the law did not build upon any strong domestic constituency or organizations for forest reform, however, these provisions ultimately faltered both in the definition of what constitutes a 'community' and in the provision of an institutional structure to support 'community forestry' (Egbe 2001).

The elected National Assembly sought to modify the draft legislation. Its main concern was that under the auction system, national timber companies would be unable to compete with international companies, and the country's forest resources would, in effect, be sold out to foreigners. Many parliamentarians were directly threatened by the reforms since they had economic interests in the forest industry. As an alternative way to promote sustainable production and value-added timber processing, the National Assembly sought to introduce a ban on log exports. This threatened the interests of the French timber companies that exported large quantities of Cameroonian logs for processing in France. The French government, acting as a patron for narrowly defined economic interests, pressured the government of Cameroon to loosen the ban.[5]

On paper, Cameroon has one of the most progressive forest laws in Africa with its provisions for the establishment of community forests. But within a reform process driven by the aim of creating a leaner and more efficient timber industry, and the associated struggles between international and national timber capital, the commitment of policy makers to equity objectives is questionable. Seven years after the enactment of the law, 104 community forest applications had been received, but only 12 had been approved (Djeumo 2001). To obtain a community forest, community members must organize one of four types of legal entities — associations, cooperatives, common initiative groups, or economic interest groups — each of which is governed by different requirements, and regulated by different ministries. The initiators are often non-residential elites and who mobilize networks of people to pose as a 'community group' and who use their social connections, information and experience to process community forest applications (Djeumo 2001; Graziani and Burnham 2001; Brown 1999). They frequently act in concert with traditional authorities, who are offered prominent positions in the new community entity, and many applications are submitted by political leaders, such as mayors and deputies, acting on the behalf of timber companies in whose fortunes they have a stake (Djeumo 2001).

Community entities must compete with industry, since potential community forest areas may also be offered on a permit basis to logging firms. In principle, community forests are given initial preference, but the application process is an onerous task for smallholder farmers. In some cases, timber corporations themselves have sponsored the formation of community forest groups, using them as a front for illegal activities, and rapidly logging the forest, with little if any benefit to the village. The first allocated community forest at Mbimboue has been completely logged out, and members of the 'community group' are now in prison (Djeumo 2001). Fear of prosecution for irregular accounting and management practices may discourage some settlements from forming community entities. Given this context, it is not surprising that Sharpe (1998) found, in a study in south-west Cameroon, that rural dwellers view recent reforms and participatory projects as another chapter in the saga of exploitation of their forests by external forces, political collaborators and traditional authorities.

Inventing Communities

The concept of the autonomous 'community' is problematic in West Africa. Migration has been common throughout the region since the 19th century. The growth of export agriculture, in particular, often has depended on migrant labour, such as the movement of Soninke from northern Mali into the Senegambia for groundnut cultivation (Manchuelle 1997), and the migrations from Niger, Burkina Faso and Mali into the cocoa and coffee belts of Ghana and Côte d'Ivoire (Hill 1956; Rouche 1954; Chaveau and Leonard 1996; Leonard 1997). Even where agriculture has developed without long-distance migrations, the concept of local communities is often fraught with difficulty. In south-west Cameroon, for example, present-day forest settlements typically are not survivals from a historical past, but rather modern formations that resulted when people from a variety of ethnic backgrounds coalesced for the task of converting forest into agricultural land (Sharpe 1998). Crosscutting patron-client networks link rural and urban worlds. The decentralization of natural resource management to local groups is further complicated by the proliferation of projects that devise their own forms of 'community participation' outside the context of local administrative bodies.

In this context, village level groups willing to work within the strictures defined by the environmental coalition backing community forestry are empowered to manage natural resource use (Hajer 1995). These strictures usually take the negative form of restrictions and prohibitions (Deme 1998). Since most local economic activities revolve around natural resource use, this gives these groups considerable power. Those who oppose the dominant environmental narratives frequently have no platform through which they can voice their dissent and aspirations. They often become targets in allocating blame for environmental degradation. Under the guise of protecting the environment, community groups exclude 'outsiders' with whom they have conflicts over resource usage. In both Côte d'Ivoire and Ghana, for example, transhumant Fulani herdsmen have been forced from their grazing lands, and their practice of burning grass early in the dry season to cause new shoots to come up has been portrayed as a threat to the environment.

In many places, community militias have been formed to take up environmental policing functions. This is most evident in the campaigns to ban bush burning that have been introduced throughout West Africa. Bush burning is an integral part of rotational farming. It is an easy land-clearance method that removes pests and weeds, improves soil structure and pH, and prevents the build up of fuels that may lead to worse wildfires at the height of the dry season. While fire ecology is now well understood, it does not fit neatly into present global concerns about carbon emissions, and hence, it is a marginalized science in today's environmental coalitions (Pyne 1997). In many West African nations, chiefs have been empowered to introduce local by-laws banning the use of fire, and community organizations have been created to prevent or regulate use of fire by farmers. In Ghana, for example, the Fire Volunteer Mobisquads have been trained to monitor bush burning. A major part of their training involves the practice of military drills. Farmers cannot clear their farms without the supervision of a Fire Volunteer, which involves payment of a supervision fee that is considered extortionary by many farmers (Amanor 2001a). This policy sweeps aside the considerable knowledge of fire management that resides in rural communities. At the same time, it assumes that a three-week training programme run by the Fire Services (who have no experience in farm-clearance), suffices to make the Fire Volunteers experts on fire management.

Community organizations are being empowered to carry out surveillance activities of the local population so that global and national environmental policies can be effectively implemented. Despite the rhetoric of democratic decentralization, environmental management is by edict. Rural people are not enabled to make their own decisions about managing natural resources. Instead, rural people essentially are provided with commands and a set of simple messages that fail to reflect the complexity of the different regional economies.

Recent literature on natural resource management stressed the need to build multi-stakeholder platforms to discuss conflicts and negotiate solutions

(Bernard and Armstrong 1998). This is particularly emphasized in cases involving pastoralists, who have suffered from environmental scapegoating and the appropriation of resources by sedentary communities (Hesse and Trench 2000). While recognizing the heterogeneity of rural people, this approach typically fails to address the appropriation of resource rights by the state and industry, and the need for political reforms to create better conditions for the democratization of rural life and downward accountability of elected representatives. Instead they still tend to rely on getting strong traditional leadership, frequently selected by the natural resource administrators, to represent the conflicting groups. The emphasis is on the ability of leaders to hold community members accountable, rather than the reverse. Without addressing issues of local democratization, community forestry projects build new patron-client networks — a strategy derived from the annals of colonial rural administration.

Alternative Strategies for Building Forest Assets

There is scope in West Africa for alternative strategies that would build forest assets in the hands of the poor. Such strategies would seek to reduce poverty, protect the environment and go beyond mere rhetoric of participation and equity. Four main avenues can be distinguished for building natural assets in the hands of low-income communities and individuals (Boyce 2003):

- *Investment:* the creation of new natural capital and the improvement of natural capital to which the poor already have access.
- *Appropriation:* the establishment of rights of the poor to natural wealth that has been treated as an open-access resource.
- *Internalization:* rewarding the poor for benefits they provide to others as environmental services.
- *Redistribution:* the transfer of natural capital from others to the poor.

Investment as a natural asset-building strategy would build upon the important roles that rural communities in West Africa historically have played in creating and augmenting stocks of forest assets, by channelling support to maintain and strengthen these value-adding processes. Despite the growing body of scientific literature on the rationales behind the adaptive strategies of African farmers, local knowledge often is sidelined by environmental programmes anxious to promote technologies that have been 'branded' in international research institutions. Current participatory approaches may solicit farmers' feedback in refining technologies emanating from international centres. But farmers participate in the programmes of development agencies, rather than development agencies participating in helping farmers to attain their own vision.

A number of the value-adding natural resource management strategies of rural West African communities have been described earlier. These include rotational bush fallowing; the use of fire to manage the agroecology; the preservation of trees through cutting and coppicing, rather than harvesting and replanting; and land-use systems in which farming and pastoralism are mutually beneficial. Successful investment strategies would not simply replicate these traditional practices; they would use them as a basis for further innovation. Such a strategic reorientation is more than a technical question. It is also a social and political question. Success will require the creation of opportunities for farmers to voice their aspirations and participate in debate about relevant development strategies.

Appropriation is already an element of contemporary participatory forest management rhetoric. The rationale is that promoting community 'ownership' of forests will lead to more efficient management. As discussed earlier, however, this approach has had two key limitations. First, there are problems in identifying the community. The community groups recognized by the state frequently are vehicles for local elites to take actions against the rest of rural society, actions that further marginalize the rural poor. Second, community participation fails to address the injustices in the framework of forest management inherited from colonial times. In the name of participation, rural citizens today are given responsibilities but not rights. Business classes allied with political elites continue to use concessions, licenses and permits to appropriate forest resources and limit the ability of rural people to trade in forest commodities.

At the same time, the current framework for community management often excludes some 'outsiders' — notably pastoralists — in the name of preventing the 'tragedy of the commons'. In so doing, it ignores interactions that have conserved and enhanced forest resources. Historically, there have been multiple rights in land in West Africa and migrations have contributed to the development of the agricultural economy. Rural populations are frequently heterogeneous and linked to larger rural economies. In such contexts, the discourse of 'community' forest management, rooted an ideal of autonomous, insular settlements, frequently leads to conflicts between various land users.

Natural asset building requires more nuanced appropriation strategies that recognize multiple rights in land, the important roles that mobile communities can play in creating and sustaining natural assets, and the importance of synergistic interactions among diverse resource-dependent communities. At the same time, such strategies would seek to defend common-pool resources against appropriation by logging companies and the state in the service of the rich and powerful. Again, such natural asset-building strategies require democratization: the creation of institutions that enable rural people to articulate their needs and make the state more accountable and transparent.

Internalization as a natural asset-building strategy would enable rural communities to capture benefits provided to others — such as watershed protection, carbon sequestration and biodiversity conservation — by virtue of their stewardship of natural resources. In West Africa, this strategy is complicated by the heterogeneity of rural communities, multiple access to different natural resources and inequalities of wealth and power within rural communities. It may be difficult to determine exactly which group of people creates or sustains forest resources, since they may be the outcome of the interactions of different groups. Compensation schemes could lead to competition to capture the value of the environmental services, disrupting the very basis on which common property regimes have been built. Moreover, given the paucity of information on West African environments, internalization strategies may introduce a bias in favour of environmental services valued by donors and policy makers, while devaluing other environmental services that may be important to rural people.

A further danger is that compensation for environmental services may be captured by local elite groups who dominate community organizations. The history of recent participatory forest management initiatives is instructive in this regard. For example, where farmers' rights to trees growing on their land are not recognized, the benefits from internalization could be captured by chiefs or community groups recognized and defined by the state. A just system of internalization can emerge only where there are democratic fora that enable people to discuss, validate and dispute, accompanied by efforts to define equitably rights in natural assets.[6]

Redistribution of rights to forest assets must be a central element of any reform process that aims to place West Africa's forest resources in the service of poverty reduction. Such redistribution must be based on recognition of the rights of rural producers to resources their work creates and preserves. This includes not only the rights of farmers to trees on their land, but also recognizes the rights of other natural resource users who play important roles in creating assets, and synergistic interactions among various producers. Given the complexity of forest resource use in West Africa, and the contests between rural users and urban-based extractive interests, it is doubtful whether any of the other strategies for natural asset building can work without a framework for the redistribution of rights. This again would require democratic structures, in which different interest groups articulate their perspectives, discuss ways of harmonizing multiple uses, mediate conflicts, negotiate practical solutions to establish codes of conduct and recognize each other's contributions to economic prosperity.

Conclusion

In the present political context in West Africa, forestry reforms have largely failed to recognize the positive environmental contributions of rural users of natural resources and to reflect their aspirations. The dominant crisis narratives devalue the livelihood strategies of rural people and deny them a voice in policy fora. 'Participatory' programmes attempt to impose hegemonic discourses and practices on rural populations. State bureaucracies resist democratic reforms. Technocentric concerns with minimizing administrative costs lead to attempts to pass the burden to local government and rural people. The lack of formally recognized rights of local communities to forest resources is paired with appropriation or control by the state in collusion with powerful vested interests.

Favourable conditions also exist, however, for the development of an alternative approach to forestry reform. A growing body of scientific knowledge is documenting the role that rural African producers have played in creating natural assets, and the rationales for their adaptive strategies in erratic and changing environments. The need for flexible, adaptive strategies has become even more apparent in today's era of rapid and uncertain environmental change. And the region is seeing an increasing movement towards democratization, backed by a popular tradition calling for accountability, transparency and policies that favour the ordinary people rather than the elites.

The current alienation of rural people from policy decisions and their lack of rights in natural resources hinder the development of flexible and sustainable forest management. Yet at present, there is a dearth of non-governmental organizations (NGOs) advocating for the rights of the poor to environmental entitlements in West Africa. Instead, most NGOs either advocate the exclusionary protection of nature from human intervention through regulations and reservations, or they merely provide technical services to communities such as tree nurseries and seedling distribution programmes. NGOs could play an important role in support of alternative strategies, by lobbying for the rights of rural people to forest resources and access to policy making, and by promoting community-based environmental organizations within communities that are truly representative.

Given their substantial investment in global environmental administration and research, international donors also will have a direct influence on the ways in which forest administration evolves in West Africa. The donors can continue to invest in research rooted in crisis narratives, and continue to support natural resource management by coalitions that attempt to enforce environmental regulation by coercive means. Alternatively, they could choose to promote more flexible systems of environmental management, building on the positive interactions between humans and nature documented in recent scientific findings. This alternative path would mean deepening the democratic representation of different rural groups in policy making and forest management.

Progressive changes in West African forest management ultimately will depend upon shifting the power relations in society and creating more secure rights in resources for forest-zone dwellers. At present, forest policies claim to protect the environment from the people, while in reality, they protect large profits for the select. These policies have failed to conserve the environment, and they have frustrated the attempts of rural people to develop viable livelihoods. The alternative is to reconceptualize forest resources as assets whose value has been, and can continue to be, enhanced by rural people. This approach will need to go beyond investment in natural capital, and beyond internalizing benefits from the provision of environmental services. It must reappropriate and redistribute rights so as to create the basis for new forms of forest management and redress the injustices to which rural people have been subjected by colonial and post-colonial frameworks of natural resource administration. A focus on environmental justice and rights can promote genuine participation and sustainable natural resource management.

Acknowledgements

Many thanks to James Boyce for constructive and useful comments on an earlier draft of this paper.

Notes

1. Some trees provide wood used for carving canoes, mortars and furniture items. Some bear fruits, including shea, locust bean, wild mango, oil palm, borassus palm and cola. Rattans and grasses are used for weaving baskets and furniture. There are many medicinal plants. Other species provide sticks used for dental cleaning and

sponges. In addition to local consumption, many NTFPs are sold in urban markets (Falconer 1994).

2. Other studies describe similar interactions. See Letouzey (1968) for Cameroon, and Spichiger and Blanc-Pamard (1973); Blanc-Pamard and Peltre (1984); Gautier (1990); Bassett and Zueli (2000) for Cote d'Ivoire.

3. During a visit to Kissidougou in 1998, farmers also identified cattle as being an important agent in this process: forest lianas began to regenerate in pastures rich in manure, and gradually formed clumps of woody vegetation from which forest islands spread.

4. Attempts to plant iroko in forest reserves have largely failed, with saplings being vulnerable to gall infection caused by the insect *Phytolyma lota*. Perhaps it is the ecology of shifting cultivation that encouraged the proliferation of iroko. While generally unsympathetic to the use of fire in farm clearance in the dry semi-deciduous forests of Ghana, Hawthorne and Abu-Juam (1995: 65) admit that 'the past economic value of the forests has been largely due to the abundance of species such as *Milicia excelsa* and *Mansonia*, which have no doubt flourished as a consequence of a history of disturbance.'

5. See Brunner and Ekoko (2000). The Cameroon Forest Law was enacted in 1994, but it proved unacceptable to the World Bank. A revised version was introduced in 1995, and implemented five years later. A central provision is that 70 per cent of logs are to be used domestically. However, under pressure from France, it made provisions for companies to continue to export more than 30 per cent of the logs, provided that they pay a progressive surtax.

6. In a review of experiences in the Americas, Rosa *et al.* (in this volume) draw similar lessons.

References

Amanor, Kojo S. (1996) *Managing Trees in Farming Systems: The Perspectives of Farmers*, Kumasi: Forestry Department.

— (1997) 'Collaborative Forest Management, Forest Resource Tenure and the Domestic Economy in Ghana', *IDRCurrents* No.15: 10–16.

— (1999) *Global Restructuring and Land Rights in Ghana: Forest Food Chains, Timber and Rural Livelihoods*, Research Report 108, Uppsala: Nordiska Afrikainstitutet.

— (2001a) 'Bushfire Management, Culture and Ecological Modernisation in Ghana', in Melissa Leach, John Fairhead and Kojo Amanor, eds., *Science and Policy Process: Perspectives from the Forest*, IDS Bulletin 233(1): 31–38.

— (2001b) 'The Symbolism of Tree Planting and Hegemonic Environmentalism', Paper presented at a Workshop on Changing Perspectives of Forests: Ecology, People and Science/Policy Processes in West Africa and the Caribbean, IDS, University of Sussex, 26–27 March.

— (2001c) 'Empowering Women through Tree Planting? Gender and global environmentalism in Northern Ghana', *Institute of African Studies Research Review* 17(1): 63–73.

Amanor, Kojo, David Brown and Michael Richards (2002) *Poverty Dimensions of Public Governance and Forest Management in Ghana*, Final Technical Report NRSP R7957 to Natural Resource Systems Project, Legon: University of Ghana and London, ODI.

Ba, H. and J. Daget (1984) *L'Empire Peul du Macina*. Nouvelles Editions Africaines. Abidjan: L'Ecole des Hautes Etudes en Science Sociales.

Barro, Abdoulaye (1998) *Senegal's Unique Case in Decentralised Natural Resource Management: The Community Based Natural Resource Management Programme*, World Bank/WBFs CBNRM Initiative. Senegal: USAID. Available at http://srdis.ciesin.columbia.edu/cases/senegal-001.htm.

Bassett, Thomas J. and J. Boutrais (2000) 'Cattle and Trees in the West African Savanna', in Reginald Cline-Cole and Clare Madge, eds., *Contesting Forestry in West Africa*, Aldershot: Ashgate.

Bassett, Thomas J. and Koli Bi Zueli (2000) 'Environmental Discourses and the Ivorian Savanna', *Annals of the Association of American Geographers* 90(1): 67–95.

Behnke, Roy H. and Ian Scoones (1993) 'Rethinking Range Ecology: Implications for Rangeland Management in Africa', in Roy H. Behnke, Ian Scoones and Carol Kerven, eds., *Range Ecology at Disequilibrium: New Models of Natural Variability and Pastoral Adaptation in African Savannas*, London: ODI, IIED and Commonwealth Secretariat.

Bernard, A.K. and G. Armstrong (1998) 'Learning and Policy Integration', in Jamie Schnurr and Susan Holtz, eds., *The Cornerstone of Development: Integrating Environmental, Social and Economic Policies*, Ottawa: IDRC and Boca Raton: Lewis Publishers.

Blanc-Pamard, C. and R. Peltre (1984) 'Dynamiques des paysages preforestiers et pratiques culturales en Afrique de l'Ouest (Côte d'Ivoire Centrale)', *Le Developpement rural en question. Memoire OSTROM*, No. 106: 55–74.

Boateng, Kwadjo (1995) 'Collaborative Forest Management Programme: Work Undertaken', Paper presented at the *Forest Department Symposium on 'The Potential for Collaboration in High-forest Management*, organized by the Forest Planning Branch, Kumasi, 28–29 November, 1995.

Boyce, James K. (2003) 'From Natural Resources to Natural Assets', in James K. Boyce and Barry G. Shelly, eds., *Natural Assets: Democratizing Environmental Ownership*, Washington DC: Island Press.

Brown, David (1999) *Principles and Practice of Forest Co-management: Evidence from West-Central Africa*, European Union Tropical Forestry Paper 2, London: ODI, and Brussels: European Commission.

Brown, David, Kate Schreckenberg, Gil Shepherd and Adrian Wells (2002) 'Forestry as an Entry Point for Governance Reform', *ODI Forestry Briefing No.1*, London: ODI.

Brunner, Jake and Francois Ekoko (2000) 'Cameroon', in Francis J. Seymour and Navroz K. Dubash, eds., *The Right Conditions: The World Bank, Structural Adjustment and Forest Policy Reform*, Washington: World Resource Institute.

Chaveau, Jean-Pierre and Eric Leonard (1996) 'Côte d'Ivoire's Pioneer Fronts: Historical and Political Determinants of the Spread of Cocoa Cultivation', in W.G. Clarence-Smith, ed., *Cocoa Pioneer Fronts since 1800: The Role of Smallholders, Planters and Merchants*, Basingstoke: Macmillan.

Cline-Cole, Reginald (1996) 'Dryland Forestry: Manufacturing Forests and Farming Trees in Nigeria', in Melissa Leach and Robin Mearns, eds., *The Lie of the Land: Challenging Received Wisdom on the African Environment*, London and Portsmouth: James Curry, NH: Heinemann, 122–139.

— (2000) 'Redefining Forestry Space and Threatening Livelihoods in Colonial Northern Nigeria', in Reginald Cline-Cole and Clare Madge, eds., *Contesting Forestry in West Africa*, Aldershot: Ashgate.

Cousins, J.E. (1946) 'Some Notes on Iroko in Onitsha and Owerri Provinces', *Farm and Forest* 7(1): 28–32.

Deme, Yacouba (1998) *Natural Resource Management by Local Associations in the Kelka region of Mali*, TIED Drylands Programme Issue Paper 74, London: TIED.

Djeumo, Andre (2001) 'The Development of Community Forests in Cameroon: Origins,

Current Situation and Constraints', *Rural Development Forestry Network Paper 25b*, London: GDI.

Dorlochter-Sulser, Kirsch-Jung, Karl Sabine and Martin Sulser (2000) *Elaboration of a Local Convention for Natural Resource Management: A case from the Bam Region, Burkina Faso*, TIED Drylands Programme Issue Paper 98, London: IIED.

Egbe, Samuel E. (2001) 'The Law, Communities and Wildlife Management in Cameroon', *Rural Development Forestry Network Paper 25*, London: ODI.

Fairhead, James and Melissa Leach (1996) *Misreading the African Landscape: Forest and Ecology in a Forest-savanna mosaic*, Cambridge: Cambridge University Press.

— (1998) *Reframing Deforestation: Global Analysis and Local realities: Studies in West Africa*, London: Routledge.

Falconer, Julia (1994) *Non-timber Products in Southern Ghana*, London: ODA (on behalf of Forestry Department, Accra).

Foggie, A. and B. Piasecki (1962) 'Timber, Fuel and Minor Produce', in J.B. Wills, ed., *Agriculture and Land Use in Ghana*, Accra: Ghana Ministry of Food and Agriculture and London: Oxford University Press.

Friends of the Earth (1992) *Plunder in Ghana's Rainforest for Illegal Profit: An Expose of Corruption, Fraud and Other Malpractices in the International Timber Trade*, London: Friends of the Earth.

Gautier, L. (1990) 'Contact forest-savane en Côte d'Ivoire centrale: evolution du recouvrement ligneux des savanes de la Reserve de Lamto (sud de V-Baole)', *Candollea* 45: 627–641.

Ghana Ministry of Lands and Forests (1998) *Decentralisation of Forest and Wildlife Sector Activities to District Assemblies*, Position Paper. Accra: Ministry of Land and Forests.

Graziani, Monica and Philip Burnham (2001) 'Legal Pluralism in the Rain Forests of South-eastern Cameroon', in Katherine Homewood, ed., *Rural Resources and Local Livelihoods in Africa*, Oxford: James Curry.

Hajer, Maarten (1995) *The Politics of Environmental Discourse: Ecological Modernization and the Policy Process*, Oxford: Clarendon Press.

Hawthorne, William D. (1996) 'Holes and Sums of Parts in Ghanaian Forests: Regeneration, Scale and Sustainable Use', *Proceedings of the Royal Society of Edinburgh*, No.104B: 75–176.

Hawthorne, William P. and Abu-Juam, Musa (1995) *Forest Protection in Ghana with Particular Reference to Vegetation and Plant Species*, Cambridge: IUCN.

Hesse, Ced and Pippa Trench (2000) *Who's Managing the Commons? Inclusive Management for a Sustainable Future*, Securing the Commons No.1. London: IIED and London: SOS Sahel.

Hill, Polly (1956) *The Gold Coast Cocoa Farmer*, London: Oxford University Press.

Intercooperation — Members of Sustainable Natural Resource Management Programme, Mali (2001) *Local Development and Community Management of Woodlands: Experience from Mali*, IIED Drylands Issue Paper. No.106, London: IIED.

Keeling, W. (1989) 'Forests Pay as Ghana loses out', *Financial Times*, 8 February, 1989.

Kellert, S.R., J.N. Mehta, S.A. Ebbin and L.L. Lichtenfeld (2000) 'Community Natural Resource Management: Promises, Rhetoric and Reality', *Society and Natural Resources* 13: 705–715.

Kone, Bather (2001) 'Biodiversity and Forests: Mali Case Study', Paper prepared for an International Workshop on Integration of Biodiversity in National Forestry Planning Programme at CIFOR Headquarters, Bogor, Indonesia, 13–16 August.

Lane, Charles R. (1998) 'Introduction: Overview of the Pastoral Problem', in Charles R. Lane, ed., *Custodians of the Commons: Pastoral land tenure in East and West Africa*, London:

Earthscan, and Geneva: UNRISD.
Leach, Melissa and Robin Mearns (1996) *The Lie of the Land: Received Wisdom on the African Environment,* Oxford: James Curry.
Leonard, Eric (1997) 'Crise ecologique, crise economique, crise d'un modele d'explotation agricole.' in B. Contamin and H. Memel-Fote, eds., *Le modele Ivorien en Question: Crises, ajustements, recompositions,,* Paris: Kathala and l'ORSTOM.
Letouzey, R. (1978) 'Notes phytogeographiques sur les Palmiers du Cameroun', *Adonsonia,* 18: 293-325.
Maley, Jean (1993) 'The Climatic and Vegetation History of the Equatorial Regions of Africa during the Upper Quarternary', In Thurston Shaw, Paul Sinclair, Bassey Andah and Alex Okpokpo, eds., *The Archaeology of Africa: Foods, Metals and Towns,* London and New York: Routledge.
— (1996) 'The African Rainforest: Principal Patterns of Vegetation from Upper Cretaceous to Quaternary', *Proceedings of the Royal Society of Edinburgh* 1048: 75–176.
— (2001) 'A Catastrophic Destruction of African Forests about 2,500 Years Ago Still Exerts a Major Influence on Present Vegetation Formations in Melissa Leach', *Science and the Policy Process: Perspectives from the Forest, IDS Bulletin,* 33(1): 13–30.
Maloney, Alfred (1887) *Sketch of the Forestry of West Africa,* London: Sampson Low, Marston, Searle and Rivington.
Mamdani, M. (1996) *Citizen and Subject: Contemporary Africa and the Legacy of Late Colonialism,* Princeton: Princeton University Press.
Manchuelle, François (1997) *Willing Migrants: Soninke labour diasporas, 1848–1960,* Athens: Ohio University Press and London: James Curry.
Moorehead, Richard (1998) 'Mali', in Charles R. Lane, ed., *Custodians of the Commons: Pastoral Land Tenure in East and West Africa,* London: Earthscan and Geneva: UNRISD.
Peluso, Nancy L. (1992) *Rich Forests, Poor People: Resource Control and Resistance in Java,* Berkeley: University of California Press.
Pyne, Stephen J. (1997) *World Fire: The Culture of Fire on Earth,* Seattle and London: University of Washington Press.
Ribot, Jesse C. (1995) 'From Exclusion to Participation: Turning Senegal's Forestry Policy Around', *World Development* 23(9): 1587–99.
— (1998) 'Theorising Access: Forest Profits along Senegal's Commodity Chain', *Development and Change* 29(2): 307–41.
— (2000) 'Rebellion, Representation and Enfranchisement in the Forest Villages of Makacoulibantang, Eastern Senegal', in Charles Zerner, ed., *People, Plants and Justice: The Politics of Nature Conservation,* New York: Columbia University Press.
— (2001a) *Science, Use Rights and Exclusion: A History of Forestry in Francophone West Africa,* Drylands Programme Issue Paper No. 104, London: IIED.
— (2001b) *Local Actors, Powers and Accountability in African Decentralizations: A Review of Issues,* Ottawa: International Development Research Centre of Canada Assessment of Social Policy Reforms Initiative.
Rouche, Jean (1954) 'Notes on Migrations into the Gold Coast.', Musée de l'Homme, Paris. Unpublished paper.
Sharpe, Barry (1998) 'First the Forest: Conservation, "community" and "participation" in South-west Cameroon', *Africa* 68(l): 25–45.
Sprichiger, R. and C. Blanc-Pamard (1973) 'Recherches sur le contact foret-savane en Côte d'Ivoire: note sur la vegetation dans la region de Beoumi', *Candollea* 36: 145-153.
United Nations Intergovernmental Panel on Forests (1997) *Proposals for Action.* Available at http://www.un.org/esa/forests/ipf_iff.html.
Van Rompaey, Renaat (2001) 'New Perspectives on Tropical Rain Forest Vegetation

Ecology in West Africa: Typology, Gradients and Disturbance Regime', *Science and Policy Process: Perspectives from the Forest, IDS Bulletin* 233(1): 31–38.

Westoby, Jack (1987) *The Purpose of Forests: Follies of Development,* Oxford: Blackwell.

Zhang, Y. (2001) 'Economics of Transaction Costs-saving Forestry', *Ecological Economics* 36: 197–204.

PART III:

CAPTURING BENEFITS

Terraces can improve both the quantity and quality of water supplies.
Photo credit: Barry Shelley.

CHAPTER 9
COMPENSATION FOR ENVIRONMENTAL SERVICES AND RURAL COMMUNITIES: LESSONS FROM THE AMERICAS

Herman Rosa, Deborah Barry, Susan Kandel and Leopoldo Dimas

Introduction

The degradation of the world's ecosystems is undermining their capacity to provide environmental services that are vital to humankind. This has fuelled experimentation with compensation schemes that reward people for managing ecosystems to provide environmental services, based on the premise that positive incentives can lead to changes in land-use practices. In the Americas, such experiments have concentrated on watershed management for hydrological services and on conservation of biodiversity and scenic beauty. If and when international negotiations yield a suitable framework for climate change mitigation, carbon dioxide sequestration could be added to the mix.

The prevailing approach to compensation has focused on payments, rather than other possible rewards such as greater provision of local public goods or enhanced social status. In many cases, payment for environmental services (PES) schemes have been characterized by designs that seek the lowest cost possible for achieving environmental goals; concentrate on single environmental services (such as carbon sequestration), sometimes at the expense of other ecosystem services; and accord priority to simplified, large-scale ecosystems, preferably controlled by a few people, so as to reduce transaction costs.

This approach can have adverse — even devastating — impacts on poor and marginalized rural communities. At the same time, it misses opportunities for tapping into the crucial roles that these communities often play in ecosystem stewardship and the provision of environmental services. When poor communities hold secure rights over lands that provide environmental services, they are most likely to benefit from compensation schemes, and the goals of environmental protection and poverty reduction are mutually supporting. More often, however, community rights to natural resources are limited and insecure. In such cases, compensation schemes can induce powerful outside interests to establish 'new' private property rights over resources previously managed by poor communities, undermining their asset base and pushing them into deeper poverty.

A review of experiences with PES schemes in the Americas sheds light on both their potential as a strategy for helping poor communities to build and sustain natural assets and their limitations in contexts marked by limited and insecure property rights for the poor. This chapter summarizes lessons from an evaluation of experiences in Costa Rica, Mexico, Brazil, El Salvador and New York, highlighting issues that need to be considered when seeking to reward poor communities for their role in ensuring the flow of environmental services.[1]

Why Focus on Poor Communities?

If given opportunities and technical resources to do so, the rural poor can not only reverse environmentally degrading impacts of past land-use practices but also invest in the enhancement of valuable environmental services. PES schemes are a potential strategy for bringing about these changes. From a pragmatic perspective, it often makes sense to focus these schemes on indigenous and peasant communities who inhabit, manage and use ecosystems of importance for conservation and environmental services provision. In particular, many countries in the Americas have now adopted legal provisions that recognize and protect the rights of indigenous peoples to their land, resources, cultural identity, self-government and participation in national affairs.

Rural communities typically have a deep relationship to the lands they occupy not only as the basis for their economic subsistence but also as a central element of their cultural identity, social organization and belief systems. These same lands often provide important environmental services. In some cases, as in the conservation of agricultural biodiversity, these services depend on the labour and knowledge of community members.[2] In other cases, such as regulation of the quality and quantity of water flows, human activities can have both positive and negative effects.

From an environmental justice perspective, PES schemes that fail to integrate the social objective of benefiting poor communities with the environmental objective of securing environmental services can turn into instruments of social exclusion, resulting in deeper and broader poverty. In such cases, environmental goals still may be met, but at a high social cost. In contrast, compensation strategies planned and implemented in concert with the needs of poor communities can improve both rural livelihoods and environmental management.

Key Issues

If coupled with a concern for equity and poverty reduction, compensation for environmental services can be an important tool for building natural assets in the hands of the poor. PES schemes can involve all four 'routes' for natural asset building: the *redistribution* and *(re)appropriation* of natural assets to secure the rights of low-income communities and individuals; *internalization* to reward them for providing benefits to others through natural resource stewardship; and further *investment* in natural assets induced by the resources and incentives that PES schemes provide.[3]

When implemented as an element of natural asset-building strategies, PES mechanisms thus can help to improve rural livelihoods while advancing environmental goals. In so doing, PES schemes can be 'consciousness-raising' in two respects. First, they can catalyze local efforts by rural communities to construct shared visions that revalourize the landscapes they manage. Second, they can raise awareness among policy makers and the public of the key roles that indigenous and peasant communities play in managing complex ecosystems that are critical for the provision of environmental services.

This section discusses key issues that arise in efforts to make PES schemes part of strategy for building natural assets in the hands of the poor: the need to integrate different levels of environmental services; the need for community participation to fashion equitable rules for PES schemes; the importance of a landscape perspective in resource management; the key role of social capital in efforts to build natural assets; the need for secure community rights; and the roles of the state, international donors and non-governmental support organizations.

Integrating Three Levels of Environmental Services

Rural communities rely heavily on the natural resource base. Producers manage ecosystems with an eye toward meeting their basic needs, including food, firewood, water and spiritual well-being (Level 1); earning incomes by selling products (Level 2); and pursuing new alternatives linked to environmental services provision, such as water or power generation for urban areas, biodiversity conservation and carbon sequestration (Level 3). Relationships at each level are crucial when considering PES schemes from the perspective of rural communities.

At the first level, where relations are internal to the community and not dependent on transactions with outside actors and markets, the key concerns are the rights of access to and control over natural resources. Closely connected with these are the management norms established by communities to ensure the continued flow of basic necessities. PES mechanisms can fail or prove detrimental if they fail to incorporate an understanding of how rural communities themselves value key environmental services for their own basic subsistence, identity and spiritual well-being.

The second level has to do with the relationship between natural resource management and income-earning strategies. In seeking better entry terms or better prices on the market, management practices can and increasingly do incorporate distinct environmental attributes or services into the production process. Where traditional production practices already incorporate 'environmentally-friendly' attributes, the main effort is one of marketing to make those attributes explicit. In other cases, practices evolve to take advantage of new opportunities. Examples that reflect both situations are organic farming, shade-grown coffee, certified sustainable forestry, ecotourism and handicraft production. At this level, the main needs include marketing efforts, certification of practices and products, training and specialized technical assistance.

At the third level, outside recognition is sought for the value of environmental services such as biodiversity conservation, water provision for urban centers, carbon sequestration to mitigate climate change and other services not readily captured in a product that secures a price premium on the market. Here, the challenge is finding other compensation mechanisms that recognize and reward ecosystem management practices that guarantee environmental services of interest to outside 'consumers'. This third level is without a doubt the most complex for communities, and it can be unviable or turn into a threat if not rooted in the two previous levels. Strengthening community strategies to maintain or enhance environmental services should support the integration of these levels and enable producers to overcome hurdles at each level.

Rules for Applying Economic Instruments to Ensure Equity

The concept of payment for environmental services emerged from economists' concepts of how to internalize 'positive externalities' in the production process. Mirroring the discussion on the use of economic instruments to curb negative externalities such as pollution by internalizing costs, PES instruments aim to maintain and expand the flow of positive externalities by internalizing benefits. Possibilities include direct payments to those responsible for maintaining certain land uses, and the development or markets for certain environmental services. Taxes and charges on consumers of environmental services can be useful for mobilizing financial resources. Payments can be targeted in exchange for specific activities that ensure the provision of environmental services.

Such economic instruments can be powerful tools for achieving environmental objectives in a cost-efficient manner. But if they are to promote equity and poverty reduction, economic instruments need to be harnessed through rules that ensure that the benefits also flow to poor rural communities. These rules relate to the requirements to participate in the PES schemes. Since these schemes involve government, donor, or other non-governmental organizations' (NGOs) interventions, international agreements and national, state and local governance structures typically define the framework for applying economic instruments. In so doing, they largely determine the potential for inclusion or exclusion. When economic instruments turn out to be effective tools for strengthening the livelihoods of poor rural communities, this is usually because the governance structures ensure this outcome (IIED 2001).

In general, the rules tend to be established by more powerful and wealthy actors. Hence, an explicit and deliberate effort is required to (i) ensure the participation of rural communities and the inclusion of their interests in the rule-making process; (ii) expand, defend and secure their rights over the resource base; (iii) enhance their technical capacities and increase their market power; and (iv) strengthen their organizations.

The equity or inequity of rules is not only a matter of who receives compensation for the provision of the environmental services, but also who consumes these services and who is required to pay for them. If PES schemes create additional costs to consumers who are already in a highly disadvantaged position, they can result in greater inequity, including perverse arrangements where low-income communities end up paying large landowners for environmental services flowing from their lands.

Fashioning equitable rules often requires a negotiation process, which may include the determination of compensation levels. Traditional methods of economic valuation are often proposed, but these may not be particularly useful in many cases. Other techniques, based on consultation and deliberation, are often more appropriate for arriving at adequate PES schemes. In Australia, for instance, the combination of multiple-criteria evaluation and a citizens' jury, informed by expert opinion, has been proposed to define values and priorities for the design of mechanisms of compensation for environmental services (Land and Water Australia 2002).

Allocation: A Landscape Perspective

A landscape can be understood as 'a geographical mosaic composed of interacting ecosystems resulting from the influence of geological, topographical, soil, climatic, biotic and human interactions in a given area' (Forest Stewardship Council 2003). A landscape perspective highlights the fact that environmental services typically are generated and distributed through a great variety of land uses, often including patchworks of forests, diverse forms of agriculture, disturbed areas and human settlements (Gliessman 1998).

This perspective moves away from idyllic and romanticized concepts of 'undisturbed nature' to the heterogeneous complexity of land uses that exist in reality. It forces us to look at all components of the landscape, and at the particular features that impact — positively or negatively — on its capacity for generating environmental services. It also makes us look at the interactions among the components, which in some cases may be critical for generating those services. For instance, the conservation of plant species in a tropical forest can be fostered by cross-pollination with individuals in neighbouring agroforestry systems or agro-ecosystems (Gliessman 1998). Within a geographic mosaic, even disturbed patches of land can play a critical role in maintaining the flow of environmental services (see also Amanor, in this volume).

Landscape mosaics, by definition are multifunctional, providing multiple environmental services at the same time. By recognizing this complexity, a landscape perspective can avoid the dangers of focusing on a single environmental service, which, as in the case of monocultures, can promote transformations that impoverish rather than enhance the landscape as a whole. The generation and long-term conservation of environmental services require integrated management schemes that harmonize and value the diverse components of the landscape. This too often involves negotiation and conflict resolution mechanisms, given the different and at times conflicting demands, interests and visions of the people present in a landscape mosaic.

A crucial issue when embarking upon PES schemes in rural areas is how to build the landscape-level effort and allocate the compensation. The case studies reviewed in this chapter provide important insights and lessons on this issue. Particularly on the collective and relatively extensive landholdings of Mexico's ejidos and Brazil's extractive reserves, decisions are made regarding how to manage the delicate balance of land uses for different needs and interests, including self-consumption, collective production, harvesting for the market, raising animals, maintenance of water and fuel sources, and the location of human settlements. At the same time, decisions must be made regarding allocations among different producers and their families, taking into account their access to resources for production for self-consumption and/or marketable products, and the management changes and payments that are necessary for the compensation mechanism to work.

Allocation poses new questions: When and how should compensations be distributed? What changes are needed to reverse land degradation processes and ensure the future flow of environmental services, and how should individuals be compensated for possible lost income? What are the trade-offs of introducing changes at a larger scale, above the level of the individual farm or even the ejido, for example by swapping a forested area for one under agriculture to improve the larger landscape? Should PES schemes stipulate or provide incentives for such changes? Could expanding the scale of management allow for changes in cropping patterns that would contribute to the provision of environmental services or increase income flows? Would collaborative efforts allow for the introduction of new activities such as eco-tourism that otherwise would not be possible? All these questions point to the wide range of options for allocating resources and compensation. The communities themselves must help to make these choices over time.

Social Capital Accumulation

'Social capital' can be understood as the organizational capacities within a locality, and the ability of community members to secure resources (knowledge, public services, access to markets, etc.) as a result of engagement in social networks or other structures beyond the locality. Key elements are relations of confidence; reciprocity and exchanges; common rules, norms, and sanctions; and connections and networks (Pretty and Ward 2001). Thus understood, social capital is crucial for the provision of environmental services, since producers and land managers within a landscape mosaic need to act in a concerted fashion to ensure that provision.

Social capital accumulation is also essential to ensure that PES mechanisms effectively benefit poor rural communities. Without strong internal organization and external linkages, poor communities cannot influence the rules of PES schemes, nor can they effectively conduct struggles to expand, defend and secure their rights to the resource base. Social organization is required to negotiate successfully with intermediaries and external agents, so that their proposals contribute to the diversification and strengthening of livelihoods strategies. Social organization likewise is needed to deal with internal distribution issues and other conflicts that arise when new benefits flow to a community.

Support organizations play essential roles in these processes. Institutions or NGOs that provide technical assistance, operational support and mediation with other institutions or markets are critical to the success or failure of PES schemes. Institutions that are endogenous to the community, and outside organizations that are sensitive to local processes and that respect local decision-making, tend to favour the development of PES schemes that benefit poor rural communities.

Yet supporting institutions also can hinder appropriation by the communities. Problems can arise when intermediary organizations and communities have conflicting concepts of PES schemes. Since outside organizations usually hold the key to funds and other benefits, there is always a danger that they will try to impose their own agenda, not respecting local knowledge or the community's right to decide whether or not to enter into particular compensation mechanisms. In this regard, it is important to avoid a preconceived goal of setting up a compensation scheme, as it may turn out that this is not a viable or desirable option for some communities.

The Precondition: Communities' Rights to Natural Resources

The control and use of natural resources are determined to a large degree by property rights. Traditional conservation schemes seek to ensure the provision of environmental services by restricting the rights of rural communities to access and use natural resources. In effect, certain 'sticks' in the bundle of property rights are appropriated by the state. In recent years, the expansion of community rights has emerged as an alternative strategy. This reflects growing recognition that turning resource users into partners is a better way to ensure the provision of environmental services than seeking to restrict their access. The expansion of community rights also can be an effective way to advance poverty reduction objectives, because it puts assets into the hands of the poor. In fact, defending and expanding community rights to natural resources itself can be a form of compensation in many cases, making livelihood strategies more secure and laying the groundwork for other, complementary compensation mechanisms.

The 'bundle of sticks' that constitute property rights to a natural resource often are divided among various agents. *Access rights* include the operational right to enter into defined areas and enjoy non-extractive benefits, such as recreation activities. *Withdrawal rights* give, in addition, the right to extract different products. *Management rights* refer to determination of patterns of resource use. *Exclusion rights* confer the power to decide who else can have access and extract resources. Finally, *alienation rights* exist when holders of these other rights can transfer them to others (Schlager and Ostrom 1992).

Poor rural communities do not need to hold every stick in the bundle to internalize benefits from the flow of environmental services. But they need secure rights to at least some of the sticks. In the extractive reserves in Acre, Brazil, for example, secure access, withdrawal and exclusion rights allow communities to be recognized and compensated for their role in maintaining the ecosystem's integrity and hence the flow of environmental services (see Hall, in this volume). Management rights, as in the case of Mexico's ejidos, go a step further by giving the communities a large say in determining land uses and production options. Land redistribution programmes that convey title to the land, such as those carried out in El Salvador in the 1980s and 1990s, can expand the scope for integrating PES schemes into the livelihoods strategies of peasant communities. The expansion and defence of the property rights of poor communities can be the decisive factor both in improving the supply of environmental services and in ensuring that the poor share in the resulting stream of benefits.

The State, International Donors and Support Organizations

The state often plays a decisive role in the orientation of PES schemes. The state can expand and defend the rights of rural communities to access, use and control natural resources, or it can undermine these rights. A policy framework that revalues rural communities and the landscapes they manage can support community strategies to improve environmental practices. The state also generally defines the framework and rules for PES schemes. Since rules made by local power holders tend to exclude poor rural communities, state intervention is often needed to strengthen the participation of rural communities in rule-making processes.

International donor agencies can also play a critical role. To minimize the risk of compensation strategies leading to social exclusion or perverse environmental effects, donor-supported initiatives should build upon community perspectives and priorities, and avoid preconceived objectives. Inappropriate external 'cooperation' can actually turn into another hurdle to be overcome by communities. International donors play a positive role when they support the strengthening of social capital and negotiating platforms, which enable rural communities to participate effectively in defining PES strategies, mechanisms and ground rules.

Intermediaries at the local, national and at times international levels are needed for activities such as research, training, certification, funds management and market access. Yet support organizations also can have a negative influence. Large numbers of intermediaries can reduce the benefits received by producers and communities. Conflicts can arise when there are differing approaches to compensation strategies between support organizations and communities. Again, it is essential that support organizations respect communities' agendas and concerns, working collaboratively with local actors, acting transparently and respecting community decisions regarding management of the resources under their control.

Experiences in the Americas

The outcomes of recent PES initiatives in the Americas have been shaped by their national and local contexts, and by the interests of the different stakeholders engaged in these initiatives. Costa Rica stands out as the only country in the hemisphere with an institutionalized, state-led, national system of payments for environmental services. Mexico offers important examples in a setting where peasant and indigenous communities have substantial access to and control over natural resources. In Brazil, in contrast, access to resources is more uneven and restricted, and PES initiatives have required the expansion and innovation of the rights of communities. In El Salvador, the management of agro-ecosystems and the restoration of degraded landscapes have been particularly important. The experience of the Watershed Agricultural Programme in New York State demonstrates the importance of careful negotiations in devising PES schemes that respond to local needs. Given such diverse contexts, it would be impossible simply to copy a successful compensation scheme from one setting, and expect it to work just as well in another. Nevertheless, these experiences furnish valuable lessons that need to be taken into account in designing PES schemes that benefit rural communities.

Costa Rica: Payments for Forest Services [4]

Costa Rica's official PES scheme began in 1996, with amendments to the Forestry Law (Ley Forestal No. 7575), and grew out of prior experience with direct subsidies for the forestry sector. The system emphasizes global environmental services (biodiversity conservation and carbon sequestration), but it is funded primarily from a domestic tax on fossil fuels. Originally, four categories were eligible for payments on a per hectare basis: forest protection, forest management, reforestation and tree plantations. Between 1997 and 2002, the programme covered more than 300,000 hectares and total payments exceeded US$80 million with 70 per cent going for forest protection.

Large and medium-sized property owners were the main recipients of these payments, an outcome favoured by the emphasis on conservation, the forestry orientation of the scheme, the requirement of property titles and the use of stringent technical criteria. Over time, however, internal criticisms and pressure from indigenous and small-scale producer organizations led to more inclusive rules. The participation of indigenous reserves increased, and in 2002 agroforestry systems were made eligible for compensation. Payments for agroforestry systems — on a basis of US$0.60 per tree — began in 2003.

The notion of valuing and compensating for environmental services is also present at the local level. Unlike the official PES scheme that emphasizes global services, local initiatives focus on protecting water resources for human consumption and energy generation. They also use more flexible criteria than the national system. For instance, those eligible for payments usually include those who work and live on the land, not just landowners.

Small-scale producers participating in such initiatives generally consider the local benefits (improved water and landscapes) and the technical assistance associated with the schemes, which permit production diversification and entry into new markets, to be more valuable than the payments themselves. Sometimes, however, conflicting visions with regard to natural resource use make it difficult or impossible to establish local-level PES schemes.

Seen from the perspective of poor rural communities, the Costa Rican experience, offers several lessons:

- First, it shows the importance of broad participation in the early stages of PES schemes to ensure their long-term legitimacy and sustainability. An accelerated institutionalization of PES schemes, without adequately including the interests of small producers and indigenous communities, generates restrictions that are difficult to overcome later.
- Second, without strong and representative organizations of small producers and indigenous communities, it is difficult to ensure participation that will result in truly inclusive schemes.
- Third, the global orientation, eligibility criteria and operational rules largely determine the capacity for inclusion in the PES schemes. In some settings, greater inclusion requires seeing beyond the forest to link up with other productive activities that are central to livelihoods.
- Fourth, a broad focus on a wide range of practices for the provision of environmental services can be important for improving, diversifying and strengthening the livelihood strategies of rural communities. The impact of PES schemes can be enhanced when they promote environmentally improved productive activities such as agroforestry, agro-tourism, eco-tourism, non-timber products and sustainable agriculture.
- Finally, the incorporation of local-level perspectives, priorities and visions can empower local communities and promote participatory management.

Mexico: Community Ownership and Environmental Services[5]

The most striking feature of the Mexican context is peasant and indigenous communities' access to and control over natural resources. They control half the country's land and 80 per cent of the forests. This resource base has fostered community-based initiatives in biodiversity protection, carbon sequestration, ecotourism and environment friendly production.

In the southern state of Chiapas, for example, more than 300 farmers participate in the Scolel Té project in which they plant, on average, one hectare of their individual 4–5 hectare parcels with trees to absorb carbon in exchange for direct payments. The Paris-based International Automobile Federation, the organizer of Formula One racing events, purchased the first 5,500 tons of carbon at a price of US$10 per ton (later raised to US$12 per ton). The payments represent modest additional income for the farmers, but more important incentives are associated with the possibilities to penetrate the timber market and integrate carbon sequestration into organic coffee production or other agro-ecological initiatives.

In Oaxaca, a union of indigenous communities, known as UZACHI, which is engaged in sustainable community forestry, has made efforts to add environmental services to their production and management strategies. Different activities are integrated through participatory territorial planning tools that define areas for subsistence farming of corn and wheat; income generation products like timber; and the protection of biological diversity, soils and water. UZACHI supports crop diversification through growing mushrooms, orchids and other ornamental plants. Together with other indigenous communities and supporting NGOs, they drew up a carbon sequestration proposal for fixing 836,000 tons of carbon through silviculture and agro-silviculture systems.

Ecotourism increasingly appears as an attractive alternative for many rural communities. Various projects have shown mixed results, however, both in social and environmental terms. In Mazunte, for example, after the government issued a ban on capturing turtles, the community looked for alternative income sources and in 1992 established a 14,000 hectare Peasant Ecological Reserve and a Joint Owners Association. Seven years later, Mazunte had tourist accommodations, restaurants, businesses on the beach and four taxis. Most of the local population lived off tourism, and there was a natural cosmetics factory and a Turtle Museum. However, this very success led to environmental stresses and the neglect of conservation. Nevertheless, ecotourism can be a promising activity when integrated into other production strategies (handicrafts, natural and organic products, etc.), especially when social organization and cohesion are strong.

Mexico's community-based initiatives provide important lessons:

- First, when communities have broad access to the resource base, organizational capacity becomes the crucial factor for establishing agreements, complying with norms, managing conflicts, dealing with external actors and applying territorial management strategies for environmental services provision.
- Second, it is necessary to develop participatory territorial planning and management instruments at different scales: from the plot or farm level, up to the landscape level where it may be necessary to harmonize different land uses.
- Third, peasant and indigenous communities rely heavily on the support

of NGOs that assist with research, technical assistance, certification, seeking financial support, promotion and marketing. Yet the different visions and approaches of NGOs and communication can create conflicts.

- Finally, existing production strategies provide the most convenient starting point for meeting the demand for environmental services, through diversification (as in the case of farmers who expand their agroforestry activities for carbon sequestration or water regulation), or by means of marketing environmental services associated with their existing crops (as in the case of biodiversity-friendly shade-grown coffee). Rather than focusing on a single environmental service, communities can supply integrated services, and combine markets for environmental services with fair trade markets or solidarity markets for products of peasants and indigenous people.

Brazil: Protection with People[6]

Compared to Mexico, indigenous and peasant communities in Brazil have much less secure access to natural resources, which generates more precarious social conditions. For those reasons, the prime lessons of Brazil relate to the expansion, innovation and defence of the rights of communities.

The traditional conservation perspective, which aims to protect natural resources by excluding people, has had a major influence in Brazil. For instance, in Vale do Ribeira, the poorest region in the state of São Paulo, more than 50 per cent of the valley is being protected in an effort to preserve the Mata Atlántica coastal forest. To compensate municipalities for foregone revenues, the Ecological Tax on the Circulation of Markets and Services (ICMS) distributes a fraction of state sales tax revenues to municipalities in proportion to the area under conservation.

In 2001, Vale do Ribeira received 37 per cent of the Ecological ICMS collected in the state. Nevertheless, the municipalities in the valley consider the compensation insufficient for the livelihoods that were lost to the creation of the reserves. Barra do Turvo, a municipality that falls to a large extent within a State Park, went as so far as to ask the Governor to suspend its Ecological ICMS quota payments (amounting to some US$50,000 per month), and instead allow small producers to use degraded areas of the park.

The traditional notion of protection without people is slowly giving way to more inclusive perspectives. For instance, in Jaú National Park — a World

Heritage Site and Brazil's second largest national park — despite a law that formally forbids human settlements within national parks, the communities living inside the park had a say in the 1998 management plan, the first participatory plan for a Brazilian national park. Nevertheless, the legal status of the lands held by traditional communities within the park is not defined.

Extractive reserves represent a more inclusive face of conservation in Brazil. Instead of restricting access and usufruct rights of the forest communities, extractive reserves expand these rights and guarantee them by law. Formal recognition of the rights of the extractivist populations living within these protected areas to harvest rubber and other non-timber products is coupled with laws against forest-clearing for ranching, timber and other operations, in effect creating new exclusion rights. In the State of Acre, for example, under the Chico Mendes Law, about US$0.20 per kilogram of rubber collected is paid to rubber-tapper associations in recognition of their stewardship of the forest and role in guaranteeing environmental services.

Family-based agro-extractivist production is critical for the livelihoods of many communities in rural Brazil. In Gurupá, on the shores of the Amazon River, for example, community livelihoods are based on the extraction of timber, açaí, palmetto, and other non-timber products, and on subsistence agriculture. Such communities could benefit from PES schemes designed to improve the productivity, profitability and sustainability of their activities.

The experiences in Brazil provide further lessons:

- First, a traditional conservation focus can have negative impacts on communities dependent on access to the resource base.
- Second, expanding access and usufruct rights, and compensating communities for their stewardship role can strengthen livelihoods while guaranteeing the flow of environmental services.
- Third, the use of a wide range of compensation mechanisms geared towards supporting the productive activities that preserve or enhance environmental services provision can provide the greatest benefits.
- Finally, it is crucial to integrate environmental objectives with social and equity objectives in the design and implementation of PES schemes, to ensure that they operate in favour of communities. Public discussion and decisions on rights, responsibilities, procedures and rules can help in achieving equitable results.

El Salvador: Environmental Services from Anthropogenic Landscapes[7]

El Salvador, a country of just over 20,000 square kilometres, provides an interesting set of features relevant to the design of PES schemes. These include the predominance of anthropogenic landscapes, the influence of traditional conservation discourses, strong social organizations and a remittance-driven economy in which accelerated urbanization is accompanied by the collapse of agricultural activities in rural areas. During the 1980s and early 1990s, one-fifth of the country's territory was redistributed in a series of land reforms, broadening rural access to the resource base. The potentially beneficial effects of this greater access were undermined, however, by the profound crisis in the agricultural sector driven by falling real prices for basic grains and an unfavourable policy environment (Acevedo 1996). In this context, local initiatives are emerging that seek to identify and reinforce synergies between production, conservation and environmental restoration in rural areas.

Given that the Salvadoran landscape is dominated almost everywhere by agro-ecosystems (notably basic grains, often on degraded hillsides, and shaded-coffee on rich volcanic soils and pastures), one would expect that the idea of such synergies would attract enthusiastic public support through adequate policy instruments, including PES schemes. Paradoxically, however, government initiatives supported by the Global Environmental Facility (GEF) and the World Bank appear to prioritize the use of compensation mechanisms as financial instruments for conservation alone. In so far as the role of agro-ecosystems in the provision of global environmental services is recognized, small producers have been largely ignored. Such was the case in the GEF–World Bank funded 'Coffee and Biodiversity' project (1998–2001) that sought to conserve biodiversity on shade-grown coffee plantations. Through the certification of 'biodiversity-friendly coffee' the project sought to enable producers to fetch price premiums on alternative coffee markets, a form of compensation for the environmental services they provide. The project worked almost exclusively with medium- and large-size farms, despite the fact that small farms (under seven hectares) not only represent 80 per cent of individual farms, but also tend to have more complex agro-ecosystems than larger farms. As mixed production systems, small farms typically provide a variety of goods besides coffee — fruit, firewood, medicinal plants and forage — buffering households from the volatile price fluctuations of the international coffee market. This livelihood strategy also impedes large-scale clearing, which has been the response of many large holdings to the current crisis caused by very low coffee prices.

While donor projects and high-profile regional initiatives such as the Mesoamerican Biological Corridor focus on the global environmental service of biodiversity conservation, hydrological services command the greatest attention within the country. The widespread loss of capacity to regulate hydrological flows has contributed to droughts, flooding, severe water supply problems (including for the San Salvador metropolitan region) and reduced hydroelectric power generation (Barry and Rosa 1996). Accordingly, various domestic initiatives that contemplate compensation for environmental services have water as their main concern.

The Environmental Committee of Chalatenango, a poor province in the north of the country, provides an example of a regional-scale water initiative. The Committee is demanding that the San Salvador metropolitan region compensate Chalatenango communities in the upper Lempa River watershed for the provision of various water-related services, including hydroelectric energy, water supply and clean-up of contaminants. At a micro-regional level, the Mancomunidad La Montañona, an association of seven municipalities in the province, is developing a territorial management strategy in which environmental services play a strategic role both in creating new economic alternatives, such as ecotourism, and providing for improved water resource management.

The experiences in El Salvador provide several lessons:

- First, seeing beyond the forests, and transcending traditional conservation perspectives, is crucial for the development of PES schemes. Improved practices in agro-ecosystems can enhance environmental services, while strengthening rural livelihoods.
- Second, strong social organization is a key precondition for success. Managing heterogeneous and fragmented landscapes for environmental services requires effective collective action that can be achieved only through local negotiating processes for environmental and territorial management. Social organization is also essential for negotiating the terms of PES schemes and ensuring an equitable distribution of benefits.
- Third, favourable policy environment for rural areas is a must. Recognizing and rewarding the role of rural communities as providers of environmental services requires an institutional framework for the management of anthropogenic landscapes and the agricultural sector that goes well beyond the scope of traditional policies in both agriculture and conservation.

- Finally, genuine participation is needed to define policies and rules. Public policies and PES schemes can and should build upon local initiatives that attempt to integrate environmental objectives into development strategies.

Lessons from New York[8]

New York City's water supply system provides its 7.4 million residents — along with some 1.5 million visitors, workers and residents of neighbouring communities — with 1.4 billion gallons of water per day. The water is obtained from the Delaware, Catskill and Croton watersheds, with the first two providing about 90 per cent of the city's water supply.

In 1989, the United States Environmental Protection Agency (EPA) promulgated a new Surface Water Treatment Rule that required the filtration of public water obtained from surface sources, unless stringent public health criteria were met and an approved watershed management strategy was put in place. The estimated capital cost of a filtration system for the Catskill/Delaware watersheds was US$6 billion, with another US$200–US$300 million per year needed for operation and maintenance costs. Faced with such daunting costs, the New York City Department of Environmental Protection instead tried in 1990 to impose new land use regulations that would have severely limited agricultural opportunities and rural livelihoods in the watershed areas. This reflected a vision of the Catskills region simply as a source of water, and of farmers as a threat. In contrast, for the farmers the watershed represented livelihoods, identity and community. They organized to resist the new regulations.

The struggle was resolved through negotiations that lasted several years and involved numerous stakeholders. In the end, the City accepted agriculture as a preferred land use for the watershed, while the farmers accepted commitments to transform their practices, with support from the City, so as to guarantee a supply of clean water. The 1997 watershed management strategy that formalized this outcome includes several initiatives to support farmers' activities that improve the quality of the water supply. Its centrepiece is the Watershed Agricultural Programme, a voluntary, locally administered programme, whereby City funds are used to implement environmentally friendly practices on watershed farms. Participating farmers receive technical assistance to develop a 'Whole Farm Plan', a comprehensive strategy for controlling potential sources of pollution on the farm. New York City authorities cover the costs associated with the implementation of new practices, which often include technical and managerial assistance, new equipment, and infrastructure improvements such as concrete floors for dairy barns.

The participating farmers are eligible for other forms of compensation, too: a Conservation Reserve Enhancement Programme pays farmers to remove streamside lands from agricultural production; a Whole Farm Easement Programme compensates farmers for forgoing development rights to their land; a Natural Resources Viability Programme helps to develop markets for the products of watershed farmers and a Catskill Family Farms Cooperative taps niche markets for vegetables and other produce helping farmers to achieve economies of scale and market power.

Lessons from New York City's watershed management strategy include the following:

- First, negotiation processes involving multiple stakeholders are necessary to harmonize opposing landscape visions and establish PES schemes adapted to the priorities of those involved.
- Second, a direct payment mechanism does not necessarily represent the most favourable or appropriate form of compensation. A package of compensations, with different components, can be more effective.
- Third, the empowerment of local actors can enhance their capabilities and generate additional incentives for the provision of environmental services.
- Finally, the state can play a key role in catalyzing processes related to compensation for environmental services.

Conclusions

Compensation for environmental services is not a cure-all for rural poverty and environmental degradation. Nonetheless, PES schemes can be valuable for diversifying livelihood strategies; improving natural resource management; catalyzing shared visions that give new value to rural landscapes; and increasing public awareness of the key role played by indigenous and peasant communities in managing complex ecosystems that provide vital environmental services.

To realize their promise for reducing poverty, PES schemes need to be part of wider strategies that expand and defend the whole basket of assets in the hands of the poor; otherwise, they could fail to benefit the poor, or even have adverse effects on them. In the lexicon of the natural assets framework, this implies that compensation for environmental services — an internalization strategy — should be coupled with asset building strategies that extend the control of the communities over the resource base through redistribution and (re)appropriation, and that mobilize investments in restoring and improving the natural assets in the hands of the poor. Compensation processes can best meet the environmental objectives and serve the needs of rural communities, if they adopt a landscape perspective, taking into account the diverse components of the landscape and their interactions. PES schemes with a broad landscape perspective can catalyze local and territorial efforts to introduce more sustainable production and management practices, and facilitate building a shared vision that revalues rural landscapes managed by rural indigenous and peasant communities. Building social capital is crucial for crafting and implementing PES schemes that guarantee the provision of environmental services, benefit communities and distribute benefits fairly within the communities. Under the right conditions, PES schemes focused on poor, rural communities can help to address both environmental and socio-economic challenges.

Notes

1. This chapter draws from the report 'Compensation for Environmental Services and Rural Communities: Lessons from the Americas and Key Issues for Strengthening Community Strategies' by Herman Rosa, Susan Kandel and Leopoldo Dimas. This report synthesizes the results of the Payment for Environmental Services in the Americas project sponsored by the Ford Foundation and coordinated by PRISMA (Programa Salvadoreño de Investigación sobre Desarrollo y Medio Ambiente). The full report and the country studies on which it is based can be downloaded at http://www.prisma.org.sv.
2. For discussion of the role of small farmers in conserving agricultural biodiversity, see Brush (2003); Boyce (2004); Mann (2004).
3. On these four routes to natural asset-building, see Boyce (2003).
4. This section is based on Camacho *et al.* (2002).
5. This section is based on Burstein *et al.* (2002).
6. This section is based on Born *et al.* (2002).
7. This section is based on Herrador *et al.* (2002).
8. This section is based on Isakson (2002).

References

Acevedo, Carlos (1996) 'Structural Adjustment, the Agricultural Sector and the Peace Process', in James K. Boyce, ed., *Economic Policy for Building Peace: The Lessons of El Salvador*, Boulder: Lynne Rienner.

Barry, Deborah, and Herman Rosa (1996) 'Environmental Degradation and Development Options', In James K. Boyce, ed., *Economic Policy for Building Peace: The Lessons of El Salvador*, Boulder: Lynne Rienner.

Born, Harry Rubens, Adalberto Veríssimo, Yann Le Boulluec Alves, Manoel Pantoja da Costa, Clarissa Riccio de Carvalho, Gemima Cabral Born and Sergio Talocchi (2002)

Payment for Environmental Services: Brazil, Proyecto Pago por Servicios Ambientales en las Américas, San Salvador: PRISMA.

Boyce, James K. (2003) 'From Natural Resources to Natural Assets', in James K. Boyce and Barry G. Shelley, eds., *Natural Assets: Democratizing Environmental Ownership,* Washington, DC: Island Press, pp. 7–28.

— (2004) 'A Future for Small Farms? Biodiversity and Sustainable Agriculture', in James K. Boyce *et al.,* eds., *Egalitarian Development in the Era of Globalization: Essays in Honour of Keith Griffin.* Northampton, MA: Edward Elgar.

Brush, Stephen B. (2003) 'The Lighthouse and the Potato: Internalizing the Value of Crop Genetic Diversity', in James K. Boyce and Barry G. Shelley, eds., *Natural Assets: Democratizing Environmental Ownership,* Washington, DC: Island Press, pp. 187–205.

Burstein, J., G. Chapela, J. Aguilar and E. De León (2002) *Informe sobre la propuesta de pago por servicios ambientales en México,* Proyecto Pago por Servicios Ambientales en las Américas. San Salvador: PRISMA.

Camacho, María Antonieta, Virginia Reyes, Miriam Miranda and Olman Segura (2002) *Gestión local y participación en torno al pago por servicios ambientales: Estudios de caso en Costa Rica,* Proyecto Pago por Servicios Ambientales en las Américas, San Salvador: PRISMA.

Forest Stewardship Council (2003) *Principles and Criteria of Forest Stewardship.* Available on the worldwide web at http://www.fsc.org/fsc/how_fsc_works/policy_standards/princ_criteria.

Gliessman, Stephen R. (1998) *Agroecology: Ecological Processes in Sustainable Agriculture,* Chelsea, MI: Ann Arbor Press.

Herrador, D., L. Dimas, V. E. Méndez and O. Díaz (2002) *Pago por servicios ambientales en El Salvador,* San Salvador: PRISMA.

IIED (2001) *The Future is Now. Equity for a Small Planet,* Volume 2, International Institute for Environment and Development.

Isakson, Ryan (2002) *Payment for Environmental Services in the Catskills: A socio-economic analysis of the agricultural strategy in New York City's watershed management plan,* Proyecto Pago por Servicios Ambientales en las Américas, San Salvador: PRISMA.

Land and Water Australia (2002) 'Using Citizens' Juries for Making Decisions in Natural Resource Management', Research Project No.ANU11.

Ley Forestal No. 7575, (1996) San José, Costa Rica.

Mann, Charles (2004) *Diversity on the Farm,* New York: Ford Foundation and Amherst, MA: Political Economy Research Institute. Available at http://www.peri.umass.edu/fileadmin/pdf/Mann.pdf

Pretty, Jules and Hugh, Ward (2001) 'Social Capital and the Environment', *World Development* 29(2): 209–227.

Rosa, Herman, Susan Kandel and Leopoldo Dimas (2003) *Compensation for Environmental Services and Rural Communities: Lessons from the Americas and Key Issues for Strengthening Community Strategies,* San Salvador: PRISMA.

Schlager, Edella and Elinor Ostrom (1992) 'Property Rights Regimes and Natural Resources: A Conceptual Analysis', *Land Economics* 68: 249–262.

More than 100 million acres of forests worldwide are now certified by
the Forest Stewardship Council.
Photo credit: Forest Stewardship Council

CHAPTER 10
CERTIFICATION SYSTEMS AS TOOLS FOR NATURAL ASSET BUILDING

Michael E. Conroy

Introduction

'Certification systems' are relatively new tools that have evolved globally to encourage and reward higher levels of social and environmental responsibility — and accountability — among producers of all sorts. They have been designed primarily to alter the performance of otherwise unreachable transnational corporations in the fields of natural-resource-based production, such as forestry, agriculture, mining and tourism. This chapter explores the question of whether these systems, which have not generally been designed explicitly as poverty alleviation tools, can, in fact, assist poor people, either individually or in community-based and small-to-medium production units, to build their natural assets as a basis for sustainable livelihoods and poverty alleviation. From the point of view of the purposes of this volume, the question is whether these systems, developed largely in the global North, have become — or could become — important new international tools for alleviating poverty in diverse international contexts.

The two leading certification systems of this time, the Forest Stewardship Council™ and the Fair Trade Certified™ system, are analyzed extensively here from the point of view of their impacts upon the poor and their ability to contribute, directly and indirectly, to the alleviation of poverty through building natural assets. Emerging certification systems in tourism and mining are also examined, but to a lesser extent, because their standards have not yet been codified, although considerable movement toward that end has occurred in both cases.

The chapter concludes that the impact of certification systems on poverty depends on how they are designed and implemented. In the forestry sector the poverty alleviating benefits have been limited, relative to the apparent global sustainable use and conservation benefits that have been analyzed. In agricultural commodity trade, however, the leading certification systems have been designed from the beginning to have a greater impact on poverty alleviation, and the benefits are now increasingly well-documented. The longer-term challenge in both these cases, and in others that are emerging, is whether rapid global uptake and the 'mainstreaming' of the certification systems create further hurdles to the benefits that poor individuals and communities can reap.

Emergence of 'Certification Systems'

A major new movement is emerging in many places around the world that shows considerable promise for transforming the global incentive structure for responsible social and environmental practices with respect to the sustainable management of natural assets. Building on about two decades of previous efforts for promoting 'corporate responsibility', 'ethical trading', 'alternative trade organizations' and on long-developing but poorly-focused 'fair trade' efforts, the new movement combines the creation of global standards for sustainable practices (in both social and ecological terms) and market-based public campaigns to bring pressure upon leading corporations to adopt those standards. It can be called 'market-based voluntary corporate accountability... with teeth'.

To date the movement is best known for the successes of the Forest Stewardship Council — and its social and environmental NGO advocacy supporters — who have created major changes in the forest products industry, including huge improvements in awareness of the minimum standards that must be met to maintain a widely-recognized 'social license' to produce and sell in that sector. Certification according to the principles and criteria of the Forest Stewardship Council has become a powerful new tool for encouraging and rewarding higher levels of social and environmental responsibility in sustainable forest management in both tropical forests, and temperate and boreal forests. But the vast majority of the forests certified to date have been large-scale operations in temperate and boreal zones. What explanation can we give for the relative slowness of certification in tropical working forests and in community-scale forestry operations worldwide?

The chapter presents data on the evolution to date of forest management certification and will explore a series of hypotheses about the relatively slow development of certification in tropical forests and at the community scale, including a) the relatively low importance of 'branding' in markets for tropical forest products, b) the challenge of outright illegal logging for tropical forest markets, c) fundamental problems of aggregation, scale and species composition vis-à-vis markets in the global North, and d) the distinctive challenges of community-scale forest product processing and marketing. I then review a number of creative options that have emerged in recent years for meeting these challenges.

In a quite different form, the movement is also increasingly known for the growing success of certified fair trade[1] coffee and other products in the United States, Europe and Japan (Conroy 2001a, 2001b, 2002). At a time when real global coffee prices have been at a 100-year low, certified fair trade coffee sales have been booming, especially in the United States, reaching US$131 million in 2002 and doubling in 2003 (Murray *et al.* 2006). By mid-2005 there were over 600,000 small-scale farmers in 32 different countries on the Fair Trade Register for producers of coffee, tea and cocoa, the list of those who qualify to participate in the system.[2] Fair Trade Certified was created specifically to benefit small-scale, often impoverished coffee producers throughout the world; it can be seen as a direct sales system that provides guaranteed minimum prices that assure these coffee producers the equivalent of an agricultural 'living wage'. Yet the very success of the movement is challenging its ability to focus on these producers. There is considerable pressure to expand the eligibility of the Fair Trade Register to coffee estates and larger coffee plantations, partly to respond to the poverty of the coffee workers they employ and partly to improve the ability of the system to apply its criteria to a much larger portion of the total coffee sector.

Common Elements of 'Certification Systems', and Reasons for Corporate Participation

Regardless of the production sector, the movement combines the same basic elements:

- Negotiation of stakeholder-based principles and criteria for social and economic responsibility, including representatives of producers, communities, and social and environmental NGOs.
- Creation of a system for third-party independent certification of the fulfillment of those standards.
- Development and marketing of a 'logo' or certification seal that can be

placed on products and that indicates that the standards have been met in certified fashion.

- NGO 'markets campaigns' designed to bring pressure on leaders in the industry (working especially at the retail end of the commodity chain) to give preference to the products carrying the certification logo.
- And consumer education campaigns to raise awareness of the need to look for the logo, emphasizing the social and environmental damage being done by firms that are not certified.

The incentive for corporate participation is clear. Participation in a certification system offers companies an opportunity to reduce the risk of criticism of the social and environmental characteristics of the products that they process and sell (Conroy 2001a). With global branding now the most dynamic force in the contemporary marketplace, every dollar invested in increased global recognition increases the vulnerability of branded firms to a well-placed, well-orchestrated campaign directed at the social and environmental characteristics of the products they sell. As with all other risk-reduction strategies, firms have learned that they must be prepared to pay for the risk reduction. Moreover, they often achieve important market advantages by making the socially responsible choice public, especially when it precedes announcements of the same sort by their competitors. Over time, given the presence of continued risk of the 'discovery' of inappropriate practices in the value chains of firms in an industry, the minimum standards that they must meet tend to rise. And the only assurance of validation of improved practices comes through independent assessment and certification.

Not surprisingly, the movement has its critics on both right and left. From the political left, some wonder whether using the market to induce change in corporate behaviour represents an inappropriate endorsement of the corporate market economy. Others question whether the movement achieves little more than temporary 'green washing' of the corporations without changing their fundamental practices. From the political right, critics argue that markets campaigns linked to standards imposed on industry are little more than 'an extortion scheme with socially-redeeming significance' (Rushford 2001: 41). But Gereffi *et al.* (2001) suggest that what has evolved here is a new form of global governance that reaches areas where neither national nor international governance has previously penetrated.

Certification, Asset-building and Poverty Alleviation

Imagine the potential if there emerged a process by which broad coalitions of NGOs agreed upon a set of strategies for moving major natural-asset-based firms towards fundamentally higher standards for their social and environmental practices. What if they found ways of presenting credible evidence to the public at large, to financial markets, and to the insurance industry that industry leaders were failing to adopt practices that would seem reasonable to a concerned non-technical majority of consumers? And what if they mapped out the value chain for those products, identifying the points of greatest leverage for a campaign to get 'downstream' firms to place pressure on 'upstream' firms to improve the quality of their production practices? It is conceivable that such leverage could change the production practices of the suppliers. Fifteen years ago, few would have imagined that this was possible.

Today, few deny that it is happening, to the great consternation of major firms all along the value chain. In fact, it is increasingly clear that new certification standards are driven less and less by sheer consumer demand (requiring huge investments in consumer education). Instead they are driven ever more by the acceptance by producing firms of the standards embodied in certification systems as the minimal indicators of product quality needed to assure investors, boards of directors and subsequent customers in the value chain, especially retailers, of the ability of the products to remain free of criticism. That is, certification systems are redefining the business-to-business relationships in value chains in ways that are not directly linked to day-to-day consumer demand.

The theoretical bases for building natural assets have been explored by Boyce (2001); Boyce and Pastor (2001); and Boyce and Shelley (2003). Boyce notes that the application of asset-building strategies (Sherraden 1992; Oliver and Shapiro 1995) to natural assets is compelling because 'strategies for building natural assets in the hands of low-income individuals and communities can simultaneously advance the goals of poverty reduction, environmental protection and environmental justice' (2001: 268). It countermands the conventional wisdom that the poor face an inescapable tradeoff between higher incomes and a better environment. And building natural assets can contribute not only increased income but also non-income benefits such as health and environmental quality.

Boyce proposes that there are four main routes to increase the amount and value of natural assets in the hands of the poor (2001: 274): a) investment in, or improvement of, the natural resources to which the poor already have access; b) redistribution of natural resources from others to the poor; c) internalization of the benefits (and avoidance of external costs) associated with the natural resources that affect the poor; and d) appropriation of rights of access for the poor to open-access resources. They recognize that building natural assets may require, or may contribute to, building social or community assets, including the community organizations that bring benefits far beyond the economic benefits of turning natural resources into natural assets in the hands of the poor.

From an economic perspective, certification systems can be seen as constituting systems designed to internalize (and, hopefully, monetize) both the economic benefits associated with more sustainable production techniques (such as the biodiversity-conserving benefits of improved forest management) and the negative economic consequences of unsustainable production — such as the water-polluting consequences of inadequate protection for stream beds and shorelines (Boyce and Pastor, 2001). There is a rapidly growing body of formal and informal analysis of certification systems that provides far more basis now for assessing their impacts and implications than was possible even a couple years ago. This literature suggests that building natural assets may require, and is facilitated by, social and political processes well beyond those captured by the strictly economic analyses.

From a governance perspective, certification systems may be seen as attempts to create non-state market-driven systems to govern the use of natural resources (Cashore 2002: 1; Cashore *et al.* 2004). And from a sociological perspective, certification systems create new commodity networks that transform the producer-consumer chain in ways that build on progressive ideas and practices related to trust, equality, and global responsibility (Raynolds 2002: 1).

These perspectives provide an expanded, overlapping framework from which to evaluate the ability of these systems to build the natural assets for the poor. Evaluation of the impact of certification systems requires two levels of analysis: broad and narrow. We can ask broad framework questions at the macro-economic and macro-social level:

- *Context*: Does the system alter the implicit or explicit regulatory context within which natural resource management decisions are being made?
- *Internalization*: Does it alter the ability of natural asset managers to internalize external benefits and costs?
- *Market Access*: Does it change the access that producers have to markets that value that internalization?

But it is important, as well, to ask the 'narrow' framework questions that focus on issues directly linked to impoverished and disempowered people and communities:

- *Minimal Entry Level*: Does the certification system specifically privilege or provide benefits for small-scale, community-based, or otherwise disempowered producers?
- *Minimal Impact Level*: Are the changes in context designed to improve the ability of impoverished or disempowered people and communities to develop sustainable livelihoods?
- *Scalability*: Can the impacts be scaled-up so that large numbers of small-scale producers are capable of benefiting?
- *Costs*: Are the actual (or most likely) costs of participation reasonable for small-scale and impoverished producers?

Experiences in Certified Forestry

The building of the Forest Stewardship Council's (FSC) certification system for sustainable forest management practices began in 1993, with the creation of the FSC itself. Developed principally by the World Wildlife Fund and other environmental NGOs, it gained the cooperation of a number of larger European forest products firms, some smaller US forest products firms and an array of social development NGOs from the global North and South. Its initial impetus came from recognition of the need to reduce the destruction of tropical forests (Mantyranta 2002, 17). The motivation for creating a system that continued to permit harvesting of tropical timber, but only if it was under sustainable harvest conditions, was significant. European NGOs began to realize that they could not continue to place effective pressure on retail markets for tropical hardwoods that came from badly-managed tropical forests unless they were able to specify a preferred set of forest management practices which they would consider acceptable. An effective reduction in the imports of tropical hardwoods into Europe during the late 1980s was generating complaints from the global South that apparently-well-intentioned boycotts against all tropical hardwoods were damaging the development potential of countries exporting those hardwoods, without any opportunity for meeting a reasonable set of standards.

The FSC organization was deliberately structured in a concertedly democratic manner. Each of three 'chambers', economic, social and environmental, was given equal representation in key decision-making; and each of those chambers was divided into equal components drawn from and representing the interests of the global South and the global North. A broad set of global principles and criteria for sustainable forest management were negotiated over a period of several years. Though drawing on scientific bases, the resulting standards were primarily a political creation. They were, in reality, the highest standards for social and environmental performance that the social and environmental groups could convince the industry representatives to accept. Local adaptations of the global standards have been approved for nine countries, they continue to be negotiated to this day in some 30 other countries; but certification is underway in more than 60 countries on the basis of the 'generic' international standards that were concluded in the mid-1990s and that are reinterpreted and modified on a continuing basis.[3]

Figure 10.1: Logo of the Forest Stewardship Council

The FSC's 10 broad guiding principles, presented in a box here, involve both social and environmental criteria. Though they might appear quite simple and reasonable from a non-forester's perspective, they represented, when first approved and disseminated, dramatic changes in the rules that the forest products industry would be asked to follow, both in the North and in the South (FSC-US 2003).

In the 10 years that have passed since its creation, the FSC has had success that is considered remarkable — even startling — to most observers. By mid-2005 FSC had certified the forest management of nearly 54 million hectares (135.9 million acres), roughly 10 per cent of the world's working forests. The rate of growth in certified acres remained higher than 50 per cent per year. More than 3850 wood processing firms had established chain-of-custody certification under the FSC, assuring consumers that products that reach the market with an FSC label can be traced back to FSC-certified forests. FSC initiatives and standard-setting exercises were underway in more than 43 countries. And there were more than 20,000 forest products in global markets that carry FSC certification.[4]

PRINCIPLES OF THE FOREST STEWARDSHIP COUNCIL

1. *Compliance with Laws and FSC Principles.* Forest management shall respect all applicable laws of the country in which they occur, and international treaties and agreements to which the country is a signatory, and comply with all FSC principles and criteria.
2. *Tenure and Use Rights and Responsibilities.* Long-term tenure and use rights to the land and forest resources shall be clearly defined, documented and legally established.
3. *Indigenous Peoples' Rights.* The legal and customary rights of indigenous peoples to own, use and manage their lands, territories and resources shall be recognized and respected.
4. *Community Relations and Worker's Rights.* Forest management operations shall maintain or enhance the long-term social and economic well-being of forest workers and local communities.
5. *Benefits from the Forest.* Forest management operations shall encourage the efficient use of the forest's multiple products and services to ensure economic viability and a wide range of environmental and social benefits.
6. *Environmental Impact.* Forest management shall conserve biological diversity and its associated values, water resources, soils, and unique and fragile ecosystems and landscapes, and, by so doing, maintain the ecological functions and the integrity of the forest.
7. *Management Plan.* A management plan — appropriate to the scale and intensity of the operations — shall be written, implemented and kept up to date. The long-term objectives of management, and the means of achieving them, shall be clearly stated.
8. *Monitoring and Assessment.* Monitoring shall be conducted — appropriate to the scale and intensity of forest management — to assess the condition of the forest, yields of forest products, chain of custody, management activities and their social and environmental impacts.
9. *Maintenance of High Conservation Value Forests.* Management activities in high conservation value forests shall maintain or enhance the attributes that define such forests. Decisions regarding high conservation value forests shall always be considered in the context of a precautionary approach.
10. *Plantations.* Plantations shall be planned and managed in accordance with principles and criteria 1–9, and principle 10 and its criteria. While plantations can provide an array of social and economic benefits, and can contribute to satisfying the world's needs for forest products, they should complement the management of, reduce pressures on, and promote the restoration and conservation of natural forests.

Ample anecdotal evidence suggests that the demand for FSC-certified timber for dimension lumber and paper products is now many times greater than the supply. Economic theory would suggest that a price premium would arise; and there is, again, anecdotal evidence that significant price premia are being paid, especially to those suppliers who can provide large quantities to major buyers. It is extremely difficult, however, to gather systematic data on price premia for the simple reason that it is not in the interest of either the supplier or the purchaser to admit that price premia are being paid. The mills and manufacturers who buy FSC-certified timber are constantly seeking to obtain the lowest possible price; so they won't publicly offer to pay price premia. Sellers of certified timber prefer not to publicize the availability of a premium because they don't want to see the premium disappear as more sellers enter the market. Off-the-record discussions with both sides indicate that the price premium comes in the form of both greater assurance of access to markets and, in a large number of cases, actual cash price premia that are being paid quietly and consistently.

Of equal importance to the evaluation of the impact of the FSC, perhaps, is the fact that those firms that have resisted the FSC standards have been forced to create alternative 'standards' which represent, in most cases, significant improvements in their own environmental management of forests, even when they don't reach the 'gold standard' established by the FSC. The Sustainable Forestry Initiative of the American Forest and Paper Association is one example (http://www.aboutsfi.org/). The Programme for the Endorsement of Forest Certification (formerly the Pan-European Forest Certification system) is another (http://www.pefc.org/internet/html/about_pefc.htm). In other words, FSC's influence on sustainable forest management has not simply been through its own rule development. FSC has also forced non-FSC companies to create less-restrictive, less-demanding competing systems that now compete with the FSC for the minds and hearts of consumers, financiers, stockholders and insurers. These continue to evolve, quite rapidly, in directions that are positive for more sustainable management of forests (Cashore *et al.* 2004).

Benefits for the Poor

The more successfully a system challenges the status quo, the more likely it is that it will be criticized by those who question the direction in which it is moving. In the paragraphs that follow, we look at some of the principal criticisms of the development of the FSC system from the point of view of its relevance to building natural assets to reduce poverty and injustice.

One of the broadest critiques of the FSC relates to the fact that the greatest successes of the FSC to date have occurred *not* in the tropical regions for which the system was initially designed but rather in the temperate and boreal forests of the global North. Less than 20 per cent of the total acreage certified by the FSC through the beginning of 2002 was located in the global South (Atyi and Simula 2002). Similarly, only 12 per cent of the total number of forest management certificates had been earned by *campesino* communities or indigenous peoples organizations, and they represent only 3 per cent of the total area certified (van Dam 2002). The conclusion reached by van Dam (2002: 4) is that 'It is therefore clear that, despite the declared intentions at the start when the FSC was first created, forest certification has ended up benefiting the richer countries, large firms, and temperate and boreal forests (rather than tropical forests).'

There are several counter-arguments. First, there is little doubt that the forest management practices in place in Europe and in some parts of the United States, based on long histories of environmental campaigning and on local and national legislation, made it easier for the forest management firms in those locations to meet FSC standards earlier, and with less effort, than in places where the *de facto* legal requirements were less demanding. It is also true that larger-scale brand-name Northern forest products companies have been the explicit focus of the markets campaigns of environmental and social NGOs in the global North. Both of these factors may have inadvertently shaped the pattern of early success in the forest management certification movement.

Second, a growing body of evidence suggests that low-income forest communities derive considerable benefits from engaging in FSC certification efforts, even if their aspirations for premium prices and greater market access are not fully met. A recent study documents, for example, that approximately 50 community forestry enterprises that have achieved FSC certification worldwide have benefitted on several levels (Molnar 2003; Rickenbach 2002):

- Certification has given greater voice to indigenous groups historically left out of forest policy deliberations.
- Many communities have re-invented their businesses, enhanced their products and established new partnerships through the certification movement.
- FSC standard setting, under international supervision, has raised greater attention to forest tenure and livelihood rights, conditions of employment, and worker health and safety than had been achievable under prior processes.

- There have been major benefits for communities in industrial concession areas, especially with respect to community relations and worker's rights.
- And in some places, as in Bolivia, communities benefit from certification as a substitute for governmental audits and controls over their access to public forestlands.

The challenges for community-level certified forests nonetheless remain striking (Molnar 2003). The costs of initial certification assessments and annual auditing are especially high, relative to potential benefits, for communities that are small and/or remote. The costs of changing forest management practices to meet certification guidelines are, in some cases, quite expensive; and they represent investments with uncertain payoffs, given the limited price premia being found by community based or small-scale certified enterprises. As plantation certification continues to expand, the price competitiveness of small-scale and community enterprises may diminish unless they are able to implement local value-adding processing of the timber, creating products of higher value that generate more local employment.

Forest management certification cannot provide a definitive solution to the issues of tenure reform, violation of indigenous rights, or perverse incentives or subsidies that encourage over-harvesting; although the incorporation of these dimensions into the principles and criteria for FSC certification has been used extensively by communities to strengthen their tenure and rights demands (Ford Foundation 2002). Studies of community-based forest enterprises in Sweden and Canada illustrate that the strongest benefits from certification are reaped by communities that already have secure title and access, developmental support and quality natural assets (Meek 2001). The communities with lowest initial levels of social, natural and physical capital derived the least benefit from certification.

The narrow issue at play here is whether the FSC should focus its collective energy on promoting small-scale and community-based certification. This was a major element of contention during the FSC's early years, when local forest community advocates and community enterprise supporters, especially in places like Mexico where the FSC was headquartered until 2003, derided the decisions of the FSC to focus on expanding total certified acreage even if that meant giving priority to large-scale certifications of natural forests and plantations. In retrospect, it is relatively easy to assert, but difficult to demonstrate, that the resulting changes in global perceptions of the standards that need to be applied to the management of the world's forests could have been achieved if the FSC had focused primarily on certification for the benefit of small-scale, community-based, or other impoverished natural resource owners. But without rapid increases in the supply of certified forest products from temperate and boreal forests, it is quiet unlikely that major retailers would have committed to giving preference to certified forest products. And the extension of benefits to tropical forests, though more difficult, is beginning to appear on a number of fronts, as discussed next.

The broader issue is whether certification per se can offset the full range of market disadvantages faced by small-scale, low-technology community enterprises in a global forest products market increasingly dominated by large-scale or plantation-based timber supply and manufacturing operations. There is ample anecdotal evidence, and some systematic evidence, that certification does alter the context within which community-based forest enterprises operate, and that it can provide access to markets where price premia are paid, but that organizational changes, technology enhancement, skill-level development and quality control improvement are necessary to take advantage of the certified markets (Ford Foundation 2002). It would be inappropriate to ask the certification institutions, such as the FSC, to be responsible for all these local improvements; but it may be quite appropriate, and necessary, to expect that national and multilateral development programmes that seek to use certification would focus on the full array of dimensions needed to take advantage of the tool.

A related concern is the suggestion that no mechanism exists for 'fair trade' pricing of forest products certified to the highest social and environmental standards. As noted by van Dam (2002: 6), certification implies that the producer takes on rigorous commitments to respect international standards that generate external environmental benefits for the rest of the world, but consumers make no commitments to pay for those benefits. A proposal floated in the United Kingdom, discussed below, calls attention to this dilemma and may provide a payment mechanism that would assure certified forest land owners the premium needed to provide the incentive for certification itself.

Experiences with Certified Fair Trade Coffee

Certified Fair Trade coffee and other products represent a kind of certification system that has been designed from the outset to focus on the poor, small-scale producers and workers. Fair trade certification systems differ substantially from the older and broader variety of fair trade as practiced by alternative trade organizations (ATOs) and ethical trade initiatives (ETIs) (Tallontire 2002: 13). ATOs are largely firms, often not-for-profit, that source from developing countries and sell directly to ethically-motivated consumers. They assert — and seek to assure consumers — that their trading relations are 'fairer' than those of commercial traders in similar products. There are, however, no common standards covering pricing and other relations between those well-intentioned traders and the people or communities from whom they purchase. They are also distinct from ETIs, more common in Europe, which combine the efforts of large-scale commercial firms, NGOs and trade unions to determine a set of standards for workers employed by producers of all sizes. However, the gap between certification and the ETIs may narrow in the future.

Certified fair trade emerged as a successor to the ATOs, partly because the demand that ATOs could generate for the products they were selling never exceeded miniscule portions of the supply of the products, and partly because confusion was caused by the varying standards and procedures used by ATOs. As noted on the website of Fairtrade Labeling Organizations International, the international association of certified fair trade groups:

In order to generate greater sales on Fairtrade[5] terms for the benefit of many more disadvantaged and marginalised producers, it was important to get commercial manufacturers involved, and to get Fairtrade into the supermarket where most people do their shopping. As long as manufacturers agreed to buy from registered suppliers according to Fairtrade criteria, their products could carry a Fairtrade seal of approval. In 1988, the Netherlands became the first country to launch the Fairtrade consumer guarantee. Today there are labeling initiatives in 17 countries, mainly in Europe, but also North America and Japan, and the products range now includes coffee, drinking chocolate, chocolate bars, orange juice, tea, honey, sugar and bananas. On sale in most major European supermarket chains, Fairtrade is now available to a much wider public with some Fairtrade products achieving 10% of national market share. (http://www.fairtrade.net/)

Benefits for the Poor

To receive the fair trade seal of approval, coffee roasters must pay a minimum of US$1.26 per pound to producers, at the site of production, for dry, unroasted coffee beans (and US$1.41 if they are also certified organic). For most of the past 10 years that price has been well above the commodity 'C' price for coffee in New York, at which most coffee is bought and sold (Conroy 2002). During the period from 2000 to 2004, when prices fell to historic lows, the effective fair trade price was double the market commodity price; and, according to anecdotal evidence from some places in Central America, nearly three times the prices actually received by farmers from commercial brokers (www.transfairusa.org). Comparable minimum price guarantees have been negotiated for cocoa, tea, bananas, sugar and a number of other fruits.

Figure 10.2: Certified Fair Trade Seal

Certified fair trade must meet other conditions as well. Membership on the Fair Trade Registry of producers is available only to very small-scale producers organized in democratically-managed cooperatives, or, in the case of tea and banana plantations to those that have well-established worker-management agreements. And they must commit to improved environmental management of their farms, with strong price incentives for moving to certified organic production. To qualify for the certified fair trade label, buyers must agree to provide payment of a significant share (up to 60 per cent) of the purchase price of the coffee at the moment of purchase, if the farmers request it, rather than holding the products until they are sold and paying only after they have been sold. Buyers are also encouraged to establish long-term purchasing arrangements with their coffee producers to increase the stability of income flows.

An important dimension of fair trade certification that makes it attractive to small-scale producers is the fact that the costs of registry, assessment and monitoring are borne by the system, not by the producers. The 17 national affiliates of the Fairtrade Labeling Organizations International (FLO) levy a 'labelling fee' of approximately US$0.10 per pound for each pound of coffee that carries the Fair Trade label, and comparable labelling fees for other products. Worldwide, that presently generates several million dollars in annual revenues that cover much of the administrative costs of the system.[6] In the case of organic production, however, certification is not costless to the producer. In Mexico, for example, the cost of organic certification to international standards includes a US$250 yearly fee, plus the travel costs of inspectors each year (US$400–500), and a fee of 0.5 per cent of the wholesale price of the coffee for the use of the organic label.

Using certified fair trade coffee as an example, the benefits to participating producers would appear, at first, to be obvious. Doubling the price for that coffee which is placed in fair trade markets should generate direct and immediate benefits for the producers; and the available evidence suggests that this is generally true (Boot et al. 2003). There is, however, new recent information that suggests that fair trade processes have considerably broader sets of impacts upon the coffee producers who are able to participate in fair trade markets (Murray et al. 2004). According to Murray et al. (2003) case studies of the impact of participation in fair trade marketing by nine cooperatives with total membership in excess of 20,000 coffee producers tend to support the following conclusions:

• Fair Trade has raised family incomes of those who participate in Fair Trade markets, relative to those who do not; it has also generated family benefits from the social development projects organized by their cooperatives with part of the price premium. The benefits included small credit programmes for family emergencies, training that has facilitated diversifying sources of income and marketing assistance to develop alternative sources of income.
• Fair Trade has promoted enhanced family stability through new employment opportunities, increasing employment for additional family members (especially when the coffee is also produced organically, which requires additional family labour) and lessening the tendency to migrate from the coffee producing regions for members of the families.
• Fair Trade has promoted community-level benefits, including the strengthening of social networks, improved community health and diversification of local economic opportunities.
• Fair Trade appears to have strengthened democratic institutions and the empowerment of poor people in the coffee growing regions where it is

most concentrated; for continued presence on the fair trade registry of producers requires monitoring visits, and some cooperatives have been de-certified when members complained that internal practices had lost their democratic nature.

- The international recognition brought by Fair Trade seems to have conferred increased credibility for the producer organizations among government and other external organizations, including improved access to financial resources for developing the processing facilities for the coffee.

- Finally, a commonly reported benefit has been an increase in self-esteem among the coffee producers themselves, as well as renewed pride in coffee farming as a sustainable livelihood.

Challenges to Fair Trade Certification

Critics of fair trade processes often confuse the older, less-well-specified fair trade efforts with those that have relatively clear standards and procedures. But some of their critiques ring true, nonetheless.

Certified fair trade may be self-limiting in terms of market access because of contradictions in its own internal goals. Certified fair trade limits itself, by current rules, to the smallest producers and their cooperatives. Some coffee wholesale buyers and roasters have argued that this does not generate the highest quality coffee, nor is it quite likely to provide coverage of a significant share of the total world supply of coffee. Total sales of certified fair trade coffee in 2002 approximated 3.0 per cent of total coffee trade; though less than 20 per cent of the coffee produced by farmers on the registry was sold through fair trade markets. The sales of all fair trade products in 1999, both certified and not certified, was estimated at US$400 million, or approximately 0.01 per cent of global trade (Littrell and Dickson 1999).

A second criticism in that fair trade certification reinforces a reformist approach to globalization by encouraging the consumption of products shipped long distances rather than those that are locally produced (Tallontire 2002: 21). The question is largely trivial in the case of coffee, since there is virtually no coffee produced in the global North; but it is illustrative of competing agendas. Reforming the trade process by improving the prices received by some small proportion (at present) of the producers in those markets may give legitimacy to trade, which some believe will never be fundamentally more equitable. And 'green washing' the images of major trans-national corporations, by giving them credibility on the basis of fair trade in a very small proportion of their purchases, may have a similar effect.

The counter argument is that fair-trade pricing, and ultimately sustainable-production pricing, may represent the most important example of an approach that could bring greater equity to fundamentally inequitable trading relations. If producer groups worldwide were to build alliances with international NGOs for the negotiation of 'fair, long term, sustainable prices', the inequities inherent in the monopsonistic purchasing at both local and international levels might be partially offset. Consumers, financiers, stockholders and insurers become the ultimate court of financial appeal for the appropriateness of these practices. Whether their motivation is altruistic or fear of NGO advocacy, firms can reap tangible economic benefits from fair-trade pricing over the long run.

Ecotourism Certification

Few industries are more dependent on the natural assets of local economies than tourism. And few industries have attempted to compete on the basis of environmental sensitivity more than the tourism industry, especially the niche component generally called 'ecotourism'. Recent research on certification systems in tourism has found that around the world in 2000 there were no fewer than 260 programmes or voluntary initiatives, and some 100-plus eco-labelling and certification programmes offering logos, seals of approval, or awards to illustrate superior tourism practices (Honey 2002).

Ecotourism today can be subdivided into three alternative tendencies, according to Honey (2002: 6–7):

a) 'Ecotourism lite' such as programmes to install water-saving showers and to encourage tourists to lessen the laundering of their sheets and towels.
b) 'Green washing' of projects that merely use environmental and ecological language in their advertising.
c) And authentic ecotourism, closely related to concepts of sustainable development, which involves social, cultural, political, ecological and economic effects of tourism, with special attention to local communities.

In her pathbreaking earlier work, Martha Honey (1999: 21–26) defined this authentic ecotourism to have eight characteristics:

- It involves travel to natural areas.
- It minimizes the impact of travellers' presence.
- It builds environmental awareness.
- It provides direct financial benefits for conservation.
- It provides financial benefits and empowerment for local communities.
- It respects local culture.
- It is sensitive to the host country's political environment and social climate.
- It supports human rights and international labour agreements.

A November 2000 conference at the Mohonk Mountain House, outside New York City, focused on creating a set of global standards for certification of authentic sustainable tourism and ecotourism. Participants in that meeting, representing a wide range of industry and NGO stakeholders, set about crafting an initial framework now known as the 'Mohonk Principles for Sustainable Tourism and Ecotourism' (Honey and Rome 2001). The conference participants delegated to the Rainforest Alliance the task of conducting a set of global negotiations on how the Mohonk Principles might be communicated widely, broadened or sharpened as necessary, and made an element of a global system for determining whether claims of sustainability could be tested against a set of well-developed standards.

In 2003, the Rainforest Alliance released the results of two years of deliberations, including discussion at the World Ecotourism Summit held in Quebec City in May 2002.[7] The shape of the recommended global system has the following characteristics (Sanabria 2002, 2003):

- A new Sustainable Tourism Stewardship Council (STSC) will be proposed as a global institution for developing and certifying compliance with a full set of multi-stakeholder standards for Sustainable Tourism.
- The standards for Sustainable Ecotourism will include fulfillment of all those required for tourism in general, but will also carry more stringent social, educational and community-involvement requirements.
- Given the large existing number of tourism certification programmes, some of which are considered to be excellent; the STSC would focus on accrediting existing programmes that meet the highest standards that will be set (implicitly, disaccrediting others).
- The STSC would begin as an international network, based on national and regional tourism initiatives already in place; it would then lead to the creation of an STSC Association, which would be an international

office designed to facilitate marketing, training and information sharing among existing certification schemes.

- STSC accreditation would then provide a basis for identifying and distinguishing to tourism mass marketers and consumers those facilities around the world that best fulfill the negotiated set of standards for ecotourism.

Whether this effort will provide significant benefits for communities will depend on the nature of the system that evolves and its costs. If a system emerges that is analogous to certified fair trade, where the principal costs of certification are financed by labelling fees paid by consumers and borne by the accreditation agency, there could be significant opportunities. It is not very likely that accreditation alone would counter all the structural obstacles faced by community-based ecotourism operations. But standards that are global, that could be reflected easily on the websites through which an rapidly-increasing portion of all ecotourism is sold, and that create a context where major operators would have an incentive to involve local communities in tangible ways, could assist with the development of sustainable livelihoods in those communities based on natural assets.

Certification of Mining Operations

There is a long history of organizing to discourage mining companies from the most egregious of their environmentally damaging practices. In recent years, some of the most effective work has been done through the Mineral Policy Centre, in Washington DC, which has developed a series of guidebooks for local communities faced with mining problems, whether it is the proposed opening of mines, mitigation of environmental damages during mine production, expansion of mines, or the closing down of mines with attendant problems of reclamation and continuing damage from tailings (http://www.earthworksaction.org/).

In 2000, the World Mining Conference, organized among mining and natural resource ministers worldwide, dedicated nearly a quarter of its annual meeting to the question of whether the world needed a common global mining certification system and whether this should be developed and supported by governments. The mining industry had begun to respond to growing concerns over its social and environmental legacy in the previous year by organizing a three-year multi-million dollar inquiry, called *Mining, Minerals and Sustainable Development*, that released its final report at the 2002 World Summit on Sustainable Development in Johannesburg (MMSD

2002). The report recognized that the mining industry has not been sufficiently responsive to public calls for improved social and environmental stewardship and that it must reform its practices if it wishes to continue to obtain the social license to function. Fundamentally defensive in stressing the critical need for mineral products and the benefits mining brings to local communities, the report nonetheless admitted that community issues require a level of planning that 'has too often not been achieved', that issues of managing waste from mines remain 'unresolved' and that in mining 'there are often problems and disagreement around issues such as compensation, resettlement, land claims of indigenous peoples and protected areas'.

The only discussion of certification during the three-year MMSD process focused on how it 'couldn't work in the mining sector because there would always be too many small-scale producers who would never comply' (personal communication, 2002). Follow-up to that meeting has included the creation of the International Council on Mining and Minerals (www.icmm.com), which continues to provide a forum for debate among industry leaders, but without much outside input, on the nature of the industry's responses to continuing challenges to its social and environmental responsibility.

Serious discussion of the creation of a global system for establishing mining standards and certifying mining practices began in 2001, through a loosely-organized global network of mining advocacy groups. Based on a meeting of many of the members of this network in 2002, a Global Mining Campaign Network began discussions with several leading mining firms that expressed interest in playing a leading role in building credibility for efforts by the mining industry.[8] Recognizing that most mineral products have no retail markets, the Global Mining Campaign is now launching a campaign focused on mining practices for gold and silver, which can be linked to major leading jewelry and watch-making firms.[9]

Earthworks, the NGO successor to the Mineral Policy Centre, produced and released in early 2005 a draft set of guidelines for responsible sourcing of gold and silver (Miranda et al. 2005). And some members of the mining industry responded positively to these guidelines as a starting point for conversations. For the NGO community, this represents a first opportunity to begin to clean up the full mining value chain by exercising pressure from the retail end, backed by the threat of NGO markets campaigns against gold and silver, and against leading name-brand firms if no progress is made.

While the link to environmental quality is clear, the impact on local communities and poverty is not. Will the standards call for greatly reduced mining, focusing on the use of 'above ground' stocks of gold and silver, including those stored in bank vaults? If so, the employment impacts on existing mining communities could be severe. Will the standards favour mining practices in the global North, rather than improving those of the global South, creating new barriers to trade? And what will be done to affect the myriad unbranded small-scale mining operations in the global South?

Summary of Potential Impacts of Certification on Poverty

The potential contributions of existing and emerging certification systems to poverty alleviation, in terms of the questions posed at the beginning of this chapter, are summarized in Table 10.1.

Table 10.1: Criteria for Assuring that Certification Systems Reduce Poverty

Fundamental Dimensions	Certification System			
	FSC	Fair Trade	Tourism	Mining
Macro Dimensions				
Context	Strong	Weak	Strong	Strong
Internalization	Strong	Weak	Strong	Weak
Market access	Strong	Strong	Not clear yet	Not clear yet
Micro Dimensions				
Minimal entry	Weak	Strong	Weak	Weak
Minimal impact	Weak	Strong	Weak	Weak
Scalability	Strong	Strong	Not clear yet	Not clear yet
Costs	Weak	Strong	Not clear yet	Not clear yet

At the beginning of this chapter, the potential ways in which certification systems can promote poverty reduction were divided into the following 'macro' and 'micro' dimensions:

Macro dimensions:

- *Context*: Does the system alter the implicit or explicit regulatory context within which natural resource management decisions are being made?
- *Internalization*: Does it alter the ability of natural asset managers to internalize external benefits and costs?
- *Market Access*: Does it change the access that producers have to markets that value that internalization?

Micro dimensions:

- *Minimal Entry Level*: Does the certification system specifically privilege or provide benefits for small-scale, community-based, or otherwise disempowered producers?
- *Minimal Impact Level*: Are the changes in context designed to improve the ability of impoverished or disempowered people and communities to develop sustainable livelihoods?
- *Scalability*: Can the impacts be scaled-up so that large numbers of small-scale producers are capable of benefiting?
- *Costs*: Are the actual (or most likely) costs of participation reasonable for small-scale and impoverished producers?

The FSC exhibits strong characteristics on the 'macro' level, largely because it has been negotiated among producers, NGOs and industry representatives to transform fundamentally the nature of sustainable production and conservation in the industry. It is weak, however, on the 'micro' dimensions, other than scalability; and its direct poverty-alleviating effects are as limited in theory as they seem to have been in practice. Certified fair trade, on the other hand, was developed explicitly to provide direct market access for small-scale, often impoverished producers; so its strongest characteristics are the micro-dimensions needed to assure that poverty is alleviated through the system.

Whether new certification systems for sustainable tourism and ecotourism, and for the responsible sourcing of minerals, develop into strong tools for poverty reduction will depend on the specifics of the systems that emerge. In both cases, there are grounds for believing that they *could* become effective tools for poverty alleviation; whether the ongoing negotiations will take them in that direction remains to be seen.

Responses to the Challenges

A number of interesting responses are emerging to the challenges to certification systems from the point of view of their ability to provide significant improvements in asset building for small-scale and impoverished producers. Although developed for individual certification systems, their applicability may extend to others.

Efforts to reduce the costs of certification for small-scale timber operations are advancing rapidly in the US Midwest. The Minneapolis-based Community Forestry Resource Centre is experimenting with a form of umbrella-certification that would provide the full range of FSC certification services at a cost of as little as US$0.20 per acre per year. The Centre proposes to offer these services to several thousand landowners simultaneously. The key to their model is the recognition that for small landowners, logging occurs relatively infrequently. Their team of consulting foresters will provide initial certification assessments based on a sample of the landowners. They will gradually develop forest management plans for all, but they would be monitored simply on the basis of a sample of those landowners who had actually done some logging each year. If successful, this model will respond to key cost concerns of small-scale landowners in both the North and the South.[10]

Another model for improving access by communities in the global South has been created by the Tropical Forest Trust (TFT), based in London. TFT is a not-for-profit organization that 'sells' its services directly to the forest products industry. Working with firms that seek to clean up the supply chains for their tropical timber, initially in south-east Asia, they contract to teach existing local suppliers how to make certain that their logging is, first, fully legal; and they then work with the suppliers to move them toward FSC certification. For example, TFT has assisted several suppliers for the European furniture manufacturer, Scancom, to become FSC certified.[11] TFT has been especially successful in navigating the difficult waters in Malaysia where significant criticism of the FSC has centred on the certification of concession lands where indigenous land claims had not been fully resolved (Majid Cooke, 1999). Recent FSC certifications there, facilitated by TFT, have been based on innovative new schemes for integrating local communities by pursuing certification of non-traditional forest products as well.

The brilliance of the TFT model is that it is almost completely supported by the firms whose supply chains are being improved. TFT has also earned the trust of European and US environmental NGOs who are willing to accept that good faith efforts are being made to move supply towards FSC certified suppliers, so long as the firms continue to support TFT. Advocacy campaigns against some of these firms have been halted, pending the results of the TFT work on the ground. And TFT has recently developed contracts with US retail forest product firms who are attempting to improve the sourcing of their imported tropical products, such as luaun plywood, a material widely used for doors and sub-flooring.

Certified fair trade institutions are beginning to explore the possibility of creating a mechanism for monitoring working conditions on coffee estates. Analogous to the mechanisms that are now in place for monitoring tea plantations, mostly in India, the expansion of fair trade certification is driven, in part, by offers by major coffee roasters to purchase significantly larger quantities of fair trade coffee if efforts are made to improve conditions on farms that are larger than the micro-farms of the cooperatives presently enrolled in the Fair Trade Registry. This change offers one opportunity to respond to the criticism that fair trade certification limits itself to a niche market by not offering to certify larger coffee producers who do produce the majority of what is presently considered the best coffee in the world. The dilemma, however, is a classic one. Given that there remains a very large over-supply of coffee, of varying quality, from farmers presently on the registry, would certification of coffee estates represent an abandonment of the largely-impoverished small-scale coffee farmers who still cannot place their coffee in Fair Trade Certified markets? Would the potential improvements of working conditions for hundreds of thousands of day labourers on coffee estates offset the reduced benefits for some on family-owned micro-farms? Or would the overall expansion of the fair trade market make the fair trade criteria a mainstream, industry-recognized fundamental quality criterion, expanding sales for all producers on the Fair Trade Registry, smaller as well as larger?

Conclusions

The building of certification systems to negotiate stakeholder-based social and environmental standards and to provide independent third-party certification of their fulfillment does have the potential to build natural assets for the reduction of poverty and injustice. Each of the systems reviewed, however, faces challenges to its effectiveness with respect to these goals, in part because poverty reduction was not necessarily among the main goals for which they were initially established (with the exception of certified fair trade).

The superimposition of a poverty reduction goal and a focus on the poor and disempowered is a relatively heavier burden for the FSC than it is for Fair Trade Certified coffee. Whether poverty reduction becomes a key focal point for the emerging certification systems in ecotourism and mining will depend greatly on the development of standards in the coming years. Those who are assisting with the development of the systems may need to focus not only on which functions are critical for the accrediting and certifying organizations themselves, but also on which asset-building functions require additional support programmes to assist poor communities to take

advantage of the opportunities provided by the certification systems
themselves.

Notes

1. 'Certified fair trade' will be used throughout this paper to refer to that form of trade
    that corresponds to the public standards and procedures of the Fairtrade Labelling
    Organizations International (FLO), as distinct from the generic kinds of 'fair trade'
    that are discussed widely by everyone from politicians in the global North to a wide
    array of NGOs, without clarity about what makes these systems somehow 'fairer'
    than ordinary commercial trade.
2. http://www.transfairusa.org.
3. For example, the standards under which certification of forest 'plantations' may take
    place is undergoing significant review during 2005–6 in often heated discussions of
    whether plantations could ever be considered 'forests' and whether certification of
    plantations can have the beneficial effect of reducing pressure on natural forests.
4. *FSC News & Notes*, Volume 3, Issue 5, June 3, 2005.
5. In this case, 'Fairtrade' as used by the Fairtrade Labeling Organizations
    International (FLO) is the same as 'certified fair trade' used throughout this
    chapter.
6. In 2005, however, coffee producers agreed to begin to pay a small levy on all of the
    coffee sold through certified fair trade to strengthen the certification and
    monitoring services of FLO and to protect better the legitimacy of the certified fair
    trade system. The International Standards Organization rules for certification
    systems require that the accreditation of certifiers who conduct the monitoring and
    auditing be separate from the establishment of standards and criteria, to avoid
    conflicts of interest. Producer contributions for the monitoring and auditing were a
    partial result of FLO changes to respond to those mandates.
7. For further information, see http://www.rainforestalliance.org/programs/tourism/
    certification/index.html.
8. For further information, see http://www.globalminingcampaign.org
9. For further information, see http://www.nodirtygold.org.
10. For further information, see http://www.forestrycenter.org/.
11. For further information, see http://www.tropicalforesttrust.com.

References

Atyi, Richard Eba'a and Marcus Simula (2002) *Forest Certification: Pending Challenges for
   Tropical Timber*, Yokahama: International Tropical Timber Organization.
Boot, Willem J., Christopher Wunderlich and Armando Bartra (2003) *Beneficial Impacts of
   Ecolabeled Mexican Coffee*, Washington DC: Consumers Choice Council.
Boyce, James K. (2001) 'From Natural Resources to Natural Assets', *New Solutions*, 11(3):
   267–288.
Boyce, James K. and Manuel Pastor (2001) *Building Natural Assets: New Strategies for Poverty
   Reduction and Environmental Protection*, Amherst MA: Political Economy Research
   Institute, University of Massachusetts.
Boyce, James K. and Barry Shelley (2003) *Natural Assets: Democratizing Environmental
   Ownership*, Washington DC: Island Press.

Cashore, Benjamin (2002) 'Legitimacy and the Privatization of Environmental Governance: How Non-state Market-driven (NSMD) Governance Systems Gain Rule-making Authority', *Governance: An International Journal of Policy, Administration and Institutions*, 15(4): 503–529.

Cashore, Benjamin, Graeme Auld and Diana Newsom (2004) *Governing through Markets: Forest Certification and the Emergence of Non-state Authority*, New Haven: Yale University Press.

Conroy, Michael E. (2001a) 'Can Advocacy-led Certification Systems Transform Global Corporate Practices: Evidence and Some Theory', Working paper of the Political Economy Research Institute, University of Massachusetts, Amherst. Available at http://www.peri.umass.edu/fileadmin/pdf/working_papers/working_papers_1-50/WP21.pdf.

— (2001b) 'Taming the Genie: What Limits for Certification Institutions?' *Certification Institutions and Private Governance: New Dynamics in the Protection of Workers and the Environment, Duke University Environmental Leadership Colloquium, December 2001.* Available at http://www.env.duke.edu/solutions/ppt_presentations.html.

— (2002) 'Certification Systems for Sustainable Tourism and Ecotourism: Can They Transform Social and Environmental Practices?' in Martha Honey, ed., *Ecotourism and Certification: Setting Standards in Practice*, Washington DC: Island Press.

Ford Foundation (2002) *Sustainable Solutions: Building Assets for Empowerment and Sustainable Development*, New York: Ford Foundation.

Forest Stewardship Council-US (FSC-US) (2003) Available at http://www.fscus.org/images/documents/FSC_Principles_Criteria.pdf.

Gereffi, Gary, Ronie Garcia-Johnson and Erika Sasser (2001) 'The NGO–Industrial Complex', *Foreign Policy*, July–August: 56–65.

Honey, Martha (1999) *Ecotourism and Sustainable Development: Who Owns Paradise?* Washington DC: Island Press.

— (2002) *Ecotourism and Certification: Setting Standards in Practice*, Washington DC: Island Press.

Honey, Martha and Abi Rome (2001) *Protecting Paradise: Certification Programmes for Sustainable Tourism and Ecotourism*. Washington DC: Institute for Policy Studies.

Littrell, M.A. and M.A. Dickson (1999) *Social Responsibility in the Global Market: Fair Trade in Cultural Products*, New York: Sage.

Majid Cooke, Fadzilah (1999) *The Challenge of Sustainable Forests*, Honolulu: University of Hawaii Press.

Mantyranta, Hannes (2002) *Forest Certification: An Ideal That Became An Absolute*, Helsinki: Metsalehti Kustannus.

Meek, Chanda L. (2001) *Sustainable for Whom? A Discussion Paper on Certification and Communities in The Boreal Region — Case Studies from Canada and Sweden*, Jokkmokk, Sweden: Taiga Rescue Network.

Miranda, Marta, David Chambers and Catherine Coumans (2005) *Framework for Responsible Mining: A Guide to Evolving Standards*, Washington DC: Earthworks.

MMSD (2002) *Breaking New Ground: Mining, Minerals and Sustainable Development. The Report of the MMSD Project*, London: Earthscan. Available at http://www.iied.org/mmsd/finalreport/index.html.

Molnar, Augusta (2003) *Forest Certification and Communities: Looking Forward to the Next Decade*, Washington DC: Forest Trends.

Murray, Douglas, Laura Raynolds and Pete Taylor (2003) *One Cup at A Time: Poverty Alleviation and Fair Trade Coffee in Latin America*. A Report of the Colorado State University Fair Trade Research Group. Ft. Collins CO: Colorado State University.

— (2006) 'The Future of Fair Trade Coffee: Dilemmas Facing Latin America's Small-Scale Producers', *Development in Practice* 16(2): 179–192.

Oliver, Melvin and Thomas Shapiro (1997) *Black Wealth, White Wealth: A New Perspective on Racial Inequality*, New York: Routledge.

Raynolds, Laura T. (2002) 'Consumer–Producer Links in Fair Trade Coffee Networks', *Sociologia Ruralis*, 42(4): 404–424.

Rickenbach, Mark G. (2002) 'Forest Certification of Small Ownerships: Some Practical Challenges', *Journal of Forestry* 100(6): 43–47.

Rushford, Greg (2001) 'Fair Trade: Does This Emperor Wear Clothes?' *Milken Institute Review*, Second Quarter: 40–48.

Sanabria, Ronald (2002) 'Accreditation: Certifying the Certifiers', in Martha Honey, ed., *Ecotourism and Certification: Setting Standards in Practice*, Washington DC: Island Press.

Sanabria, R., Skinner, E., Font, X., Maccarrone-Eaglen, A., Sallows, M. and Fredriksen, M. (2003) 'Sustainable Tourism Stewardship Council: Raising the Standards and Benefits of Sustainable Tourism and Ecotourism Certification', New York: Rainforest Alliance. Available at http://www.ra.org/programs/tourism/initiatives/stewardship-council.html.

Sherraden, Michael (1992) *Assets and the Poor: A New American Welfare Policy*, New York: M.E. Sharpe.

Tallontire, Anne (2002) 'Challenges Facing Fair Trade: Which Way Now?' *Small Enterprise Development: An International Journal of Microfinance and Business Development* 13(3): 12–24.

van Dam, Chris (2002) 'La Economía de la Certificación Forestal: ¿Desarrollo sostenible para quien?' Paper presented at the *Congreso Iberoamericano de Desarollo y Medio Ambiente 'Desafíos locales ante la globalización*, November 2002, Quito, Ecuador: FLACSO-Quito.

Payatas, the largest municipal landfill in Metropolitan Manila.
Photo credit: Sid Balatan.

CHAPTER 11
WASTES AS ASSETS:
LIMITS AND POTENTIALS

Eugenio M. Gonzales

Introduction

In the 1980s, a photograph of scavengers, some of them children, picking through garbage at Manila's 'Smoky Mountain' dumpsite came to represent poverty in the Philippines. In 1995, the government closed the over-filled dumpsite, announcing plans to convert it into a low-cost housing development and an industrial zone. But the 1997 Asian financial crisis caught up with the project, and the promise of a better life for the scavengers remained unfulfilled.

The closure of Smokey Mountain threatened to deprive scavengers and their families of their only source of livelihood. A year before the closure, they were already following the re-routed garbage trucks more than 20 kilometres away to what is now the largest dumpsite in the country — Payatas in Quezon City (Rivera 1994, 53). If the garbage mountain represented poverty, why did the poor follow it? The reason is that to the 4,000– 8,000 families who depend on the Payatas dumpsite, garbage is not a symbol of poverty: it is an asset (Tuason 2002, 1).

This chapter describes how poor families living in the Payatas dumpsite earn an income and create jobs for their neighbours by recovering and recycling wastes. A few, who have become traders and small producers, have managed to penetrate the country's biggest supermarkets and even the export market with their recycled products. The scavengers of Payatas have shown that waste recovery and recycling can simultaneously help to reduce poverty and protect the environment. However, several recent trends threaten the poverty-reduction potential of waste recovery and recycling.

Low-income communities and their allies must explore a number of options to counter these threats. The options involve natural asset building via strategies that combine investment, redistribution, internalization and appropriation.

Although based on a case study in the Philippines, this chapter's analysis may be applicable to other countries too. The degree of applicability will depend on, among other things, the extent to which the poor have access to waste materials, regulations on waste handling and market structures for waste recovery and recycling.

Materials Conservation and the Poor

Materials conservation can be achieved in four distinct ways: by *reducing* the consumption of materials; by *re-using* materials; by *recovering* used materials and delivering these to another party who has further use for the materials; and by *reprocessing* or *recycling* the materials into other forms that are useful to others.

In metro Manila, low-income groups are mostly involved in recovering waste materials through the activity known as 'scavenging'. Only a small percentage is involved in reprocessing or recycling, because these require larger investments and more complex systems. For example, recycling plastic beverage containers requires high-volume cleaning, grinding and extruding machines that are beyond the means of low-income groups. At the same time, their poverty forces them to limit their own consumption of materials and maximize the re-use of whatever possessions they have.

Waste recovery involves the following activities:

- *sorting* out reusable and recyclable materials in the waste container or the dumpsite, and selling these to designated buyers employed by 'junk shops';
- *transporting* the materials to the junk shop;
- *consolidating* and *segregating* the materials in different sections within the junk shop;
- *cleaning* of the materials if buyers require this;
- *storage* of the materials until a specific volume and price are reached;
- *delivery* to or pick-up by companies who recycle the materials.

Each of these activities adds value and price to the materials. Most low-income groups are engaged only in the sorting process, after which control passes to 'junk shop cartels'. Some are hired as labourers in the junk shops, but few of the poor are able to move up to become junk shop owners or recyclers themselves.

Recycling Flows

The usual notion of wastes, whether these are liquid, solid, or gaseous, is that they are pollutants discarded in environmental 'sinks': bodies of water, landfills and the atmosphere. This notion assumes a linear flow of materials from their original form as natural resources to their ultimate disposal as wastes. Figure 11.1 depicts this flow, in which natural resources are extracted, processed, converted, distributed to consumers and finally deposited into environmental sinks.

A more complex but more accurate representation of the flow and processing of materials is shown in Figure 11.2, which includes the enormous opportunities for recycling 'waste' at different stages of the production and consumption process. Five basic types of 'Recycling Flows' are identified:

- Recycling Flow 1 is known as *home scrap* because the waste is recycled within the processing plant.
- Recycling Flow 2, *prompt scrap*, requires the intervention of an intermediary commercial firm to collect scrap and redirect it back into basic processing.
- Recycling Flow 3, *commercial scrap*, is composed of packaging waste, and is the staple business of most commercial recycling firms.
- Recycling Flow 4, *post-consumer scrap*, is the recyclable component of the household waste stream that enters municipal solid waste.
- Recycling Flow 5, *re-used scrap*, is a household or community-level recycling practice that has all but disappeared in modern economies, but is now undergoing a resurgence in the case of clothing.[1]

In general, the opportunities for home, prompt and commercial scrap recycling flows, are implemented more fully than opportunities for post-consumer and re-used scrap recycling, for several reasons:

- *Quantity* — the volume of recyclable materials.
- *Homogeneity* — their quality and consistency.
- *Contamination* — the degree to which different materials and substances are mixed together.
- And *location* — the number of points at which the materials are first discarded as waste.

Figure 11.1: Linear View of Materials Flow

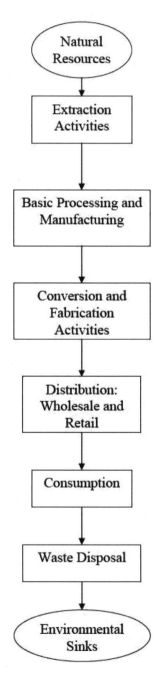

Figure 11.2: (Re) Cyclical View of Materials Flow

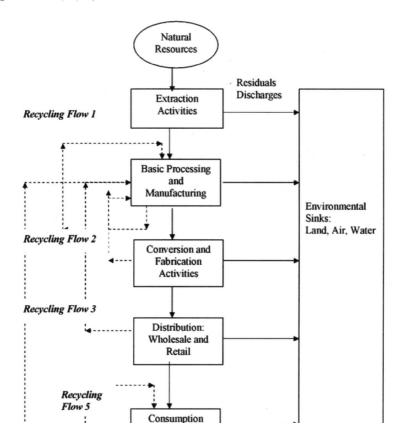

Source: Modified from Box 1.3 in Turner *et al.* 1994, 19.

The home scrap recycling flow, for example, is characterized by high volume, high homogeneity, low contamination and a single source location. Post-consumer scrap, on the other hand, is characterized by low volume, low homogeneity, high contamination and multiple locations.

As Turner *et al.* (1993, 22) observe, four additional factors can also affect the recycling effort:

- The *relative prices* of secondary, or recycled, versus primary raw materials as inputs into production processes.
- The *end-use structure* (number of uses and grades of material required) for any given recyclable material: for example, mixed waste papers and mixed colour glass typically have fewer uses than single-grade wastes.
- *Technological progress* in the secondary and primary materials industries.
- And *historical and cultural factors* that condition the degree of 'environmental awareness' in society.

Low-income groups have some opportunities to participate in and generate income from the flow of prompt, commercial and post-consumer scrap, but to do so they have to deal with junk shop owners, garbage collection agencies and firms, and other more economically empowered entities with an interest in these flows.

Two further recycling flows can tap materials after they have entered the waste stream. If effective facilities are established to separate compostables before these reach the dumpsite, these can be processed and delivered to extractive activities such as agriculture and forestry. This is shown as *compost scrap* (Recycling Flow 6) in Figure 11.3. The final recycling flow, shown as *dumpsite scrap* (Recycling Flow 7) in Figure 11.3, is seen primarily in countries in the South, where recovery activities are allowed at municipal dumpsites. This yields a flow of materials back to basic processing, conversion and fabrication, and distribution activities. This is the main flow in which low-income groups in the Philippines, including the scavengers of Payatas, participate.

Limitations

Recycling has its limits: there will always be some materials that cannot be recycled, simply because these have lost all usefulness. There are also certain materials that should not be recycled, particularly, toxic and hazardous waste. The Philippines generated 19 million metric tons of toxic and hazardous waste per year in the mid-1990s, equivalent to roughly 275 kilograms per capita (Philippines Department of Environment and Natural Resources 1997: 11). The vast majority of this — 17 million tons — was generated by the semiconductor industry and consisted of massive quantities of wastewater. Until now, there is no major facility that can handle these and other toxic and hazardous wastes in the Philippines.

Moreover, recycling can be quite costly, and itself can be a source of pollution. Paper recycling factories, for example, discharge effluents that can harm rivers and waterways if not properly managed. Treating these effluents is costly. Recycled paper is often more expensive than paper made from virgin wood pulp. It can be argued, however, that the cost of virgin paper is often understated, because the cost of replacing the forests that produce the pulp is not included. Moreover, because 100 per cent recycled paper is darker, it is not preferred as a printing or writing material.

Figure 11.3: Additional Recycling Flows

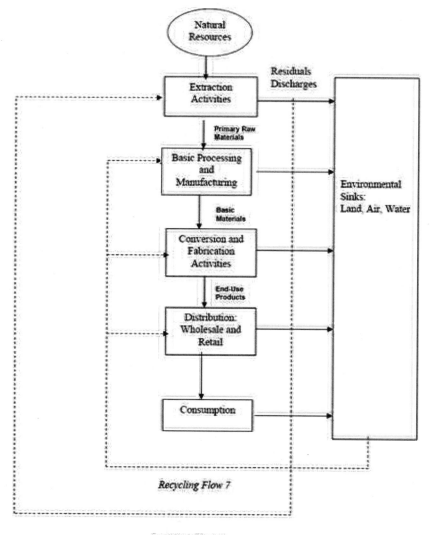

These economic and technological limitations are a continuing challenge for the development of recycling industries.

The Philippine Urban Context

Rural-to-urban migration, population growth and inadequate waste disposal facilities have created immense pressure on urban environments in the Philippines. As a result, garbage has become an issue that easily mobilizes the ordinary urban citizen into political action. Local government officials often allocate a substantial portion of their budgets to garbage collection for fear that they could lose the next election on that issue alone.

The Philippines' largest urban center is Metro Manila, with a population of more than 10 million. Four dumpsites, Smoky Mountain, Carmona, Payatas and San Mateo, served the metropolis in recent years. One by one, these have been closed, mainly because they were filled to and beyond their capacity. In early 2001, the last destination for Metro Manila's garbage, the San Mateo landfill, was closed following protests from the residents of the host town and surrounding areas.[2] Tired of the stench, dirt and disease that the garbage trucks carried through their communities, non-governmental organizations (NGOs), people's organizations and ordinary citizens blocked the roads leading to the landfill. Even local politicians joined the barricades when they saw the citizens' resolve. The landfill remains closed to this day.

Mountains of garbage piled up on city streets as the 11 cities and six towns of Metro Manila were left to fend for themselves. Illegal dumpsites sprang up in rural areas without the required environmental permits and systems, and the health of both urban and rural communities was endangered. The reopening of the Payatas dumpsite and the opening of a new landfill in Rodriguez town outside of Metro Manila has now eased the situation, at least temporarily.

The Ecological Solid Waste Management Act (Republic Act 9003), signed into law in early 2001, has encouraged recycling as one response to the landfill crisis. Of the 5,350 metric tons of waste generated daily in Metro Manila in the late 1990s, only six per cent was being recycled (JICA-MMDA 1998, 2–7, 5–11). A coalition of urban environmental NGOs, including the Recycling Movement of the Philippines, the Earth Day Network, Mother Earth, *Linis Ganda* (literally, Clean [is] Beautiful), Concerned Citizens Against Pollution and Greenpeace (Philippines), campaigned for the passage of this Act. The scavenger communities in Payatas and their organizations, like the *Lupang Pangako* Urban Poor Association and the Payatas Scavengers Association, were not involved in the campaign, although their leaders were told that they would benefit from the Act's passage.

No systematic studies on recycling have been conducted since the implementation of the Act. Based on the increase in the number of junk shops in Metro Manila, however, the Earth Day Network estimates that the recycling rate may have risen as high as 15 per cent. Local governments are now looking for economical and effective facilities for composting and recycling wastes, and the national government and foreign donors are providing funding and other incentives for such projects.

Making a Living in Payatas

Payatas is the country's largest open dumpsite, occupying 20 hectares (50 acres) of land in Quezon City, the largest component city of Metro Manila. The dump started operations in the early 1970s. Today, despite its lack of the liners and piping systems required of sanitary landfills, it receives around 1,200 tons of trash per day. Roughly, 6,000 waste-pickers make or supplement their livings by combing through this mountain of garbage (JICA-MMDA 1998, 2–5).

On July 10, 2000, more than 200 waste-pickers lost their lives in Payatas when a huge section of the garbage mountain collapsed after strong rains. Because of this tragedy, the government closed the site.[3] After a few months, however, the dump was opened again on the request of the waste-pickers themselves, although the collapsed section of the dump has been permanently closed. The tragedy attracted more NGOs and government agencies to provide health, livelihood and other assistance to the Payatas scavengers, but their lives remain difficult.

How do the scavengers make a living? Figure 11.4 is a simplified overview of the waste stream. From the source, which may be a residence, a commercial entity, or a factory, waste is collected by garbage trucks contracted by local governments or the source itself. Some garbage is also collected by itinerant waste-pickers using simple 'push-carts', who shout at the top of their voices to households to bring out their recyclables — newspapers, bottles, used paper, scrap metal, etc. — which they buy at prices that vary with market conditions. There are also itinerant waste-pickers who have no capital, and just pick through garbage receptacles that they encounter in their route, resulting in garbage being strewn on roads and sidewalks. Although they recover some materials for recycling they also perform a dis-service to the environment.

When the garbage trucks collect waste from the source, the truck crews also do their own sorting of recyclable items. Before the truck reaches the dumpsite, these are dropped off at junk shops along the way. In this way, the crew earns money to supplement their low wages. At the dumpsite entrance, as the trucks line up to pay fees to the local government (around Philippine pesos (PhP) 600 or US$12 per truck), young boys jump onto the back of the truck to pick quickly through the load. These boys, called 'jumpers', usually are hired by junk shop owners to do this work. About a kilometre from the entrance, in the actual dumping area, hundreds of waste-pickers wait. They are called '*mangangalahig*', after the pointed tool called a '*kalahig*' that they use to pick through the garbage. They assemble behind the truck and immediately sift through the garbage as it falls off. They have mastered the art of avoiding being buried by the garbage or run over by the truck, but sometimes accidents happen.

Figure 11.4: Picking through the Waste Stream

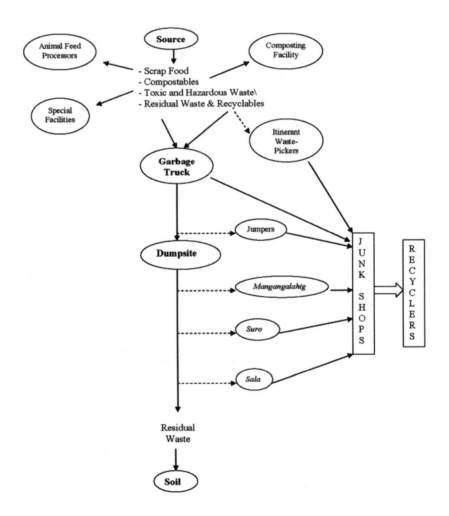

Scavengers who lack the physical abilities of the jumpers and the *mangangalahigs* are forced to rely on more tedious but less competitive ways to pick through the waste. They go to areas of the dump that are being levelled by bulldozers, in hope that the bulldozers inadvertently will unearth garbage that may still be of value. There are fewer waste-pickers, and consequently less competition, in these locations. Those who do this job are called *'suro'*, the local term for 'dredging'. A few of them have been run over by bulldozers.

The final stage of waste picking is performed by the *'sala'*, literally 'to sift through'. They go to the areas of the dump that have already been burned or are still burning. Using tongs, some of them sift through the ash looking for metal and other items of value. Others extract whole clumps of ash and use nearby waterways to remove the ash, hoping to find useful items. However, their chances of recovering items of much value are slim. Ironically, the least rewarding job in the dumpsite is also the riskiest.[4] The *sala* are constantly subjected to smoke and flames. Most of those who died in the July 2000 accident at Payatas were *salas* buried under smouldering garbage.

From this discussion, it should be clear that getting the earliest access to recyclable materials is the key to success. Those who get the 'leftovers' face the greatest risks and get the lowest returns. Indeed, the dumpsite itself is not the most strategic asset for resource recovery, since the waste stream has already been screened and the most valuable items extracted before it reaches the dump.

The junk shop node meanwhile acts as the gateway to the market both for recyclable materials and information about them — price, quality, minimum volumes and new demand for materials. The junk shop is one step away from the dumpsite, and often a step ahead of it. Owners seek to get their materials close to the source, so as to maximize volume, quality and homogeneity, and minimize transport costs. The scavengers generally see the junk shop as a necessary evil: it depresses prices, monopolizes information and sometimes even threatens to arrange their eviction from the dump. With loans and technical assistance from NGO allies, a few waste-pickers have managed to become junk shop owners or recycler-buyers themselves, and several of them have started to look beyond the dumpsite for more economic opportunities in the recycling arena. The next section presents profiles of two former waste-pickers who are now small entrepreneurs, but have not forgotten their roots and remain active in the waste-pickers organization. They still live on the fringes of the dumpsite, earning their livelihoods in waste recovery and recycling.

From Scavengers to Entrepreneurs

In 1993, the Vincentian Missionaries Social Development Foundation, under the leadership of Father Norberto Carcellar and the late Brother Oquet Anayan, started a Savings and Credit Programme for the scavengers of the Payatas dumpsite. At that time, the dump occupied only five of its present 20 hectares. The Foundation's programme catered mainly to women, using a modified Grameen Bank approach that emphasized savings rather than outside funding as a source of capital. The Foundation organized the borrowers into a people's organization, the *Lupang Pangako* (or 'promised land') Urban Poor Association, Inc. (LUPAI), registered in June 1997 with the Securities and Exchange Commission of the Philippines.

From an initial seed capital of PhP 100,000 (around US$2,000), donated by a government charity agency in 1993, LUPAI now manages around PhP 15 million (US$300,000) in savings accounts for its 7,000 members (Tuason 2002, 4). Today, many LUPAI members engage in microenterprises that provide goods and services to the scavengers and other residents of the area surrounding the dumpsite. In addition to the revolving credit programme, LUPAI has piloted a Community Mortgage Programme through which some of its members have acquired ownership of the land where their houses now stand. The programme has also provided funds for improving streets and water systems.

In addition, LUPAI works with other organizations, like the Payatas Scavengers' Association, on advocacy to improve the living conditions in the dumpsite. At dialogues with Quezon City and national government agencies, they air grievances and give recommendations, especially on land and livelihood issues.

Jaime Salada, one of the original leaders of LUPAI, has lived in Payatas since 1989. He invented a 'laundry brush' (see Figure 11.5) made from discarded plastic foam insulation and plastic netting. Most Philippine households wash clothes by hand, using a stiff brush whose hard bristles can damage clothes. Jaime's gadget is softer and easier to handle. In the dump he saw mountains of discarded insulation sheets, made of 3-inch foam plastic coated with aluminum foil on one or both sides. Jaime removed the foil and cut the plastic into small 1-inch x 3-inch pieces. These make up the core of the brush. He then wrapped these with softer rubber foam and plastic netting, sewn to produce a handy, light-weight clothes scrubber. In the beginning, all the materials Jaime used were recovered from the dump; he simply washed them before assembling them into brushes. Now, only the core comes from the dump. He buys clean rubber foam and netting of different colours to make his product more attractive.

Once a waste-picker, Jaime is now a recycler-entrepreneur. He has transformed waste materials into a new product that has penetrated the mainstream market. In the process he has created livelihoods for his neighbours through contracting and direct employment. Because the brush is easy to make, many have copied Jaime's product. He does not mind this, however, because he has continually improved his product while lowering his costs. From an original unit price of PhP 12 (US$0.24), he now sells thousands of brushes at PhP 3.00 (US$0.06) per piece to some of the largest supermarket chains in the country. At the same time, he is always on the lookout for new products that can be made from waste materials in the dumpsite.[5]

Figure 11.5: Jaime Salada and his 'Laundry Brush'

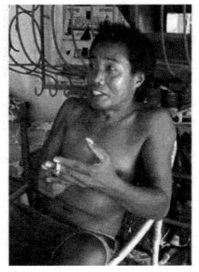

Edita de la Cuesta received a PhP 4,000 (US$80) loan from the Vincentian Savings and Credit programme in 1994, and used this as working capital to establish a recycling business. Initially, she specialized in polypropylene sacks that she washed by hand and sold as a cheap packaging material. Later she began to buy the used sacks from other waste-pickers and sold these in volume to interested buyers. Now she has her own junk shop (see Figure 11.6) and two pickup trucks that regularly collect a variety of recyclable materials from waste-pickers in Payatas. Her workers clean and stack plastic and glass bottles, scrap metal, aluminum cans and sheets, and other materials in her shop. Although Edita now maintains PhP 180,000 (US$3,600) in her LUPAI savings account, and has a business loan of PhP 200,000 (US$4,000) from the organization, she remains humble and unassuming. She has become a favourite interviewee of journalists because she is very well-informed. Her modest concrete house just outside the dumpsite served as LUPAI's rescue coordination centre during the July 2000 tragedy.

Figure 11.6: Edita de la Cuesta in her Junk Shop

Edita's business is now feeling the effects of the Ecological Solid Waste Management Act. Because the law requires waste segregation at the source, new junk shops that are closer to the beginning of the waste stream have sprouted all over Quezon City. Whereas, Edita used to buy PhP 16,000 (US$320) worth of materials from waste pickers on an ordinary day, now she says she is lucky to buy one-fourth of that amount. Nevertheless, she does not complain about the law. She understands its importance in cleaning up the city's environment and reducing the pressure on dumpsites and landfills. Her brother-in-law told her about some new plastic recycling processes and machines in Malaysia, and she is now looking into the economics of launching such a venture in the Philippines.

Jaime and Edita illustrate some of the potentials and limitations of turning wastes into assets. They have risen from poverty under truly challenging circumstances. With a little help from their allies and co-members, they now compete in the open market, using their knowledge and skills to move continually up the value chain of the waste recovery and recycling industry. They have used other assets — including market information, technology and individual drive — to add value to wastes and to derive value from them. Jaime now combines new materials with recycled ones to produce a competitive product. Edita is looking for new technology to add value to her materials and adjust to the country's new policy environment.

By encouraging segregation and recycling at the source, however, the success of the Ecological Solid Waste Management Law is reducing the volume of waste that reaches the dumpsite. Indeed, the law has proved to be an exceptionally effective piece of environmental legislation, and junk shops have sprung up around the metropolitan area to absorb the segregated recyclables. For the scavengers of Payatas, this means more competition.

Recycling for Environmental Protection and Poverty Reduction

The environmental benefits of waste recycling include reduction of the use of virgin raw materials, soil quality improvement, reduced pressures on landfill space, and reduced air and water pollution from landfills and trash strewn elsewhere. Although all of these benefits may have motivated the NGOs who campaigned for the passage of RA 9003, an activist deeply involved in the campaign believes that the government passed the law primarily in response to the increasing difficulty of finding new, socially acceptable landfill sites.

The reduced use of virgin materials also has major environmental impacts. For example, paper recycling conserves forests, the sources of pulp for paper manufacturing. Composting — the reprocessing and recycling of organic wastes for agricultural use — reduces the demand for petrochemical-based fertilizers, as well as reducing pressures on landfill space. By the year 2010, it is estimated that 42 per cent of Metro Manila's trash will consist of 'kitchen waste', most of which is compostable (JICA-MMDA 1998, 3–8). Composting also reduces air and water pollution attributable to organic decomposition in landfill sites, public markets and residential areas.

Waste recycling can contribute to poverty reduction, too, as the Payatas case shows. A 1996 survey in Payatas found that families earned an average of PhP 4,550 (US$175 at the prevailing exchange rate) per month (Tuason 2002, 1), and an income about 20 per cent higher than the legislated minimum wage. Because they live and work in the same vicinity, waste-pickers do not have to pay for daily transportation. As a part of the 'informal economy', their earnings are not subject to income and other taxes. The dump also provides some household needs for free, including building materials, furniture, clothes and personal accessories.[6]

These benefits are threatened, however, by the scavengers' lack of 'job security'; that is, their lack of secure rights to access the waste stream. Instead, they can be evicted from the dumpsite at any time (Abad 1991, cited by Rivera 1994, 11–2). The Quezon City government plans to close the dump soon because it is already filled beyond its capacity. The income of scavengers has already fallen, as upstream recycling has increased with government regulation and incentives. Whereas, in previous years a scavenger typically earned PhP 200 per day, now he or she is lucky to earn PhP 65 per day.

Health risks pose another continuing threat to the waste-pickers. The German Doctors' Health Care Development Centre, a NGO operating a clinic inside the Payatas dumpsite, reported that in August 2002 alone they had 339 cases of tuberculosis. This implies a rate of morbidity more than eight times higher than the national average. Toxic and hazardous wastes are a particularly important health issue for the waste-pickers. The clinic does not have records for toxic and hazardous waste victims because these are usually taken directly to hospitals, but there have been reports of toxic waste dumping — most commonly paint and paint residues — in the dead of the night.

What Is to Be Done?

What are the prospects for the 4,000 low-income families who depend on the Payatas dumpsite, and for other waste-pickers in the Philippines given the implementation of the Ecological Solid Waste Management Act? Can they remain dependent on wastes as their main asset? Should they continue living in and around the dump?

In the early 1990s, a survey carried out in Payatas found that 28 per cent of the respondents had some other source of income besides waste picking (Rivera 1994, 69). When asked what they would do if the dump were closed, more than half said they would go back to their home provinces outside

Metro Manila, nearly one-third said they would try to find another job in the city, and 12 per cent said they would follow the wastes to a new dumpsite if there was one (Rivera 1994, 109). These data suggest that the scavengers themselves believe that they need not depend on the dumpsite as their only or main asset. With the implementation of solid waste law, they may have no choice but to generate alternative livelihood activities around the site, or to move to get work in the new recycling facilities and junk shops being set up closer to the sources of waste. The natural assets framework suggests a number of possible courses of action.

Investment

The increase in recycling at the source, in response to landfill closures and the Ecological Solid Waste Management Act, has decreased scavengers' incomes from recycling at the sink. Town and city governments are now looking for ways to redirect part of their budgets for garbage collection to investments in recycling and composting facilities. In the late 1990s, the total expenditure for solid waste management by the local governments of Metro Manila was estimated at PhP 2.8 billion (US$56 million) per year (JICA-MMDA 1998, 2–25). The national government and the World Bank are making loans available for new projects within the Bank's US$100 million Local Government Finance and Development Project (World Bank 2002). These funds could help scavengers advance in doing what they do best — sorting, cleaning, processing and creating value out of waste materials. Scavenger organizations and allies should explore how they can tap these available funds to support the improvement of their recovery and recycling activities. For example, the development of a simple, inexpensive technology for recycling low-grade plastic could yield great benefits.

A 'livelihood master plan' needs to be formulated by the scavengers and their allies. Building on the forward-looking initiatives and ideas of waste-pickers, like Jaime Salada and Edita de la Cuesta, such a plan would identify key products and technologies that could have a significant impact on the livelihoods of the waste-pickers. The scope of the plan should include on-site and off-site activities, and non-agricultural and agricultural alternatives, that build on the strengths and experience of the waste-pickers and provide further capacity-building. Government and NGO investments could then be based on this plan.

Near the Payatas site, for example, there are many open spaces that could be utilized for urban agriculture, including 444 hectares of public land known as the National Government Centre. Government buildings occupy

some of this land, but much of the rest could be leased at concessional rates
to low-income groups to engage in urban agriculture. At present, the
ownership status of many of the lands surrounding the dumpsite remains
unknown, and the national government is now undertaking studies and
surveys to determine to whom they belong. Some owners have been
identified, and people's organizations like LUPAI are attempting to acquire
some of these lands using government assistance.

The plan can also look further ahead. Payatas junk shop dealers like Edita
can use their long experience and reliable market linkages to establish junk
shops closer to the sources of wastes, elsewhere in Metro Manila. Beyond
Payatas, another target for investment by government and the private sector
is composting. Although many simple household-level composting products
and technologies are appearing in the market, there is a need for larger
composting units that can serve villages and even cities. An effective
technology could transform a large proportion of the waste stream from a
useless, unsanitary, difficult material into an asset for degraded agricultural
lands. To succeed, such technology would also need to minimize the health
and contamination risks associated with poor segregation of wastes at the
source. The easiest way to achieve this may be to start by collecting more
homogeneous and cleaner compostable wastes from fruit, vegetable and
food markets, recovering the compostables before they reach the dump.

Finally, investments should be made not just in the waste management
system itself, but also in the people who have managed wastes for so long,
for little income and at great risk to their health and well-being. Investments
in 'human capital' — education, training and health — are a necessary
complement to other forms of investment.

Redistribution

Those who benefit most from the garbage problem in the Philippines are big
contractors with the capital to buy and maintain large fleets of dump trucks.
Ironically, these contractors are the least interested in waste segregation at
the source: they find it easier to collect mixed wastes and dump them in
landfills. Scavengers, by contrast, view waste as an asset, and they potentially
can derive more income from this asset if it is segregated. For this potential
to be fulfilled, however, redistributive measures must be undertaken to
secure access to waste streams for low-income groups.

An example of such redistributive action is the solid waste management
programme of the Ayala Group of companies, operated through its social
development arm, the Ayala Foundation. The Ayala Group is the largest

real estate and property development company in the Philippines and it owns much of the property in Makati, Metro Manila's premier financial district, including the country's most upscale commercial centre. The Foundation works with waste-picker associations in collecting recyclable materials from the companies whose offices are located in the financial district. The waste stream is literally diverted to waste-picker associations for material recovery before garbage contractors collect it. The Ayala Commercial Center has hired a junk shop operator from Payatas to collect its 36 tons of garbage per day. Employees of shops in the commercial centre, including Kentucky Fried Chicken and McDonald's, are trained and encouraged to segregate wastes, making it easier for waste-pickers to get clean recyclable materials, and reducing the volume of waste to be collected (Gonzalez 2002, 5–10). Redistribution of access to the waste stream has resulted in a win-win situation for the environment and poverty reduction.

While the actions of the Ayala Foundation may be promoted as a benefit to waste-pickers, cost was also a consideration. The junk shop from Payatas actually quoted a lower price for garbage collection services than the biggest solid waste management company in Metro Manila. It was able to do so because the operator could get additional income from recovering the recyclable materials in the garbage, while the big company only collected, compacted and unloaded the garbage in disposal sites. In effect, the junk shop can earn from service fees plus recyclables, while the big company depends only on service fees. To compete more effectively with the big contractors, however, small junk shop operators need additional capital to buy hauling equipment.

In some cases, as this example suggests, redistributive measures can take the form of information on opportunities and linkages to the solid waste management market. This is a rapidly growing market, thanks to the new solid waste law, but junk shop operators and waste-pickers need to know how to do business with big companies like Ayala, including how to fill out pre-qualification forms, how to bid on contracts and, generally, how to build a business relationship. Assistance in forging these linkages is badly needed by organizations of the poor. Some NGOs, like Philippine Business for the Environment, already publish information on the waste materials that companies are willing to give away for free. Others, like *Linis Ganda*, link junk shops with middle and upper-class buyers. These types of information and linkages can be an important component of redistributive measures.

Another important arena for redistribution is the allocation of permits for new junk shops. Currently, the junk shop business around Payatas is dominated by those who are favoured by the village head, or *barangay* captain whose endorsement is required for permits to open new shops. *Barangay* elections are therefore an important venue to campaign for more transparent and democratic allocations of these permits.

Internalization

By reducing the volume of waste that would otherwise remain in landfills, scavengers perform a valuable environmental service, one for which they deserve to be paid. Yet instead of being rewarded for this service, they currently pay for access to recyclables by exposing themselves to health risks and other dangers. They are not polluters, yet they pay the costs of pollution.

The total financial cost of handling solid waste in Metro Manila is estimated to be around PhP 2,200 (US$44) per ton. Landfill investment and operation costs are estimated to cost a further PhP 600 (US$12) per ton. The Payatas scavengers extract an estimated 65 tons of recyclables per day (JICA-MMDA1998, 2–25, 2–5). If the scavengers were paid for the environmental service of removing this material from the waste stream, they could earn roughly PhP 180,000 (US$3,600) per day or PhP 66 million (US$1.3 million) in one year. This is equivalent to 30 per cent of the average yearly income of all the waste pickers in Payatas. In other words, with internalization of the benefits they provide to society by conserving scarce landfill space, the scavengers could get a pay raise amounting to almost one-third of their present income.

Appropriation

The Payatas dumpsite is not an open-access resource: the Quezon City government controls both the entry and exit of garbage. All trucks have to pay an 'entrance fee' before they are allowed to unload their trash, and all waste-pickers have to wear an Identification Card before they are allowed to sort newly arrived garbage (although a few manage to sneak in unnoticed). Around 10 per cent of the fees go to the *barangay* or village council for its operations and projects. The rest goes to the city government, which in turn maintains the dumpsite (e.g., paying for road repairs, drainage, security, traffic control and bulldozing). The city government's control over the dumpsite was strengthened after the loss of hundreds of lives because of the accidents at Payatas. Residents report that the main government official responsible for the dumpsite seems to act with fairness, and allows all types of waste pickers, including the sometimes troublesome 'jumpers', to earn their share from the dwindling recyclables of Payatas. This situation is clearly better than a chaotic open-access regime. In maintaining something closer to a common property model, the city government has protected access rights appropriated by low-income groups.

By treating wastes as assets, these strategies for investment, redistribution, internalization and appropriation would not only help the Philippines to solve its 'garbage crisis', but also help the country's scavengers to secure sustainable livelihoods. If the control and eventual closure of municipal dumpsites like Payatas leads to the proliferation of illegal dumpsites across the country, both the environment and public welfare will be the victims. If, instead, creative strategies are adopted to address the crisis, it could be turned into an opportunity to advance the twin goals of environmental protection and poverty reduction.

Notes

1. In the US and Europe, used clothes are being donated or sold in large volumes to raise funds for charity or to be sold in countries like the Philippines, where cheap imported used clothes (often smuggled in duty-free as 'donations') are now encroaching on the local clothing market.
2. Garbage trucks had to pass through the city of Antipolo and the town of San Mateo, both located outside Metro Manila, on the way to the landfill.
3. Some environmental activists have said that the tragedy was a turning point in their campaign for the Ecological Solid Waste Management Act that was finally passed in late 2000.
4. See Rivera (1994, 78–82) for a more detailed account of the ways of recovering items of value from the garbage once it has reached the dump.
5. Jaime spent more than half of our interview time sounding me out on potential new products for his business.
6. Rivera (1993, 65–7) describes these and other non-income benefits.

References

Abad, Ricardo G. (1991) 'Squatting and Scavenging in an Urban Environment: The Adaptation of Smokey Mountain Residents', *SA 21: Selected Readings*, Quezon City: Ateneo University Office of Research and Publications.

Anantansuwong, Dararatt (2002) 'Recyclable Waste Business for Sustainable Development: A Case Study from Thailand', Paper presented to the Foundation for a Sustainable Society, Inc. and the Sasakawa Peace Foundation, Regional Conference on Civil Society — Business Collaboration in Environmental Protection, Manila, 27 February.

Ecological Solid Waste Management Act, Republic Act 9003 (2001) Republic of the Philippines

Gonzalez, Manolita (2002) 'Ayala Foundation's Solid Waste Management Programme', Paper presented to the Foundation for a Sustainable Society, Inc. and the Sasakawa Peace Foundation, Regional Conference on Civil Society — Business Collaboration in

Environmental Protection, Manila, 27 February.

Japan International Cooperation Agency [JICA] — Metropolitan Manila Development Authority [MMDA] (1998) *The Study on Solid Waste Management for Metro Manila.*

Philippine Department of Environment and Natural Resources (1997) *Metro Manila Toxic and Hazardous Waste Management Study Final Report,* Vol. 1, Main Report, Entec Europe Limited.

Rivera, Roberto N. (1994) 'Payatas: Adaptation and Maladaptation among Scavenging Communities', M.A. Thesis, Ateneo de Manila University Graduate School.

Tuason, Celia (2002) Untitled. Vincentian Missionaries Social Development Foundation, Inc. Quezon City. Unpublished paper.

Turner, R. Kerry, David Pearce and Ian Bateman (1993) *Environmental Economics: An Elementary Introduction,* Baltimore: The Johns Hopkins University Press.

The zebra is among the wildlife that draws tourists to Zimbabwe.
Photo credit: IUCN Regional Office for Southern Africa.

CHAPTER 12
COMMUNITY RIGHTS
AND WILDLIFE STEWARDSHIP:
ZIMBABWE'S CAMPFIRE PROGRAMME

James C. Murombedzi

Zimbabwe's Communal Areas Management Programme for Indigenous Resources (CAMPFIRE) is based on the idea that resource management problems are the result of the absence of both institutional capacity and incentives to manage resources sustainably. In 1989, the government introduced CAMPFIRE, a new system that assigns group ownership rights to communities and provides institutions for resource management for the benefit of these communities (Martin 1986). This was implemented through an amendment to the Parks and Wildlife Act of 1975 that enables the government to delegate 'appropriate authority' over wildlife to 'communal representatives'.

The chapter explores whether CAMPFIRE has succeeded in devolving ownership over wildlife to communities and in generating benefits for these communities. I begin by evaluating the extent to which CAMPFIRE has achieved resource tenure reform by assigning clear and unambiguous rights to communities. I then seek to establish the extent to which benefits from wildlife management have become integrated into household livelihood strategies.

Communal Tenure

The CAMPFIRE programme is designed principally for the communal lands of Zimbabwe and aims to strengthen communal tenure regimes. Communal lands, formerly known as Reserves and later as Tribal Trust

Lands, are areas that were designated for the African population of the country during the colonial era, alongside the expropriation of lands for the white settler community and subsequent policies aimed at creating labour reserves and undermining African agricultural livelihoods (Phimister 1986).

There is considerable debate concerning the nature of the tenure system in the communal areas today. According to Cheater (1989), communal tenure in Zimbabwe is largely an ideological construct used in the colonial era to rationalize the racial division of land and to create an effective basis for the indirect control of natural resources through the chiefs, and continued by the post-colonial state to justify its own control over land (see also Ranger 1985, 1988; Drinkwater 1991). Scoones and Wilson (1989) and Bruce (1998) view the attachment of communities to a discrete piece of land as a function of the colonial system of indirect rule, which passed control over land to chiefs and headmen as a substitute for direct political power. Pre-colonial self-allocation of land (Bruce 1990), together with significant inequalities in landholding size among the indigenous African population (Ranger 1985, 1988) and African readiness to purchase land in freehold areas (Bourdillon 1987), suggest that the 'communal' nature of traditional land tenure in Zimbabwe may have been overstated.

The post-colonial Communal Lands Act of 1982 in effect vests ownership of communal lands and resources with the state, and assigns Rural District Councils (RDCs) the power to regulate their use. According to the Act, access to communal land is to be governed by customary law relating to the allocation, occupation and use of land. At the same time, Communal Land by-laws produced by the Ministry of Local Government provide for the planning and control of land use within council areas. In some RDCs, the constituency also includes owners and occupiers of lands held under private freehold or leasehold tenure. In such cases, the landholders have full control over the planning and use of their land, and the role of the RDC is simply to provide services.

The National Parks and Wildlife Act (1975), as amended in 1982, gives authority over wildlife to the RDCs for the communal areas and to the landowners for the private/leasehold tenure sector. In the communal areas, therefore, residents typically do not determine how wildlife is going to be managed or how the 'benefits' so generated are to be utilized. These decisions tend to be made by the RDC and other 'outsiders'. At the same time, communities have to pay a variety of taxes and charges to the RDC for the management of 'their' wildlife. Communities do not have an intrinsic right to use wildlife themselves, only the right to benefit from the use of wildlife by others. Owners and occupiers of private lands, on the other hand, can decide on appropriate wildlife uses and are free to appropriate all the benefits of use, sharing some of these benefits with their communal lands neighbours in the case of 'conservancies'.

CAMPFIRE: Devolution of Resource Management?

Because of the absence of formal resource management institutions in most communities a significant component of CAMPFIRE has been the development of new forms of communal organization for wildlife management. This has involved the creation of village, ward and district wildlife management committees, in a process led by the Zimbabwe Trust, a local non-governmental organization that has become the lead implementing agency for CAMPFIRE. These new committees are, in effect, sub-committees of the devolved local government units: the Village Development Committee, the Ward Development Committee and the RDC, respectively.

This institutional development process has not extended to defining local rights over the wildlife resource. Instead, management tends to be based on RDC control over wildlife, completely divorced from other local systems of rights to communal resources. Most local people still do not view themselves as the joint owners of wildlife resources, but rather continue to see them as belonging to either the government or the RDC (Murombedzi 1994).

In the absence of clear rights to wildlife for the local communities, institutional development has tended to ignore the existing traditional institutions for land and resource management. This has contributed to the alienation of communities from the CAMPFIRE initiative. Lack of government recognition has not compromised traditional leaders' role in managing and regulating the use of communal resources. 'Traditional leadership', Cousins (1998, 7) remarks, 'draws much of its legitimate authority from its embeddedness in the social and cultural life of rural communities, where discourses of "tradition" associated with cultural identity are still persuasive for many'.

To the extent that CAMPFIRE ignores local rights and knowledge systems, it is informed by a centralizing and 'modernizing' ethic. This is a huge contradiction in a programme that is supposed to create community forms of resource ownership. In an attempt to stimulate the further devolution of authority over wildlife from the RDCs to the 'producer communities', the Tenure Reform Commission of 1994 recommended that new village assemblies be created as communal property associations, with clear and unambiguous rights to communal lands and resources. The commission based this recommendation on the CAMPFIRE programme's demonstration of the capacity of communities to manage resources over which they have clearly defined rights. Ironically, the CAMPFIRE programme itself would benefit from the implementation of this principle.

Wildlife Management Benefits

Quantification of economic benefits that have been generated from the various modes of wildlife utilization under CAMPFIRE also has been the subject of inquiry. The general conclusion has been that revenues have contributed significantly to the well-being of participating communities. With a few exceptions (Bond 1997; Murombedzi 1992, 1994), however, these studies have not compared the benefits of CAMPFIRE with those from other potential land uses, nor looked into the opportunity costs of participating in the programme. Moreover, little empirical data exists on the costs that households incur through wildlife predation on livestock. Calculations of benefits typically do not include the revenues accruing to the safari operators. Neither do they place values on the rights secured (or lost) by the communities. Instead 'benefit' in CAMPFIRE refers to the revenues that accrue to communities and RDCs.

'Unless the revenues from wildlife are translated into disposable individual or household incomes', Murphree (1997, 22) observes, 'decisions on wildlife/livestock options will be skewed towards livestock, even in situations where it is apparent that the wildlife option is collectedly more productive.' Accordingly, some of the revenues from wildlife utilization are distributed to households. In practice, since communities have little control over wildlife management, little or no equity in the form of wildlife utilization rights, and few opportunities to provide goods and services to the wildlife utilization industry, their participation in CAMPFIRE often amounts to little more than the receipt of handouts.

The level of household benefit is affected by several factors, chief among which is population density. Wildlife populations generally are most dense in those areas where human population densities are lowest, the pastoral and agricultural potential of the land being constrained by natural climatic factors, inadequate infrastructure, or both. These marginal areas often are adjacent to national parks and other protected areas. The households in these wards have, at least potentially, the highest revenues from safari hunting and other wildlife utilization operations.

CAMPFIRE-induced Immigration

With extremely low human population density and very high wildlife population density (due to its proximity to the Mana Pools National Park) Masoka ward in the Dande communal lands has among the highest revenues of all the communities participating in CAMPFIRE. Increases in human population density could reduce earnings considerably, as humans compete with wildlife for key resources such as arable land and water (Bond 1997). Consequently, one might expect that households with significant proportions of their incomes accounted for by wildlife earnings would seek to limit population expansion. Yet the contrary appears to be the case in Masoka and other CAMPFIRE wards with low population densities and high wildlife revenues.

Because of the historical distribution of land in Zimbabwe and the shortcomings of the post-independence land reform programme, there has been a high rate of migration among communal lands, and in particular to more marginal, less densely-populated lands. Accurate figures on migration are not available, but it is conceivable that more households have migrated to other communal lands than have been officially relocated in the government resettlement programme. Spontaneous resettlement in communal lands has occurred against official government policy and all attempts by the RDCs to a regulated land settlement and land use.

Masoka, with one of the highest wildlife revenues per household in the CAMPFIRE programme, also appears to have one of the highest rates of in-migration compared to other wards (Nabane 1995). Although officials have explained the potential impacts of migrants on wildlife habitat, the people of Masoka themselves continue to strive to attract more people to settle in the ward, fully aware that this will have the effect of reducing the amount of revenue per household. At the beginning of the CAMPFIRE programme, the Masoka community erected a solar-powered electric fence around an area of some 18 square kilometres to safeguard crops and livestock from wildlife predation. Today, the community wants to reposition the fence to accommodate expansion. How can we explain these dynamics, and what are their implications?

The people of Masoka argue that the settlers are not necessarily newcomers, but rather mostly the descendants of Masoka families who are 'coming home' from wage labour employment. They also say that the non-indigenous people settling in the ward are accepted mainly on compassionate and humanitarian grounds. In fact, however, most of the settlers are not descendants of Masoka families. In many cases they are retired labourers from Malawi and Zambia or their descendants, who have decided to settle in Zimbabwe and do not have legally recognized claims to official resettlement land. When confronted with this information, the people of Masoka admit that this is so, but argue that newcomers are a small community of only a few hundred households.

Masoka people encourage settlement in their ward because they believe it is the only way that they can quickly constitute a large enough constituency to leverage 'development' from the government. Today their children have to leave home to attend secondary school, more than a 100 kilometres away, because they are too few to warrant government investment in a secondary school in Masoka itself. Their nearest neighbours are 60 kilometres away, and so no bus operator will offer service to Masoka because there are too few passengers to warrant the trip. In any case, the road to Masoka is impassable in the wet season, and the government will not invest in its improvement since there are too few cotton growers in Masoka to justify the expense.

The settlers are agriculturists, and as they clear land for agriculture they encroach into wildlife habitat. The long-term residents are fully aware of the potential impact on their own wildlife revenues, but the 'development' option appears to be more attractive to them, despite the advice of numerous anthropologists and development practitioners. From this example, we may be tempted to conclude that at least at this stage in CAMPFIRE, participating communities view the programme as a temporary windfall, rather than a long-term development strategy. Thus, even in wards where CAMPFIRE revenues contribute significantly to household incomes, wildlife habitat continues to be lost to agricultural expansion.

Similar dynamics have been observed elsewhere. For example, Dobola ward in the Binga communal lands, one of the major wildlife producing areas for Binga's CAMPFIRE programme, experienced an influx of more than 300 households in the early 1990s. The connivance of powerful politicians in facilitating this movement of people is well-documented (Dzingirai 1994). Earlier immigrants facilitated the settlement of newcomers to minimize their own wildlife predation-related costs. North Gokwe likewise is rapidly becoming a very densely populated district, from a very low population density only a few years ago. In all these cases, the long-term residents appear to encourage immigration because of the perceived developmental benefits of higher population densities. Rather than a potential development resource, wildlife appears to be seen as the archetype of under-development. For the settlers, one attraction of the CAMPFIRE areas is the eradication of the tsetse fly, which makes agro-pastoralism less risky. Tsetse fly eradication programmes also opened up roads in previously unserviced areas, thus, providing some rudimentary infrastructure. Coupled with overcrowding in other communal lands and the slow pace of land reform, these appear to be sufficient incentives for farmers to resettle into these marginal areas despite the low and erratic rainfall and poor soils. They view wildlife as a wasting asset: valuable in subsidizing the settlement process, but an impediment to long-term investment.

Cotton production is important in most CAMPFIRE wards where there is a high rate of immigration. Researchers do not appear to have attempted to measure cash crop production systematically and compare it to wildlife revenues in any of these wards. What has been demonstrated, however, is that most migrants into these areas are enterprising frontiersmen and women who wish to invest in expanded cash crop and livestock production. They see the 'less developed' and sparsely populated communal lands of the Zambezi valley as a place that offers both land for cotton production and adequate grazing for livestock (Dzingirai 1994; Derman 1990). By settling in communal lands, they avoid the perceived bureaucratic constraints of the formal resettlement programme. Moreover, even in the CAMPFIRE communities, the government's agricultural extension services continue to be geared towards encouraging the expansion of arable agriculture, rather than realigning land use to favour wildlife production. The tsetse fly eradication programmes of the Zambezi valley are also justified on the basis of their potential to open up new lands for settlement and agriculture, and the huge mid-Zambezi Valley settlement scheme was a policy response to spontaneous settlement in areas that had been eradicated of the fly (Derman 1990).

Employment in the Safari Industry

Employment generation is often cited as one of the benefits of CAMPFIRE. While there has been no attempt to document the number of jobs created in the communities participating in the programme, it is evident that the safari industry is capital-intensive rather than labour-intensive. Moreover, the management of wildlife by communities is undertaken by elected committees and volunteer labour, rather than by dedicated organizations employing staff.

The safari industry continues to be dominated by whites, with very little participation of blacks as skilled workers (hunters and guides). The majority of black employees in the industry are cooks and camp attendants. Although the success of hunts often depends on the skills and knowledge of local trackers, who are an integral part of every safari operation, they are treated as unskilled labourers, rather than being recognized as qualified guides and remunerated accordingly.

The historical domination of the safari industry by whites can be traced to appropriation of rights from the local population by the colonial state. The racist conditions under which the industry developed in Zimbabwe persist to this day almost unchanged. In their desire to perpetuate for their clients the myth of a wild, pristine African experience, most safari operations prohibit local access into the hunting camps except as lowly paid labourers. The livestock and dogs of the local populations are harassed or shot if seen as interfering with hunting operations, because they defile the 'pristine' wilderness. Individual safari operators also impose restrictions on local activities in the hunting areas, ranging from total prohibition of access to some forms of negotiated access, restrictions made possible by the lack of clarity of the nature of local rights in the CAMPFIRE programme.

In some places, locals have insisted that community members should be attached to hunting operations for monitoring or training purposes. But there is no evidence that CAMPFIRE's training programmes actually have resulted in substantial skills acquisition by the local people. To date, not a single community trainee has qualified as a guide. Local people attached to monitor hunting operations often are left stranded in the village ostensibly due to lack space for them in the hunting trucks. Where local monitors do manage to participate in the hunt, the treatment they receive is often deplorable: they are viewed as a nuisance, rather than representing an aspect of cooperation between the hunter and community.

Conclusions

In CAMPFIRE, wildlife management continues to be driven mainly by external interests rather than by local dynamics stimulated by proprietorship. The RDCs use their authority to provide services to a broad band of wildlife resource users and to mediate conflicts among them. In addition regulating the conditions under which outsiders access the wildlife resources, they seek to control potentially negative local community activities such as livestock grazing, arable expansion and poaching.

The economic focus of wildlife management has been on supplying market demands for safari hunting and tourism. The greatest beneficiaries of the wildlife management services provided through CAMPFIRE are the safari operators, who receive increased security of access to the wildlife, as well as protection from local community threats. Land reorganization and land use planning also help to provide long-term security for wildlife habitat. Meanwhile, the management of natural resources on which household livelihoods depend, perhaps more than on wildlife revenues, is ignored. Communities do not manage natural resources in isolation, yet CAMPFIRE attempts to introduce an exclusive wildlife management regime without reference to existing diffuse systems of rights and management.

Even in most of the successful CAMPFIRE wards, the wildlife benefits that accrue to households are viewed as an insufficient basis for long-term livelihoods. Participants evidently are prepared to lose the wildlife in return for immigration that they hope will spur the central government to provide social overhead capital. In many places, household CAMPFIRE revenues have been declining, mainly due to the increased number of households participating in the programme (Bond 1997). Case studies demonstrate that most households in communal areas in Zimbabwe invest significant amounts of income into agricultural production and that such investments typically far exceed CAMPFIRE revenues (Murombedzi 1994).

Because of the weak tax base for most local authorities, wildlife immediately became the most taxable commodity in CAMPFIRE areas. For this reason, and also because of the traditional mistrust of local people by local government officials, it has become increasingly difficult to further devolve proprietorship of wildlife to local communities. Nowhere in CAMPFIRE has wildlife come to represent a viable mechanism for household-level accumulation. It is seen as beneficial not to the extent that it contributes to household incomes, but to the extent that it subsidizes the local authorities. Yet here, too, in so far as CAMPFIRE revenues finance community-level investments, this is done not to improve wildlife management, but rather to improve agricultural productivity, for example, via the construction of warehousing facilities for agricultural inputs and produce, and investment in agricultural processing technology such as mills.

Attempts to entice people's participation in conservation through the distribution of revenues from some forms of resource utilization, without at the same time devolving rights to these resources to local people, will not necessarily improve stewardship of resources. Rights of access to the wildlife resource itself need to be part of this equation. The focus of CAMPFIRE on 'high-value' forms of wildlife utilization marginalizes other local needs, including hunting. Even when wildlife is harvested for local communities, this is done by 'professionals' in orgies of butchery as in the Nyaminyami annual impala cropping programme (Murombedzi 1994). In contrast, community-based licensing and monitoring systems would cut costs and offer local people opportunities to directly utilize the wildlife themselves.

CAMPFIRE is being implemented predominantly in marginal ecosystems where there are obvious climatic limitations to arable agriculture and pastoralism, and where the programme postulates that wildlife management is the most productive form of land use. If this is to become a viable land use in such areas, CAMPFIRE must offer a solution for the crisis of accumulation faced by their residents. Quantitatively, accumulation means more inputs and implements, more land for arable agriculture, more access to marketing points and so on. Qualitatively, it means the adoption of new and more sophisticated production technologies, better land protection and the allocation of land to more productive uses (Baker 1989).

Viewed through this lens, the CAMPFIRE premise is that it will foster accumulation by allocating land to a more productive land use — wildlife utilization — and ensuring that its benefits accrue to the individual household. Yet even in Masoka, where land use planning has been devolved to the local community, this has been insufficient to stop the expansion of arable agriculture. Accumulation in the CAMPFIRE wards continues to be seen as the expansion of arable agriculture and livestock. In this context, CAMPFIRE implementation instead has sought to constrain the ability of households to accumulate through arable expansion or livestock acquisition, by means of land use planning and restrictions on the importation of cattle and donkeys (for draught power) into districts that did not have them because of tsetse fly infestation. In practice, wildlife revenues have provided a rather small carrot to encourage individuals to conserve wildlife, while restrictions have provided a more imposing stick.

At present, then, it is debatable whether land use allocation will be determined by local economic imperatives. It is more likely that the households in CAMPFIRE wards will continue to be constrained by RDC policies to participate in wildlife management, and that the programmes therefore will be contested. In situations where wildlife management only contributes marginally to the local and household economies, individuals will not be motivated to manage the wildlife beyond a minimum threshold determined by existing coercive measures rather than by individual commitment. In other words, where households face conservation costs that continue to be greater than the benefits, wildlife management will remain top-down and authoritarian. This is likely to change only if and when communities secure greater rights to wildlife resources.

References

Baker, J. (1989) *Rural Communities under Stress: Peasant Farmers and the State in Africa*, Cambridge: Cambridge University Press.

Bond, I. (1997) 'An Assessment of the Financial Benefits to Households from CAMPFIRE: The Wildlife Benefit-cost Ratio', *CAMPFIRE News*, 15, Harare: CAMPFIRE Association.

Bourdillon, M.F.C. (1987) *The Shona Peoples*, Gweru: Mambo Press.

Bruce, J.W. (1990) 'Legal Issues in Land Use and Resettlement', Background paper for the Agriculture Division, Southern Africa Department of the World Bank, *Zimbabwe Agriculture Sector Memorandum*.

Bruce, J.W. (1998) 'Learning from the Comparative Experience with Agrarian Land Reform', *Proceedings of the International Conference on Land Tenure in the Developing World with a focus on Southern Africa*, Cape Town: University of Cape Town.

Cheater, A.P. (1989) 'The Ideology of "Communal" Land Tenure in Zimbabwe: Mythogenesis Enacted', *Africa* 60(2): 188–206.

Cousins, B. (1998) 'How Do Rights become Real? Formal and Informal Institutions in South Africa's Tenure Reform programme', *Proceedings of the International Conference on Land Tenure in the Developing World with Focus on Southern Africa*, Cape Town: University of Cape Town.

Derman, B.W. (1990) *The Unsettling of the Zambezi Valley: An Examination of the Mid-Zambezi Rural Development Project*, CASS Working Paper, Harare: University of Zimbabwe, Centre For Applied Social Sciences.

Drinkwater, M. (1991) *The State and Agrarian Change in Zimbabwe's Communal Areas*, London: Macmillan Publishing.

Dzingirai, V. (1994) *Politics and Ideology in Human Settlement: Getting settled in the Sokomena Area of Chief Dobola*, CASS Working Paper, Harare: University of Zimbabwe, Centre For Applied Social Sciences.

Farquharson, L. (1993) 'Commercial Wildlife Utilization in Zimbabwe: Are Commercial Farms the Appropriate Model for CAMPFIRE?' Dissertation, Montreal: McGill University.

Martin, R.B. (1986) *Communal Areas Management Programme for Indigenous Resources (CAMPFIRE)*, Harare: Government of Zimbabwe, Department of National Parks and Wildlife Management, Branch of Terrestrial Ecology.

Moyo, S. K. (1998) Speech by S.K. Moyo, Minister of Mines, Environment and Tourism, reproduced in *CAMPFIRE News*, 17: 8.

Murombedzi, J.C. (1992) *Decentralization or Recentralization? Implementing CAMPFIRE in the Omay Communal Lands of the Nyaminyami District*, CASS Working Paper, Harare: University of Zimbabwe, Centre for Applied Social Sciences.

— (1994) 'The Dynamics of Conflict in Environmental Management Policy in the Context of the Communal Areas Management Programme for Indigenous Resources', D.Phil. Dissertation, Harare: University of Zimbabwe, Centre for Applied Social Sciences.

Murphree, M.W. (1997) 'Congruent Objectives, Competing Interest and Strategic Compromise: Concept and Process in the Evolution of Zimbabwe's CAMPFIRE Programme', Paper presented at the Conference on 'Representing Communities: Histories and Politics of Community-based Resource Management', June, Helen, Georgia.

Phimister, I. (1986) 'Discourse and the Discipline of Historical Context: Conservationism and Ideas about Development in Southern Rhodesia', *Journal of Southern Africa Studies* 12: 264–75.

Ranger, T.O. (1985) *Peasant Consciousness and Guerrilla War in Zimbabwe*, London: James Currey.

— (1988) 'The Communal Areas of Zimbabwe', *Land in Agrarian Systems Symposium*,

Urbana-Champaign: University of Illinois.

Scoones, I. and K. Wilson (1989) 'Households, Lineage Groups and Ecological Dynamics: Issues for Livestock Development', in B. Cousins, ed., *People, Land and Livestock: Proceedings of a Workshop on the Socio-economic Dimensions of Livestock Production in Zimbabwe's Communal Lands*, GTZ and Harare: Centre for Applied Social Sciences, University of Zimbabwe.

PART IV:

DEFENDING THE COMMONS

A Romani woman in her kitchen garden in Hungary.
Photo credit: Krista Harper.

CHAPTER 13
INTERNATIONAL ENVIRONMENTAL JUSTICE:
BUILDING THE NATURAL ASSETS OF THE WORLD'S POOR

Krista Harper and S. Ravi Rajan

Introduction

Across the globe, vibrant social movements are emerging that link together issues of resource access, social security, environmental risks and disaster vulnerability. Although all people suffer the effects of pollution, global warming and resource exploitation, poor people are especially vulnerable since they live closer to the margin of survival and are less able to afford cushions from environmental ills. Moreover, as in the case of the United States described by Manuel Pastor in this volume, poor communities often face disproportionately heavy burdens from environmental degradation. Increasingly, low-income urban and rural communities around the world are organizing to fight for environmental justice — that is, for more equitable access to natural resources and environmental quality, including clean air and water. These new environmental movements connect sources and sinks; North and South; ecology and equity; and asset building and hazard vulnerability. They have begun to articulate new ideas about the quality of life, and the meaning of development and modernization.

There is mounting recognition that environmental pollution and natural resource degradation are not simply 'quality of life' issues primarily of concern to middle-class people of the global North. In cities of both the North and the South, residents of poor neighbourhoods often are most exposed to air fouled by car exhaust, diesel fumes, and deliberate and accidental industrial emissions. As urban growth accelerates worldwide, neighbourhoods struggle for access to green space, public transportation, sanitation, and clean water and air. Poor communities have the least access to these public goods. Some researchers estimate that as much as one fifth of developing countries' disease burdens can be attributed to environmental pollution vectors such as poor water quality, lack of sanitation facilities and exposure to industrial wastes (Blacksmith Institute 2000, 2). In rural areas, the poor are often most dependent on natural resources from fisheries to forests, rivers to rangelands, for their immediate subsistence and survival.

Research on environmental inequalities has identified three reasons why poor communities are often disproportionately affected by pollution and environmental deterioration:

1) *Siting*: Poor neighbourhoods are more likely to have environmental hazards and pollution dumped on them, especially if their residents belong to historically disenfranchised racial ethnic groups (Bullard 1994).

2) *Move-in*: In some instances, the poor are compelled by economic circumstances to move to more polluted or degraded areas where property values are lower, a process sometimes called 'market dynamics' (Been 1999).

3) *Vulnerability*: Even if exposure to environmental hazards were the same across the entire population, the poor would be hurt more by virtue of their inferior access to good nutrition, health care, insurance and private amenities such as bottled water and air conditioning (Leatherman 2005).

This chapter sketches the contours of what can be described as the international 'environmental justice' movement. We begin by exploring the dimensions of environmental inequity among countries, between the nations of the global South and North. We then explore environmental injustice within countries of the South. Because of the sheer scale of this subject — the literally countless dramas being played out across the globe — we do not attempt to be comprehensive, but instead use typical examples to draw out some common features of such movements. In particular, we explore the relationship between environmental injustice and the social attributes of age, race, ethnicity, class and gender.

Against this backdrop, we explore what communities are doing across the world to combat environmental contamination and resource depletion. We suggest that the 'natural assets' approach — based on investment, redistribution, internalization of benefits and appropriation — is a valuable tool for understanding community strategies for securing ecologically sustainable livelihoods. We conclude with some thoughts on what external agencies and catalysts can do to support these efforts.

The Environment and Inequality among Countries

Environmental inequalities exist between the industrialized countries of the 'global North' and the developing countries of the 'global South'. Many countries of the former 'Second World' (eastern Europe and the former Soviet Union) face environmental threats similar to those in the global South. The global North exploits the ecology of poorer countries in three main ways:

- as a source of raw materials;
- as a sink where the North can dispose of pollution and negative environmental 'side effects';
- through 'coercive conservation' that aims to preserve wild ecosystems and biodiversity without consideration for the human communities living in or near these habitats.

Figure 13.1: Environmental Inequalities among Countries of the Global North and South

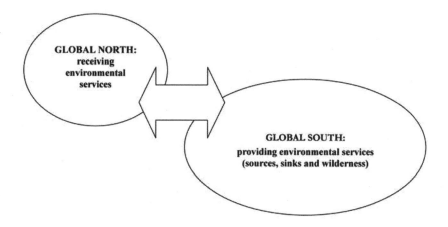

The South as 'Source': Minerals Extraction and Agribusiness

Since the beginning of colonialism, Asia, Africa and the Americas were seen by the colonizers as a source of natural wealth to be exploited. European explorers sailed to the Americas in search of El Dorado, the legendary 'City of Gold'. Although they never found it, they did find tremendous mineral wealth and lands to produce export crops including cotton, sugar, tea, coffee, and later, fruit. Five centuries later, mineral extraction and agribusiness continue to play an important role in trade between the global North and South, with grave environmental consequences.

The mining industry vividly illustrates the global North's exploitation of the South as a source of natural wealth. When Papua New Guinea (PNG) was under Australian rule in the 1950s, for example, colonial administrators sold gold prospecting rights to multinational corporations without consulting local communities that would be impacted. After PNG achieved independence in 1975, the national government persisted in encouraging mineral exploration to attract foreign direct investment. In a well-publicized case, an Australian-based firm opened the Ok Tedi gold-mining operation near the source of the Fly River. While some members of indigenous groups benefited from employment in the mines, toxic sediments killed off the river ecosystem's fish and birds, and devastated the livelihood of the Yonggom people who live downstream. Yonggom activists successfully sued for compensation and damages to cover the rehabilitation of the river. Company shareholders, in turn, threatened to close the mine, leaving the task of cleaning up to the PNG government (Kirsch 2002; Johnson and Jorgenson 1994).

The Costa Rican banana plantation economy provides an example of the Northern exploitation of Southern environments through agribusiness. Banana plantations in the Sarapiquí rainforest have pushed out ecologically sound traditional agroforestry production by peasants. Taking advantage of government concessions for foreign direct investment, Standard Fruit Company cleared the forests to make way for mono-crop banana cultivation, importing workers from surrounding regions and countries. When bananas dropped in value in the world market after a period of high profits, Standard Fruit scaled back production, leaving behind large tracts of destroyed forestlands and unemployed, landless workers (Vandemeer and Perfecto 1995).

The South as 'Sink': Toxic Exports and the Dirty Industries

In recent decades, rich countries have also used poor countries as a 'sink' for pollution and waste. Ironically, improvements in environmental quality resulting from the enactment of stricter environmental standards in the global North sometimes have contributed to the growth of polluting industries and the dumping of toxic wastes in the South, as corporations and entire industries actively seek sites with fewer environmental regulations (Clapp 2001).[1]

One of the first cases of hazardous waste dumping in South Africa to catch the attention of the international press came when Thor Chemicals, Inc., moved its mercury reclamation processing facility from the corporation's home in England to a small village in South Africa's KwaZulu-Natal province, 40 miles north of Durban. After one year of operation, water samples in the village registered mercury levels over 1500 times the level deemed toxic by US Environmental Protection Agency, and dangerously high levels of mercury were found in Durban's water supply as well (Lambrecht 1989; Fondaw 2001). Environmental health researchers reported that communities downstream from the facility were at risk of mercury poisoning by consuming the contaminated fish (Oosthuizen and Erlich 2001).

The infamous 'Summers memo' epitomizes the view of the South as a sink. In February 1992, an internal memo by Lawrence Summers, the World Bank's chief economist at the time, discussed the transfer of pollution and dirty industries from industrialized countries to less-developed countries (LDCs). 'Just between you and me, shouldn't the World Bank be encouraging *more* migration of the dirty industries to the LDCs?', Summer wrote. He continued, 'I think the economic logic behind dumping a load of toxic waste in the lowest wage country is impeccable and we should face up to that.' (*The Economist* 1992) When the memo was leaked and subsequently publicized by environmental organizations, Summers claimed that his comments were intended simply to provoke a debate within the World Bank. Given the reality of toxic dumping in South Africa and other poor countries, however, the Summers memo seemed to confirm activists' worst fears about the callous indifference of many policymakers to international environmental inequalities.

The South as 'Wild': Coercing Conservation

A final dimension of international environmental inequalities emerges when the global South is treated as a repository of 'wild Nature' that must be protected from local people. 'Coercive conservation' — wilderness preservation programmes that ignore local people's traditional relationships with the land — arises from the Western (especially US) wilderness ethic that places high value on untouched 'nature without people'. [2]

In Africa, wildlife conservation dating from the colonial era has served as a means to control indigenous populations' use of the landscape (Ranger 1989). The Masai tribe, for example, has inhabited the savannas of what is now Kenya and Tanzania for 500 years, but in the 1950s British colonial administrators resettled them on smaller tracts of land to promote nature tourism. With limited access to their traditional rangelands, the Masai now raise their herds in a severely degraded environment threatened by desertification (Neumann 1998).

In recent decades, national and international conservation campaigns have further displaced Masai cattle-herders and other local people by banning them from nature preserves. While the park systems welcome foreign tourists on safari, they consider the local inhabitants who graze or hunt on the newly enclosed commons to be 'poachers' and punish them accordingly. As part of its campaign to protect the African elephant, the World Wildlife Fund furnished the Kenyan Wildlife Service with money that was used to arm sanctuary rangers in the fight against suspected ivory poachers. By the early 1990s, Kenyan rangers had shot and killed over 100 people in their efforts to protect the elephant (Peluso 1993).

In many places, such coercive conservation policies have fostered a widespread perception that environmentalists care more about 'nature' than they do about people. International environmental organizations have often legitimized and financially supported authoritarian governments, and have wrested access to land and resources out of the hands of local residents. For non-coercive conservation to become a reality, local communities must participate meaningfully in all aspects of planning, implementation and evaluation (see also Murombedzi in this volume).

The Environment and Inequality within Countries

Environmental injustice exists not only among nations, but *within* them as well. In rich countries and poor countries alike, certain populations bear disproportionate burdens from the effects of environmental degradation. Within countries, people often experience environmental inequalities along lines of class, race, ethnicity and nationality; urban/rural divisions; age and gender. This section will briefly examine these aspects of environmental inequalities.

Class

Around the world, environmental problems often affect most strongly the lives of poor and working people. Both individually and collectively, poor people everywhere have fewer political and material resources for avoiding environmental risks. Poor agricultural workers from India to Mexico and California face the worst health impacts of pesticide drift. Here, the reason is that being poor, they are forced to take on the most hazardous jobs.

In yet other cases, poor communities find themselves situated in toxic dumps or lethal cancer clusters. For example, in the Bhopal gas disaster, the vast majority of those who inhaled the toxic fumes that emanated from the Union Carbide factory were poor workers who could not afford to live in any place other than near the hazardous factory (Rajan 2001). With broken windows and inadequate ventilation, the houses of slum dwellers neighbouring the plant offered little protection from the clouds of gas and fumes (Centre for Science and Environment 1985). Poor communities often lack the political resources that would enable them to prevent the siting of hazardous industrial plants and dumps or to collect compensation for damages. In Bhopal, the state cut funding for long-term epidemiological research, after only six years, leaving citizens' organizations to collect data on their own (Dhara 2002; Fortun 1998). Without adequate medical monitoring prior to and following the chemical explosion, state bureaucrats frequently dismissed poor people's claims of disaster-related illness as 'compensation neurosis' or the consequence of 'normal' poor hygiene and nutrition (Rajan 2001). In such contexts, the threat of exposure is compounded by lack of adequate scientific research by state regulatory agencies that could either establish their risks, or which could allow them to seek compensation.

Figure 13.2: Environmental Inequalities *within* Countries of the Global North and South

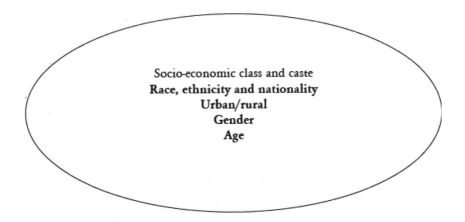

Socio-economic class and caste
Race, ethnicity and nationality
Urban/rural
Gender
Age

Race, Ethnicity and Nationality

In many places, racial, ethnic and national minorities are more likely to be exposed to pollution and environmental degradation. In the United States, for example, toxic waste sites are sited disproportionately near African-American communities (Bullard 1994), and migrant farmworkers from Mexico face chronic occupational exposures to pesticides because they fear deportation and job loss (Pulido 1996). In metropolitan areas across the country, African-Americans, Latinos and Asian-Americans often live in those neighbourhoods most exposed to toxic industrial emissions (Ash and Fetter 2004; see also the chapter by Manuel Pastor in this volume). In Eastern Europe, where they were once forbidden to own land, the Roma (Gypsy) minority today faces housing discrimination, high unemployment and dumping of toxic wastes in their villages and neighbourhoods (Harper 2007; Filcak 2004a, 2004b). In Southeast Asia, ethnic minorities contend with deforestation by powerful logging interests that threatens their traditional livelihoods (Hurst 1990, Fahn 2003). In Nigeria, the Ogoni people have seen their environment ravaged by multinational oil companies (Human Rights Watch 1999). The pattern is clear: political disenfranchisement translates into a precarious grip on assets.

Urban/Rural Divisions

Environmental problems affect urban and rural people in different ways. Urban people typically face greater exposure to air pollution and traffic hazards. In Budapest, Hungary, for example, pediatricians recorded higher levels of lead in the blood of children living in the centre of the city than in samples taken from suburban children (Harper 2006). In some of China's urban industrial centres, more than two-thirds of the children are afflicted by lead poisoning (Chu 2002).

Rural people, in contrast, often suffer from the depletion of natural resources to meet urban demands. They bear the weight of the city's 'ecological footprint', while experiencing fewer of the infrastructure or other benefits of urban life. In some cases, the effects on rural people are devastating. The lands of the Kayapó people in Brazil, for example, were flooded when the government dammed the Xingu River to generate electricity for urban populations (Turner 1993; Zimmerman *et al.* 2001). Native Americans living near nuclear test sites in Nevada and people living near the Lop Nur atomic testing range in China have suffered alike from the majority population's perception of 'remote' rural land as wastelands suitable for extreme environmental damage (Kuletz 1999; Johnston 1994).

Age

The elderly and the very young are often especially vulnerable to environmental hazards. Elderly people tend to be less mobile than other community members, and often spend their entire day within the neighbourhood. This helps to explain why elderly residents of West Harlem, in New York City, became key community organizers when the neighbourhood's air quality was threatened by a sewage treatment plant (Checker 2001).

At the same time, children are especially prone to environmental risks because of their ongoing physical development. A World Health Organization (WHO) survey reported that, 'two-thirds of the preventable diseases occurring worldwide from environmental causes occur among children' (WHO 1997, 199). As the least mobile members of society, children are exposed to toxins in the places where they live and play (Stephens 1996). Environmental groups focusing on children's health are now flourishing across Eastern Europe and the former Soviet Union, from the mothers' movement for clean food in southern Poland to the anti-nuclear activism of Ukraine's Mama 86 (Glazer and Glazer 1998; Bellows 2003).

Gender

Environmental degradation affects men and women in different ways. Because labour is often divided along gender lines, men and women face different environmental hazards at work and at home. Women tend to be less mobile and hence more dependent on the immediate environment for their livelihoods. In rural India, women are forced by deforestation to walk further in search of fuel wood; at the same time, they are exposed to high levels of hazardous pollutants from the smoke they inhale while they cook (Agarwal 1986).[3] In their traditional role as family care-givers, women are especially sensitive to environmental health problems (Douglass *et al.* 2002). Penny Newman, a leader of the Citizens' Clearinghouse for Hazardous Wastes in the United States, characterizes the crusade against toxics as 'a movement of housewives' because of the crucial role that mothers play as grassroots community activists (Gottlieb 1993).

Individuals and communities may experience several overlapping aspects of environmental inequality at the same time. In the Brazilian Amazon forest, female rubber tappers have fought alongside male organizers in demanding sustainable forest management and equitable access to resources. Women often take roles on the front lines of *empades*, the strike lines protecting stands of rubber trees from clear-cutting. Led by the late Chico Mendes, the rubber tappers' union succeeded in establishing the Xapuri extractive reserve (see the chapter by Anthony Hall in this volume). Many of the women found that they had limited access to markets where they could sell rubber gathered in the new reserve, however, and decided to form a separate organization, the Women's Group of Xapuri (Campbell 1996). The group's emergence highlights the cross-cutting elements of class, rural identity and gender in the distribution and use of natural resources.

Communities are Organizing for Environmental Justice

Debunking the myth that only affluent citizens of the global North can afford to worry about the environment, poor communities across the globe have long mobilized to protect nature and environmental quality. These groups asserted their rights to clean air, water and other open access resources — resources 'available in theory to all, but available in practice only to those with the power to appropriate them' (Boyce 2003, p. 9). In so doing, they have increased the natural assets of low-income people, bringing benefits in terms of economic opportunities, public health and social status. This section looks at examples of grassroots activism in China's cities, in South African mining towns, on Russia's Far Eastern shore, in the shantytowns of Bangkok, on the riverbanks of central and Eastern Europe, and in rural sectors of India. As they work to solve problems at the local level, these community-based organizations take part in the growing movement to redress environmental inequalities within and among countries.

Fighting for Clean Air in Urban China

The 10 million people living in Tianjin, China's third largest metropolis, are no strangers to smog. Sunlight filters on the northern port city through a blanket of brownish haze so thick that it can be seen in satellite photos taken from space. Exhaust fumes and particulate matter choke the air and clog residents' lungs as they ride their bicycles to work. After years of suffering from respiratory illnesses, the residents of one Tianjin neighbourhood joined together to take a company to court to prevent the expansion of a coal-burning plant that belched out foul-smelling smoke — and won compensation for past damages as well as a promise that the company would adopt cleaner design in the new plant (Plafker 2002).

Tianjin is by no means the only Chinese city plagued by severe air pollution. Residents of Beijing speak of autumn as the 'dirty season', since it is marked by a sharp rise in the city's already elevated air pollution levels (China Economic Times 2001). Sulphur dioxide and particulate matter pose especially grave threats to health. The effects of breathing polluted air are particularly serious for the children of China. A recent national study found that half of all urban youth in China are afflicted with lead poisoning (Chu 2002).

For many years, pollution was widely regarded as the inevitable price to be paid for China's 'economic miracle'. 'The worst pollution is poverty', state officials told a Western environmental consultant who visited the country in the early 1980s (Shen 2001, p. 26). Twenty years later, officials and the public are increasingly aware of the costs of unregulated industrial growth. According to a report published by the Chinese government in 1999, the health costs of air and water pollution were over US$46 billion per year — equivalent to almost seven per cent of the country's GNP (Pan 2001).

Today change is in the air, heralded by a recent wave of citizens' class-action lawsuits against big polluters. The plaintiffs in the Tianjin case were represented by Wang Cangfa, an environmental lawyer and the founder of the Centre for Legal Assistance to Pollution Victims (CLAPV). Founded in 1998 and run entirely by volunteers, CLAPV staffs China's first environmental hotline and has received over 100 calls a month since it opened (Plafker 2002). The Centre also offers workshops on environmental law for legal professionals and journalists, and provides free legal assistance to victims of air and water pollution. In another case, Wang Cangfa has defended groups of farmers from the outskirts of Beijing whose livestock and produce were ruined by industrial effluents (Brettel 2002).

The emerging Chinese environmental movement includes government-organized groups as well as non-governmental organizations set up by committed individuals (Knup 1997). These groups are tackling the problems of urban air and water pollution, and bringing citizens' grievances to the attention of the courts and state environmental protection agencies. China now faces the challenge of developing a more consistent environmental monitoring and enforcement system, to enable the country to move beyond 'end-of-pipe' solutions and compensation (Shen 2001).

Asbestos Activism in South Africa

In South Africa, mine workers and rural villagers are joining forces to fight pollution from the asbestos industry. Since the fall of the apartheid regime, many asbestos mining corporations have left South Africa. Their mines and mills have closed, leaving thousands of workers unemployed. Although jobs have disappeared, the asbestos industry left visible scars on the landscape and the bodies of those working in and living near the mines. Asbestos contamination has emerged as one of South Africa's major environmental health challenges. Defunct companies have left behind an estimated 121 mining sites — sites the South African government must now rehabilitate at great cost. Winds have spread asbestos fibers as far as 100 kilometres from their source. Residents of villages near the former mines have found drifts of asbestos fibers and dust in their gardens, playgrounds and streets. Because villagers construct their buildings from handmade bricks of mud and plaster, many homes and schools are contaminated. Asbestos contamination causes a range of painful and deadly respiratory ailments, including asbestosis, lung cancer and mesothelioma. These asbestos-related diseases (ARDs), common among former miners and mill workers, also develop through prolonged secondary exposure to asbestos tailings. In some villages near mine complexes, more than a third of the inhabitants suffer from ARDs (Jacobs *et al.* 2001).

In the Northern Cape and North-west provinces of South Africa, trade unions and village associations are organizing to clean up the pollution left by the asbestos mining industry, and building coalitions to address the health needs of people affected by ARDs. The National Union of Mineworkers is working in partnership with the Environmental Justice Networking Forum and local advocacy groups, such as Concerned People against Asbestos in the town of Prieska.

They have used lobbying, litigation, advocacy and education to advance their goals, pressing the South African government for assistance and participating in the 1998 Parliamentary Asbestos Summit. A group of over 7,000 former miners and other people afflicted with asbestosis has filed suit in the United Kingdom in the Cape Plc. case. The case was settled in June 2003, by which time 776 claimants had already died (Altenroxel 2003).

Combating the Tragedy of the Corporate Commons in Russia's Far East

In Sakhalin Island, on Russia's far eastern shore, activists are fighting to protect the Bering Sea's fisheries and wildlife from petroleum drilling. The residents of the island are a long way from Moscow, where Russian officials make decisions affecting their environment. Since the break-up of the Soviet Union, the Russian government has sought to attract foreign direct investment by licensing multinational corporations to conduct offshore oil exploration and drilling. Exxon is shifting operations from Alaska, with its stricter regulatory environment, in favour of large-scale exploration and drilling off Sakhalin (Carlton 2002). While the government in Moscow gains income from the sale of licenses, the people of Sakhalin Island face the collapse of the local fishing and food processing industries (Barranikova and Lisitsyn 2001). Despite promises by both Exxon and the Russian government that oil exploration will create new jobs for local residents, hopes for sustainable economic development through oil are not borne out by past experiences in other parts of the world (Wilson 1999).

Offshore oil exploration has had particularly dire consequences for the Nivkhi people, an indigenous group living on the northern coast of Sakhalin Island whose traditional way of life is based on the herring, smelt, salmon and other fish of the Bering Sea. Since the collapse of the Soviet Union, the public transportation infrastructure of Sakhalin Island has fallen apart, isolating the rural communities of the northern coast. The Nivkhi, along with other residents, find themselves more dependent than ever on the natural environment — fishing, hunting and gathering for survival (Wilson 1999; Meier 2000). Nivkhi fishermen report that recent fish catches have been inedible because of strong chemical odours and festering ulcers on the fish (Barranikova and Litsyn 2001).

Sakhalin Environmental Watch (SEW), a Russian non-governmental organization, is fighting to protect the island's natural resources and the rights of local people. SEW organized a coalition of local people, including indigenous groups, representatives of the local fishing industry and environmentalists (Boyd and Cook 1998/1999). Environmental activists from SEW have conducted research on the state of fisheries near offshore oil exploration projects in the Bering Sea, drawing on the local knowledge of Nivkhi fishermen (Barranikova and Litsyn 2001). They have also organized international exchanges with Alaskan communities affected by the 1989 Exxon Valdez oil spill, who offered testimony on the long-term ecological and economic damages resulting from the spill (Steiner 1999).

Yet SEW's impressive ability to draw upon multiple forms of ecological expertise and to forge cooperation among community groups may not be enough to protect the Sakhalin environment. Considerable progress was made in the 1990s towards building a government environmental protection agency and encouraging the growth of environmental organizations, but Russian President Vladmir Putin then clamped down on environmentalism as a threat to national security and economic growth. In summer of 2000, for example, Putin closed down the Committee on Ecology (Russia's environmental protection agency) and the Russian Forestry Service (Cox

2000). The ability of non-governmental organizations to promote change depends, in part, on the presence of responsive government institutions, but the avenues for citizen participation in environmental decision-making in Russia remain strictly limited (Gordon 2006).

Greening the Slums: Community Activism in Bangkok

Across Asia, cities have been growing at a breakneck speed in recent decades. As the centre of Thailand's economic growth, metropolitan Bangkok has expanded rapidly since the early 1960s. The economic growth and urbanization have not, however, resulted in a better urban environment for city dwellers. Instead, Bangkok's residents now contend with traffic congestion, air pollution and high levels of lead and other toxins in the environment. A city built on rivers and canals, Bangkok now faces a shortage of potable water. Only two per cent of the metropolitan population is linked to the municipal sewer system.

Although all Bangkok residents are victims of the city's rapid environmental deterioration, poor communities suffer most acutely. Bangkok's slums are located mainly in marginal and industrial zones that are most vulnerable to floods, unmonitored trash disposal and industrial waste dumping. Roughly one million of Bangkok's seven million residents live in these slums, many of which are 'illegal', being built on land owned by the city or private firms, limiting the residents' political power to improve their living conditions (Douglass *et al.* 2002).

In one Bangkok slum, however, residents have organized to improve the community's environment, expand small businesses and provide badly needed social services. In 1990, the 1,000 members of the Wat Chonglom squatter settlement began a community development programme, drawing on interest-free loans secured from Citibank by two professors at nearby Mahidol University. The community began by cleaning up trash that had accumulated under the slums' raised buildings and sidewalks. Buoyed by this initial success, the residents of Wat Chonglom connected houses to a piped water system, built a community hall and day-care centre, and repaired and painted family homes. Women took an especially active role in setting the agenda and implementing these neighbourhood improvements. The project quickly benefited the urban environment, public health and safety, and these improvements in turn fostered new income opportunities as residents opened new food stalls, beauty parlors, video stores and other small businesses. Can Wat Chonglom's successes be repeated in other slums? A research team from the University of Hawaii gives a qualified 'yes', concluding that Wat Chonglom's transformation was enabled by a combination of strong community groups, access to partnership with a local university, and access to external funds and loans (Douglass *et al.* 2002). These social and economic assets empowered residents to reappropriate and improve their natural environment.

Central and Eastern Europe: The Struggle for Clean Water

In Romania and Hungary, environmental organizations have been working quietly for over a decade to improve air and water quality. When a massive toxic release into the Danube River system occurred in early 2000, thousands of citizens in both countries mobilized to defend their right to clean water and a safe environment. On January 30, the tailings dam breached at a gold-processing facility in Baia Mare, Romania, releasing roughly 100,000 cubic metres of water containing high levels of cyanide and heavy metals into nearby streams. Within three days the toxic plume had flowed into Hungary, where it reached the Tisza River, a major tributary of the Danube. A month later, the spill had passed through Hungary, Serbia and Bulgaria, and back into Romania en route to the Black Sea. When the plume reached the Danube's delta at the Black Sea coast, a research team of the United Nations Environmental Programme recorded cyanide at 0.058 milligrams per liter, almost six times the Romanian Environmental Protection Agency's permissible concentration level.

All told, the disaster affected about 2000 kilometres of the Tisza and Danube Rivers. The cyanide killed thousands of tons of fish, poisoned waterfowl and threatened many communities' drinking water supplies. Heavy metals deposited in the river's sediment will continue to affect life for many decades.

The responsible mining operation, Aurul SA, was a joint venture begun in 1992 between the private Australian mining company, Esmeralda, and the state-owned Romanian mining concern, Remin. Ironically, the Romanian government had heralded Esmeralda's involvement as an opportunity to introduce more environmentally sound practices in the already heavily mined region. Following an environmental impact assessment, the plant began processing in April 1999. After the spill, the Romanian authorities levied a fine on Aurul SA amounting to US$166. This was obviously insufficient to cover the damages or to deter irresponsible behaviour in the future, but the fine was small because the owners were deemed to be in compliance with Romanian standards.

In the post-communist era, Romania has attracted foreign investment with its mineral wealth, coupled with its relatively lax environmental standards for extracting that wealth. In this respect, current policies share a curious commonality with the communist government's views ·on the environment, when officials accepted ecological degradation as an unfortunate but necessary side-effect of industrialization and growth. In both periods, Romanian development strategy has emphasized mineral extraction and processing, with a change to foreign direct investment and public-private partnerships in the post-communist period. The president of an environmental organization in Szolnok, a Hungarian city affected by the spill, described Aurul SA as 'the perfect example of eco-colonialism — taking advantage of the lack of regulations and unemployment' (Harper and Ash 2001).

In opposition to the conventional wisdom that people must choose between jobs and the environment, communities in Romania and Hungary are rallying for sustainable livelihoods. In Baia Mare, the site of the spill, a city where life expectancies are 10 years shorter than the Romanian national average and the WHO has recorded some of the highest blood lead levels ever found, residents are literally fighting for their lives (Csagoly 2000). Members of the Baia Mare environmental organization ASSOC (Association of Professional NGOs for Social Assistance in Baia Mare) point out that while mining operations and heavy industry contribute wages to the local economy, this comes at the expense of other economic producers whose livelihoods are damaged by polluted air, water and soil. For example, farmers in and around Baia Mare cannot find markets for their produce, and residents cannot safely eat fruits and vegetables from their home gardens. ASSOC has been active in informing residents of environmental threats and setting up public forums where farmers and other citizens present their grievances to local authorities. Following the cyanide spill, they initiated collaborative projects with Hungarian environmental groups downstream. Today they are coordinating a programme that trains high-school science teachers throughout the region to monitor key environmental health indicators, and they are working to rehabilitate rivers and groundwater supplies, as other organizations in the region seek viable economic alternatives to the mining industry.

Building Sustainable Forestry in Rural India

Pioneering forest management programmes in India have sought to preserve the commons by building partnerships between local communities and government agencies. Such efforts, generically known as Joint Forest

Management (JFM) aim at involving forest communities in micro-level decision-making about subsistence use, commercial development and afforestation (Mishra 1999).

In many Indian states, for example, traditional approaches to policing forests resulted in militant conflict with local populations. These conflicts have their roots in the very purpose for which forest departments were created by the colonial government in the 19th century. Then, as continues to be largely the case now, the primary purpose of conservation was to ensure the steady supply of timber to meet the demands of the state. The needs of local resource users were subordinated to that of the state, which directed its forestry departments to protect the forests from theft by local peoples. (Rawat 1991; Rangarajan 1996; Saberwal 1999; Sivaramakrishnan 1999). In adopting such a philosophy, the Indian colonial and post-colonial state followed the tradition established first in France and Prussia (Rajan 1998, 2006).

In recent years, forest departments in some Indian states, such as West Bengal, began creating forest protection committees that provided employment, compensation and a proactive role for local communities in conserving local forests. Joint Forest Management, as the programme is known, envisages developing partnerships between the forest department and forest users. Such partnerships are forged on the principles of mutual trust and jointly defined roles and responsibilities, with forest protection and development as the goal. Under the JFM programme, 'the user (local communities) and the owner (government) manage the resource and share the cost equally' (Joint Forest Management website 2004).

The origins of JFM go back to 1972, when the convergence of two factors, deforestation and demand by local communities for forest resources, led to a government initiated experiment in the fringe forest villages of the Arabari development block in Midnapore district of West Bengal. Local villagers were charged with protecting coppices of Sal (*Shorea robusta*) trees and in return received free usufructary rights on non-timber forest products, a promise of 25 per cent share of sale of Sal poles and employment. The success of this experiment led to the more widespread advocacy of 'social forestry'. In the ensuing three decades, the JFM model has evolved and has been adopted across many states of the Indian union (People's Commission on Environment and Development in India website 2004).

The experience with JFM has demonstrated that qualitatively new relationships, re-configuring how power, compensation and expertise are negotiated, can be formed between users and regulatory bodies (Gadgil and Guha 1995; Chambers *et al.* 1989; Jeffery and Sundar 1999; Poffenberger and McGean 1996; Saxena 1997). Moreover, in recent times, such ideas have become an important element of governmental policy in India (Planning Commission, Government of India 2003).

Conclusions

The work of environmental justice movements around the world is part of a larger transformation in the role of public participation in development policy. Traditionally, local people were cast in the role of 'users and choosers' of plans conceived in the offices of development agencies, an approach that failed to tap their knowledge, skills and commitment to improving living conditions. The community-based initiatives described in the previous section reveal the power of local activists as creative 'makers and shapers' of efforts to protect and maintain healthy and livable environments.[4] Their struggles remind us that no landscape is a wasteland and no people are expendable.

The recurrent themes of rights and justice in environmental movements around the world — both within and across national borders — points to a new conception of environmentalism itself. Rather than a movement simply to protect the environment, we are witnessing the development of movements to protect people, by defending their rights to healthy environments and sustainable livelihoods based on access to natural assets. By rejecting the false dichotomy between the well-being of nature and the well-being of the poor, struggles for environmental justice promise to reinvigorate the global quest for a sustainable future.

Notes

1. While the 1992 Basel Convention on the Control of Trans-boundary Movements of Hazardous Waste regulates the export of waste, its 'recycling' clause permits any toxic wastes labelled as recyclable material to be exported.
2. On 'coercive conservation', see Nancy Peluso (1993).
3. Following pioneering research on the latter problem by epidemiologists and health workers, there is now a movement afoot to improve the environmental quality of stoves (Kammen 1995).
4. On the contrast between 'users and choosers' versus 'makers and shapers', see Cornwall and Gaventa (2001).

References

Agarwal, Bina (1986) *Cold Hearths and Barren Slopes: Wood Fuel Crisis in the Third World*, London: Zed Books.

Altenroxel, Lynne (2003) 'Pay-out for Ill Miners Cut by Half', *The Mercury*, 30 June. Accessed at http://www.themercury.co.za/index.php?fSectionId=283&fArticleId=178656.

Ash, Michael and Robert Fetter (2004) 'Who Lives on the Wrong Side of the Environmental Tracks? Evidence from the EPA's Risk-screening Environmental Indicators Model', *Social Science Quarterly* 85(2): 441–462.

Barannikova, Natalia and Dmitri Lisitsyn (2001) 'Oil and Water Don't Mix', *Pacific Environments* 2(3). Available at http://www.pacificenvironment.org/articles/oilandwater.htm.

Been, Vicki (1999) 'Locally Undesirable Land Uses in Minority Neighbourhoods. Disparate Siting or Market Dynamics?' 103 *Yale Law Journal* 1383.

Bellows, Anne (2003) 'Exposing Violences: Using Women's Human Rights Theory to Reconceptualize Food Rights,' *Journal of Agricultural and Environmental Ethics* 16(3): 249–280.

Blacksmith Institute (2000) 'The Hidden Tragedy: Pollution in the Developing World', New York: Blacksmith Institute. Available at http://www.blacksmithinstitute.org/hidden.pdf.

Boyce, James K. (2003) 'From Natural Resources to Natural Assets', in James K. Boyce and Barry G. Shelley, eds., *Natural Assets: Democratizing Environmental Ownership*, Washington DC: Island Press.

Boyd, Michelle and Gary Cook (1998/1999) 'Whales of the Asian Pacific in Peril', *Earth Island Journal* 14(1).

Brettell, Anna (2002) 'Environmental Disputes and Public Service Law: Past and Present', *China Environment Series* 4: 66–69.

Bullard, Robert (1994) *Unequal Protection: Environmental Justice and Communities of Colour*, San Francisco: Sierra Club.

Campbell, Connie, with the Women's Group of Xapuri (1996) 'Out on the Front Lines but Still Struggling for Voice', in Rocheleau, Dianne *et al.*, eds., *Feminist Political Ecology*, New York: Routledge.

Carlton, Jim (2002) 'In Russia with Fragile Ecology: Stymied in Alaska, Oil Companies Find Russian Rules Aren't as Strict', *Wall Street Journal*, September 4, A1.

Centre for Science and the Environment (CSE) (1985) The State of India's Environment, 1984–1985: *The Second Citizen's Report*, New Delhi: CSE.

Chambers, R., Saxena, N.C. and Shah, T. (1989) *To the Hands of the Poor: Water and Trees*, New Delhi: Oxford.

Checker, Melissa (2001) 'Like Nixon Coming to China: Finding Common Ground in a Multi-ethnic Coalition for Environmental Justice', *Anthropological Quarterly* 74(3): 135–146.

China Economic Times, 24 October, 2001.

Chu, Henry (2002) 'China Is Passing Pollution to a New Generation, Study Finds', *Los Angeles Times*, 19 June, A3.

Clapp, Jennifer (2001) *Toxic Exports: The Transfer of Hazardous Wastes from Rich to Poor Countries*, Ithaca, NY: Cornell University Press.

Cornwall, Andrea and John Gaventa (2001) 'From Users and Choosers to Makers and Shapers: Repositioning Participation in Social Policy', *Institute for Development Studies Working Paper No. 127*, Sussex, UK: Institute for Development Studies.

Cox, Rory (2000) 'Putin Sets Back Ecological Clock', *Pacific Environments* 2(2).

Csagoly, Paul (2000) 'After the Tisza Disaster', *The Bulletin* 9(3) (2000): 9–11.

Dhara, V. Ramana (2002) 'What Ails the Bhopal Investigations? (And is there a Cure?)', *International Journal of Occupational and Environmental Health* 8: 371–79.

Douglass, Mike, *et al.* (2002) 'Urban Poverty and the Environment: Social Capital and State-Community Synergy in Seoul and Bangkok', in Peter Evans, ed., *Livable Cities: Urban Struggles for Livelihood and Sustainability*, Berkeley: University of California.

The Economist (1992) 'Pollution and the Poor: Lawrence Summers' Memo', *The Economist* 322: 18–19, 8 February.

Fahn, James (2003) *A Land on Fire: The Environmental Consequences of the South-east Asian Boom*, Boulder: Westview.

Filcak, Richard (2004a) 'Climate Change and Poverty: The Case of Disadvantaged Roma Communities in Central and Eastern Europe', in conference proceedings: *Just Climate? Pursuing Environmental Justice in the Face of Global Climate Change*, Ann Arbor: University of Michigan.

— (2004b) 'Environmental Justice Cures a Variety of Ills', *Local Governance Brief — Quarterly Policy Journal of the Local Government and Public Service Reform Initiative*, Budapest, Hungary: Open Society Institute (Summer).

Fondaw, Corey (2001) 'Thor Chemicals and Mercury Exposure in Cato-Ridge, South Africa', *University of Michigan Environmental Justice Case Studies*. Available at http://www.umich.edu/~snre492/Jones/thorchem.htm.

Fortun, Kim (1998) 'The Bhopal Disaster: Advocacy and Expertise', *Science as Culture* 7(2): 193–216.

Gadgil, Madhav and Ramachandra Guha (1995) *Ecology and Equity : The Use and Abuse of Nature in Contemporary India,*. New York: Routledge.

Glazer, Penina Migdal and Myron Peretz Glazer (1998) *The Environmental Crusaders : Confronting Disaster and Mobilizing Community*, University Park, PA: Pennsylvania State.

Gordon, David (2006) Muzzling Russia's Independent Voices', *San Francisco Chronicle*, January 4, p. B9.

Gottlieb, Robert (1993) *Forcing the Spring: The Transformation of the American Environmental Movement*, Washington DC: Island Press.

Harper, Krista (2006) *Wild Capitalism: Environmental Activists and Post-socialist Political Ecology in Hungary*, New York: East European Monographs.

— (2007) 'Does Everyone Suffer Alike? Race, Class and Environmental Justice in Hungary', in Carl Maida, ed., *Sustainability and Communities of Place*, New York: Berghahn.

Harper, Krista and Michael Ash (2001) 'The Tisza Chemical Spill', in Char Miller, *et al.* eds., *History in Dispute 7: Water and the Environment Since 1945: Global Perspectives*, Columbia, SC: Manly.

Human Rights Watch (1999) 'The Price of Oil: Corporate Responsibility and Human Rights Violations in Nigeria's Oil Producing Communities'. January. Available at http://www.hrw.org/reports/1999/nigeria.

Hurst, Philip (1990) *Rainforest Politics: Ecological Destruction in South-east Asia*, London: Zed Books.

Jacobs, Nancy, *et al.* (2001) 'Asbestos-related Disease in South Africa: Opportunities and Challenges Remaining Since the 1998 Parliamentary Asbestos Summit', A report presented to South Africa's Parliamentary Portfolio, Committee on Environmental Affairs Tourism, 12 October.

Jeffery, R. and Sundar, N. (1999) *A New Moral Economy for India's Forests? Discourses of Community and Participation*, New Delhi: Sage.

Johnston, Barbara Rose (1994) 'Experimenting on Human Subjects: Nuclear Weapons Testing and Human Rights Abuse', in Barbara Rose Johnston, ed., *Who Pays the Price? The Socio-cultural Context of Environmental Crisis*, Covelo, CA: Island.

Johnston, Barbara Rose and Daniel Jorgensen (1994) 'Mineral Development, the

Environment, and Human Rights: The Ok Tedi Mine, Papua New Guinea', in Barbara Rose Johnston, ed., *Who Pays the Price? The Sociocultural Context of Environmental Crisis*, Covelo, CA: Island.

Joint Forest Management website (2004) URL: http://www.teriin.org/jfm/jfm.htm

Kammen, Daniel (1995) 'Cookstoves for the Developing World', *Scientific American* 273(1): 72–75.

Kirsch, Stuart (2002) 'Anthropology and Advocacy: A Case Study of the Campaign against the Ok Tedi Mine', *Critique of Anthropology* 22(2): 175–200.

Knup, Elizabeth (1997) 'Environmental NGOs in China: An Overview', *China Environment Series* 1: 9–15.

Kroll-Smith, Steve, Phil Brown and Valerie J. Gunter (2000) *Illness and the Environment: A Reader in Contested Medicine*, New York: New York University Press.

Kuletz, Valerie (1999) *The Tainted Desert*, New York: Routledge.

Lambrecht, Bill (1989) 'Waste Pollutes Drinking Water in South Africa', *St. Louis Post-Dispatch*, 26 November.

Leatherman, Thomas (2005) 'A Space of Vulnerability in Poverty and Health: Political-Ecology and Biocultural Analysis,' *Ethos* 33(1): 46–70.

Meier, Andrew (2000) 'Pollution on Sakhalin: Man's Gain May Be Nature's Loss', *Time Europe* 156(19): 6.

Mishra, T. R. (1999) 'Forestry Research in India', *Economic and Political Weekly*. April 17–24.

Neumann, Roderick P. (1998) *Imposing Wilderness: Struggles over Livelihood and Nature Preservation in Africa*, California: University of California Press.

Oosthuizen, Jacques and Rodney Ehrlich (2001) 'The Impact of Pollution from a Mercury Processing Plant in KwaZulu-Natal, South Africa, on the Health of Fish-eating Communities in the Area: An Environmental Health Risk Assessment', *International Journal of Environmental Health Research* 11(1): 41–50.

Pan, Philip P. (2001) 'Cancer-stricken Chinese Village Tries to Pierce a Wall of Silence', *Washington Post*, 5 November, p. A19.

People's Commission on Environment and Development in India website (2004) Section on 'Vanishing Forests.' Available at http://www.pcedindia.com/peoplescomm/forest_4a.htm.

Peluso, Nancy (1993) 'Coercing Conservation: The Politics of State Resource Control', *Global Environmental Change* 3(2).

Plafker, Ted (2002) 'Chinese Activists Take to the Courts', *International Herald Tribune*, August 28.

Planning Commission, Government of India (2003) *Successful Governance Initiatives and Best Practices: Experiences from Indian States*, New Delhi: Academic Foundation Press.

Poffenberger, Mark and Betsy McGean (1996) *Village Voices, Forest choices: Joint Forest Management in India*, Delhi: Oxford University Press.

Pulido, Laura (1996) *Environmentalism and Economic Justice: Two Chicano Struggles in the Southwest*, Tucson, AZ: Arizona.

Rajan, S.R. (1998) 'Imperial Environmentalism or Environmental Imperialism? European Forestry, Colonial Foresters, and the Agendas of Forest Management in British India 1800–1900', in R. Grove, V. Damodaran and S. Sangwan, eds., *Nature and the Orient*, Delhi: Oxford University Press, 324-72.

— (2001) 'Toward a Metaphysic of Environmental Violence: The Case of the Bhopal Gas Disaster', in Nancy Lee Peluso and Michael Watts, eds., *Violent Environments*, Ithaca, NY: Cornell, 380–98.

— (2006) *Modernizing Nature: Forestry and Imperial Eco-development 1800–1950*, New York: Oxford.

Rangarajan, Mahesh (1996) Fencing the Forest: Conservation and Ecological Change in India's Central Provinces, 1860–1914, New York: Oxford University Press.

Ranger, Terrence (1989) 'Whose Heritage? The Case of the Matopo National Park', *Journal of Southern African Studies* 15(2): 217–49.

Rawat, Ajay Singh (1993) *Indian Forestry: A Perspective,* New Delhi: Indus.

Saberwal, Vasant (1999) *Pastoral Politics: Shepherds, Bureaucrats and Conservation in the Western Himalaya,* New York: Oxford University Press.

Saxena, N.C., (1997) *The Saga of Participatory Forest Management in India,* Jakarta: CIFOR.

Shen, Thomas T. (2001) 'Concept and Policies for Preventing Pollution and Poverty in China', *Sinosphere* 4(1): 25–8.

Shivaramakrishnan, K. (1999) *Modern Forests: State-making and Environmental Change in Colonial Eastern India,* New York: Oxford University Press.

Steiner, Rick (1999) 'Oil Spills: Lessons from Alaska for Sakhalin', *Economic Development and the Environment on the Sakhalin Offshore Oil and Gas Fields II,* Hokkaido, Japan: Hokkaido University Slavic Research Center. Available at http://src-h.slav.hokudai.ac.jp/sakhalin/eng/71/contents.html.

Stephens, Sharon (1996) 'Reflections on Environmental Justice: Children as Victims and Actors', *Social Justice* 23(4): 62.

Turner, Terrence (1993) 'The Role of Indigenous Peoples in the Environmental Crisis: The Example of the Kayapo of the Brazilian Amazon', *Perspectives in Biology and Medicine* 36(3): 526.

Vandermeer, John and Yvette Perfecto (1995) *Breakfast of Biodiversity: The Truth about Rainforest Destruction,* Oakland, CA: Food First.

Wilson, Emma (1999) 'Conflict or Compromise? Traditional Natural Resource Use and Oil Exploitation in Northeastern Sakhalin/Noglikskii District', *Economic Development and the Environment on the Sakhalin Offshore Oil and Gas Fields II,* Hokkaido, Japan: Hokkaido University Slavic Research Center.

World Health Organization (WHO) (1997) *Health and Environment in Sustainable Development: Five Years after the Earth Summit,* Geneva: WHO.

Zimmerman, Barbara, *et al.* (2001) 'Conservation and Development Alliances with the Kayapó of South-eastern Amazonia, a Tropical Forest Indigenous People', *Environmental Conservation* 28(1): 10–22.

A performance by the Toxic Avengers theater group dramatizes an incident in which an immigrant worker suffered brain damage at a toxic waste facility in East Palo Alto, California.
Photo copyright David Bacon, 2006.

CHAPTER 14
ENVIRONMENTAL JUSTICE: REFLECTIONS FROM THE UNITED STATES

Manuel Pastor

Introduction

Across the United States, a vibrant social movement for 'environmental justice' has emerged. Based initially on the recognition that US minority groups have borne a disproportionate burden of environmental hazards, environmental justice (EJ) advocates have long since shifted from simply resisting 'environmental racism' to embracing a positive concept of equal access to environmental and social goods.

The connection between this movement and the asset-building framework has been limited, however, in part because of the nascent nature of the latter, in part because of the immediate preoccupations of the former. Resisting hazards would seem to land one squarely in the usual deficit model: the community is characterized by its lack of clean water, or by the higher risks induced by toxic pollutants in the air. Moving from resistance to the challenge of defining a wealth-building strategy is a useful next step for both the EJ movement and the asset-building framework alike.

In this chapter, I sketch a bridge between the United States environmental justice movement and the asset-building framework. I begin by reviewing the broad political development of the movement and the research on which it has been based. As we will see, there has been some debate over the extent of environmental inequity and this is an issue that even those who are sympathetic to the movement's aims and basic assertions must address in a straightforward fashion. Of particular concern are three issues: (1) Is the pattern of environmental inequity simply a manifestation of market outcomes rather than racial or class discrimination? (2) Is the pattern a result of moves to higher-risk areas by minority residents driven by choice rather than dictate? and (3) Are there real and consequential effects in terms of wealth and health, in which case paying attention to environmental inequity could yield dividends for communities struggling for local improvement and empowerment? To address these questions and the relationship to organizing, I review the research conducted in southern California by several colleagues and me, and discuss its connection to the efforts by local environmental justice advocates.

In the second half of the chapter, I explore the relationship between environmental inequities and the state of assets in affected communities. Five forms of capital are negatively affected by environmental inequity: *productive capital*, because polluted lands impede investment and development; *financial capital*, because such lands present liability risks that make financing difficult; *social capital*, because hazards tend to locate where social power and cohesion are low, often exacerbating those conditions; *human capital*, because air toxics have significant impacts on health and learning; and *natural capital*, because of direct damages to land, air, water and a broader sense of environmental well-being. As a result, struggles for environmental justice can lead to increases in the assets available to poorer communities: reversing their role as an 'environmental sink' and laying claim to the natural assets at stake can have a complementary effect on other types of wealth.

I conclude the chapter with some thoughts on what the United States environmental justice experience might offer to those considering natural assets in international and comparative frames. I suggest four key lessons: the utility of considering natural assets in urban as well as rural contexts; the notion that the debate about environmental inequity can be an entry point to broader considerations about equal access to social opportunities; the need to deconstruct broad notions of both nation and the environment to sort out who is winning and losing; and the potential for the EJ movement to make powerful links between local actions for equity and the broader social good of environmental sustainability and economic prosperity.

Environmental Justice in the United States Context

Origins of Environmental Justice

Many analysts date the emergence of the movement against environmental racism in the United States to a set of landmark protests in Warren County,

North Carolina in 1982, when a largely African-American rural community was chosen as the landfill site for burial of polychlorinated biphenyls (PCBs) (Bullard 1994a). The protests prompted the US General Accounting Office, under pressure from the Congressional Black Caucus, to conduct and issue a 1983 study that seemed to confirm that landfills were disproportionately located in Black communities, at least in the southern United States. A subsequent study by the Commission for Racial Justice of the United Church of Christ (1987) correlated toxic facilities and minority communities on a national scale. These results, along with anger in local communities about ongoing attempts to site waste incinerators and other hazards, helped fuel the organizing of the first People of Colour Environmental Leadership conference held in Washington DC, in October 1991.

The period before and after the Summit saw a plethora of new fronts in the struggle. In Los Angeles, California, groups from largely black South Central and the largely Latino Eastside came together to resist the placement of a hazardous waste incinerator in an industrial zone between their neighbourhoods, a remarkable crossing of racial and geographic lines. In Oakland, California, People United for a Better Oakland (PUEBLO) organized to eradicate lead poisoning among children and obtained the most comprehensive lead abatement programme at that time on the West Coast. In the same period, residents in Louisiana's petrochemical corridor (known as 'Cancer Alley') resisted the imposition of a major industrial plant. Throughout the United States system of Indian reservations, indigenous peoples launched struggles against the dumping of uranium waste, a practice denounced as 'radioactive colonialism' by Ward Churchill and Winona LaDuke.[1]

This emerging EJ movement represented a significant break with traditional US environmentalism in several ways. The first was simply the complexion of the actors: US environmental movements had traditionally been dominated by whites, and these new movements were largely, although not exclusively, based in communities of colour. The second was in scope: while the traditional environmental movement emphasized preserving natural landscapes and endangered species, the EJ movement seemed more concerned with social and urban landscapes and threatened peoples. A third difference was in roots: while the traditional movements were based in environmental protection *per se*, most of the EJ leadership came to the struggle through a civil rights prism in which equal access to environmental quality was viewed in the context of a variety of other access issues. Environmentalism, in other words, was less the goal than equity, although many EJ proponents did argue that communities of colour had special relationships with nature, and that traditional community notions of harmony with the Earth could serve as a guidepost for the broader environmental community.[2]

Finally, there has been a difference in the ways in which science has been deployed in the EJ movement. Brookings Institution scholar Christopher Foreman (1998) has suggested that traditional environmentalists tend to favour 'rational' processes of debate regarding objective scientific research on hazards and their risks. As Guana (1998) points out, such frameworks tend to produce negotiation between businesses and their hired experts, environmental organizations and their (hired and sometimes volunteer) experts, and government regulators. By contrast, EJ activists favour 'democratic' epistemologies in which community participation facilitates story-telling about lived experiences; in Foreman's view, this simply leads to 'theatrics', but in the minds of many EJ advocates, this allows for community empowerment. Thus, in recent years, groups like the Environmental Health Coalition (1998) in San Diego have mobilized local mothers to test air quality and report the results to authorities and the public, and California's Communities for A Better Environment has used simple community-based monitoring technologies — essentially buckets that can be used to sample facility emissions — to force refineries and others to reduce pollution (O'Rourke and Macey 2003). While these efforts have sometimes been attacked for yielding 'unscientific' data, the results are often quite solid and have informed and mobilized local communities.

The central point here is that the US environmental and environmental justice movements have followed distinct trajectories. Many mainstream environmental organizations have now adopted EJ as a concern, and some have done important work documenting and challenging disparities (Sandweiss 1998). But relations have frequently been uneasy. One recent example: an attempt in 2001 to locate an environmentally efficient power plant, using state-of-the-art technology, in South Gate in south/central Los Angeles County was supported by environmentalist groups, but resisted by one of the most important EJ groups in California because of the burden it would add to already over-exposed populations. Eventually, the EJ proponents carried the day (Martin 2001a, 2001b; see also Pastor *et al.* 2005). There have been similar tensions around emissions-trading schemes, with some environmentalists supportive, and most EJ activists worried that the resulting 'hot spots' — locations where firms choose to purchase permits rather than clean up — will be in low-income communities and communities of colour (Chinn 1999).

Despite the fact that this movement is based in communities not frequently known for their political clout, and that the broader environmental movement has not always been supportive, EJ activists have made surprising progress on the policy front. A Presidential Executive Order issued in 1994 directed all federal agencies to 'address, as appropriate, disproportionately high and adverse human health or environmental effects of its programs, policies and activities on minority populations and low-income populations in the United States' (Executive Order 12898, 1994). The federal Environmental Protection Agency (EPA) has used EJ as a key rationale for prioritizing clean up and redevelopment of polluted 'brownfields' sites in minority communities, a topic we explore later as a wealth enhancement strategy. In late 2000, the California legislature passed Senate Bill 115, a measure that directs the state's Office of Planning and Research to coordinate EJ initiatives with the federal government and across state agencies, and the subsequent years have seen a series of related legislation dealing with children's health, cumulative exposure and other matters.

This flurry of activity does not reflect a sudden realization by enlightened government actors but rather the concerted political pressure of EJ activists and others. California's recent attention to the question, for example, is politically rooted: environmental inequity has been a key concern of Latino lawmakers who are new to power but old to pollution, and happen to represent critical swing voters in state elections. Community organizing and mobilization — exactly the social elements crucial to asset development in the emerging community-building framework — have been both the impetus and outcome of the EJ movement.

Research and Action

As this history shows, activism and research have often gone hand-in-hand in the EJ movement. The anti-landfill struggle in Warren County prompted a study, which subsequently justified community concerns. The United Church of Christ study fed the movement's efforts and gave activists a solid base from which to lobby. While EJ groups may embrace a democratizing epistemology, they have frequently deployed friendly experts and supportive statistics in their work; indeed, proving disproportionality has occupied much of the time of activist groups and their allies.

Of course, empirical research is not uniformly supportive of the EJ hypotheses. In the early 1990s, several sociologists based at the University of Massachusetts, Amherst, argued for both smaller geographic scales and more multivariate work; employing both innovations, they demonstrated that racial differences in proximity to toxic storage and disposal facilities were not significant once controls were introduced for income, access to industry and other relevant explanatory factors (Anderton *et al.* 1994a, 1994b). This work represented a methodological improvement over previous research — and the results called into question the base for EJ concerns, particularly around race.

These national-level findings have been criticized for both methodological reasons and data deficiencies (Been 1995; Bullard 1996). Boyce (2002) has cogently argued that the Anderton *et al.* results in fact show significant disparities by race once you move beyond the immediate site and into adjoining residential neighbourhoods. However, other careful studies have also failed to find evidence of environmental inequity. Given the mixed and controversial bag, many have accepted Bowen's (2001) view that definitive patterns are hard to encounter. However, a recent broad national study by three researchers who were sceptical about EJ claims did find evidence of significant disparities by race and class, depending on the geographic scale of analysis used (Lester *et al.* 2001). Since these researchers initially thought they were embarking on a refutation of EJ proponents, this is a particularly striking result.

What are the key issues that have been raised in these various research efforts?[3] First, there is the question as to whether race has effects separate and apart from those of class. The practical problem posed by studies that show income to be significant and to dominate race is simple: in United States law, discrimination by race is actionable in court while displacement of hazards into poor communities is viewed as an outcome of the market.[4] Even poor communities whose main self-identification is by class may search to demonstrate racial disparity to be able to move the levers of public policy and the courts.

But there is also a theoretical issue at stake: a correlation between hazards and poverty may simply reflect the fact that those who must place hazards are seeking the lowest costs in terms of land and compensation to residents. That is, the geographic distribution of hazards might actually reflect 'rational market criteria' rather than bias in the planning process.[5] Of course, such a distribution could also reflect class power — but the observational equivalence with the pure market outcome allows apologists to have their day. On the other hand, finding disparities by race *after* controlling for income suggests clear evidence of a power dimension in siting decisions — and this, in turn, sets the analytical platform for interpreting the effect of income too as a result of vertical class-based command and control rather than simply the horizontal allocative function of markets.[6]

The debate about the role of market dynamics is also implicit in a second key issue addressed by critics of EJ: whether hazards were placed in minority and poor communities or whether minorities and the poor were attracted by virtue of low land prices. If the former is the case, then the fault most likely lies in discriminatory siting practices and the remedies would focus on addressing the imbalance in political power that allows some communities to be targeted. If the latter is the case, then any contemporary correlation between hazards and colour could be the result of individual choice rather than group imposition, and the search for remedies would be reasonably circumscribed to providing full information and preventing any housing discrimination that crowds minorities into undesirable locations.

Many EJ activists dismiss this timing issue, suggesting that whatever its cause, disproportionate exposure presents a potential health problem that should be addressed. However, if 'minority move-in' is important, then cleaning up an area and driving up housing prices may simply cause residents to move to a cheaper and more polluted area, reproducing the same social inequality that we saw before. Moreover, from a natural assets perspective, the timing issue is quite important: if the poor *are* simply choosing to obtain low-cost housing in a higher-risk environment, then what appears to be environmental inequity could actually be consistent with no net loss in assets (i.e., individuals consciously trading off their own environmental health or human capital for monetary savings or financial capital).[7] Disentangling this question is, therefore, key to knowing whether assets are being gained or lost.

A third issue relates to consequences. Some analysts have suggested that even if there are disparities in proximity to hazards too little is known about actual health risks, and that the differences in environmental exposure may not be significant (Foreman 1998; Bowen 1999, 2001). Foreman, in particular, has also argued that the activist focus on corporate-induced hazards, such as toxic storage and disposal facilities, has led to a de-emphasis on other epidemiological factors, including individual behaviour with regard to smoking or drinking; in his view, political targeting is taking precedence over health.

Several recent national-level studies have tried to address this issue by making use of exposure risk indicators based on toxic air releases; the results suggest that race is indeed correlated with the allocation of potential health effects (Bouwes *et al.* 2003; Ash and Fetter 2004). But while these efforts establish the plausibility of enhanced risk, the transmission to illness is generally unspecified. Actually confirming or disputing the risk-illness connection — and specifying the exact physiological routes — requires detailed epidemiological studies that are difficult and expensive to mount. In the meantime, many communities may be getting sick. At the same time, the perception of health risk itself, and the other environmental disamenities that result from dirty air and toxic fumes impose costs in terms of both the quality of life and housing values.

Research and Action in Los Angeles

These three challenges of investigating an independent role for race and power, understanding imposition versus choice using chronological evidence and examining the consequences of disparity have formed the parameters of a research programme in which I have been involved for the last six years. Conducted with colleagues at Occidental College in Los Angeles and at Brown University, we have focused on the southern California area, partly because it is one of the most polluted regions in the United States and partly because of an organic connection to an ongoing set of political struggles there. As with the early national research profiled above, our work has been inspired by a community organization concerned about these issues.[8]

Our community partner has been Communities for a Better Environment (CBE). CBE, originally called Citizens for a Better Environment, was once a more technocratic and more Anglo organization based in the San Francisco Bay Area, with a small satellite operation in the southern part of the state. The southern California office was transformed, however, by the involvement of Carlos Porras, a Latino political activist who came from prisoner rights, union and civil rights traditions to the issue of environmental quality in the Los Angeles area. The shift to broaden the agenda had many aspects, including changing the name from 'Citizens' to 'Communities' when Porras and other emerging organizers in southern California argued that the original name was off-putting to many concerned residents who were not US citizens and whose human rights to a clean environment had been violated for exactly that reason.

CBE's southern California operations expanded rapidly in the wake of the new orientation and the results were impressive. The organization battled the Southern California Air Quality Management District, managing to: (1) secure the end of an emissions-trading programme that allowed local refineries to avoid facility clean-up by purchasing old polluting vehicles and taking them off the road, a programme that did improve regional air quality but ran the risk of producing toxic hot spots in the largely Latino neighbourhoods abutting the refineries, (2) force the agency to adopt a new set of environmental justice principles that are far-reaching in scope and scale, and (3) reverse an 'irreversible' ruling setting a very high number of permissible cancers because of the emissions per new facility. Our research relationship with CBE has consisted of support for a series of action projects, such as an assessment of the environmental justice aspects of an expansion of the Los Angeles International Airport, as well as more general research establishing the parameters of the environmental justice problem in southern California.

This broader research programme has targeted the questions raised here. First, we have conducted studies regarding the distribution of toxic storage facilities and emissions from plants listed in the Toxic Release Inventory (TRI) maintained by the US Environmental Protection Agency (Boer *et al.* 1997; Sadd *et al.* 1999). In both cases, we have found a significant disparity in proximity by race, even after controlling for income, local land use patterns, per cent of employees in manufacturing, population density and other reasonable variables. We also found that the relationship between income and proximity to these hazards is best modeled by an 'inverted U' rather than a straight line. The poorest communities tend to suffer less because they have relatively few industrial activities nearby. The richest communities escape proximity by virtue of their political power. Working-class communities bear the brunt of exposure, with communities of colour bearing an especially high burden. This pattern suggests that power, not market dynamics, is the driving factor.

In another study, we took up the second broad research question of timing (Pastor *et al.* 2001). Using a laborious archival research process, we dated the arrival of nearly all high-capacity toxic storage and disposal facilities in Los Angeles County, and then linked those data to a geographically consistent small-area file of demographic data that spanned the period 1970–1990. The results suggested that hazards had indeed been *placed in* these working class communities of colour, with race again playing an independent role even after accounting for other explanatory variables. The affected neighbourhoods did experience demographic change after siting but at no more rapid a pace than the rest of the dynamic southern California area.

The third issue raised above has to do with risk arising from disproportionate exposure to hazards. This issue has bedeviled both organizers and researchers for years, partly because of the tremendous difficulties and uncertainties associated with risk estimation and management. We explored this issue to some degree in our early study of facility-based toxic releases, in which we found that the *degree* of toxicity of the releases rises with percentage of minority residents and increases in the other key variables (Sadd *et al.* 1999). But this degree was calculated in a crude way, involving a sorting of census tracts into three groups: those without releases, with non-carcinogenic releases and with carcinogenic releases.

A more direct approach involves tract-level estimates of lifetime individual cancer risk and a respiratory hazard index, both based on exposure to 148 ambient air toxics from mobile and stationary sources. These indices were derived by combining estimates of ambient air toxics concentrations with corresponding toxicity data. Exposure data were derived from a Cumulative Exposure Project, which estimated average concentrations of 148 air toxics for every census tract in the contiguous United States (US EPA 1998). Emissions data used in the model take into account large stationary sources, small-scale service industries and fabricators (such as dry cleaners, auto body paint shops and furniture manufacturers) and mobile sources (such as cars, trucks and aircraft). The modeling algorithm takes into account meteorological data and simulation of atmospheric processes (Morello et al. 2000; Rosenbaum et al. 1999; Rosenbaum et al. 2000). The concentration data and toxicity information were then used to calculate individual lifetime cancer risks and a respiratory hazard index associated with outdoor air toxics exposures over a lifetime (see Morello et al. 2001). Importantly, mobile sources are the main contributing factor to risk in the southern California area we studied.

To be clear, the variable we use is not the actual incidence of cancer; rather, we have the estimated likelihood of cancer assuming that an individual resides in this tract for their entire life. Matching these geographic data with the demographic characteristics of local residents yields the striking pattern evidenced in Figure 14.1: while higher incomes do alleviate exposure rates, minorities face more ambient air pollution and hence higher cancer risks at every income level. The disparate pattern by race and ethnicity holds even in a multivariate setting where we control for variables such as home ownership (a measure of both geographic commitment and political power), housing value (a measure of wealth), local land use and population density.

We have recently begun to explore another potential consequence of environmental disparity: the effects of pollution exposure on schools, children and learning. We first looked at the relationship between the demographic make-up of schools and the risk levels pertaining to their location. As the universe of study we chose the Los Angeles Unified School District (LAUSD). With over 700,000 students in 1999, LAUSD is the second most populous school district in the United States, and covers an area encompassing 704 square miles within Los Angeles County. Using the respiratory and cancer risk measures discussed earler, we utilized geo-coded data for school ethnic composition to estimate risks by race.

As can be seen in Figures 14.2a and 14.2b, the cancer and respiratory risks are significantly higher for minority children ('excess cancer risk' in Figure 14.2a means the estimated risk compared to 'background rates' that would exist with no exposure to air toxics). Note that once again, Asians have a higher risk than Anglos, although they do not lead the pack as in Figure 14.1; the difference here is that we are not controlling for income, and since Asian households tend to have higher incomes than African-Americans and Latinos, this is likely to reduce risk in the neighbourhoods where their children attend school. While the increased cancer risk for minority children may grab immediate attention, the respiratory risk may be particularly troubling given what is now reported as an 'epidemic' of asthma among urban youth (see Hegner 2000; for more on school risk, see Schettler *et al.* 2001). Again, the differentials in both cancer risk and respiratory hazards persist even when we introduce other explanatory variables, such as local land use and income levels (Pastor *et al.* 2002).

Figure 14.1: Distribution of Estimated Lifetime Cancer Risk from Ambient Hazardous Air Pollutant Exposures by Race/Ethnicity and Income, Southern California

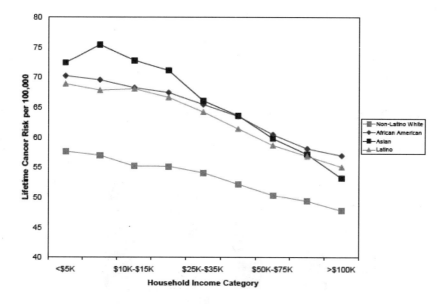

Source: Morello-Frosch *et al.* (2001).

Most recently, we have tried to track the effect of these differentials on learning outcomes using a school-wide performance measure called the Academic Performance Index. The appropriate measure in this case is the respiratory index, since there is substantial research showing a link between respiratory problems, such as asthma, and learning challenges. Figure 14.3 shows the simple relationship between schools broken into thirds by respiratory risk and the associated performance score; as can be seen, performance is indeed lower in the schools in which children face the highest respiratory risks.

Figure 14.2a: Excess Cancer Risk for Schoolchildren by Race, Los Angeles Unified School District

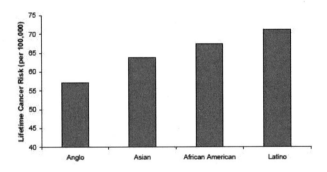

Source: Data taken from Pastor et al. (2002).

Figure 14.2b: Respiratory Risk for Schoolchildren by Race, Los Angeles Unified School District

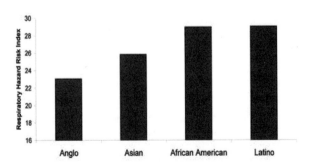

Source: Data taken from Pastor et al. (2002).

Again, researchers might reasonably worry that the lower scores for schools in more polluted areas might reflect collinearity with other explanatory factors. But in a set of multiple regressions in which respiratory risk is coupled with other variables such as percentage of students on free lunches, percentage of students learning English, percentage of teachers with an emergency credential, parents' education background, etc., there is still a negative and statistically significant effect of the risk variable on academic performance.[9] The implications for human capital formation in poor minority communities would seem obvious.

Putting together the results, at least for the area we have studied extensively, yields a clear and disturbing picture: there is indeed a problem of disproportionate exposure by race and class; this seems to reflect power in decision-making rather than 'efficient' market allocation; and it has important consequences for health and academic achievement.

The tough conditions portrayed have given rise to equally tough environmental justice organizations. While the group with which we have worked, Communities for a Better Environment, is one of the leading organizations in southern California, there are many others. The Labour/Community Strategy Centre, for example, has challenged oil refineries in low-income areas and led a struggle to keep bus rates low and public transportation accessible (Mann 1996; Pastor 2001a). Concerned Citizens of South Central and the Mothers of East L.A. successfully fought the siting of an incinerator near their neighbourhoods. In the seeming heart of environmental darkness has emerged the light of community empowerment. Building on this — to go from the necessity of rejecting disamenities to a positive vision of how to create wealth for poor communities — is the next challenge for the EJ movement in Los Angeles and nationwide.

Environmental Justice and Assets

While the patterns of environmental inequity may be striking and the community challenges may be inspiring, the relationship of environmental justice to assets and asset-building strategies has not been much explored. This is partly because activists and concerned policy makers have often rightly focused on preventing further damage rather than building new wealth, an understandable impulse given the severity and urgency of the threats many communities face. Nevertheless, there are five different assets that are touched by, and might be enhanced by, attempts to improve environmental justice: productive capital, financial capital, social capital, human capital, and of course, natural capital.

To bring out this potential, it is useful first to recast the assertions of EJ through the prism of property rights and the associated claim to environmental benefits, including improved health, higher property values and enhanced income. While many EJ proponents have eschewed the language of property rights, partly because private property and market logic has been so often turned against them, one can understand the movements that seek to combat hazards as asserting community-based property rights over environmental sinks. In so doing, these movements contest other forces who seek to gain income and benefits from those sinks without community permission.

Figure 14.3: Academic Performance Index Score by Environmental Ranking

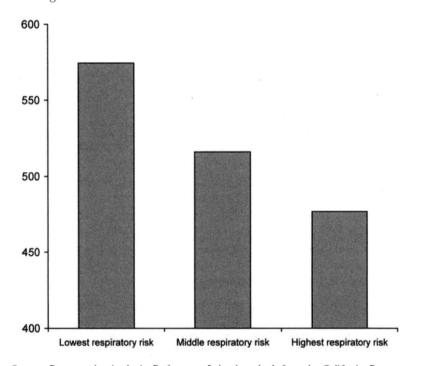

Sources: Data on the Academic Performance Index by school from the California Department of Education; school locations geocoded and attached to respiratory risk index following the procedure indicated in Pastor et al. (2002).

In this view, environmental inequity arises when the community's property claim — that is, the right to determine how much pollution a neighbourhood will tolerate and for what tradeoffs — is usurped by a particular firm and/or by the larger society in the form of inadequate regulation. When the net benefits are distributed widely and the direct costs are concentrated — as when a whole region's toxic waste is disposed of in one particular neighbourhood, and the profits and employment engendered by waste firm operations accrue to individuals outside that area — the affected community is clearly suffering a negative externality without receiving any compensation in return. This represents a violation of the community's property rights.

Of course, if a community itself decides to utilize the sink, or to trade rights to the sink for other certain benefits, then this is consistent with choice. But there is little direct evidence that communities are themselves making these choices, and even less evidence that they secure benefits from having done so. In the area we have studied most extensively, Los Angeles County, job growth is actually the lowest in those communities that host hazards (Boyce and Pastor 2001). The instances of inequity pointed to by the EJ movement are generally impositions, and they tend to bring negative effects along a wide range of dimensions of wealth and health.

Assets, Wealth and Environmental Justice

How can the EJ movement help enhance wealth and community development? The most direct route is through the recuperation of despoiled assets into *productive capital* that can be used to create community income. Perhaps the possibility of such a transformation is clearest in the case of rural communities that have seen lands ruined and productivity threatened by chemical spills, toxic dumping, unsafe hog farming and similar practices; clean-up in these areas can restore the agricultural and other income-earning potential of the land and directly lift income flows. But there is a clear analogue to the rural problem and potential in urban 'brownfields'.

Brownfields are contaminated lands that have become difficult to recycle to new uses. As Dixon (2003) notes, there are three broad categories of brownfields: those that are well-located for business and are 'lightly contaminated'; those that have attractive locations and moderate levels of contamination; and those that are highly contaminated and/or are located far from marketable opportunities. For the first and second category, the key impediment to productive redevelopment of the site is less the cost of the clean-up than the uncertainty around property rights and liabilities. Briefly, US law, partly in response to pressures from the environmental movement, generally requires that the owner of a property must take financial responsibility for the clean-up of any toxics located on a site. Unless there are egregious violations that result in the formal designation of the property as a Superfund or other special site, most owners do not have to face this issue until the time of sale. At that time, a prospective buyer may conduct an inspection and discover some degree of toxic contamination. The nature of clean-up is such that its cost cannot be fully known until the job begins.

Because of this uncertainty, sales fall through. Current owners sue past owners — who may have sold the property when toxics were not considered such a problem — and the property remains unused or underutilized. When corporate owners 'mothball' a site to sidestep liability issues, this avoids private costs, but it leaves the surrounding communities saddled with health hazards and unproductive land. To encourage a way out of this dilemma, the United States government and various state governments have devised programmes in which developers are relieved of future liability provided that they clean up sites to relevant standards.

Partly because of patterns of poverty and housing discrimination, US minorities tend to live in older industrial areas where brownfields are in relative abundance. Firms seeking to establish new plants often avoid these areas and choose 'greenfields' on the edges of urban areas; this gives an additional thrust to the processes of housing sprawl and the suburbanization of employment that have left many people of colour far from the available jobs (Wilson 1996). As Pastor (2001b) notes, between 1970 and 1990, job density rose more rapidly outside the central cities, worsening the problems of 'spatial mismatch' in which available employment is located far from the dwellings of inner-city residents. Revitalizing brownfields therefore offers hope for low-income communities to create employment opportunities close to home (US EPA 1996).

Ensuring that the community reaps benefits is, however, not automatic. This requires community participation in the redevelopment process itself, which can translate into specific requirements regarding local hiring, minority ownership opportunities and community land ownership (see, for example, Watson 2003; Medoff and Sklar 1994 on the Dudley Street Neighbourhood Initiative in Boston). Some business leaders worry that community involvement and tough requirements for local benefits will stymie the redevelopment process. However, a study by the United States government (US EPA 1999), prompted by the concern that environmental justice mandates might slow brownfields redevelopment, found instead that community involvement actually helped accelerate the process because political problems are dealt with earlier in the negotiations. In short, incorporating equity concerns up front can actually speed the brownfields process and help build productive capital.

The second form of wealth that environmental justice can help build is *financial capital*. The brownfields movement is again illustrative. While the apparent obstacle to development is liability, the manifestation of the issue is financial: banks will not lend to developers until future claims regarding responsibility for clean-up are clear. Otherwise the bank itself can wind up holding the bag for past owners' pollution. Settling property claims and cleaning up sites in the brownfields redevelopment process can free financial flows, and this can have positive spillover effects for several reasons.

The first is simply that by putting together brownfield financing, banks may become more accustomed to lending in areas that they have traditionally redlined; in this sense, environmental justice struggles can contribute to ending the broader credit blockade faced by many US minority communities (Turner and Skidmore 1999; Squires 1992; Oliver and Shapiro 1995). The second is that brownfield deals often involve new financial strategies, including the coupling of private and public development monies as well as new models like community land trusts; this can introduce bankers to new modalities for financing community development.

There is also a strong indirect benefit on financial capital. Environmental hazards tend to dampen the growth in housing property values. In the United States, the main form of wealth for the average household is home ownership. The purchase of a home introduces a buyer to the financial sector, and increases in home values can generate the collateral needed for borrowing to start a business or get an education. In this sense, environmental negatives can limit access to financial capital. By equalizing the distribution of hazards and/or forcing clean-up, the EJ movement can have positive impacts on equalizing access to credit as well.

Environmental justice also draws upon and reinforces *social capital*. The strength of social capital — that is, the vibrancy of ties between community members as well as the health of formal community groups — turns out to be one of the best defences against disproportionate siting. In our study of siting practices in Los Angeles County (Pastor *et al.* 2001), we discovered that the neighbourhoods most likely to have a toxic facility placed in close proximity were those that were either roughly split between blacks and Latinos or those undergoing rapid demographic change between groups. Our working hypothesis is that these are conditions under which the usual bonds of community are not as strong as they might be; this weakens political power, makes mobilization more difficult and increases susceptibility to polluters. Building social capital is therefore one key to achieving environmental justice.

As the same time, environmental justice struggles themselves can build social capital. After all, the environment is a prime organizing issue. Residents in affected communities have an immediate 'hook' on which to hang their concerns and environmental inequity can seem like a sort of capstone to all the other injustices perpetuated on low-income communities: on top of unequally distributed jobs, education and healthcare comes inequitable access to a clean environment. Thus, while polluters have been able to take advantage of communities with weak social bonds, EJ organizers have been able to use the sense of grievance to move community leaders to address a variety of issues. Such bonding is critical for protecting natural assets: as Cole (1992) notes, lawyers can help communities to win injunctions, but it is a mobilized community that will ensure enforcement and thus protect their local environment.

Wealth enhancement also comes in the form of *human capital*. One route is simply through human health, a key baseline factor for productive participation in the economy. As noted earlier, the research on the link between environmental exposures and health outcomes is, like the research on racial disparities, somewhat controversial. Part of the problem is that many of the communities that are over exposed to hazards are also subject to other disparities, including access to health care; disentangling the contribution of environmental factors is a challenge (Institute of Medicine 1999). The strict standards of epidemiological methods, including the need to firmly establish physiological mechanisms and biological pathways, also have made it difficult to establish direct causal links, except in the case of lead (Institute of Medicine 1999).

However, there is accumulating evidence on the impact of air pollutants on respiratory problems, and certain chemicals have been clearly linked with cancer. Communities have a clear sense that reduction in exposure will prolong life and improve health. As the research outlined here suggests, disproportionate pollution may also harm school performance and hence that form of human capital development; given the other impediments to success faced by inner-city communities, this seems like a high penalty indeed. Partly as a result, environmental justice advocates are increasingly embracing the 'precautionary principle' — the notion that in the absence of proof that exposure causes no harm, public policy should be directed to limiting exposures.

Finally, environmental justice is also clearly about *natural capital*. While the initial focus of many environmental justice groups has been on avoiding negatives — that is, minimizing the misappropriation of a community's natural capital in the form of sinks — there is an increasing stress on achieving positive environmental outcomes. One key frontier for many urban movements has been gaining community access to open space, collective gardens and the like. Some of these activities can lead directly to measurable gains in income; others, like pocket parks in dense urban areas, lead to less measurable but equally important gains in the quality of life, especially for young people (Pinderhughes 2003; Hynes 2003).

All these forms of asset enhancement can be mutually reinforcing. Regaining control of productive assets in the form of brownfields can open the gates of credit; enhancing human capital can raise earning capacity and allow the acquisition of productive capital; social capital in the form of a strong community seems critical to making progress on any front; and natural capital itself is at stake in the struggle. EJ movements therefore represent one way both to raise assets and to protect the natural environment, while offering a broad challenge to the general distribution of wealth, power and opportunity in society.

Lessons from the US Environmental Justice Movement

What are the implications of the US EJ movement for an international perspective on natural assets? Those of us in the North are often hesitant about suggesting what might be learned from our experiences. This caution stems partly from justified concerns about ideological imperialism as well as an acute awareness that what fits well in one circumstance may fit poorly in another. But there may be useful lessons in this case, partly because the EJ movement is itself rooted in what might be termed the 'South within the North' — that is, low-income communities and communities of colour who have fought within the United States to find their voice and reclaim their assets.

One key implication stems from the urban character of much of the EJ movement. There is a tendency to think of environmental quality as a rural issue, and of the natural assets approach as therefore a good fit in the countryside, but it is clear that vibrant environmental struggles and crucial forms of natural capital are also present in metropolitan areas. In the United States, EJ groups have countered the notion that cities are merely 'sacrifice zones', in contrast to a traditional environmentalism instinct that stressed preservation of national parks and wilderness areas. Instead, EJ groups have worked to avoid the abuse of their neighbourhoods as environmental sinks, lobbied for new forms of accessible open space, and sought to transform brownfields into productive natural assets.

EJ analysts and activists also have begun to tackle broader issues of sprawl and the construction of metropolitan space itself (Bullard *et al.* 2000; Pulido 2000; Urban Habitat Programme 1998). This challenge to US urban form can be instructive where hyper-urbanization is bringing choking traffic, despoiled landscapes and faltering levels of employment. It is not enough to point to the unequal consequences for the poor. We must take on, and reverse, the incentive structures that result in environmentally and socially insensitive patterns of development. Steering business from greenfields to brownfields, and encouraging a better match between jobs and housing, can both protect the environment and ameliorate the conditions that cause poverty.

A second insight concerns the potential for the environment and natural assets to serve as a starting point in a broader debate about inequity, injustice and power. For years, I asked my students in an introductory economics class two hypothetical questions. The first was whether a community affected by a polluting firm had the right to shut the firm down; the answer was generally a strong 'yes'. The second question was whether a community that would be negatively affected by a plant shutdown had the right to keep the firm open; the answer was almost always a strong 'no', even when I stipulated that the company proposing to shed employees was profitable (albeit at a lower rate than might be garnered elsewhere).

The asymmetry of their responses suggests how much progress we have made in recognizing environmental externalities, and how little we have made in seeing the economic activity in the same way. The right to a clean and healthy environment has a legal basis in many state and national constitutions (Boyce and Pastor 2001); moreover, there are popular conceptions of environmental rights that seem to be held by the broad public. Many other aspects of social and economic justice are not codified in the form of rights. In a market society, for example, unequal distributions are often viewed as the reflection of an underlying distribution of talents, and attempts to promote social and economic justice are seen as well-meaning luxuries to be taken up when the economy is booming and wasteful expenditures are affordable. As for racial justice, while discrimination may be legally outlawed, the right to full justice — which might, for example, include reparations to African-Americans who carry the legacy of slavery much in the same way we might require polluters to compensate communities who have had their local environments trampled — remains ideologically off-limits.

Many EJ leaders have used the acceptance of environmental rights as a way to broaden the notion of the public good and raise the questions of social, racial and economic justice. The environment is an entry point where broad human rights are recognized and inequity seems to be disdained (few argue that the rich deserve cleaner air, at least outside the rarified realms of neoclassical economics). But if people deserve clean air, why do they not deserve good schools, safe neighbourhoods, decent employment and other amenities that comprise our built and social environments? EJ movements, thus, serve as a way to raise issues of broader economic fairness and to affirm that poverty reduction is integral to environmental protection itself.

A third implication of the EJ research and activism reviewed here has to do with the importance of deconstructing broad categories of both 'the nations' and 'the environment'. As Boyce (2006) has argued in analyzing environmental degradation, the key questions are: who wins, who loses and why are the winners able to impose costs on the losers? In a powerful paper for the World Conference against Racism, Robert Bullard (2001) points out that environmental racism operates at both an *intra-national* and *inter-national* level. Drawing parallels between the struggle of the South to avoid dumping by dirty industries and the EJ struggles of people of colour in various US communities, Bullard argues that the dynamics of oppression are similar (see also Bullard *et al.* 2005).

But Bullard wisely avoids the simplistic argument that treats the South as a unitary whole of the dispossessed. Anyone familiar with environmental conditions in the developing world knows that the opportunities are also unequally distributed within those countries: indigenous people in Ecuador, for example, face the environmental consequences of refinery production while local elites — among them those Ecuadoreans who profit the most from oil extraction — are able to shuttle from beaches to mountains to enjoy what nature, rather than oil companies, has to offer. Highlighting the gains and losses within particular countries helps clarify the issues and facilitates the search for those who share common problems.

A final key implication has to do with the link between the local and the global, the particular and the universal. Many of the EJ movements in the United States seem to be highly localized: they start from particular community-based grievances about serving as society's dumping ground, and challenge the particular racial and other power mosaics that have made such disparities possible. This local character, however, has not prevented the development of ties among groups facing the commonalities of domination, poverty and poor environmental health. There are now a number of national networks in the United States built from local community groups, and there are growing international ties among communities involved in environmental justice battles.

Moreover, in both their rhetoric and their practice it is clear that EJ groups in the United States are not simply seeking a reallocation of hazards to higher-income white neighbourhoods; rather, they are hoping that successful resistance will force corporations and governments to adopt source reduction, pollution prevention and the broader goal of environmental sustainability. This organizing wisdom is supported by an emerging body of evidence (Boyce *et al.* 1999; Morello-Frosch 1997) that suggests that equity is positively associated with overall environmental protection — that is, when societies are prevented by more equal levels of income and power from simply displacing the problem to certain communities, there is more of an incentive to minimize the wasteful impacts of industrial production in a way that will benefit all.

The link to the global environment is clear. Just as local US groups have rebutted the accusation of parochial self-interest by arguing that steering environmental disamenities away from the poor and communities of colour will, in fact, result in pressure for clean-up, so too must we ensure that the struggle for environmental justice in the North does not result in displacement of environmental burdens to the South, but rather contributes to a new and more profound sense of the commons that we share in this planet.

Establishing this new sense of the global commons — and of everyone's right to a more effective, equitable and democratic use of the Earth's precious natural resources — would represent a true internationalization of the natural assets framework. While much remains to be done on both the organizing and research fronts, it seems that looking at environmental equity through the natural assets lens, and looking at natural assets in terms of the distributive and power issues that have been central to environmental justice, could help us to better realize the shared goals of community control, social equity and environmental sustainability.

Notes

1. See Churchill and LaDuke (1986); many of the examples are drawn from Bullard (1994b).
2. The analysis here is similar to that taken by Camacho (1998) in his closing chapter. The original statement of EJ principles from the First People of Colour Environmental Leadership Summit included an affirmation of 'the sacredness of Mother Earth, ecological unity and the interdependence of all species'.
3. We are raising here some of the big issues of causation and consequence. Another important issue has been the question of scale, especially which geographic level is appropriate for documenting patterns and whether controls for spatial

autocorrelation and other econometric problems are appropriate.

4. Recent court rulings have made action on the grounds of race more problematic, in part because the Supreme Court seems to be moving in the direction of requiring that discriminatory intent as well as impact be demonstrated. The most important ruling came in April 2001, in *Sandoval v. Alexander*, a seemingly unrelated case involving English-only tests for driving licenses in Alabama, in which the Court ruled that private lawsuits against state government agencies must show a discriminatory intent as well as an effect. Some have argued that this will effectively stop EJ claims based on outcomes, while others suggest that that the door is still partly open. For now, most EJ-supportive lawyers seem to favour filing administrative rather than legal claims.

5. In this view, communities with low levels of economic activity may even seek such facilities as they try to encourage economic development (see Been 1994). The results of more careful studies do not square with this notion since, as noted below, the best regression fit is often a U-shaped specification of income.

6. See Hamilton (1995) for a cogent explanation of the power-based explanation for the location of environmental hazards.

7. This, of course, assumes that individuals are making the choice rather than being forced to relocate by external pressures of gentrification or by the policies of government agencies like redevelopment agencies. In the real world, such political or power dynamics appear to play a large role.

8. Another reason for the regional focus is methodological: we have contended that hazard levels are rooted in a region's particular industrial structure and that what should therefore count is the distribution by race *within* the region. In a fascinating new study, Ash and Fetter (2004) provide evidence that this really matters: using fixed effect regression techniques, they show that Latinos, for example, live in less polluted cities but live in more polluted areas within cities. Thus, the race effect might 'wash out' at a national level but would still be important in any particular social geography.

9. Indeed, this result holds even if we control for the per cent of students who are minority, which as we know is highly correlated for other reasons with the distribution of respiratory risk. See Pastor *et al.* (2004).

References

Anderton, Douglas L., Andy B. Anderson, Peter H. Rossi, John Michael Oakes, Michael R. Fraser, Eleanor W. Weber and Edward J. Calabrese (1994a) 'Hazardous Waste Facilities: "Environmental Equity" Issues in Metropolitan Areas', *Evaluation Review* 18: 123–40.

Anderton, Douglas L., Andy B. Anderson, John Michael Oakes and Michael R. Fraser (1994b) 'Environmental Equity: The Demographics of Dumping', *Demography* 31: 229–48.

Ash, Michael and T. Robert Fetter (2004) 'Who Lives on the Wrong Side of the Environmental Tracks? Evidence from the EPA's Risk-screening Environmental Indicators Model', *Social Science Quarterly*, 85(2): 441–62.

Been, Vicki (1994) 'Locally Undesirable Land Uses in Minority Neighbourhoods: Disproportionate Siting or Market Dynamics?' *The Yale Law Journal* 103: 1383–1422.

— (1995) 'Analyzing Evidence of Environmental Justice', *Journal of Land Use and Environmental Law* 11: 1–37.

Boer, Joel T., Manuel Pastor, Jr., James L. Sadd and Lori D. Snyder (1997) 'Is There Environmental Racism? The Demographics of Hazardous Waste in Los Angeles

County', *Social Science Quarterly* 78(4): 793–810.

Bouwes, Nicolaas, Steven M. Hassur and Mark D. Shapiro (2003) 'Empowerment Through Risk-Related Information: EPA's Risk Screening Environmental Indicators Project', in James K. Boyce and Barry G. Shelley, eds., *Natural Assets: Democratizing Environmental Ownership*, Washington DC: Island Press.

Bowen, William M. (1999) 'Comments on 'Every Breath You Take...: The Demographics of Toxic Air Releases in Southern California', *Economic Development Quarterly* 13(2): 124–134.

— (2001) *Environmental Justice through Research-based Decision-making*, New York: Garland Publishing.

Boyce, James K. (2006) 'Power Inequalities and the Political Economy of Environmental Protection', in Jean-Marie Baland, Pranab Bardhan, and Samuel Bowles, eds., *Inequality, Collective Action, and Environmental Sustainability*, Princeton: Princeton University Press, 314–348.

Boyce, James K., Andrew R. Klemer, Paul H. Templet and Cleve E. Willis (1999) 'Power Distribution, the Environment and Public Health: A State-level Analysis', *Ecological Economics* 29: 127–140.

Boyce, James K. and Manuel Pastor (2001) *Building Natural Assets: New Strategies for Poverty Reduction and Environmental Protection*, Amherst, MA: Political Economy Research Institute.

Bullard, Robert D. (1994a) 'Environmental Justice for All', in Robert D. Bullard, ed., *Unequal Protection: Environmental Justice and Communities of Color*, San Francisco: Sierra Club Books.

— (1994b) *Unequal Protection: Environmental Justice and Communities of Color*. San Francisco: Sierra Club Books.

— (1996) 'Environmental Justice: It's More Than Waste Facility Siting', *Social Science Quarterly* 77(3): 493–499.

— (2001) 'Confronting Environmental Racism in the 21st Century', Working Paper, Environmental Justice Resource Centre, Clark Atlanta University: UN Research Institute for Social Development.

Bullard, Robert D., Glenn S. Johnson and Angel O. Torres (2000) *Sprawl City: Race, Politics and Planning in Atlanta*, Washington DC: Island Press.

— (2005) 'Addressing Global Poverty, Pollution and Human Rights', in Bullard, Robert D., ed., *The Quest for Environmental Justice: Human Rights and the Politics of Pollution*, San Francisco, California: Sierra Club Books, 279–297.

Camacho, David E. (1998) *Environmental Injustices, Political Struggles: Race, Class and the Environment*, Durham, NC: Duke University Press.

Chinn, Lily N. (1999) 'Can the Market be Fair and Efficient? An Environmental Justice Critique of Emissions Trading', *Ecology Law Quarterly* 26(1): 80–125.

Churchill, Ward and Winona LaDuke (1986) 'Native America: The Political Economy of Radioactive Colonialism', *Insurgent Sociologist* 13: 51–68.

Cole, Luke W. (1992) 'Empowerment as the Key to Environmental Protection: The Need for Environmental Poverty Law', *Ecology Law Quarterly* 19(4): 619–683.

Dixon, K.A. (2003) 'Reclaiming Brownfields: From Corporate Liability to Community Asset', in James K. Boyce and Barry G. Shelley, eds., *Natural Assets: Democratizing Environmental Ownership*, Washington, DC: Island Press, 57–76.

Environmental Health Coalition (1998) *Toxic Turnaround: A Step-by-Step Guide to Reducing Pollution for Local Governments*, San Diego, CA: Environmental Health Coalition.

Executive Order 12898 (1994) *Federal Actions to Address Environmental Justice in Minority Populations and Low-income Populations*, 12 February, 1994.

Foreman, Christopher H. Jr. (1998) *The Promise and Peril of Environmental Justice,* Washington DC: Brookings Institution.

Guana, Eileen (1998) 'The Environmental Justice Misfit: Public Participation and the Paradigm Paradox', *Stanford Environmental Law Journal* 17(1): 3–72.

Hamilton, James T. (1995) 'Testing for Environmental Racism: Prejudice, Profits, Political Power?' *Journal of Policy Analysis and Management* 14(1): 107–132.

Hegner, Richard E. (2000) *The Asthma Epidemic: Prospects for Controlling an Escalating Public Health Crisis,* Washington DC: National Health Policy Forum, George Washington University.

Hynes, Patricia (2003) 'The Chelsea River: Democratizing Access to Nature in a World of Cities', in James K. Boyce and Barry G. Shelley, eds., *Natural Assets: Democratizing Environmental Ownership,* Washington DC: Island Press.

Institute of Medicine (1999) *Toward Environmental Justice: Research, Education and Health Policy Needs,* Washington DC: National Academy Press.

Lester, James P., David W. Allen and Kelly M. Hill (2000) *Environmental Injustice in the United States: Myths and Realities,* Boulder, CO: Westview Press.

Mann, Eric (1996) *A New Vision for Urban Transportation: The Bus Riders Union Makes History at the Intersection of Mass Transit, Civil Rights and the Environment,* Los Angeles, CA: Labor/Community Strategies Center.

Martin, Hugo (2001a) 'Proposed South Gate Power Plant Faces Fierce Opposition', *Los Angeles Times,* 10 January, 2001.

— (2001b) 'Firm Drops Plan for South Gate Generator', *Los Angeles Times,* 9 March, 2001.

Medoff, Peter and Holly Sklar (1994) *Streets of Hope: The Fall and Rise of an Urban Neighbourhood,* Boston, MA: South End Press.

Morello-Frosch, Rachel (1997) 'Environmental Justice and California's "Riskscape": The Distribution of Air Toxics and Associated Cancer and Non-cancer Risks among Diverse Communities', Ph.D. Dissertation, University of Carolina, Berkeley.

Morello-Frosch, Rachel, Manuel Pastor and Jim Sadd (2001) 'Environmental Justice and Southern California's "Riskscape": The Distribution of Air Toxics Exposures and Health Risks among Diverse Communities', *Urban Affairs Review* 36(4): 551–578.

Morello-Frosch, Rachel A., T.J. Woodruff, D.A. Axelrad and J.C. Caldwell (2000) 'Air Toxics and Health Risks in California: The Public Health Implications of Outdoor Concentrations', *Risk Analysis* 20(2): 273–291.

Oliver, Melvin L. and Thomas M. Shapiro (1995) *Black Wealth, White Wealth: A New Perspective on Racial Inequality,* New York, NY: Routledge.

O'Rourke, Dara and Gregg Macey (2003) 'Community Environmental Policing: Assessing New Strategies of Public Participation in Environmental Regulation', *Journal of Policy Analysis and Management* 22(3): 383–414.

Pastor, Manuel Jr. (2001a) 'Common Ground at Ground Zero? The New Economy and the New Organizing in Los Angeles', *Antipode* 33(2): 260–289.

— (2001b) 'Geography and Opportunity', in Neil Smelser, William Julius Wilson, Faith Mitchell, eds., *America Becoming: Racial Trends and Their Consequences,* Volume 1, Washington DC: National Academy Press.

Pastor, Manuel Jr., James Sadd and John Hipp (2001) 'Which Came First? Toxic Facilities, Minority Move-in and Environmental Justice', *Urban Affairs Review* 23(1): 1–21.

Pastor, Manuel Jr., James Sadd and Rachel Morello-Frosch (2002) 'Who's Minding the Kids? Toxic Air, Public Schools and Environmental Justice in Los Angeles', *Social Science Quarterly* 83(1): 263–280.

— (2004) 'Reading, Writing and Toxics: Children's Health, Academic Performance and

Environmental Justice in Los Angeles', *Environment and Planning C: Government and Policy* 22: 271–290.

— (2005) 'The Air is Always Cleaner on the Other Side: Race, Space and Air Toxics Exposures in California', *Journal of Urban Affairs* 27(2): 127–148.

Pinderhughes, Raquel (2003) 'Poverty and the Environment: The Urban Agriculture Connection', in James K. Boyce and Barry G. Shelley, eds., *Natural Assets: Democratizing Environmental Ownership*, Washington DC: Island Press.

Pulido, Laura (2000) 'Rethinking Environmental Racism: White Privilege and Urban Development in Southern California', *Annals of the Association of American Geographers* 90(1): 12–41.

Rosenbaum, A., D.A. Axelrad, T.J. Woodruff, Y. Wei, M.P. Ligocki and J.P. Cohen (1999) 'National Estimates of Outdoor Air Toxics Concentrations', *Journal of the Air & Waste Management Association* 49: 1138–1152.

Rosenbaum, A., M. Ligocki and Y. Wei (2000) *Modeling Cumulative Outdoor Concentrations of Hazardous Air Pollutants: Revised Final Report*, Systems Applications International, Inc. Available at http://www.epa.gov/CumulativeExposure/resource/resource.htm.

Sadd, James L., Manuel Pastor, Jr., Joel T. Boer and Lori D. Snyder (1999) 'Every Breath You Take ...: The Demographics of Toxic Air Releases in Southern California', *Economic Development Quarterly* 13(2): 107–123.

Sandweiss, Stephen (1998) 'The Social Construction of Environmental Justice', in David E. Camacho, ed., *Environmental Injustices, Political Struggles: Race, Class and the Environment*, Durham, North Carolina: Duke University Press.

Schettler, Ted, Jill Stein, Fay Reich and Maria Valenti (2001) *In Harm's Way: Toxic Threats to Child Development*, Boston, MA: Greater Boston Physicians for Social Responsibility. Available at http://www.igc.org/psr.

Squires, Gregory D (1992) *From Redlining to Reinvestment: Community Responses to Urban Disinvestment*, Philadelphia, PA: Temple University Press.

Turner, Margery Austin and Felicity Skidmore (1999) *Mortgage Lending Discrimination: A Review of Existing Evidence*, Washington DC: Urban Institute.

United Church of Christ (UCC), Commission for Racial Justice (1987) *Toxic Wastes and Race in the United States: A National Report on the Racial and Socio-economic Characteristics of Communities with Hazardous Waste Sites*, New York: Public Data Access, Inc.

United States Environmental Protection Agency (1996) *Environmental Justice, Urban Revitalization and Brownfields: The Search for Authentic Signs of Hope*, Washington DC: US EPA. Available at http://www.epa.gov/swerosps/bf/nejachtm.htm.

— (1998) *Cumulative Exposure Project*, Washington DC: US EPA. Available at http://www.epa.gov/CumulativeExposure.

— (1999) *Brownfields Title VI Case Studies: Summary Report*, Washington DC: US EPA. Available at http://www.epa.gov/brownfields.

United States General Accounting Office (1983) *Siting of Hazardous Waste Landfills and their Correlation with Racial and Economic Status of Surrounding Communities*, Washington DC: US GAO.

Urban Habitat Programme (1998) *What If We Shared? Finding's from Myron Orfield's San Francisco Bay Area Metropolitics: A Regional Agenda for Community and Stability*, San Francisco, CA: Urban Habitat Programme.

Watson, Greg (2003) 'Can Natural Assets Help Address Urban Poverty?' in James K. Boyce and Barry G. Shelley, eds., *Natural Assets: Democratizing Environmental Ownership*, Washington DC: Island Press.

Wilson, William Julius (1996) *When Work Disappears: The World of the New Urban Poor*, New York: Alfred A. Knopf, Inc.

Battersea Power Station, a coal-fired electricity generation plant
built in London in the 1930s.

CHAPTER 15
EQUITABLE CARBON REVENUE DISTRIBUTION UNDER AN INTERNATIONAL EMISSIONS TRADING REGIME

Nathan E. Hultman and Daniel M. Kammen

Introduction

Scientists believe with high certainty that the impacts of current greenhouse gas emissions have started but may not be completely felt for 100 years or more.[1] The long-term nature of the climate problem requires fundamental, long-term changes in how economies produce goods and services. One of the most likely policies to encourage the transition to reduced use of fossil-fuel energy is a system of overlapping national and international emissions permits (Victor *et al.* 2005; Hultman 2004). The Kyoto Protocol set up one international trading system, but even if this Protocol ultimately fails, the movement towards a global emissions market is likely to continue for several reasons. First, most major polluting countries have endorsed the aims and the mechanisms of Kyoto. Second, the European Union has already implemented a broad coverage emissions-trading system parallel to Kyoto's. Third, many large industrial and energy corporations — including the major European energy oil companies — have endorsed the mechanisms of the Kyoto Protocol, and some have initiated their own emissions trading systems.

The world therefore is likely see the emergence of multiple linked markets for greenhouse gas emissions permits over the next five to ten years. These systems, implemented soundly, should help reduce humanity's impact on the global climate by internalizing some of the costs of climate change. At the same time, these permits will be assets that have an economic value and provide economic benefits. Therefore, they represent a tool that could be used to reduce poverty by distributing these assets to people with few conventional sources of capital.

In this chapter, we discuss institutional structures that could help bring equitable benefits from this atmospheric asset distribution. First, we review the arguments for creating tradable permits. Then, we discuss the implications of the international allocation of emissions permits, and how a country with an agreed emissions cap can decide to distribute permits within its borders. Finally, we review some potential obstacles to equitable asset distribution, and discuss steps that communities, foundations, governments and non-governmental organizations (NGOs) might take to advance a sustainable and progressive solution to atmospheric emissions.

From Sink to Asset: Approaches to Managing Carbon Storage

Alternative Approaches to Reducing Environmental Damage

Several policy mechanisms exist for reducing the overexploitation associated with open-access resources. A government with highly structured legal systems and powerful enforcement capabilities can regulate the common resource according to a certain formula; this formula is optimally set to ensure that the total exploitation is not at a level that threatens the viability of the resource. This approach, often called the 'command-and-control' or 'regulatory' approach, is attractive in its simplicity, but in a diverse economy with differing costs of abatement, it can lead to large disparities in the cost of compliance.

As an alternative to the regulatory approach, the government can set a price for the resource, allowing producers to decide on their own how much of the resource to consume. This price can be set directly as a tax (for example, US$5 per ton CO_2 emitted), or indirectly via a system in which the government sets a total emission limit and then allows firms and individuals to buy and sell permits or allowances to emit up to this cap (Weitzman 1974). These methods — taxes, permits, or a hybrid[2] of the two — have the potential to reduce the total cost of meeting environmental targets, since those polluters for whom abatement is cheaper than buying a permit (or paying the pollution tax) cut emissions, while those for whom abatement is more expensive pay to continue polluting.

In addition to reducing total cost of compliance, these market-based methods have other economic and environmental advantages. First, because firms who surpass the requirements that would have been set by regulation are able to benefit financially, there are stronger incentives to invest in pollution-control technology. In the long run, this helps push technological changes that further reduce the cost of compliance. Second, these schemes establish the principle that the polluter pays for the use of 'environmental sinks' — in contrast to regulatory approaches in which the discharge of wastes into the air or water bodies is free as long as it remains within prescribed guidelines. Importantly, the question of whom the polluter pays is often not addressed. Depending on how environmental sinks are shared, market-based pollution reduction can become a tool to enhance distributional equity as well as economic efficiency.

International Emissions Permits

Recent international policies to regulate global atmospheric resources have taken the form of permit or allowance trading systems. The Kyoto and EU approaches define property rights for portions of the commons and assign those rights to emitters. Because the atmosphere provides continuous benefits in the form of pollution abatement services, it can be thought of as an economic asset that yields dividends to the planet's people and organisms. This asset clearly has a large value as these services are necessary for life, but defining this value even roughly has proven difficult given the complex nature of the Earth system, the challenge of reaching scientific understanding of it, and our inability to predict future human and biospheric needs. Though some estimates have been made for the value of nature's services (de Groot 1994; Vitousek 1997; Daily 1997), we can never know precisely how much the atmosphere is worth; nevertheless, many estimates of the possible damages of climate change have been made (Tol 2005).

Policies to convert one aspect of the atmosphere — its ability to absorb carbon — from an open-access resource to a legally recognized and monetized asset will move its price closer to its fundamental value (at the least, from zero to positive). For this shift to happen, governments must elaborate a legal system of tradable emissions rights and distribute the permits to the entities that will trade them. The most contentious question in developing such a system is precisely this allocation of emissions rights. Since everybody has until now had free access to the atmosphere, distributing rights to it has prompted argument about the appropriate shares for each country.

This problem is sometimes cast as a question of whether to allocate permits on the basis of what countries or industries have emitted in the recent past. This method, often called 'grandfathering', is politically convenient in that large incumbent polluters essentially can continue with business as usual. However, it also rewards inefficient resource use and ignores the benefits that have already accrued to users because of their greater use of the common resource. Other authors have argued for allocations that take account of historical emissions already in the atmosphere which continue to affect Earth's radiative balance (Agarwal and Narain 1991; Smith 1991). Another perspective maintains that the atmosphere is a common heritage of humankind and should therefore be allocated to individuals rather than countries; this perspective provides an ethical framework to support an equitable allocation of current and future rights.

Expected Characteristics of the International Carbon Market

The UN meetings in Bonn and Marrakesh both framed and approved rules governing emissions trading under the Kyoto Protocol, and the Protocol entered into force in 2005. The major developed countries (except the United States and Australia, which have not ratified the Protocol) must adhere to agreed emission limits for the period 2008–12.[3] Table 15.1 presents these the Kyoto targets, alongside emissions data for the years 1990 and 2000. These caps reflect a modified version of grandfathering, with permits allocated approximately according to each country's past emissions. Developing countries — including large emitters such as China and India — do not have these targets under the Kyoto Protocol, but many have stated their willingness to consider the adoption of binding targets once the developed countries begin to reduce their own emissions. Since the period governed by Kyoto ends in 2012, preliminary negotiations have begun on allocating targets for the so-called 'second commitment period' starting in 2013.

Although the Kyoto Protocol has been rejected by the current administration in the United States, markets for greenhouse gas emissions tied to the UN Framework Convention on Climate Change (FCCC) are being introduced. For example, the United Kingdom introduced a voluntary multi-sector trading plan in early 2002, and Denmark implemented an early mandatory programme that covers the electricity generation sector (Rosenzweig *et al.* 2002). The European Commission later introduced a proposal for mandatory multi-sector EU-wide emissions trading that began in 2005. Despite the official United States stance, the Chicago Climate Exchange provides a voluntary mechanism for US companies to initiate internal greenhouse tracking and trading programmes. Under the Kyoto Protocol, such parallel programmes may be linked through a central registry maintained by the FCCC (see Figure 15.1).

Table 15.1: Historical Emissions and Kyoto Protocol Targets

Region	Greenhouse Gas Emissions billion tons CO2e/year		
	1990	2000	KP Target
World	21.81	23.63	na
Developing countries	6.92	9.64	na
Annex I countries	14.90	13.99	13.46
European Union	3.33	3.28	2.76
United States	4.98	5.76	4.55
Non-EU, non-US OECD	1.84	2.20	2.05
Russia and Eastern Europe	4.75	2.74	4.19

Sources: Historical emissions are converted from data compiled by the US Energy Information Administration (2002) and do not include land-use change (LUC) emissions arising, for example, from changes in forest cover. Kyoto targets are based on net emissions reported to the UN Framework Convention on Climate Change Secretariat (2000) and include LUC emissions. Most Annex I countries reported LUC emissions ranging between 10 per cent and 10 per cent of reported energy-related emissions; for Annex I as a whole, LUC amounts to a 10 per cent reduction in energy-related emissions.

Estimate of International Carbon Market Size

Several methods exist to characterize the total amount of wealth at stake in these allocation processes. The most important consideration for the long-term is how much benefit the global atmosphere provides to humankind by absorbing greenhouse gases. In the near term, a crude but simple way to get an idea of the expected order of magnitude of this market is to take a short time horizon in which the policy context is relatively clear, and multiply the expected number of permits to be issued by an expected market price. The most pertinent contemporary example is to take the Annex I emissions limits (shown in Table 15.1), excluding the United States because of its stated aim to stand clear of the Kyoto Protocol, and multiply these by an estimated short-term clearing price for carbon.

Modeling studies and historical experience (see Tables 15.2 and 15.3) suggest a clearing price somewhere between US$3 and US$12 per ton of carbon-dioxide equivalent (CO_2e). If we conservatively assume an expected price at the low-end of the scale, given US non-participation, we can take US$5 per ton of CO_2e as a rough approximation. A simple minimum estimate of the value of this global atmospheric scarcity rent, then, assuming global emissions of 22 billion tons of CO2 equivalent per year, would be roughly

Figure 15.1: Schematic Diagram of International Emissions Permit Trade

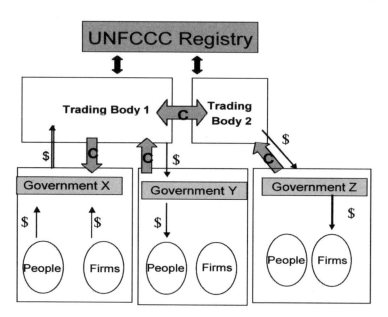

Note: Grey arrows represent carbon permit flows; thin black arrows represent monetary flows; thick black arrows represent information sharing. Different country governments (represented as X, Y and Z) can decide how to distribute revenue from domestic auctions or international purchases; in this diagram, Country X has opted for a carbon tax, Country Y has allocated dividends from the sale of permits to its citizens and Country Z has grandfathered its permits to the private sector ('firms').

US$100 billion per year.[4] Under Kyoto, non-US Annex I countries have permits totaling approximately 9 billion tons of CO_2e per year, for a value of about US$45 billion.[5]

As an additional indication of the potential size of the market, we can note that private investors and some governments have already implemented a number of carbon reduction projects to generate carbon credits. Table 15.4 presents a sample of such initiatives as of 2002. Together these projects represent an investment of over US$500 million, which is substantial given that at the time there were no legally binding carbon-reduction requirements in place; companies were engaging in projects primarily to learn the regulatory process and hedge their emissions exposure in anticipation of future regulation. With the advent of the binding emissions trading systems in the EU and the entry-into-force of Kyoto, the carbon market has expanded to over 100 million tons CO_2e per year with values ranging from a few dollars per ton to over US\$20 per ton, depending on the permit quality and legal context (Lecocq and Capoor 2005).

Table 15.2: Summary of Model Estimates of Global Emissions Market Characteristics

Gases covered	Permit price	Quantity traded	Trade volume	% CDM	Study
	\$/ton CO2 2001	Mt CO2	billion USD 2001		
CO2 only	4-15 (10)	1700-3100 (2400)	7-48 (24)	60-64 (62)	Springer 2001
CO2 only	28	1200	17-34	50	UNCTAD 2000
Six-GHG	3-9 (5)	1600-3000 (2300)	10-14 (12)	56-65 (61)	Springer 2001

Note: Springer (2001) and the UN Conference on Trade and Development (2000) reviewed approximately 15 existing modeling studies of the near-term carbon market. Most of these studies included the United States as a consumer of permits; the estimates most likely represent the upper limit on the prices in an ex-US carbon market. For example, the International Energy Agency (2001) has estimated that US non-participation will reduce international carbon permit prices by 34 to 90 per cent. Averages and standard deviations calculated by authors. CDM = Clean Development Mechanism (see text for details).

Table 15.3: Historical Experience with Carbon Prices

Commodity	Vintage years	Price (US\$/tC02e)	Notes
Annex B VER	1991-2007	0.60-1.50	Vintages before first Kyoto Commitment period
Annex B VER	2008-2012	1.65-3.00	First Kyoto Commitment Period
CDM VER	2000-2001	1.15-3.50	
Dutch ERU	2008-2012	4.40-7.99	
Danish Allowance	2001, 2002	2.14-4.17	2002 showed lower peak prices
UK Allowance	2002	5.76-9.36	

Note: VER denotes verified emissions reductions; CDM denotes the Clean Development Mechanism; ERU denotes emission reduction units. Annex B countries are approximately the same as Annex I countries.
Source: Modified from Rosenzweig, Varilek and Janssen (2002).

Table 15.4: Examples of Projects to Generate Carbon Credits

Investment type	Holdings (\$M)	Emphasis	Investors	Regions
Pure Carbon Funds				
World Bank PCF	145	Carbon	Govt, Private	CDM & JI
ERUPT	32	EE, Cogen, RE, Forest	Govt	CEE
Australian GHG Friendly	varies	Landfill Meth, RE, capture, EE	Private	Australia
Private Equity with carbon enhancement				
Dexia-FondElec En Eff & Em Redn Fund	63.9	EE	Multilat, Private	CEE
Ren En & En Eff Fund	65	RE, EE in emerging mkts	Govt, Private	Em Mkt
FondElec Latam Clean En Svcs Fund	25	EE, microgen, RE	Private	Latam
Black Emerald Leasing	?	RE, Fuelcell, biogas	Private	Europe
Planned Forestry Funds & Companies				
Hancock New Forests Australia	200	sust forest	Private	Australia
GMO Renewable Resources	50	sust forest	Private	US, CEE, CDM
COOL	?	carbon & forestry	Private	Latam
Other Planned				
UBS Global Alternative Climate	50	carbon	Private	CDM & JI
Natsource	?	en technology	Private	

Note: EE denotes energy efficiency; RE is renewable energy; CEE is Central and Eastern Europe.
Source: Modified from Bürer (2001).

International Carbon Capital Transfers

Whatever the total size of the market, not all the emission permits are traded across national borders. While we know that countries with high emission abatement costs will be net purchasers of permits, the long-term cross-border financial flows that would result from this asset creation are still unclear. Nevertheless, several studies have elucidated a possible range of expected international trade. At the low end, Grubb, Vrolijk and Brack (1999), for example, suggest that only about six per cent of the total Annex I permits would be traded internationally; this calculation, however, was limited to trading within the Annex I group of countries. For global trading, the results presented in Figure 15.2 indicate a possible range of 1.2–3.1 billion tons (Gt) of CO_2e per year, with a best guess of about 2.4 billion tons per year, equivalent to about 20 per cent of outstanding Kyoto permits.[6] Using our earlier rough estimate of US$5 per ton as the price, we could thus expect cross-border activity in the range of US$8–US$10 billion per year. While this is less than the total value of the permits, it is nevertheless substantial.

Developing countries are particularly interested in how much of these cross-border transactions might flow to their jurisdictions. The studies summarized in Figure 15.2 indicate that approximately 55–65 per cent of cross-border trades would involve developing countries through the Clean Development Mechanism (CDM). The CDM is an international institution established under the Kyoto Protocol that helps developed countries implement emissions-reduction projects in the developing world. Even though the host countries' emissions are not bound by current international agreements, they are thus able to add credits to developed countries' accounts. These studies suggest that developing countries could expect to see around half of the cross-border trades, or about US$4–5 billion using our conservative estimates.[7]

Table 15.5 presents a comparison of some capital flow projections across regions under alternative trading systems, as estimated by UNCTAD (2000). These figures assume US participation, and thus the world will most likely see lower dollar volumes in the near future. For trading limited to Annex I, the former Soviet Union could expect to receive up to US$10 billion annually. Under a global permit market — which is unlikely in the near future, but possible, in a decade or two — UNCTAD estimates that up to US$35 billion per year could flow to developing countries and the former Soviet Union. In the most likely near-term case of limited engagement of developing countries through CDM, flows could reach US$20 billion annually. This is equivalent to roughly 13 per cent of current net foreign direct investment flows to these countries.

Table 15.5: Capital Flow Projections by Region and Mechanism

| Region | Trading System | | | |
| | Annex I & FSU | Global Market | CDM | net FDI |
	flows to region in billion US$ 2002			
Former Soviet Union	10.5	6.2	5.1	29.1
Asia				
China	na	11.1	9.0	
India	na	2.9	2.4	
Latin Am, Africa, other Non-Annex I	na	4.4	4.4	62.0
Total market value	50.1	34.9	20.3	159.0

Note: Annex I and Former Soviet Union (FSU) column refers to trading that is limited to those regions; Global Market column refers to flows expected under a global permit trading system; CDM column refers to expected flows under Kyoto CDM linked to Annex I emissions trading. Net foreign direct investment (FDI) flows to each region are provided for comparison; for the FSU this figure includes Eastern Europe.
Source: Modified from UNCTAD (2000) and Institute of International Finance (2002).

Long-term Carbon Market Projections

In the near future, carbon permits will be a modest but significant source of revenue for those countries or companies who are able to sell them. Before turning to the design of policies to distribute this revenue, it is important to consider whether this market will increase substantially over time. In the future, the number of permits will need to decrease to address the scientific fundamentals of climate stabilization. To reach a steady state in which human emissions are balanced by natural uptake, emissions will have to decrease by a further 50 per cent so as to diminish to 10 billion tons of CO_2e per year. The associated change in prices and traded quantities will depend on the degree to which the policy-driven permit scarcity is offset by economic 'decarbonization' and technological change. These trends are quite difficult to forecast over decadal time scales, and so the debate about long-term climate economics continues.

The effect of permit scarcity on the size of the market depends on the price elasticity of demand for carbon fuels.[8] For example, if the price elasticity of demand is 0.5, then increasing the price of carbon by 10 per cent would decrease consumption by 5 per cent. In this case, as the number of permits is reduced, demand pushes up the price of carbon more rapidly as the quantity falls; thus, fewer permits end up generating more total revenue.

If the carbon revenues are distributed across the population on an equal per capita basis, as in the Sky Trust system described in the next section, this means that stricter emissions limits will *increase* the carbon dividends for majority of people, thereby generating support for stricter environmental protection.[9] In contrast, in a relatively elastic system (with price elasticity greater than one), a contraction in the number of permits would not be offset by a commensurate rise in carbon prices, and total carbon revenue would fall.

In the short run, the capital infrastructure is inflexible and the elasticity is low. The problem comes in forecasting this elasticity over the time scale that is meaningful to climate policy, namely in the next 10–50 years. Indeed, much of the debate about the costs of compliance with Kyoto can be understood as a debate over the rate at which the price elasticity of demand can change (US Department of Energy and Inter-laboratory Working Group on Energy-efficient and Clean-energy Technologies 2000; Krause 2000). A related question is how this elasticity varies between developed and developing countries. The price elasticity is of particular importance in determining whether an egalitarian distribution of revenues would yield incentives for or against public support of more fossil fuel reductions: if demand is inelastic, bigger cutbacks generate larger dividends for redistribution, and hence political support for the repeated tightening of standards that would be necessary for ultimate stabilization of atmospheric greenhouse gas concentrations.

Given the uncertainty of future paths, it is useful to specify a range of options that span the 'reasonable' set of possibilities. The Intergovernmental Panel on Climate Change (IPCC) has conducted such an exercise, producing a set of emissions scenarios under various conceivable global economic development pathways (Nakicenovic and Intergovernmental Panel on Climate Change. Working Group III 2000). Figure 15.2, which plots six of the main scenarios that span the range of possibilities, shows that carbon emissions can take widely differing paths depending on both government policy and market functioning. The uncertainty is greater the further one projects into the future. In discussing long-term economic impacts, one must therefore remember that these figures may change dramatically and in unpredictable ways over the coming decades.

Distribution of Carbon Revenues

In the short term, the annual carbon market turnover will certainly be noticeable, but not particularly large relative to the global economy.

Nevertheless, given that the natural Earth system can absorb about 10 billion tons of CO_2 per year, states will be legislating into existence a valuable asset. As Victor (2001) has pointed out, the US$45 billion annual value calculated earlier is just an annual dividend from an asset — the sink capacity — of much greater value. Conservatively assuming that this is a risk-free asset, and taking five per cent as the long-term risk-free rate, this dividend implies an approximate perpetuity value of US$900 billion. Though politicians so far have avoided addressing the long-term ownership of this asset, the next set of international commitments could begin to recognize more equitable ways of assigning ownership to atmospheric carbon rights. In this way, negotiators could start to move carbon income away from arbitrarily chosen historical polluters to a wider and more deliberately chosen set of recipients.

Figure 15.2: IPCC Future Scenarios to 2100

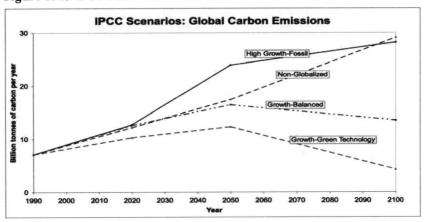

Note: Growth-fossil category plots IPCC scenario A1F1; Growth-balanced=A1B; Growth-GreenTech=A1T; Non-Globalized=A2.
Source: Modified from Nakicenovic, Nebojsa and IPCC (2000).

In discussing how potential revenues can be distributed, we need to distinguish between the international allocation of permits and the intra-national allocation of permits. The international allocation derives primarily from the UN-sponsored agreements on climate change, including the Kyoto Protocol; in these agreements, the negotiating groups delineate which parties receive permits to emit and how much each receives. This process exists to partition rights on a global basis, recognizing that the atmosphere is a global resource with global access.

However, each individual country then has to decide how to meet their target under the international regime. Again, countries have the options of mitigating their emissions through direct regulation, or a market-based system of taxes or permits, or a hybrid system. While all these approaches are likely be used in some form across the 150 or so countries that are expected ultimately to engage in binding commitments, we will discuss primarily the options for distributing the revenue that would accrue from sales of permits, both internationally to satisfy obligations under the UNFCCC and under domestic permit-trading systems.

International Distribution of Carbon Revenues

In principle, permits could be sold directly from one government to another, bought and sold through a supranational entity. Such an entity could merely serve as a market-maker for trades between countries, or if vested with the appropriate authority, it could actually distribute the proceeds from permit sales to the owners of the assets. If one accepts that the atmosphere is owned equally by individual citizens, a supranational trust would distribute carbon revenue to those owners. This would be an international version of the 'Sky Trust' that has been proposed domestically for the United States (Kopp *et al.* 1999; Americans for Equitable Climate Solutions 2000; Barnes and Breslow 2001).

This centralized route has significant logistical and political drawbacks. It would require international administrative institutions to transfer a large amount of funds, raising sovereignty concerns that are unlikely to be placated in the foreseeable future. Moreover, most developed countries would be net 'losers' in financial terms — paying more into the trust than they would receive in dividends — presenting a political obstacle. Thus, while a global trust has theoretical elegance, in the near term the world will almost certainly see a system of internationally negotiated permit rights coupled with domestically defined distribution systems.

The discussion of emissions permits revolves primarily around the *atmosphere's* capacity to hold excess carbon. But carbon can also be absorbed and stored in the *biosphere* — forests and grasslands, particularly. While in theory this 'carbon sequestration' is an Earth system service that provides benefits to the entire population, in practice the physical boundaries of terrestrial biosphere carbon sinks has meant that they have been viewed primarily as property of individual countries and not as part of the international common resource. Thus, under the Kyoto framework, carbon absorbed by a forest in Sweden can be subtracted against industrial emissions from Sweden in figuring out its obligations. This raises many questions of equity, especially if countries are now to be compensated for forest regrowth in the wake of past deforestation (Agarwal and Narain 1991).

Domestic Distribution of Carbon Revenues

Once a country has an international allocation, it will be able to buy or sell permits as needed. Countries that over-comply with their cap or that host credit-generating projects will be able to generate revenue through the international market for greenhouse gas emissions permits. Furthermore, countries that implement a domestic system of tradable permits or carbon fees will generate revenues at home. It is important to note that individual countries are not *forced* to wait for an international allocation (à la Kyoto) to implement a domestic system: as sovereign states, they can decide on emissions targets unilaterally or in smaller groups.

Regardless of the origin of the international framework, once a country decides to raise carbon prices to control greenhouse gas emissions, it has three broad options for distributing the resulting revenue within its borders:

- Retain in governmental budget;
- Distribute to corporations doing business in country; or
- Distribute to citizens or residents.

In the government option, the revenues from carbon taxes or permit sales go to the treasury and become part of the budget. The distributional outcome thereby becomes subject to the political process of the country. The government could decide to tap the carbon revenue for its discretionary budget. Alternatively it could use the revenue to reduce other tax burdens, either targeting specific industries, or citizens, or as a broad-based tax cut. In the United States, for example, possibilities include social security payroll tax reductions and cuts in corporate income taxes (Phillips 2001; US Congressional Budget Office 2001).

If the country decides to grant permits directly to corporations, as part of a grandfathered allocation, these private entities are able to continue their previous emissions free of charge. This policy effectively grants corporations ownership of the GHG revenue stream. While the government may recoup some of this revenue through taxes or a hybrid permit auction, the remaining revenue accrues to the corporation, and, by extension, to its owners.

The third option is to distribute the benefits directly to the people of the country. This distribution could take two forms:

- A periodic distribution of dividends accruing from the national sale of permits (Barnes 2001).
- A one-time distribution of 'emission endowments' that provide periodic dividends and are assets that can be traded on a secondary market (McKibben and Wilcoxen 1999).

Each of these could be distributed universally with each citizen getting an equal share, or in some other way that might, for example, redress economic hardships caused by climate change policies or actual climate change. Sky trusts are a universal mechanism for distributing dividends.

Hybrid schemes are possible. For example, the government could retain a fraction of sky-trust revenue to invest in renewable energy research and development, and adjustment programmes for workers in carbon-intensive industries that are rendered less competitive by having to pay for their environmental externalities.

Multiple national sky trusts would have several attractions. First, the majority of people would be net winners in purely financial terms, receiving more in annual dividends than they would pay in higher carbon prices. This enhances their political viability. Second, low- and middle-income households tend to be net winners, while high-income (and high-consumption) households tend to pay more into the fund then they get back in dividends. The sky trust thus has a progressive impact on income distribution (Barnes and Breslow 2001). Third, multiple national sky trusts would not be dependent on painstakingly developing an international consensus on the procedures and institutions necessary to allocate emission rights internationally. Fourth, they would be compatible with an equitable international allocation that could be negotiated during the second, third, or later commitment periods under the UNFCCC. Fifth, national sky trusts potentially could serve to refine administrative procedures through institutional experimentation and learning. Finally, a system of functioning national sky trusts could serve as a stepping stone to an eventual global sky trust.

Perspectives on the Distribution Options

One can evaluate these alternative carbon asset distribution options from many perspectives. In this section, we briefly discuss four perspectives: ethical, legal, economic and political.

Ethical Perspectives

The ethical argument has been spelled out extensively by ecological economists, environmental thinkers, political scientists and legal scholars, among others. The basic idea is simple: that the atmosphere, as a global common resource, should be shared equitably among the people of the world. With this overarching framework, two questions arise: whether natural debts incurred in the past should be included in this equitable sharing; and whether 'equitable' means equal per capita allocation or should incorporate other economic criteria as well.

Within the scholarly debates on ethical perspectives, nobody argues explicitly for grossly unequal distribution of rights to the atmosphere. One can argue, however, that some element of grandfathering can have theoretical as well as pragmatic benefits. For example, resources that in the past have been free arguably should not be burdened suddenly with a high cost, as the resource users were operating in a legal and scientific world that did not recognize any limit; their ethical obligation may be considered to begin from the point of learning and recognition, rather than from the point of causation.

Legal Perspectives

A related argument has been advance by legal theoreticians. The principal question is whether existing international law provides an adequate foundation for the concept of the atmosphere as the 'Common Heritage' of humankind, or merely a weaker 'Common Concern' of humankind (Baslar 1998; Arend 1999). Some precedents for the former exist in the treatment of common resources under international environmental law, such as the Antarctic Treaty and Amendments, the UN Convention on the Law of the Sea and the conventions governing lunar mineral exploitation. Existing legal instruments and decisions do not necessarily imply a universal right to the benefits of the atmosphere, and there is even some disagreement as to whether the atmosphere meets the legal definition of a commons (Buck 1998). Nevertheless, the precedents are encouraging in that the international community has explicitly delineated the common ownership of other shared resources.

Economic Perspectives

One objection to the option of granting permits to corporations free of charge is that not all people are managers or shareholders. Consumers may capture some surplus via the lower prices that firms could charge, but owners could appropriate a large part of this windfall. Furthermore, any surplus passed along to consumers would not be equally distributed: those who consume more (typically, high-income households) would reap more than those who consume less (typically, lower-income households). Thus, granting free permits to corporations would probably end up enriching those who already have substantial wealth, without providing much benefit to the 'average' citizen who arguably has an equally legitimate claim to the atmosphere.

The sky trust proposal differs from a corporate allocation in three ways:

- First, by allocating an equal share to each person, the sky trust embodies a specific ethical judgment regarding entitlements.
- Second, the sky trust has a *payout ratio* — the fraction of revenues that is returned to shareholders as dividends after other costs are paid — that is extremely high relative to the payout ratio of a typical corporation. Proposed payout ratios in sky trusts vary from 75 per cent to 100 per cent, whereas corporate payout ratios are often less than 10 per cent.[10]
- Third, most sky trust proposals provide for an equal dividend to everybody, without giving individuals the option of either buying or selling their entitlement.

While necessarily initiated through the national legislative process, such a system could be separated from the government.

From an economic perspective, if one could somehow demonstrate that the government can use the revenue more effectively than individuals, then the government should retain the revenue. Defining 'effectiveness' for governments is a difficult task, and given the mixed record of government spending, one must make a strong case for governmental retention of carbon revenues. One area that is particularly compelling, however, is government-sponsored research and development: because private firms often cannot capture the full benefits of innovations, government sponsorship to yield public spillover benefits has been repeatedly vindicated (Duke and Kammen 1999).

Specifically, carbon revenue could be used for investment in developing long-term approaches for reducing carbon emissions. Currently the United States, for example, arguably under-invests in alternative energy research and development. Federal investments in *all* energy research amount to less than 0.4 per cent of US energy revenues, compared to over 12 per cent in many areas of the life-sciences (Kammen and Margolis 1999). Using even a small fraction of the carbon revenue could create more opportunities for the shift to renewable energy, and thus make further reductions in carbon emissions more likely (US Congressional Budget Office 2001; US Department of Energy and Interlaboratory Working Group on Energy-efficient and Clean-energy Technologies 2000). In addition, targeting some carbon revenue for governmental-sponsored adjustment assistance could mitigate social problems caused by reduced use of fossil fuels.

Political Perspectives

The political argument over distribution mechanisms will pit strong ethical arguments against entrenched economic interests. One likely compromise is to divide the problem into short and long time horizons. In the short-term, this would allow atmospheric dividends to continue to accrue mainly to those who enjoy them now (mostly corporations based in developed countries), while moving towards a more equitable long-term redistribution of rights (Kinzig and Kammen 1998; Baer *et al.* 2000).

If it is decided that atmospheric carbon revenue should be distributed directly to citizens, the possible pitfalls of distribution mechanisms take on greater importance. Without a strong legal and administrative system, the money may not reach its rightful owners, either because the infrastructure (records, registries, banks, etc.) is not in place to deliver it, or because knowledgeable insiders divert the cash from the intended recipients. In such cases, it is possible that alternative institutional arrangements can achieve a partial distribution of carbon income while maintaining integrity. For example, the Bonn Agreements and Marrakesh Accords to the Framework Convention on Climate Change established an Adaptation Fund, which is to draw funding from a tax on Clean Development Mechanism projects. Decisions adopted at Marrakesh also direct the Global Environmental Facility (GEF) to help fund capacity building and technology transfer in developing countries. Recycling carbon revenue through the Adaptation Fund or earmarked GEF money would redistribute wealth to poorer countries and provide a source of funds for climate-friendly sustainable development.

Conclusions

Because of the importance of bringing large developing countries into the international regulatory framework, the politics of atmospheric rights could realign behind a more equitable allocation. To argue that the revenue from higher carbon prices should be distributed directly to citizens, one needs to demonstrate one or more of the following: (a) the right to share in carbon revenue stems from an ethical argument based on common ownership; (b) the citizens can use the money more effectively than the government; and (c) the political landscape is sufficiently malleable to make this a reality.

Without a strong international norm that encourages countries to adopt an egalitarian distributional standard, it is hard to imagine that more than a few industrialized countries would willingly forgo the large asset values necessary for an international allocation scheme based on equal per-capita emissions rights. Long-term equity in emissions rights, therefore, while conceivable, would require development of an international norm that defines the atmosphere as the common heritage of humankind.

Within individual countries, a system of national sky trusts could provide a means for ensuring that atmospheric scarcity rent flows to the poor as well as the rich. By constructing a legal endowment in the natural asset of the atmosphere, such a system could align environmental protection with wealth creation for the poor. We have noted several administrative and political obstacles to the implementation of an interlocking system of national sky trusts. Even if this goal proves unattainable in the short term, smaller steps can help move towards this ideal of harmonizing environmental protection and poverty reduction via the definition of natural assets.

Governments have primary, but not exclusive, power over both international allocation and domestic distribution policies. As a first step, governments should define and defend their own long-term positions on equity questions, for example, by agreeing to the principle of equalizing per-capita emissions rights over time. Such actions can help to build consensus and cooperation for the longer term, and potentially make room for more compromise in the shorter term. NGOs can press domestically for international agreements delineating the principle of universal human ownership of the atmosphere (Schreurs and Economy 1997). This strategy of norm definition has worked well for some other issues as in the international campaign to ban land mines, in which intensive lobbying based upon ethical grounds was able to bolster a new area of international law (Finnemore and Sikkink 1998). Philanthropic foundations with a charter to support equity, human rights and environmental protection can target this area of climate policy as a long-term goal. Local communities also can participate in the process, in particular by showing their national governments that cutting emissions is not only possible but economically desirable.

International and domestic climate change policies that define and allocate rights to emit carbon have already emerged. By moving towards a more equitable international allocation, and by implementing domestic revenue distribution policies that focus on citizens, government research and development and adjustment assistance, these policies could simultaneously build wealth for the poor and reduce the risk of over exploiting the atmospheric commons. The result can be a sustainable and progressive solution to global climate change.

Acknowledgements

We thank the Natural Assets Project team for stimulating discussions and interactions. Nathan E. Hultman was supported by the NASA Earth Systems Science Programme, and Daniel M. Kammen gratefully acknowledges the support from the Energy Foundation.

Notes

1. Though we refer primarily to the predominant anthropogenic greenhouse gas of carbon dioxide, and often use 'carbon' as shorthand, the theoretical concepts developed here can include the non-CO_2 greenhouse gases as well. Accordingly, we adopt the common designation of 'CO_2-equivalent', or CO_2e, to refer to greenhouse gases as a whole.
2. For example, to mitigate the price uncertainty under a cap-and-trade system, the government can set a ceiling for the carbon price by implementing a fixed penalty rate. Denmark used this type of system for its early domestic carbon permit plan.
3. Annex I is a designation in the UN Framework Convention on Climate Change (FCCC) and reproduced in the Kyoto Protocol as Annex B. Annex I countries are: Australia, Austria, Belgium, Bulgaria, Croatia, Czech Republic, Denmark, Estonia, Finland, France, Germany, Hungary, Iceland, Ireland, Italy, Japan, Latvia, Liechtenstein, Lithuania, Luxembourg, Monaco, Netherlands, New Zealand, Norway, Poland, Portugal, Russian Federation, Slovakia, Slovenia, Spain, Sweden, Switzerland, U.K., Ukraine and USA.
4. Barnes and Breslow (2003) perform a similar calculation for the United States, using a much higher carbon price. Our US$100 billion figure uses a carbon price of around US$5 per ton CO_2e, and assumes that this would cut emissions to a near-term target of 21.81 billion tons per year globally.
5. In the language of the international agreements, the term 'quantified emission limitation and reduction obligation' is sometimes used as longhand for 'permits'.
6. This figure includes the US permits to be consistent with the models' assumptions.
7. Again, the studies in Table 15.2 assume US participation.
8. Elasticity is defined as the percentage change in consumption divided by the percentage change in price. Things that are more 'necessary', such as basic foods and energy, tend to have lower elasticity than luxury items, which can be more easily foregone if prices rise.
9. Elasticities are not constant over demand, and would most likely become smaller as the quantity of permits decline, enhancing this effect.

10. A 75 per cent payout ratio results from earmarking 25 per cent of the proceeds for renewable energy R&D, adjustment assistance and so on.

References

Agarwal, Anil and Sunita Narain (1991) *Global Warming in an Unequal World: A Case of Environmental Colonialism*, New Delhi: Centre for Science and Environment.

Americans for Equitable Climate Solutions (2000) *Sky Trust Initiative: Economy-wide proposal to reduce US carbon emissions*, Washington DC: Americans for Equitable Climate Solutions. Available at http://www.aecs-inc.org/indexn.html.

Arend, Anthony C. (1999) *Legal Rules and International Society*, New York: Oxford University Press.

Baer, Paul, John Harte, Barbara Haya, Antonia V. Herzog, John Holdren, Nathan E. Hultman, Daniel M. Kammen, Richard B. Norgaard and Leigh Raymond (2000) 'Climate Change — Equity and Greenhouse Gas Responsibility', *Science* 289(5488): 2287.

Barnes, Peter (2001) *Who Owns the Sky? Our Common Assets and the Future of Capitalism*, Washington DC: Island Press.

Barnes, Peter and M. Breslow (2003) in James K. Boyce and Barry G. Shelley, eds., *Natural Assets: Democratizing Environmental Ownership*, Washington, DC: Island Press, 135–149.

Baslar, Kemal (1998) *The Concept of the Common Heritage of Mankind in International Law*, The Hague: M. Nijhoff Publishers.

Buck, Susan J. (1998) *The Global Commons: An Introduction*, Washington DC: Island Press.

Bürer, Mary Jean (2001) 'Funds Offer Carbon "kicker"', *Environmental Finance*(COP-7 Supplement): 18–20.

Daily, Gretchen C. (1997) *Nature's Services: Societal Dependence on Natural Ecosystems*, Washington DC: Island Press.

de Groot, R.S. (1994) 'Environmental Functions and the Economic Value of Natural Ecosystems', in Jansson, A.M., M. Hammer, C. Folke and R. Costanza, eds., *Investing in Natural Capital : The Ecological Economics Approach to Sustainability*, Washington DC: Island Press.

Duke, Richard and Daniel M. Kammen (1999) 'The Economics of Energy Market Transformation Programmes', *Energy Journal* 20(4): 15–64.

Finnemore, M. and K. Sikkink (1998) 'International Norm Dynamics and Political Change', *International Organization* 52(4): 887–917.

Grubb, Michael, Christiaan Vrolijk and Duncan Brack (1999) *The Kyoto Protocol: A Guide and Assessment*, London, England: Royal Institute of International Affairs.

Hultman, Nathan E (2004). 'Emerging Carbon Markets and the Future of Climate Policy', *Georgetown Journal of International Affairs* 5(1): 123–129.

Institute of International Finance (2002) 'Emerging Market Indicators', *The Economist*, 4 May 2002, pp.101–102.

International Energy Agency (2001) *International Emission Trading: From Concept to Reality*, Paris: OECD Press.

Kinzig, Anne P. and Daniel M. Kammen (1998) 'National Trajectories of Carbon Emissions: Analysis of Proposals to Foster the Transition to Low-carbon Economies', *Global Environmental Change-human and Policy Dimensions* 8(3): 183–208.

Kopp, Raymond, R. Morgenstern, W. Pizer and M. A. Toman (1999) *A Proposal for Credible Early Action in US Climate Policy*, Washington DC: Resources for the Future.

Available at http://www.weathervane.rff.org/features/feature060.html.

Krause, Florentin (2000) *Solving the Kyoto Quandary: Flexibility with no Regrets*, El Cerrito, Calif.: International Project for Sustainable Energy Paths.

Lecocq, Franck and Karan Capoor (2005) *State and Trends of the Carbon Market*, Washington DC: World Bank. Available at www.carbonfinance.org.

Margolis, Robert M. and Daniel M. Kammen (1999) 'Evidence of Under-Investment in Energy R&D in the United States and the Impact of Federal Policy', *Energy Policy* 27(10): 575–584.

McKibben, Warwick J. and Peter J. Wilcoxen (1999) *Designing a Realistic Climate Change Policy that Includes Developing Countries*, Washington DC: Brookings Institution.

Nakicenovic, Nebojsa and Intergovernmental Panel on Climate Change: Working Group III (2000) *Special Report on Emissions scenarios: a special report of Working Group III of the Intergovernmental Panel on Climate Change*, Cambridge: Cambridge University Press.

Phillips, M. (2001) *Returning Carbon Permit Proceeds to the Economy: Three options*, Washington DC: Americans for Equitable Climate Solutions.

Rosenzweig, Richard, Matthew Varilek and Josef Janssen (2002) *The Emerging International Greenhouse Gas Market*, Arlington, VA: Pew Center on Global Climate Change. Available at http://www.pewclimate.org.

Schreurs, Miranda A. and Elizabeth Economy (1997) *The Internationalization of Environmental Protection*, Cambridge: Cambridge University Press.

Smith, Kirk R. (1991) 'Allocating Responsibility for Global Warming: The Natural Debt Index.' *Ambio* 20(2): 95-96.

Springer, Urs (2001) *The Market for GHG Permits Under the Kyoto Protocol: A Survey of Model Studies*, St. Gallen, Switzerland: University of St. Gallen.

Tol, Richard S. J. (2005). 'The Marginal Damage Costs of Carbon Dioxide Emissions: An Assessment of the Uncertaintites', *Energy Policy* 33: 2064–2074.

United Nations Conference on Trade and Development (2000) *Greenhouse Gas Market Perspectives: Trade and Investment Implications of the Climate Change Regime*, United Nations, New York: UNCTAD/DITC/TED/Misc.9.

United Nations Framework Convention on Climate Change (2000) *National Communications from Parties Included in Annex I to the Convention: Greenhouse Gas Inventory Data from 1990 to 1998*, FCCC/SBI/2000/11. Bonn, Germany: UNFCCC Secretariat. Available at http://www.unfccc.de.

United States Congressional Budget Office (2001) *An Evaluation of Cap-and-trade Programs for Reducing US Carbon Emissions*, Washington, DC: US CBO.

United States Department of Energy and Interlaboratory Working Group on Energy-efficient and Clean-energy Technologies (2000) *Scenarios for a Clean Energy Future*, ORNL/CON-476 & LBNL-44029. Washington DC: United Stated Department of Energy. Available at http://www.ornl.gov/ornl/Energy_Eff/CEF.htm.

United States Department of Energy —— Energy Information Administration (2002) *World Carbon Dioxide Emissions from the Consumption and Flaring of Fossil Fuels, 1980–2000*, Available at http://www.eia.doe.gov/emeu/international/environm.html.

Victor, David G. (2001) *The Collapse of the Kyoto Protocol and the Struggle to Slow Global Warming*, Princeton: Princeton University Press.

Victor, D. G., J. C. House and S. Joy (2005) A Madisonian Approach to Climate Policy, *Science*, Sep 16, 309(5742): 1820–1821.

Vitousek, Peter M. (1997) 'Human Domination of Earth's ecosystems', *Science* 277(5325): 494–499.

Weitzman, Martin (1974) 'Prices vs. Quantities', *Review of Economic Studies* 61(4): 477–491.

In India, a protest against environmental 'CO$_2$lonialism.'
Photo credit: Centre for Science and Environment.

CHAPTER 16
GREENHOUSE JUSTICE:
AN ENTITLEMENT FRAMEWORK FOR
MANAGING THE GLOBAL
ATMOSPHERIC COMMONS

Sunita Narain and Matthew Riddle

Prologue

I first learned about global warming in the late 1980s. My colleague Anil Agarwal and I had spent over two years traversing Indian villages, searching for policies and practices to reforest wasted common lands. We quickly learned to look beyond trees, at ways to deepen democracy so that these commons could be regenerated. In India forests are mostly owned by government agencies, but it is poor communities that actually use them. It quickly became clear that without community participation, afforestation was not possible. This is because our forests are not wilderness areas, but habitats of people and their animals. For people to be involved the rules for engagement had to be respected, and to be respected, the rules had to be fair.

At the time, India had a 'green' environment minister. Data released by a prestigious US research institution had convinced her that it was the poor who contributed most substantially to global warming — they did 'unsustainable' things like growing rice and keeping farm animals. Anil and I were pulled into the global climate debate when a flummoxed state Chief Minister called us. He had received a government circular that asked him to discourage rural people from keeping animals. 'How do I do this?' he asked us. 'Do the animals of the poor really disrupt the world's climate system?' We were equally puzzled. It seemed absurd. We had been arguing for quite a while that the poor were victims of environmental degradation. Here they were now, cast as complete villains. How?

With this question, we embarked on our climate research journey. As we began to grasp climate change issues, we learned that there was not all that much difference between managing a local forest and managing the global climate. Both were common property resources. In both cases, what was needed most of all was a property rights framework that would encourage cooperation. We advanced two main arguments:

- *First, the world needs to differentiate between the greenhouse gas emissions of the poor — say, from subsistence paddy or animals — and those of the rich — say, from cars. Survival emissions are not equivalent to luxury emissions.*
- *Second, managing a global commons means cooperation among countries. As a stray cow or goat is more likely to chew saplings in the forest, any country can affect the global climate if it emits beyond what the atmosphere can take. Cooperation is possible — and this is where our forest experience came in handy — only if benefits are distributed equally.*

On this basis, we developed the concept of per capita entitlements — to define each nation's share of the Earth's atmosphere — and used these entitlement rights to propose rules of engagement that were fair and equitable (Agarwal and Narain 1991). We suggested that countries using less than their share of the atmosphere could trade their unused quota, and that this would give them the incentive to invest in technologies that would not increase their emissions. But in all this, as we told the climate negotiators with whom we met, think of the local forest, and learn that the issue of equity is not a luxury: it is a prerequisite.

— Sunita Narain

Introduction

Climate change is about the economy: the links among carbon dioxide emissions, economic growth and distributional equity. In the past two decades, the industrialized countries have managed to delink sulphur dioxide emissions from economic growth, so that emissions have fallen even as national income has risen. They have failed to do the same, however, with carbon dioxide emissions. Per capita carbon dioxide emissions remain tightly related to a country's level of economic development and standard of living. It is evident that as long as the world economy is carbon-based — driven by energy from coal, oil and natural gas — growth cannot be delinked substantially from carbon dioxide emissions.

According to the Synthesis Report of the 2001 Inter-governmental Panel on Climate Change (IPCC), the only time the world managed to de-link carbon dioxide emissions from economic growth was during the oil crisis of the 1970s, when rising energy prices led to a brief divergence of the emissions and GDP trends in the developed world. Otherwise, trends have been closely linked. So, for example, when the break-up of the former Soviet

Union led to a decline in national income, this brought with it a sharp drop in its CO_2 emissions (IPCC 2001).

As long as the world energy economy remains carbon-based, equitable sharing of 'atmospheric space' will be a critical issue, especially for poor developing countries that need space for future economic growth. The enormous inequity in carbon dioxide emissions today is clear when we compare the United States per capita emissions to those of South Asian nations. In 1996, one US citizen emitted as much carbon dioxide as 19 Indians, 30 Pakistanis, 49 Sri Lankans, 107 Bangladeshis, or 269 Nepalis (see Table 16.1). Although the gap has narrowed somewhat over time, this extraordinary disparity makes it very difficult for political leaders, especially in countries with an electoral democracy, to agree to a common action plan unless there is a clear recognition of the need for equity in sharing available atmospheric space. Without global equity, global solidarity will not be possible.

Table 16.1: Comparison of Per Capita Carbon Emissions of USA and South Asian countries

Country	Per capita emissions (tons of carbon)		Number of citizens equivalent to one US citizen	
	1990	1996	1990	1996
USA	5.18	5.37	1	1
Bangladesh	0.04	0.05	130	107
India	0.22	0.29	24	19
Nepal	0.01	0.02	518	269
Pakistan	0.16	0.18	32	30
Sri Lanka	0.06	0.11	86	49

Source: Marland et al. 1999.

It is equally important to consider the issue of equity within nations. It is clear that the poor of the world are not using their 'ecological space', including their share of the carbon-absorptive capacity of the biosphere. In any framework of carbon-emission entitlements, above all it is the entitlement of the poor within the poor nations that needs to be secured.

How will the concept of equity be operationalized in global negotiations? This chapter presents a conceptual framework for consideration.

Stabilizing the Earth's Climate

To combat global warming, governments of the world must ensure that greenhouse gas (GHG) concentrations do not build up beyond an acceptable level. According to the IPCC studies, if concentrations of carbon dioxide (CO_2), the most important greenhouse gas, stabilize at 450 parts per million (ppm), global average temperature will increase by 1.5–3.9° C from 1990 levels over the course of several centuries (IPCC 2001a, 100). Although this temperature rise exceeds natural variability, it could allow many — though not all — ecosystems to adapt, and thus can be taken tentatively as an upper limit on the tolerable rate of climate change.

To stabilize the atmospheric concentration at 450 ppm, cumulative CO_2 emissions will have to be limited to a total of about 600–800 billion tons of carbon (btC) between now and the end of the 21st century, by which time annual emissions should diminish to less than 3 btC per year. Under a business-as-usual scenario, cumulative emissions will be about twice as high as this, at 1500 btC, with annual emissions reaching 20 btC per year by 2100 and still accelerating upward. The world can expect a warming of 1.4–5.8° C above 1990 levels and a sea level rise of 9–88 centimetres (cm) by the end of the century under this scenario (IPCC 2001b, 13–16). This will adversely affect natural habitats, agricultural systems and human health, and it will have especially severe implications for coastal and island ecosystems and their human communities.

The 450 ppm stabilization trajectory, despite being a dramatic departure from business as usual, itself is not without considerable risks. It would commit the world to a non-trivial degree of climate change, and could subject the global climate system to a radical shock because of non-linear effects that existing climate models fail to take into account. Evidence from prehistoric climatic records increasingly supports the view that the climate system can change very rapidly, with dramatic ecological impacts. Relatively small human-induced changes could be amplified by feedback mechanisms that cannot be controlled by human beings (Kartha et al. 1998; Alley 2002.)

In the year 2000, the atmospheric concentration of CO_2 was around 370 ppm, up from less than 300 ppm in 1990. Stabilizing atmospheric concentrations poses an extremely daunting challenge. The global North must reduce its current carbon emissions substantially, and the South must begin stabilizing and eventually reducing its own per capita carbon emissions, even as economies industrialize and motorize in the years to come. Climate scientists Bert Bolin and Haroon Kheshgi (2001) estimate that for stabilization at 450 ppm, global per capita carbon emissions would have to decrease from the present 1.1 ton per capita per year to less than 0.5 tons by the middle of this century. Stabilization even at 550 ppm — the scenario now accepted by the European Union — would require a rapid decrease of emissions (Onigkeit and Alcamo 1998).

International negotiations have seen growing acceptance of emissions trading as the most economically effective strategy for reducing GHG emissions reduction, and equal per capita entitlements and North-South convergence as the key to equity and global solidarity. But there has been relatively little discussion on what constitutes ecologically effective action. To deal with global warming, nations not only have to undertake energy efficiency measures. Ultimately they have to move towards a zero-carbon energy-based economy, eliminating the use of fossil fuels altogether. Though the two are not mutually exclusive, a focus on energy efficiency measures could pose a serious risk to prospects for a zero-carbon energy transition. Such a focus could 'lock in' fossil fuels for a much longer time than desired, and 'lock out' renewable energy sources. A market-based Clean Development Mechanism, which seeks least-cost options for CO_2 reductions by fostering trading in emissions rights across countries, likewise could end up becoming part of the problem rather than a part of the solution. Although a zero-emissions future looks more technically promising today than ever before, the transition will not take place by itself. Governments must take a proactive role in promoting it here and now.

Renewable Energy Technologies

A rapid shift towards renewable energy technologies (RETs) is not only the best option to combat climate change; it is the only option. If the world waits for most of its oil, gas and coal resources to be exhausted before making this transition, something that probably will not occur before the end of this century, then the risk of serious climate change will be inordinately high.

The 20th century actually saw a major transition away from renewable energy towards a fossil fuel-based global economy. Between 1900 and 2000, world energy use grew more than ten times. Even though the energy from RETs increased nearly five-fold during the century its share in total energy use dropped from 42 per cent to 19 per cent (Brown *et al.* 1999, 23). The challenge for the 21st century is to reverse this trend, to restore a much bigger share for RETs. This will require a switch from traditional RETs to new ones.

New RETs are already growing faster than any other method of electricity generation. Favourable market developments, including lower interest rates, because of higher up-front capital costs compared to fossil fuel-based systems, enabled wind power to become the fastest-growing energy source in the 1990s (Gray 1999). Over the decade, installed wind power capacity worldwide grew by more than 25 per cent per year (Brown *et al.* 1999a: 16). Meanwhile annual production of photovoltaics is doubling every five years (Priddle 1999). Technological advances are also taking place in the use of hydrogen fuel cells. Their cost has fallen dramatically, though it must fall still further to compete with the internal combustion engine. Modern biomass energy, including new technologies that produce ethanol from agricultural wastes, also offers immense potential.

These technological developments have led energy experts to be cautiously optimistic about the future of RETs. A major study conducted by the Vienna-based International Institute for Applied Systems Analysis and the World Energy Conference, entitled *Global Energy Perspectives,* forecasts that with appropriate 'technology push and policy pull', RETs could contribute nearly 40 per cent of the global primary energy supply by 2050, and net carbon emissions could be below 1990 emissions by as much as 15 per cent. In this scenario, industrialized countries would cut their carbon emissions by about 75 per cent from 1990 levels, and developing countries would stay within 2.5 times their 1990 carbon emissions.

But the study warns that because of the long capital turnover rates (the time it takes to recover investment) of energy supply technologies and infrastructures, it is research investments made in the next few decades that will shape the technology options available to the world in mid-century. The more the world gets locked into fossil fuel-based systems, especially efficient and low-cost fossil fuel systems, the longer it will take to get out of them. If the huge energy investments that will be made by developing countries in the next three to four decades lock them into a carbon energy economy like that of the industrialized countries, this will result in an enormous build-up of greenhouse gases. The governments of the world will have to play a key role in 'reinventing the energy system' in the 21st century, just as they played a key role in determining the modern carbon-based energy supply structure since the 19th century.

Today the biggest obstacles in the way of renewable technologies are low fossil fuel prices and fossil fuel subsidies in many countries. These are exacerbated by declining public sector research and development for RETs, along with plummeting private sector research and development as the deregulation of energy markets increasingly promotes a focus on short-term returns (Kartha *et al.* 1998). Rapid expansion in the use of zero-carbon technologies will come only with proactive official policies aimed at increasing research investment, and at creating favourable economic conditions so that mass production can further bring down their costs.

It was the government of California, for example, that forced car manufacturers to take fuel cells seriously. The state's decree that by 2004 one-tenth of all cars sold in the state must be zero-emission vehicles led car makers and specialist fuel cell companies to invest more than US$1.5 billion on fuel cells.[1] Similarly, when Iceland pledged in 1999, to become the world's first hydrogen-powered economy, in response to severe automobile pollution in Reykjavik, the country's capital, this immediately attracted Shell, Daimler-Chrysler and Norsk Hydro. The country hopes to replace all cars, buses and fishing fleet engines with fuel cell-powered transport.

Developing countries are best positioned to take a lead in creating a global market for zero-carbon energy technologies, however, because they have two great advantages: they have more potential for solar energy than most Western countries; and they have hundreds of thousands of villages that are not yet connected to carbon-based power grids. For the more than two billion people who today have no access to electricity, providing access to RETs would constitute a new path of rural development. If the South follows the fossil fuel-based historic industrialization of the North, it will face a severely compromised climatic system. The South, therefore, has to 'get it right the first time'.

Towards a Framework for Equitable Entitlements

Addressing the problem of global climate change is not only an economic and environmental issue. Above all it is a moral and ethical issue. It will require the greatest cooperative enterprise that the world has ever seen, and this can happen only if there is a sense of fairness in the burden-sharing arrangements. Even if coercion might work in the short term, it would not succeed for long. Long-term cooperation will come only with a fair deal.

The crux of any fair deal will be the concept of equal per capita entitlements to greenhouse gas emissions. This principle was incorporated in the work plan at the Fourth Session of the United Nations' Framework Convention on Climate Change (UNFCCC) Conference of the Parties in Buenos Aires in 1998, at the insistence of the developing countries. Efforts to define a per capita carbon budget must confront several issues.

Net versus Gross Emissions: Sharing the World's Common Sinks

Annual changes in the atmospheric concentration of CO_2 are determined by the amount of CO_2 that is released into the atmosphere (gross emissions) and the amount that is reabsorbed by plants and microorganisms on land and in the ocean. The difference between the two, net emissions, is added to the atmosphere each year. Each country's contribution to global warming can be best understood by looking at net emissions: their gross emissions minus their share of the Earth's carbon absorptive capacity.

To calculate national net emissions, we need a way to allocate shares of the world's carbon absorptive capacity among countries. One natural way to do so is to divide it evenly on a per capita basis. Another approach is to consider the oceanic sinks to be global common property that should be divided evenly, but to count terrestrial sinks, such as forests and grasslands, as national property. The oceans currently absorb about two billion tons of carbon annually, a little more than half of the total absorption by all sinks of 3.8 btC (IPCC 2001b, 185).[2] If oceanic sink capacity were allocated equally among all the people of the world, this would give a per capita sink availability of 0.32 tC per year. This exceeds the gross emissions per capita in many developing countries. In other words, no matter which method is used to allocate terrestrial sinks, these countries today have *negative* net emissions: they are using less than their share of the Earth's carbon absorptive capacity. Under an international entitlement framework, these countries could trade their unused emission rights, or bank them for future use. The gross emissions of the industrialized countries, on the other hand, are far beyond this level, and some developing countries, including China and Egypt, have also surpassed it.

Historical Emissions and Greenhouse Equity

A study by the International Project for Sustainable Energy Paths (IPSEP), prepared for the Dutch government in 1989, started from the premise that to limit global warming, a total of only 300 btC could be released between 1985 and 2100. If this global carbon emissions budget were allocated among countries on the basis of population, then the developed countries would have already exhausted their entire quota (48 btC) by the year 1999, even if they had limited their annual CO_2 emissions to 1986 levels. Developing countries would be able to emit CO_2 (at their 1986 rate) until the year 2169.

The IPSEP study further observed that developed and developing countries have been emitting CO_2 at vastly different rates for a long time. If historical carbon emissions were backdated to 1950, and permissible emissions again distributed between industrialized and developing countries on the basis of population, then the developing countries could continue to emit CO_2 (at their 1986 rate) until 2241, whereas the industrialized countries would have already exhausted their entire quota by 1986. As these calculations suggest, an equitable allocation of the world's carbon budget that took historical emissions into account would provide the industrialized countries with so little space for reform as to be politically unfeasible.

Ad Hoc Emission Budgets and Entitlements

The most common approach is to propose atmospheric concentration limits at various future dates on an *ad hoc* basis, allowing for some build up of greenhouse gases in the atmosphere. These targeted atmospheric concentrations are then translated into a global emissions budget that can be distributed among nations. In this approach, both the targets and the emissions caps needed to meet them would be subject to periodic scientific reviews, and therefore the national entitlements would be subject to review, too. A country that does not use its budget during a particular year again could have the right to trade its unused share. Alternatively, nations could simply agree on an *ad hoc* per capita entitlement to which all countries eventually will converge (see Figure 16.1). This target could be more or less ambitious, but again it would be subject to periodic review, allowing changes based on new scientific information.

Figure 16.1: Alternative Approaches to Equitable Per Capita Carbon Emission Entitlements

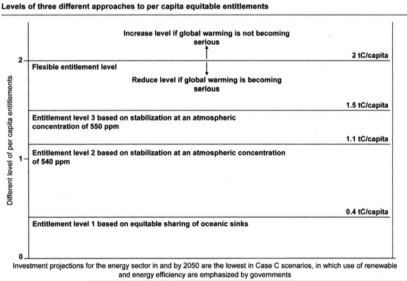

Levels of three different approaches to per capita equitable entitlements

Increase level if global warming is not becoming serious

2 tC/capita

Flexible entitlement level

Reduce level if global warming is becoming serious

1.5 tC/capita

Entitlement level 3 based on stabilization at an atmospheric concentration of 550 ppm

1.1 tC/capita

Entitlement level 2 based on stabilization at an atmospheric concentration of 540 ppm

0.4 tC/capita

Entitlement level 1 based on equitable sharing of oceanic sinks

Different level of per capita entitlements

Investment projections for the energy sector in and by 2050 are the lowest in Case C scenarios, in which use of renewable and energy efficiency are emphasized by governments

Source: Nebojsa Nakicenovic et al (ed) 1998, Global Energy Perspectives, Cambridge University Press, Cambridge

There is already much 'pragmatic *ad hoc*ism' in international climate negotiations. The emissions limits for the industrialized countries that are specified in the Kyoto Protocol, for instance, are pegged to their 1990 emission levels. The choice of 1990 as the base year was quite arbitrary, but it was accepted in order to provide a baseline for industrialized countries to show that they are reducing their emissions. The choice of the percentage by which each industrialized country is to reduce its emissions was also *ad hoc*; once again, targets were agreed simply in the interest of moving ahead.

Whatever approach to setting per capita entitlements is adopted, acceptance of the principle of equity could help to get North-South cooperation moving through emissions trading. Equity would combine the principles of *equal entitlements* and *convergence*; in other words, all nations would agree to reach the same level of per capita emissions entitlements at some future date.[3] Those nations whose emissions exceed their entitlements will slowly reduce their emissions to reach this level, while those whose emissions are below their entitlements have space to grow.

Entitlements and the Transition to Renewables

Equal per capita emissions entitlements offer the most just and effective way of getting developing countries to engage with the climate change problem. If low-level polluters were able to trade their unused emissions rights with high-level polluters, this would provide an incentive to keep their emissions growth path as low as possible. The transition to renewable energy technologies could be spurred if emissions trading were restricted to financing for zero-carbon energy projects. The Clean Development Mechanism (CDM), set up by the Kyoto Protocol, allows industrialized countries to meet part of their emission reduction commitments by funding projects to reduce net emissions in developing countries. If CDM projects were restricted to zero-carbon energy technologies, the shortrun costs to industrialized countries of using CDM to meet emissions reduction targets would be higher than alternatives such as improvements in the operating efficiency of conventional power plants or the substitution of natural gas for coal, options favoured by the United States and some other industrialized countries. In the long run, however, bearing the upfront cost of the RET route will boost technologies whose price is coming down rapidly, lowering future emissions reduction costs.

A study carried out for the World Bank, for example, estimates the additional capital cost of switching from coal-based power to solar thermal power in India to be about US\$500,000 per megawatt (MW) of installed capacity. In other words, if through a CDM transaction the industrialized countries paid India US$25 billion to offset their own carbon emissions, this could finance some 50,000 MW of solar power plants, enough to provide about one-fifth of India's electricity use. This would dwarf existing worldwide solar capacity — cumulative worldwide production of photovoltaic panels through 2003 was only 3,145 MW (Jiménez 2004). Investment on this scale could play a critical role in bringing down the world price of solar power.

Once the pro-renewables strategy is accepted, the case for equitable per capita emissions entitlements takes on a new urgency. Its most important appeal is not that it creates a framework to force all countries to converge to a sustainable level of emissions at some future date, but rather that it creates a framework for engaging developing nations to kick start the movement towards a zero-carbon energy transition. Once the world seriously begins moving towards such a transition, the entitlement framework will become increasingly redundant. The greatest advantage of a system of equitable and tradable emissions entitlements is that it would provide an 'enabling economic environment for technology transfer' as foreseen in Article 10 of the Kyoto Protocol (Agarwal and Narain 1998a, 1998b).

Entitlements within Countries

Just as an international agreement must provide an equitable allocation of carbon emissions among countries in order to be effective, a national programme for reducing emissions must provide an equitable allocation of emission rights among the people of the country. One way to do this would be through a 'sky trust' (Barnes 2001; Brenner et al. 2005). A fee would be charged to those who release CO_2 into the atmosphere. This would be levied most easily at the point where fossil fuels enter the economy, with the cost passed along to the ultimate consumers. The money would be deposited in a trust fund from which dividends would be distributed to everyone in the country on an equal per capita basis. The result would be that individuals whose consumption is responsible for more than their share of carbon emissions would pay more into the trust fund than they receive back in dividends, while those who emit less than their share would receive more than they pay in higher carbon prices.

An equitable intra-national system for emissions assignment along these lines could further promote zero-emission technologies. India, for instance, had per capita carbon emissions of only 0.2 tons per year in the 1990s, and per capita consumption of energy of only 330 kilowatt hours per year

(Gupta *et al.* 2001, 56). Yet these figures hide huge disparities. The urban-industrial sector is energy-intensive and wasteful, while the rural subsistence sector is energy-poor and frugal. Currently it is estimated that only 31 per cent of India's rural households use electricity. Connecting all of the country's villages to a carbon-based electricity grid will be expensive. It is here that the option of leapfrogging to off-grid solutions based on RETs is most economically viable. If India's carbon emission entitlements were assigned on an equal per capita basis, so that the country's richer citizens in effect pay the poor for their excess energy use, this would provide both the resources and the incentives for current low-energy users to adopt zero-emission technologies. In this way, again, an equitable rights-based framework would stimulate powerful demand for investments in new renewable energy technologies.

Conclusion

The threat posed by global warming can no longer be taken lightly. A major worldwide commitment is needed to reduce carbon emissions to stabilize atmospheric concentrations quickly and minimize the chance of devastating climate changes. This will require cooperation between industrialized and developing nations. This can be achieved only if all sides agree that the commitments made by each country are fair and equitable. The principle of convergence toward equal per capita emissions rights provides the best starting point for negotiations over how to achieve an equitable solution.

A transition to renewable sources of energy clearly will be necessary to cut carbon emissions sufficiently. Those regions of the world that currently use relatively little fossil-fuel energy must avoid the carbon-intensive path of development that industrialized countries have followed, and move directly to the use of zero-carbon technologies. An equitable distribution of emission rights, at both the international and intra-national levels, could play a crucial role in encouraging this transition by providing poor countries, and poor communities within developing countries, with money and incentives to invest in renewable energy technologies. The foundation for sustainable management of the global atmospheric commons is a just distribution of entitlements.

Notes

1. The initial deadline was the year 2004 (Economist 1999). This was subsequently extended by the California Air Resources Board.
2. For comparison, annual emissions in the 1980s amounted to 7.1 btC.

3. It may be argued that any system of per capita entitlements would be unjust to those nations that have stable populations, and could provide an incentive for population growth. It is rather far-fetched to think that anyone would have more babies simply because she wants to increase her country's emissions quota, but this problem could be dealt with by setting the global distribution of population-based entitlements with reference to an agreed base year, such as the year of agreement.

References

Agarwal, Anil and Sunita Narain (1991) *Global Warming in an Unequal World: A Case of Environmental Colonialism*, New Delhi: Centre for Science and the Environment.

— (1998a) 'Sharing the Air', *Down to Earth* 15 August 1998: 41–42, New Delhi: Society for Environmental Communications.

— (1998b) *Towards a Non-carbon Energy Transition*, November 1998: 1–4, Dossier Fact Sheet 3, New Delhi: Centre for Science and the Environment.

Alley, Richard B. (2000) *The Two-mile Time Machine: Ice Cores, Abrupt Climate Change and Our Future*, Princeton: Princeton University Press.

Barnes, Peter (2001) *Who Owns the Sky? Our Common Assets and the Future of Capitalism*, Washington DC: Island Press.

Bolin, Bert and Haroon Kheshgi (2001) 'On Strategies for Reducing Greenhouse Gas Emissions', Proceedings of the National Academy of Sciences, Washington DC as quoted in Jiahua Pan 2002, 'Understanding Human Development Potentials and Demands for Greenhouse Gas Emissions with Empirical Analysis Using Time Series and Cross-sectional Data', Working Paper 2002–10, Global Change and Economic Development Programme, Chinese Academy of Social Sciences.

Brenner, Mark, Matthew Riddle and James K. Boyce (2005) 'A Chinese Sky Trust? Distributional Impacts of Carbon Charges and Revenue Recycling in China', Amherst, MA: Political Economy Research Institute, Working Paper No. 97.

Brown, Lester *et al.* (1999) *State of the World 1999*, Washington DC: World Watch Institute.

Economist (1999) 'Fuel Cells Meet Big Business', *The Economist* 24 July 1999.

Gray, Tom (1999) 'Wind is Getting Stronger and is On Course for the Next Decade', *Renewable Energy World* 2(3), UK: James & James Science Publishers Ltd.

Gupta, J. *et al.* (2001) *An Asian Dilemma: Modernising the Electricity Sector in China and India in the Context of Rapid Economic Growth and the Concern for Climate Change*, The Netherlands Free: University of Amsterdam.

IPCC (2001a) *Climate Change 2001; Synthesis Report*. Contribution of Working Groups I, II, III to the Third Assessment Report of the Inter-governmental Panel on Climate Change, Cambridge: Cambridge University Press.

IPCC (2001b) *Climate Change 2001: The Scientific Basis*. Contribution of Working Group I to the Third Assessment Report of the Inter-governmental Panel on Climate Change, Cambridge: Cambridge University Press.

Jiménez, Viviana M. (2004) 'World Sales of Solar Cells Jump 32 Per cent', *Eco Economy Indicators*, Washington DC: Earth Policy Institute, 20 October.

Kartha, Sivan *et al.* (1998) '"Meaningful Participation" for the North and South', Presented at SEI/CSE Workshop on Towards Equity and Sustainability in the Kyoto Protocol, Buenos Aires, 8 November.

Marland, Gregg *et al.* (1999) *National Carbon Dioxide Emissions from Fossil Fuel Burning, Cement Manufacture and Gas Flaring*, USA: Oak Ridge Laboratory.

Nebojša, Nakićenović *et al.* (1998) *Global Energy Perspectives*, Cambridge: Cambridge

University Press.

Onigkeit, Janina and Joseph Alcamo (1998) *Stabilisation Targets and Convergence of Per Capita Emissions*, Workshop Report: First Answers Towards Buenos Aires, Centre for Environmental Systems Research, University of Kassel, Germany and the National Institute of Public Health and the Environment (RIVM). Presented at the Seventh International Workshop on using Global Models to support Climate Negotiations, The Netherlands, 21–22 September 1998.

Priddle, Robert (1999) Energy and Sustainable Development, *IAEA Bulletin* 41(1), Vienna: International Atomic Energy.

ABOUT THE CONTRIBUTORS

Anil Agarwal founded the New Delhi-based Centre for Science and Environment (CSE) in 1980, and directed it until his death at the age of 54 in 2002. The CSE studies the relationship between the environment and development, and seeks to foster public consciousness about the need for sustainable development. Anil Agarwal also chaired the world's largest network of environmental NGOs, the Nairobi-based Environment Liaison Centre, and served as a member of the World Water Commission. He won numerous awards, including the Padma Bhushan Award bestowed by the President of India.

Kojo Sebastian Amanor is an associate professor at the Institute of African Studies, University of Ghana, Legon. His publications include *Land, Labour and the Family in Southern Ghana: A Critique of Land Policy under Neoliberalisation* (Nordic Institute of African Studies, 2001); *The Management of Trees on Farms: The Perspectives of Farmers* (Ghana Forestry Department, 1996) and *The New Frontier: Farmers' Responses to Land Degradation* (Zed Press, 1994).

Deborah Ann Barry has worked in Central America and Mexico for over 30 years on sustainable agriculture, land-use management and public policy development. Currently, she is senior research associate with the Center for International Forestry Research, based in Washington, DC, prior to which she was a programme officer for the Ford Foundation in Mexico City for seven years. She is co-editor of *The Community Forests of Mexico: Managing for Sustainable Landscapes* (University of Texas Press, 2005).

James K. Boyce is a professor of economics at the University of Massachusetts, Amherst, and director of the Program on Development, Peacebuilding and the Environment at the Political Economy Research Institute (PERI). His books include *The Political Economy of the Environment* (Edward Elgar, 2002) and *Investing in Peace: Aid and Conditionality after Civil Wars* (Oxford University Press, 2002). He is co-editor of *Natural Assets: Democratizing Environmental Ownership* (Island Press, 2003).

Michael E. Conroy is a programme officer at the Rockefeller Brothers Fund and senior lecturer in the School of Forestry and Environmental Studies at Yale University. Previously he was a senior programme officer at the Ford Foundation, and professor of economics at the University of Texas.

José De Echave is director of the Mines and Communities Programme at CooperAcción, a non-governmental organization in Peru that was founded in 1997. CooperAcción defends the rights of mining communities, promotes environmentally sound technologies and fosters dialogue among social organizations, the private sector and government.

Leopoldo Dimas is a senior researcher at PRISMA (Programa Salvadoreño de Investigación sobre Desarrollo y Medio Ambiente) an applied research and reference centre on environment and development issues based in San Salvador, El Salvador.

Eugenio M. Gonzales is the former Executive Director of the Foundation for a Sustainable Society, Inc. in the Philippines, an endowment that provides financial and technical assistance to non-governmental organizations, cooperatives and entrepreneurs for economically viable and ecologically sound community-oriented enterprises. Previously he taught in the Department of Industrial Engineering and Operations Research at the University of the Philippines, Diliman.

Anthony Hall is Reader in the Department of Social Policy at the London School of Economics and Political Science. Before joining the LSE, he worked at Reading University and as Country Representative in Brazil for Oxfam. His books include *Sustaining Amazonia: Grassroots Action for Productive Conservation* (Manchester University Press, 1997), *Amazonia at the Crossroads: the Challenge of Sustainable Development* (Institute of Latin American Studies, University of London, 2000) and *Global Impact, Local Action: New Environmental Policy in Latin America* (Institute for the Study of the Americas, University of London, 2005).

Krista Harper is an assistant professor of anthropology and public policy at the University of Massachusetts, Amherst. As a Fulbright scholar, she has conducted research on environmental and human rights movements in Eastern Europe. She is the author of *Wild Capitalism: Environmental Activists and Post-socialist Political Ecology in Hungary* (East European Monographs, 2006).

Nathan E. Hultman is an assistant professor of science, technology and international affairs at the School of Foreign Service, Georgetown

University. He received his doctorate in Energy and Resources from the University of California, Berkeley (2003), where he was a NASA Earth Systems Science Fellow.

Narpat S. Jodha is a senior research associate and policy analyst at the International Centre for Integrated Mountain Development in Kathmandu, Nepal, and a fellow of the World Academy of Art and Science. He is the author of *Life on the Edge: Sustaining Agriculture and Community Resources in Fragile Environments* (Oxford University Press, 2001).

Daniel M. Kammen is the Class of 1935 Distinguished Professor of Energy in the Energy and Resources Group and the Goldman School of Public Policy at the University of California, Berkeley, where he is also the founding director of the Renewable and Appropriate Energy Laboratory (RAEL) and co-director of the Berkeley Institute of the Environment. He previously taught at Princeton University. His publications include the book *Should We Risk It? Exploring Environmental, Health and Technological Problem Solving* (Princeton University Press, 2001).

Susan Kandel is a senior researcher at PRISMA (Programa Salvadoreño de Investigación sobre Desarrollo y Medio Ambiente) an applied research and reference centre on environment and development issues based in San Salvador, El Salvador.

Karyn Keenan is an environmental lawyer and activist who works with communities affected by commercial resource extraction, with a focus on mining activity in Latin America. She currently works with the Halifax Initiative, a Canadian coalition that seeks to transform the international financial institutions to achieve poverty eradication, environmental sustainabiltiy and equitable wealth redistribution.

John Kurien teaches at the Centre for Development Studies (CDS) in Trivandrum, India. His publications include *Property Rights, Resource Management and Governance: Crafting an Institutional Framework for Global Marine Fisheries* (CDS, 1998) and *Responsible Fish Trade and Food Security* (FAO/UN, 2005).

Stephen F. Minkin was an early proponent of environmental restoration of floodplain fisheries, and a founding member of the Centre for Natural Resource Studies in Bangladesh, where his research focused on the importance of fish species biodiversity for human welfare. He has also written extensively on the origins and medical transmission of HIV/AIDS.

RECLAIMING NATURE

James Murombedzi is the World Conservation Union (IUCN) Regional Representative for Southern Africa, based in Harare. Prior to joining IUCN, he was Programme Officer in the Ford Foundation's Environment and Development programme in Southern Africa, and lecturer at the University of Zimbabwe, where he carried out research on the devolution of natural resources management in the region.

Sunita Narain is the director of the Centre for Science and Environment (CSE) in New Delhi, India. She is co-author with Anil Agarwal of the CSE publications *Global Warming in an Unequal World: A Case of Environmental Colonialism* (1991); *Towards a Green World: Should Environmental Management Be Built on Legal Conventions or Human Rights?* (1992); and *Dying Wisdom: The Rise, Fall and Potential of India's Water Harvesting Systems* (1997).

Manuel Pastor is a professor of Latin American and Latino studies at the University of California, Santa Cruz, where he directs the Center for Justice, Tolerance and Community. His books include *Regions That Work: How Cities and Suburbs Can Grow Together* (University of Minnesota Press, 2000), co-authored with Peter Dreier, Eugene Grigsby and Marta Lopez-Garza and *Searching for the Uncommon Common Ground: New Dimensions on Race in America* (W.W. Norton, 2002), co-authored with Angela Glover Blackwell and Stewart Kwoh.

M. Mokhlesur Rahman has worked on fisheries and natural resource management in Bangladesh for the last 20 years. He is a founding member of the Centre for Natural Resources Studies (CNRS) and currently its executive director. He received an MS in Zoology with a specialization in fisheries from Dhaka University in 1979. He has worked on fisheries and wetlands for DANIDA, Caritas Bangladesh, the Food and Agricultural Organization of the United Nations and the United Nations Development Programme.

S. Ravi Rajan is an associate professor of environmental studies at the University of California, Santa Cruz. He received a doctorate in environmental history at Oxford University. He the author of *Modernizing Nature: Forestry and Imperial Eco-development, 1800–1950* (Oxford University Press, 2006). He was a core-group member of the Bhopal Group for Information and Action in the 1980s and currently serves on the boards of Pesticides Action Network and the International Media Project.

Matthew Riddle is a doctoral candidate in economics at the University of Massachusetts, Amherst.

Herman Rosa is director of PRISMA (Programa Salvadoreño de Investigación sobre Desarrollo y Medio Ambiente) an applied research and reference centre on environment and development issues based in San Salvador, El Salvador, and coordinator of the Payment for Environmental Services Project, funded by the Ford Foundation.

Peter Rosset is a researcher at the Centre for the Study of Rural Change in Mexico (CECCAM), co-coordinator of the Land Research Action Network (www.landaction.org), an associate of the Centre for the Study of the Americas (CENSA) and visiting scholar in Environmental Science, Policy and Management at the University of California, Berkeley. He resides in San Cristóbal de las Casas in Chiapas, Mexico.

Elizabeth A. Stanton is a researcher at the Global Development and Environment Institute in Medford, Massachusetts, and a doctoral candidate in economics at the University of Massachusetts, Amherst. She has been programme director of the Center for Popular Economics, and has taught at the University of Massachusetts, Amherst, the School for International Training, Castleton College, and Fitchburg State College. She is co-author, with James K. Boyce, of *Environment for the People* (Political Economy Research Institute, 2005).

Ken Traynor is a researcher for the trade and environment programme at the Canadian Environmental Law Association (CELA) in Toronto. CELA is a non-profit, public interest organization established in 1970 to protect the environment and to advocate environmental law reforms. It offers a free legal advisory clinic for the public, and assists citizens and groups who are otherwise unable to afford legal assistance.

INDEX

Z